Two, Three...
Many Vietnams

Two, Three . . .
Many Vietnams

a radical reader on the wars in Southeast Asia and the conflicts at home

edited by

The Editors of *Ramparts*
with Banning Garrett
and Katherine Barkley

Canfield Press, San Francisco
a department of Harper & Row, Publishers, Inc.
New York, Evanston, London

The group which the United States wants to intimidate and terrorize by way of the Vietnamese nation is the human group in its entirety.

—JEAN-PAUL SARTRE

TWO, THREE . . . MANY VIETNAMS: A RADICAL READER ON THE WARS IN SOUTHEAST ASIA AND THE CONFLICTS AT HOME

 For information address Harper & Row, Publishers, Inc., 49 East 33rd Street, New York, N.Y. 10016.

Standard Book Number 06-383867-2

Library of Congress Catalog Card Number: 79-142862

Dedicated to:

Third World peoples fighting for liberation

Contents

Preface

As the conflict in Asia widens and the death toll mounts, as this country's domestic schism deepens and the war commitments expand, it is more and more apparent that Vietnam is a critical turning point not merely in America's relations with the world, but also in her relations with herself.

For the better part of this century, America's leaders have promoted a liberal conception of America's domestic order and world role, and it has been accepted by most forces in the political arena. Now with the Vietnam war, however, this image of America as a democratic melting pot and international peacemaker has been challenged in the deepest, most irrevocable way, and it has been done by America's own deeds—by the most destructive, predatory, and unjustifiable war in a quarter of a century; by the immeasurable waste of human and material resources and the conscious, calculated withholding of that wealth from the oppressed and exploited ethnic groups, conquered and ravaged in America's past.

As this gap between the American image and the American reality turned into the blood and fire of Vietnam, the recognition provoked at first a profound moral crisis throughout this nation. A new political generation set out in the '60s to square the American reality with the values of equality and self-determination embodied (or so they had been taught) in the structure of American politics and history. But as the depth of America's resistance to change, its commitment to war and order, asserted itself—as Vietnam became Laos and Cambodia, as Selma became Watts and Detroit, as Berkeley became Jackson and Kent State—the mind of the new political generation became mature under fire, sweeping outwards and backwards in time: from Korea to the Philippines, from the Little Bighorn to the Alamo.

The moral crisis assumed a sociological dimension. The very framework of American society and its history were now perceived with different eyes. It was seen that the American dream itself had been built on false foundations: the democratic political ideals were long ago overwhelmed by an economic reality where the rich prosper and control; the rhetoric of peace between independent nations was betrayed from the outset by a commitment to imperial manifest destiny—at first to annex and settle within her own continental limits, and later, spurred by the expansionist corporate economy, to dominate the oceans and lands beyond.

Thus, from the initial moral crisis created by Vietnam there began to develop among many dissenters a perspective that can only be described as revolutionary. In this perspective the aim of political activity is seen as a fundamental reconstruction of institutions, not merely a changing of policies and people in power. For only by a basic transformation of economic and political forms can America's destructive course be halted and new directions—embracing new orders of priorities and social concerns—be undertaken.

Ramparts—itself a product of the changing consciousness of America's new political generations—was the first mass circulation magazine to challenge the moral and political basis of the war. A series of articles exposing the nature of the conflict, and the machinations behind it, included "The Vietnam Lobby," ex-Green Beret Don Duncan's "I Quit," "Children of Vietnam," "Madam Nhu and MSU," and Noam Chomsky's "The Fire This Time." In these articles *Ramparts* blazed a trail which other journals and papers followed cautiously at first, and then, as the impossibility of winning became clearer, more adventurously, until the time when discontent with the war was so widespread that the expose of the My Lai massacres could be syndicated in establishment papers across the country.

Many people have misunderstood the significance of this change and consequently overestimated the potential benefits which might accrue from the spread of such "anti-war" sentiments. A mere cease-fire, as the original Geneva Accords showed, may only be the prelude to a larger war, if the potential sources of such a war (e.g., the presence of the U.S. in Indochina) are not properly dealt with.

In short, the change to a cautious peace orientation among establishment pundits, from bank presidents and newspaper publishers to politicians, is largely attributable to the fact that no one likes a losing war, least of all those responsible for the management of human affairs. Many recently emerged advocates of peace are merely advocates of the tactical view that Washington is "over-committed"—whereas Washington is in fact *wrongly* committed, to the wrong sides and the wrong priorities in the major social conflicts of our time. As *Ramparts* pointed out in an editorial during the October-November 1969 Moratorium:

> The disillusionment of the establishment policymakers over Vietnam goes no deeper and no further than the cost disadvantages they see in the war. "To say that the burden of this war must now be lifted," says [McGeorge] Bundy, "is not at all to say that it should never have been fought." . . . What the crises of the last decade have taught us, however, is that what is needed is not another changing of the guard but a changing of the system. The job of the radicals in the Moratorium is to convince the new protesters that Vietnam is no simple aberration, but rather the natural overgrowth of a system that seeks to lock the third world into a permanent state of inden-

tured servitude. "Changing the system" must first of all mean a liquidation of the global empire that has grown to such mammoth proportions in the post World War II era. If that empire is not broken up, then withdrawal from Vietnam will merely mean cutting losses in one war to save energy for the next. . . .

No major political figure of either party, from McCarthy to Kennedy, McGovern to Lindsay, has yet called for a withdrawal from the American Empire. Yet that is the real key to peace. Everything else can only be illusory. If the resources of the underdeveloped world are not left to those nations to control and develop, and if the U.S. military arm is not withdrawn—not only from Southeast Asia, but from all of Asia, Africa and Latin America—then we are destined to walk down the already visible path of national suicide, and even perhaps global annihilation.

The invasion of Cambodia in May 1970 was a dramatic indication of Washington's commitment to maintaining the Indochina outpost of the American empire, despite its pledges of de-escalation and withdrawal. The historic nationwide student strike in response to the invasion was an equally dramatic indication of the potential for domestic resistance to such an openly aggressive imperial policy. Whether the forces of resistance have yet assimilated the lessons of the last quarter century of America's cold war crusade only time will tell. TWO, THREE . . . MANY VIETNAMS is an effort to distill those lessons in terms of the Southeast Asian War, and thus to build the consciousness necessary to make future Indochinas impossible.

The editors of *Ramparts* wish to thank Banning Garrett and Katherine Barkley of the Pacific Studies Center, who wrote the introductions and compiled the bibilography and ancillary materials.

David Horowitz

Map 1. Indochina

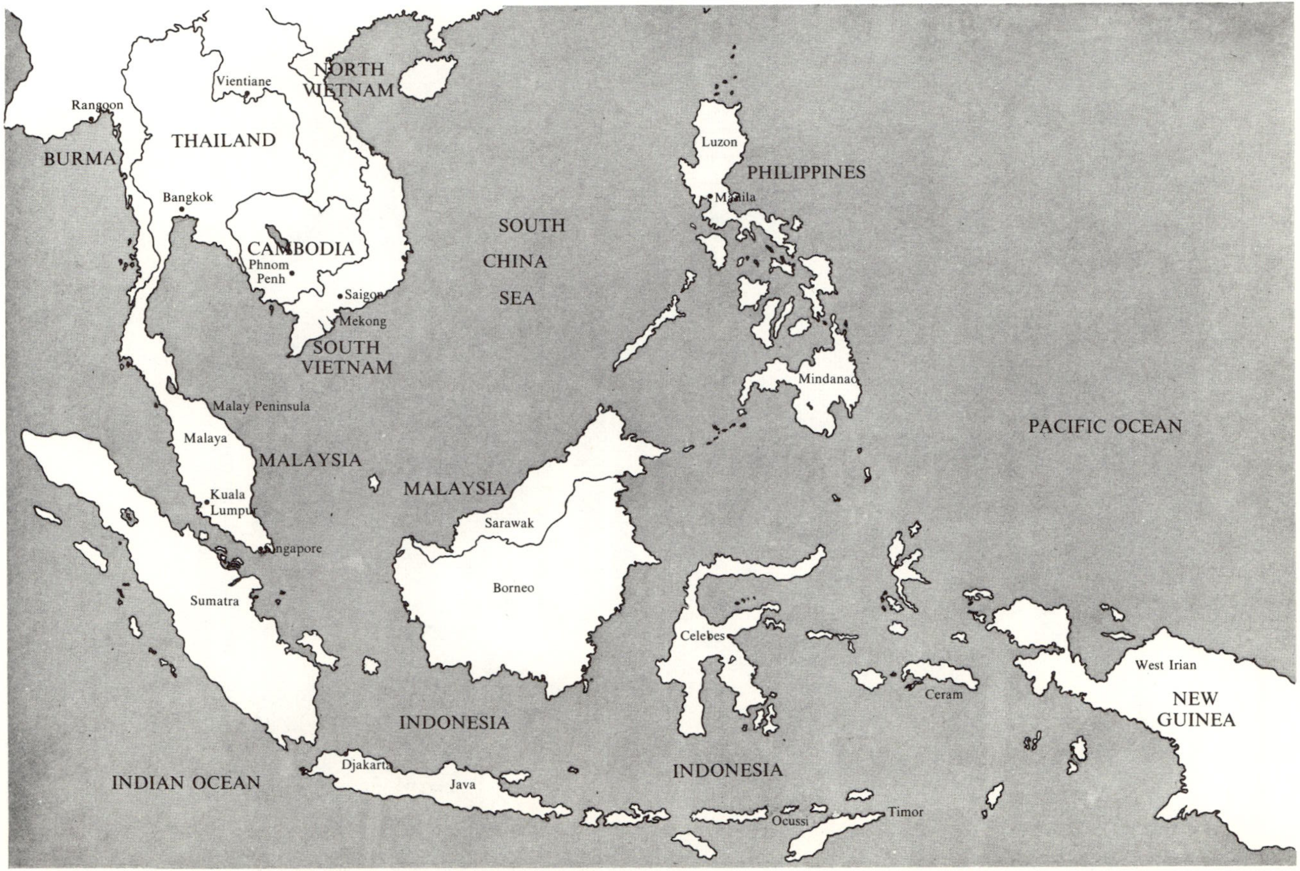

Map 2. Indochina and Indonesia

WAR IS NOT HEALTHY FOR CHILDREN OR OTHER LIVING THINGS.
(Photo by David Goldstein.)

chapter one

VIETNAM

Since the 1950s, American involvement in Vietnam has been justified within the so-called Free World as an important attempt to "contain" or restrict communist expansion. The precedent for this involvement was set by the Truman Doctrine of 1947, when President Harry S Truman, sanctioning U.S. intervention against a nationalist uprising in Greece, divided the world into two camps—free and communist, or "good" and "evil"—and proclaimed the United States to be the global protector of democracy and national self-determination. In much the same way, England had justified establishing its global empire with the pretext of taking up the White Man's Burden to train Africans and Asians in the "art of self-government" and Christian morals.* But the twentieth-century Pax Americana is proving to be far more brutal than the old Pax Britannica under which Third World peoples had suffered for several centuries before.

Like so many other Americans, DONALD DUNCAN, author of the first selection, had enthusiastically joined the anti-communist crusade during the '50s and went to Vietnam as a Green Beret hoping to help save a "free people" from communism. Instead, as he reveals in his writings, Duncan found that there was no freedom under Ngo Dinh Diem, who in 1955 had been put into power in South Vietnam by the U.S.; that his military training was explicitly racist; and that Americans in Vietnam were contemptuous of the people and government they were sent to defend. The only Vietnamese Americans respected, in fact, were the enemy—the National Liberation Front soldiers—who, unlike the soldiers in the South Vietnamese Army, had proved to be brave and disciplined fighters. The NLF troops, Duncan found, not only were motivated to fight—more important, they were supported by the Vietnamese people. And American military action, Duncan realized, was creating communists rather than suppressing them. Although U.S. and South Vietnamese officials attempted to rationalize away his discoveries, for Duncan the nature of American involvement had become clear: under the cloak of anti-communism, the

*John A. Hobson, *Imperialism,* rev. ed. (Ann Arbor, Mich.: University of Michigan Press, 1965).

United States, with the familiar colonial air of "doing what is best for the people," was actually spreading imperial domination to Vietnam.

Duncan quit the Green Berets in 1965, but the U.S. has continued to escalate its strategy of institutionalized genocide. In the next essay in this chapter, "After Pinkville," NOAM CHOMSKY describes the role of some American social scientists in designing this strategy. Realizing that in Vietnam the people themselves, not invading troops, are the "enemy," they have argued for the use of forced urbanization, whereby bombs and artillery are used to force people in the rural population—the "sea" of peasants in which guerrillas can "swim"—out of their villages and into urban areas and concentration camps where they can be controlled. The aim of this strategy, according to Chomsky, is to destroy the social organization of the Vietnamese peasants, which for decades has given them the strength to fight against foreign domination—in short, the American answer to people's war is to eliminate the people. With this strategy, the United States can pull out several hundred thousand troops; move back to defensive positions; obliterate the countryside with bombs, artillery, and defoliants; and control the people in concentrated and easily defended areas. By "urbanizing" the country, therefore, the U.S. could continue indefinitely its presence in Indochina with a minimum loss of American lives. As Chomsky suggests, the very nature of U.S. strategy in Vietnam is explicitly racist and genocidal.

In "On Genocide," which is the introduction to the proceedings from Bertrand Russell's 1967 war tribunal in Stockholm, JEAN-PAUL SARTRE carefully addresses himself to the question of genocide and he points out that although Hitler openly advocated the deliberate and systematic destruction of the Jews, the U.S. need not make a similar statement of purpose in order to have similar intentions. However, as he explains, genocide is never an accident of history, but rather the result of the economic organization and political objectives of a society and the contradictions existing within it. To illustrate his analysis, Sartre contrasts European colonialism with American neo-colonialism. The European powers destroyed native cultures, massacred some colonized peoples in order to terrorize the rest into subjugation, and refused to integrate the native groups into the European culture, thus fragmenting the native populations into classes that could be exploited for their labor. However, once these colonized people learned the arts of people's war or guerrilla war and could no longer be terrorized into submission, the colonial powers realized the only way to maintain control was by the complete liquidation of the insurgents. Yet such total genocide would also eliminate the raison d'etre of colonialism—the colonized economy—and consequently the Europeans found their only possible solution was to grant independence to the nationalist movements.

In contrast to European colonial powers, the United States has attempted, as in Vietnam, to take over control of countries that have already achieved independence. However, since the U.S. has no overriding economic interest in Vietnam, it has no inherent reason—resources, markets, or labor—to limit genocide. In fact, the real reasons for the U.S. presence there, Sartre argues, are to establish bases for containing Communist China and to demonstrate to the Third World that national liberation struggles will be defeated. Given these motivations, Sartre concludes:

> Of course, it would be preferable, for propaganda purposes, if the Vietnamese would submit before being exterminated. But it is not certain that the situation wouldn't be clearer if Vietnam were wiped off the map. Otherwise someone might think that Vietnam's submission had been attributable to some *avoidable* weakness. But if these peasants do not weaken for an instant, and if the price they pay for their heroism is *inevitable* death, the guerrillas of the future will be all the more discouraged.

So far, American genocidal strategy has failed to destroy the Vietnamese social structure, at least in North Vietnam. British correspondent RICHARD GOTT, in his March 1970 reports from Hanoi, reprinted in this chapter, observed a healthy, disciplined society. Although almost everything built since 1954 was destroyed, Gott found the North Vietnamese optimistic, purposeful, and determined, with none of the deference and cultural isolation that characterized them before their revolt against French colonialism. In fact, Gott remarked, "I never met a single person who did not look as though he knew exactly what he was doing and why he was doing it."

In another selection, PETER WEISS asks how it is possible that the North Vietnamese could withstand three years of almost continuous U.S. bombardment. What, he wonders, enabled the North Vietnamese to maintain social unity and production? In his 1968 trip to North Vietnam he found his answer in the cultural life of the people. The writers he interviewed live, work, and fight with the people. Their literature is for and about these people; its purpose is to communicate the goals and experiences of people's war—to create identification with the struggle and to give hope in times of despair. The poets and novelists see their writing as a weapon to be used by the peasants and workers in their efforts to change the world and as a way of placing their struggle in the perspective of their past—a history of peasant-led resistance to oppression. "This seeking out of its [Vietnam's] own history," Weiss writes, "this investigation of the remote past, is part of the process of rebirth with which revolutionary activity began." On the foundations of the past and traditional culture—a culture that was distorted by French colonialism—the Vietnamese have built one that both expresses the revolution and holds the revolution together. For them, Weiss points out, "a success in the artistic, scientific, or educational areas is always seen as a victory over the aggressor who wants to destroy the social foundations of Vietnam."

According to Berkeley professor FRANZ SCHURMANN, author of the last selection, the Vietnamese leadership found that as the U.S. escalated its attacks, the patriotism of the people—their identification with the national revolutionary culture—in addition to their ideology and organization, held them together and enabled them to continue fighting. But even the American left, Schurmann feels, has little understanding of the Vietnamese, their culture, their feelings about their struggle for *national* liberation. Most Americans see the Vietnamese as organization men—dedicated, even fanatical, communists. It is the responsibility of the American left, Schurmann believes, to present the Vietnamese as real people to the American public. Moreover, he argues:

> By making the Vietnamese and not just the Vietnam war real, the left may discover that its own ability as revolutionaries to love America will give it a source of strength and solidarity it does not have now, where each does his own thing. Even more, the portrayal of the Vietnamese as a real people may finally make the American people aware that there is only one meaningful political force in South Vietnam—the National Front for the Liberation of South Vietnam.

"I Quit": Memoirs of a Special Forces Hero

Don Duncan

When I was drafted into the Army, ten years ago, I was a militant anticommunist. Like most Americans, I couldn't conceive of anybody choosing communism over democracy. The depth of my aversion to this ideology was, I suppose, due in part to my being Roman Catholic, in part to the stories in the news media about communism, and in part to the fact that my stepfather was born in Budapest, Hungary. Although he had come to the United States as a young man, most of his family had stayed in Europe. From time to time, I would be given examples of the horrors of

Reprinted from *Ramparts,* February 1966.

life under communism. Shortly after basic training, I was sent to Germany. I was there at the time of the Soviet suppression of the Hungarian revolt. Everything I had heard about communism was verified. Like my fellow soldiers, I felt frustrated and cheated that the United States would not go to the aid of the Hungarians. Angrily, I followed the action of the brute force being used against people who were armed with sticks, stolen weapons and a desire for independence.

While serving in Germany, I ran across Special Forces. I was so impressed by their dedication and élan that I decided to volunteer for duty with this group. By 1959, I had been accepted into the Special Forces and underwent training at Fort Bragg. I was soon to learn much about the outfit and the men in it. A good percentage of them were Lodge Act people—men who had come from Iron Curtain countries. Their anticommunism bordered on fanaticism. Many of them who, like me, had joined Special Forces to do something positive, were to leave because "things" weren't happening fast enough. They were to show up later in Africa and Latin America in the employ of others or as independent agents for the CIA.

Initially, training was aimed at having United States teams organize guerrilla movements in foreign countries. Emphasis was placed on the fact that guerrillas can't take prisoners. We were continuously told, "You don't have to kill them yourself—let your indigenous counterpart do that." I was later to witness the practice of turning prisoners over to ARVN (Army of the Republic of Vietnam) for "interrogation" and the atrocities which ensued.

Throughout the training there was an exciting aura of mystery. Hints were continually being dropped that "at this very moment" Special Forces men were in various Latin American and Asian countries on secret missions. The anticommunist theme was woven throughout. Recommended reading would invariably turn out to be books on "brain washing" and atrocity tales—life under communism. The enemy was *the enemy.* There was no doubt that *the enemy* was communism and communist countries. There never was a suggestion that Special Forces would set up guerrilla warfare against the government in a fascist-controlled country.

It was a long time before I could look back and realize that this conditioning about the communist conspiracy and *the enemy* was taking place. Like most of the men who volunteered for Special Forces, I wasn't hard to sell. We were ready for it. Artur Fisers, my classmate and roommate, was living for the day when he would "lead the first 'tick' of the first team to go into Latvia." "How about Vietnam, Art?" "To hell with Vietnam. I wouldn't blend. There are not many blue-eyed gooks." This was to be only the first of many contradictions of the theory that Special Forces men cannot be prejudiced about the color or religion of other people.

After graduation, I was chosen to be a Procurement NCO for Special Forces in California. The joke was made that I was now a procurer. After seeing how we were prostituted, the analogy doesn't seem a bad one. General Yarborough's instructions were simple: "I want good, dedicated men who will graduate. If you want him, take him. Just remember, he may be on your team someday." Our final instructions from the captain directly in charge of the program had some succinct points. I stood in shocked disbelief to hear, "Don't send me any niggers. Be careful, however, not to give the impression that we are prejudiced in Special Forces. You won't find it hard to find an excuse to reject them. Most will be too dumb to pass the written test. If they luck out on that and get by the physical testing, you'll find that they have some sort of a criminal record." The third man I sent to Fort Bragg was a "nigger." And I didn't forget that someday he might be on my team.

My first impressions of Vietnam were gained from the window of the jet while flying over Saigon and its outlying areas. As I looked down I thought, "Why, those could be farms anywhere and that could be a city anywhere." The ride from Tan Son Nhut to the center of town destroyed the initial illusion.

My impressions weren't unique for a new arrival in Saigon. I was appalled by the heat and humidity which made my worsted uniform feel like a fur coat. Smells. Exhaust fumes from the hundreds of blue and white Renault taxis and military vehicles. Human excrement; the foul, stagnant, black mud and water as we passed over the river on Cong Ly Street; and, overriding all the others, the very pungent and rancid smell of what I later found out was *nuoc mam,* a sauce made much in the same manner as sauerkraut, with fish substituted for cabbage. No Vietnamese meal is complete without it. People—masses of them! The smallest children, with the dirty faces of all children their age, standing on the sidewalk unshod and with no clothing other than a shirtwaist that never quite reached the navel on the protruding belly. Those a little older wearing overall-type trousers with the crotch seam torn out—a practical alteration that eliminates the need for diapers. Young grade school girls in their blue butterfly sun hats, and boys of the same age with hands out saying, "OK—Salem," thereby exhausting their English vocabulary. The women in *ao dais* of all colors, all looking beautiful and graceful. The slim, hipless men, many walking hand-in-hand with other men, and so misunderstood by the newcomer. Old men with straggly Fu Manchu beards staring impassively, wearing wide-legged, pajama-like trousers.

Bars by the hundreds, with American-style names—Playboy, Hungry i, Flamingo—and faced with grenade-proof screening. Houses made from packing cases, accommodating three or four families, stand alongside spacious villas complete with military guard. American GI's abound in sport shirts, slacks and cameras; motorcycles, screaming to make room for a speeding official in a large, shiny sedan, pass over an intersection that has hundreds of horseshoe impressions in the soft asphalt tar. Confusion, noise, smells, people—almost overwhelming.

My initial assignment was in Saigon as an Area Specialist for III and IV Corps Tactical Zone in the Special Forces Tactical Operations Center. And my education began there. The officers and NCOs were unanimous in their contempt for the Vietnamese.

There was a continual putdown of Saigon officials, the Saigon government, ARVN, the LLDB (Luc Luong Dac Biet—Vietnamese Special Forces) and the Vietnamese man-in-the-street. The government was rotten, the officials corrupt, ARVN cowardly, the LLDB all three, and the man-in-the-street an ignorant thief. (LLDB also qualified under "thief.")

It occurred to me that if the people on "our side" were all these things, why were we then supporting them and spending $1.5 million dollars a day in their country? The answer was always the same: "They are anticommunists." This was supposed to explain everything.

As a result of this insulation, my initial observations of everything and everyone Vietnamese were colored. I almost fell into the habit, or mental laziness, of evaluating Vietnam not on the basis of what I saw and heard, but on what I was told by other biased Americans. When you see something contradictory, there is always a fellow countryman willing to interpret the significance of it, and it won't be favorable to the Vietnamese. This is due partially to the type of Vietnamese whom the average American meets, coupled with typical American prejudices. During his working hours, the American soldier deals primarily with the Vietnamese military. Many (or most) of the higher-ranking officers attained their status through family position, as a reward for political assistance, and through wealth. Most of the ranking civilians attained their positions in the same manner. They use their offices primarily as a means of adding to their personal wealth. There is hardly any social rapport between GI Joe and his Vietnamese counterpart.

Most contact between Americans and Vietnamese civilians is restricted to taxi drivers, laborers, secretaries, contractors and bar girls. All these people have one thing in common: they are dependent on Americans for a living. The last three have something else in common. In addition to speaking varying amounts of English, they will tell Americans anything they want to hear as long as the money rolls in. Neither the civilian nor military with whom the American usually has contact is representative of the Vietnamese people.

Many of our military, officers and enlisted, have exported the color prejudice, referring to Vietnamese as "slopes" and "gooks"—two words of endearment left over from Korea. Other fine examples of American democracy in action are the segregated bars. Although there are exceptions in Saigon, Nha Trang, Da Nang and some of the other larger towns, Negroes do not go into white bars except at the risk of being ejected. I have seen more than one incident where a Negro newcomer has made a "mistake" and walked into the wrong bar. If insulting catcalls weren't enough to make him leave, he was thrown out bodily. There are cases where this sort of thing has led to near-riots.

After my initial assignment in Saigon, which lasted two and one-half months, I volunteered for a new program called Project Delta. This was a classified project wherein specially selected men in Special Forces were to train and organize small teams to be infiltrated into Laos. The primary purpose of dropping these teams into Laos was to try and find the Ho Chi Minh trail and gather information on traffic, troops, weapons, etc. This was purely a reconnaissance intelligence mission, but the possibility of forming guerrilla bases later was considered. There was some talk of going into North Vietnam, but not by Project Delta. Another outfit, Special Operations Group, was already doing just that. SOG was a combined forces effort. The CIA, Air Force, Navy, Army and detached Special Forces personnel were all in on the act.

Project Delta was paid for by Uncle Sam from CIDG (Civilian Irregular Defense Group) funds. We had to feed, billet and clothe the Vietnamese. Free beer was supplied and lump sums of money were agreed on, some to be paid after completion of training and more to be paid when the teams returned.

Originally, it was thought that the teams would be composed of four Vietnamese and two Americans. Although many of the people we were training had natural aptitudes for the area of operations, strong and effective leadership was lacking. It was emphasized constantly to the Pentagon and to the ambassador by those intimately involved in the training program, that if any degree of success was to be realized it was imperative that Americans must accompany the teams.

When at the last minute we received a firm "No Go" for the United States personnel, we asked, "Why?" The answer was that it was an election year [1964] and it would cause great embarrassment if Americans were captured in Laos. Anything of that nature would have to wait until after the election. The reaction to this decision on the part of the Americans was one of anger, disappointment and disgust.

And like everyone, I was disappointed. This was the one thing, if I had to single out one, that made me really start questioning our role in Vietnam. It suddenly occurred to me that the denial of American participation was not based on whether it was right or wrong for us to be going to Laos. The primary concern was the possible embarrassment to President Johnson during an election campaign. Toward this end we sent people on a mission that had little or no chance of success. It became apparent that we were not interested in the welfare of the Vietnamese, but in how we could best promote our own interests. We sent 40 men who had become our friends. These were exceptionally dedicated people, all volunteers; six returned, the rest were killed or captured.

When the project shifted to in-country operations, Americans went on drops throughout the Viet Cong-held areas of South Vietnam. One such trip was into War Zone D north of Dong Xoi, near the Michelin plantation. There is no such thing as a typical mission. Each one is different. But this one revealed some startling things. Later I was to brief Secretary of Defense McNamara and General Westmoreland on the limited military value of the bombing, as witnessed on this mission.

I had seen the effect of the bombing at close range. These bombs would land and go for about 15 yards and tear off a lot of foliage from the trees, but that was it. Unless you drop these things in somebody's hip pocket they don't do any good. For 28 hours they bombed that area. And it was rather amusing because, when I came out, it was estimated that they had killed about 250 Viet Cong on the first day. They asked me how many Viet Cong did I think had been killed and I said maybe six; I was giving them the benefit of the doubt at that. The bombing had no real military significance. It would only work if aimed at concentrated targets such as villages.

One of the first axioms one learns about unconventional warfare is that no insurgent or guerrilla movement can endure without the support of the people. While doing research in my job as an area specialist, I found that, in province after province, the Viet Cong guerrillas had started as small teams. They were now in battalion and regimental strength. Before I left, the Viet Cong could put troops in the field in division strength in almost any province. Such growth is not only impossible without popular support, it actually required an overwhelming mandate.

We were still being told, both by our own government and the Saigon government, that the vast majority of the people of South Vietnam were opposed to the Viet Cong. When I questioned this contradiction, I was always told that the people only helped the Viet Cong through fear. Supposedly, the Viet Cong held the people in the grip of terror by assassination and torture. This argument was also against doctrine. Special Forces are taught that reliable support can be gained only through friendship and trust. History denied the "terror" argument. The people feared and hated the French, and they rose up against them. It became quite obvious that a minority movement could not keep tabs on a hostile majority. South Vietnam is a relatively small country, dotted with thousands of small villages. In this very restricted area, companies and battalions of Viet Cong can maneuver and live under the very noses of government troops; but the people don't betray these movements, even though it is a relatively simple thing to pass the word. On the other hand, government troop movements are always reported. In an action against the Viet Cong, the only hope for surprise is for the government to move the troops by helicopters. Even this is no guarantee. General Nguyen Khan, while still head of the Saigon government, acknowledged that Viet Cong sympathizers and agents were everywhere—even in the inner councils—when he made the statement: "Any operation that lets more than four hours elapse between conception and implementation is doomed to failure." He made these remarks in the last days of his regime, right after a personally directed operation north of Saigon ended in disaster.

To back up the terror theory, the killing of village chiefs and their families were pointed out to me. Those who were quick to point at these murders ignored certain facts. Province, district, village and hamlet chiefs are appointed, not elected. Too often petty officials are not even people from the area, but outsiders being rewarded for political favors. Those who are from the area are thought of as quislings because they have gone against their own by cooperating with Saigon. Guerrillas or partisans who killed quislings in World War II were made heroes in American movies. Those who look on the Viet Cong killings of these people with horror, and use them as justification for our having to beat them, don't realize that our own military considers such actions good strategy when the tables are reversed. When teaching Special Forces how to set up guerrilla warfare in an enemy country, killing unpopular officials is pointed out as one method of gaining friends among the populace. It is recommended that special assassination teams be set up for this purpose.

I know a couple of cases where it was suggested by Special Forces officers that Viet Cong prisoners be killed. In one case in which I was involved, we had picked up prisoners in the valley around An Khe. We didn't want prisoners but they walked into our hands. We were supposed to stay in the area four more days, and there were only eight of us and four of them, and we didn't know what the hell to do with them. You can't carry them. Food is limited, and the way the transmission went with the base camp you knew what they wanted you to do—get rid of them. I wouldn't do that, and when I got back to operation base a major told me, "You know we almost told you right over the phone to do them in." I said that I was glad he didn't, because it would have been embarrassing to refuse to do it. I knew goddamn well I wasn't going to kill them. In a fight it's one thing, but with guys with their hands bound it's another. And I wouldn't have been able to shoot them because of the noise. It would have had to be a very personal thing, like sticking a knife into them. The major said, "Oh, you wouldn't have had to do it; all you had to do was give them over to the Vietnamese." Of course, this is supposed to absolve you of any responsibility. This is the general attitude. It's really a left-handed morality. Very few of the Special Forces guys had any qualms about this. Damn few.

Little by little, as all these facts made their impact on me, I had to accept the fact that, communist or not, the vast majority of the people were

GIs terrify a South Vietnamese farmer by making him hold an empty rifle. *(Photo by Joseph W. Carey, BBM.)*

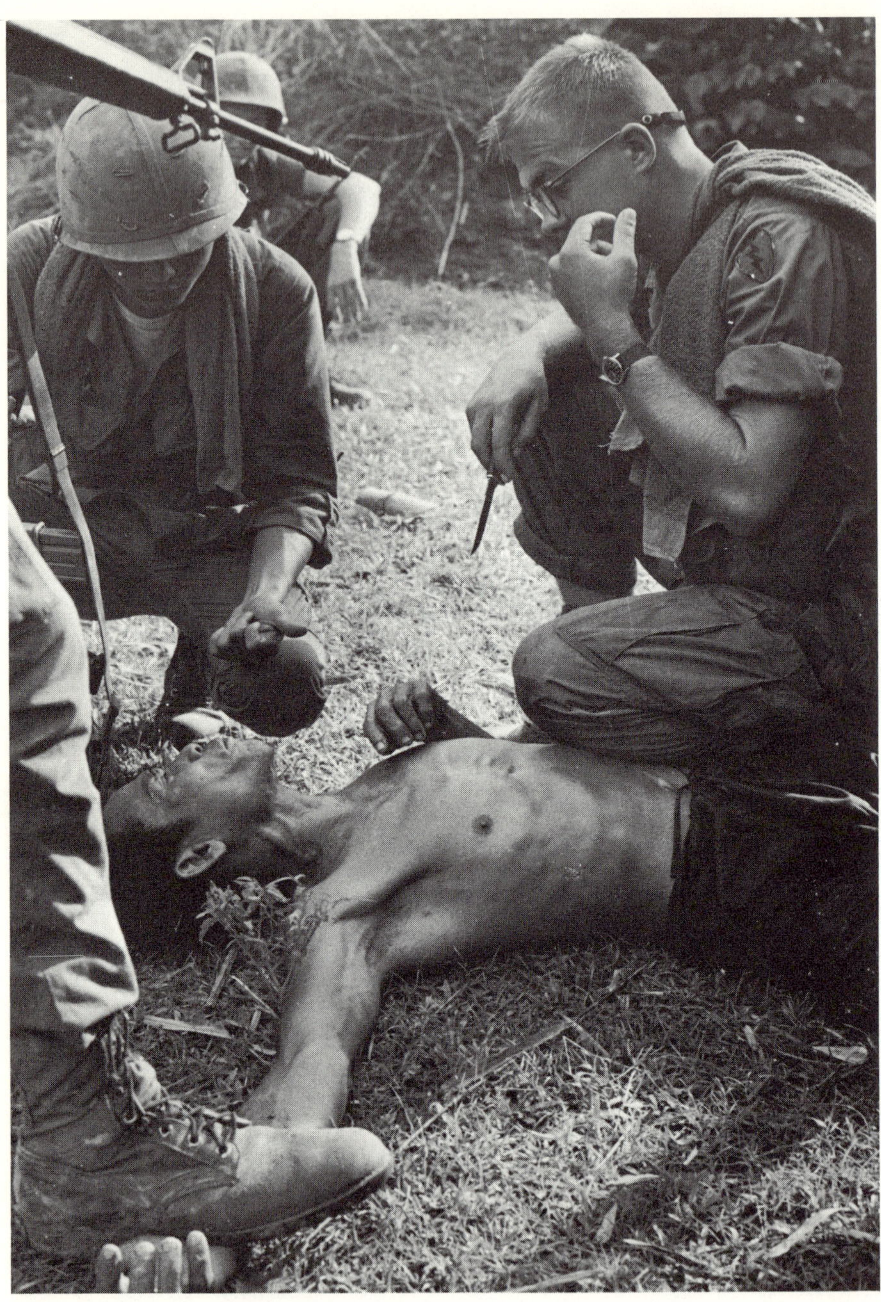

Same farmer being interrogated by a U.S. Army captain and South Vietnamese translator. *(Photo by Joseph W. Carey, BBM.)*

pro-Viet Cong and anti-Saigon. I also had to realize that the position, "We are in Vietnam because we are in sympathy with the aspirations and desires of the Vietnamese people," was a lie. If this is a lie, how many others are there?

I suppose that one of the things that bothered me from the very beginning in Vietnam was the condemnation of ARVN as a fighting force: "The Vietnamese are cowardly . . . the Vietnamese can't be disciplined . . . the Vietnamese just can't understand tactics and strategy . . . etc., etc." But the Viet Cong are Vietnamese. United States military files in Saigon document time and again a Viet Cong company surrounding two or even three ARVN companies and annihilating them. These same files document instances of a Viet Cong company, surrounded by ARVN battalions, mounting a ferocious fight and breaking loose. I have seen evidence of the Viet Cong attacking machine gun positions across open terrain with terrible losses. This can't be done with undisciplined bandits. For many years now the tactics and strategy of the Viet Cong have been so successful that massive fire power and air support on our side are the only things that have prevented a Viet Cong victory. These are all Vietnamese. What makes the difference? Major "Charging Charlie" Beckwith, the Special Forces commander at Plei Me, used the words "dedicated," "tough," "disciplined," "well-trained" and "brave" to describe the Viet Cong—and, almost in the same breath, condemned the Vietnamese on our side.

It became obvious that motivation was the prime factor in this problem. The Viet Cong soldier believes in his cause. He believes he is fighting for national independence. He has faith in his leaders, whose obvious dedication is probably greater than his own. His officers live in the same huts and eat the same food. His government counterpart knows that *his* leaders are in their positions because of family, money or reward for political favors. He knows his officers' primary concern is gaining wealth and favor. His captains and majors eat in French restaurants and pay as much for one meal as the soldier makes in a week. The officers sleep in guarded villas with their mistresses. They find many excuses for not being with their men in battle. The soldier hears his officers lie about their roles in battle. The soldier knows that he will be cheated out of his pay if possible. He knows equipment he may need is being sold downtown. His only motivation is the knowledge that he is fighting to perpetuate his government—a system that has kept him uneducated and in poverty. He has so many promises made to him, only to be broken, that now he believes nothing from his government.

I have seen the South Vietnamese soldier fight well, and at times ferociously, but usually only when in a position where there is no choice. At those times he is fighting for survival. On Project Delta there were many brave Vietnamese. When I knew them well enough to discuss such things, I asked them, "Why do you go on these missions time and again? You are volunteers. Why do you not quit and do less dangerous work?" The answer was always the same: "We are friends. We fight well together. If we quit, it will make the project bad." Never, "We are fighting for democracy . . . freedom . . . the people . . ." or any cause. The "enemy" he was fighting had become an abstraction. He was fighting, and fighting well, to sustain the brotherhood of his friends. The project had created a mystique of individualism and eliteness. He felt important. Trust and faith was put in him and he returned it in kind. The Americans didn't condescend to him. The life of every American on the team was dependent on the Vietnamese, and we let them know we were aware of it. We found out early that appealing to them on the basis of patriotism was a waste of time. They felt that they were nothing more than tools of the scheming Saigon politicians.

ARVN troops and their commanders know that if they don't bother the Viet Cong they will be safe from Viet Cong attacks. I'll never forget what a shock it was to find out that various troop commanders and district chiefs were actually making personal deals with "the enemy." The files in Saigon record instances where government troops with American advisors were told by the Viet Cong to lay down their weapons and walk away from the Americans. The troops did just that and the Viet Cong promises of safety to the troops were honored.

In an effort to show waning popularity for the Viet Cong, great emphasis was placed on figures of Viet Cong defections. Even if the unlikely possibility of the correctness of these figures is accepted, they are worthless when compared to ARVN desertions. The admitted desertion rate and reports of incidents of draft dodging, although deflated, were staggering. Usually, only those caught are reported. Reading OPSUMS (Operational Summaries) and newspapers while in Vietnam, I repeatedly saw references made to hundreds of ARVN listed as missing after the major battles. The reader is supposed to conclude that these hundreds, which by now total thousands, are prisoners of the Viet Cong. They are definitely not listed as deserters. If this were true, half of the Viet Cong would be tied down as guards in POW compounds—which, of course, is ridiculous.

This lack of enthusiasm and reluctance to join in battle wasn't difficult to figure. The majority of the people are either anti-Saigon or pro-Viet Cong, or both, and ARVN is drafted from the people.

I was not unique among my contemporaries in knowing most of these things. However, whenever anybody questioned our being in Vietnam—in light of the facts—the old rationale was always presented: "We have to stop the spread of communism somewhere . . . if we don't fight the commies here, we'll have to fight them at home . . . if we pull out, the rest of Asia will go Red . . . these are uneducated people who have been duped; they don't understand the difference between democracy and communism. . . ."

Being extremely anticommunist myself, these "arguments" satisfied me for a long time. In fact, I guess it was saying these very same things to myself over and over again that made it possible for me to participate in the things I did in Vietnam. But were we stopping communism? Even during the short period I had been in Vietnam, the Viet Cong had obviously gained in strength; the government controlled less and less of the country every day. The more troops and money we poured in, the more people hated us. Countries all over the world were losing sympathy with our stand in Vietnam. Countries which up to now had preserved a neutral position were becoming vehemently anti-American. A village near Tay Ninh in which I had slept in safety six months earlier was the center of a Viet Cong operation that cost the lives of two American friends. A Special Forces team operating in the area was almost decimated over a period of four months. United States Operations Mission (USOM), civilian representatives who had been able to travel by vehicle in relative safety throughout the countryside, were being kidnapped and killed. Like the military, they now had to travel by air.

The real question was whether communism was spreading in spite of our involvement—or because of it.

The attitude that the uneducated peasant lacked the political maturity to decide between communism and democracy and that ". . . we are only doing this for your own good," although it had a familiar colonialistic ring, at first seemed to have merit. Then I remembered that most of the villages would be under Viet Cong control for some of the time and under government control at other times. How many Americans had such a close look at both sides of the cloth? The more often government troops passed through an area, the more surely it would become sympathetic to the Viet Cong. The Viet Cong might sleep in the houses, but the government troops ransacked them. More often than not, the Viet Cong helped plant and harvest the crops; invariably government troops razed them. Rape is severely punished among the Viet Cong. It is so common among the ARVN that it is seldom reported for fear of even worse atrocities.

I saw the Airborne Brigade come into Nha Trang. Nha Trang is a government town and the Vietnamese Airborne Brigade are government troops. They were, in fact, originally trained by Special Forces, and they actually had the town in a grip of terror for three days. Merchants were collecting money to get them out of town; cafes and bars shut down.

The troops were accosting women on the streets. They would go into a place—a bar or cafe—and order varieties of food. When the checks came they wouldn't pay them. Instead they would simply wreck the place, dumping over the tables and smashing dishes. While these men were accosting women, the police would just stand by, powerless or unwilling to help. In fact, the situation was so difficult that American troops, if in town at the same time as the Vietnamese Airborne Brigade, were told to stay off the streets at night to avoid harm.

The whole thing was a lie. We weren't preserving freedom in South

Vietnam. There was no freedom to preserve. To avoid opposition to the government meant jail or death. Neutralism was forbidden and punished. Newspapers that didn't say the right thing were closed down. People are not even free to leave and Vietnam is one of those rare countries which doesn't fill its American visa quota. It's all there to see once the Red film is removed from the eyes. We aren't the freedom fighters. We are the Russian tanks blasting the hopes of an Asian Hungary.

It's not democracy we brought to Vietnam—it's anticommunism. This is the only choice the people in the village have. This is why most of them have embraced the Viet Cong and shunned the alternative. The people remember that when they were fighting the French for their national independence it was the Americans who helped the French. It's the American anticommunist bombs that kill their children. It's American anticommunism that has supported one dictator after another in Saigon. When anticommunist napalm burns their children, it hardly matters that an anticommunist Special Forces medic comes later to apply bandages.

One day I asked one of our Vietnamese helicopter pilots what he thought of the last bomb raid. "I think maybe today we make many Viet Cong." In July, when Mr. McNamara asked me how effective the bombing was in War Zone D, I told him, "It's an expensive defoliant. Unless dropped in a hip pocket it was only effective in housing areas." He didn't seem surprised. In fact, his only comment after my recital of my team's experiences in War Zone D was when he turned to General Westmoreland who was sitting on my right. "I guess we still have a small reaction problem," McNamara said. Ambassador Taylor said nothing.

While I was in Vietnam, the American and/or Saigon government was forever carping about North Vietnam breaking the Geneva Accords. Yet my own outfit, Special Forces, had first come to Vietnam in civilian clothes, traveling on civilian passports, for the specific purpose of training and arming the ethnic groups for the CIA, a violation of the Geneva Accords. The Saigon respect for the Accords was best symbolized by a political cartoon in the Saigon Post. It showed a man urinating on a scroll labeled "Geneva Accords 1954." When the troops of Project Delta uncovered the arms cache at Vung Ro Bay, General Nguyen Khan, pointing at the weapons, happily presented them to the three ICC men as proof to the world that Hanoi was breaking the Accords. Evidently they were too polite to point out that the cache had been found by men wearing U.S.-supplied uniforms, carrying American weapons; men who had been trained by Americans and were being paid by Americans. Neither did they mention that the general had flown to this spot in an American helicopter and that the weapons were being loaded onto an American-made ship manned by American-trained sailors.

It had taken a long time and a mountain of evidence but I had finally found some truths. The world is not just good guys and bad guys. Anticommunism is a lousy substitute for democracy. I know now that there are many types of communism but there are none which appeal to me. In the long run, I don't think Vietnam will be better off under Ho's brand of communism. But it's not for me or my government to decide. That decision is for the Vietnamese. I also know that we have allowed the creation of a military monster which will lie to our elected officials—and that both of them will lie to the American people.

For those people who, while deploring the war and bombings, defend it on the basis that it is stopping communism, I repeat the words of the Vietnamese pilot: "I think maybe today we make many Viet Cong." The Nazi bombing of London didn't make the Londoners quit. We have no monopoly on feelings for the underdog. People of other nations will continue to be increasingly sympathetic to this small agrarian country that is being pounded by the richest and most powerful nation in the world.

When I returned from Vietnam I was asked, "Do you resent young people who have never been in Vietnam, or in any war, protesting it?" On the contrary, I am relieved. I think they should be commended. I had to wait until I was thirty-five years old, after spending ten years in the Army and 18 months personally witnessing the stupidity of the war, before I could figure it out. That these young people were able to figure it out so quickly and so accurately is not only a credit to their intelligence but a great personal triumph over a lifetime of conditioning and indoctrination. I only hope that the picture I have tried to create will help other people come to the truth without wasting ten years. Those people protesting the war in Vietnam are not against our boys in Vietnam. On the contrary. What they are against is our boys *being* in Vietnam. They are not unpatriotic—again, the opposite is true. They are opposed to people, our own and others, dying for a lie, thereby corrupting the very word democracy.

There are those who will believe that I only started to feel these things after I returned from Vietnam. In my final weeks in that country I was putting out a very small information paper for Special Forces. The masthead of the paper was a flaming torch. I tried in my own way to bring a little light to the men with whom I worked. On the last page of the first issue were the names of four men—all friends of mine—reported killed in action on the same day. Among them was Sgt. Horner, one of the men I "procured" for Special Forces when he was stationed at the Army Presidio in San Francisco.

To those friends I wrote this dedication:

We can best immortalize our fallen members by striving for an enlightened future where Man has found another solution to his problems rather than resorting to the futility and stupidity of war.

Master Sergeant Donald Duncan left the United States Army in September of 1965 after ten years of service, including six years in the Special Forces and 18 months on active duty in Vietnam. While in Viet-

nam he received the South Vietnamese Silver Star, the Combat Infantry Badge, the Bronze Star and the United States Army Air Medal. He was nominated for the American Silver Star and was the first enlisted man in Vietnam to be nominated for the Legion of Merit. He participated in many missions behind enemy lines in War Zone D, Vung Tao and the An Lao Valley. In March 1965, he turned down the offer of a direct commission to the rank of captain. Instead he left Vietnam on September 5, 1965, and received his honorable discharge four days later.

After Pinkville

Noam Chomsky

On October 15, 1965, an estimated 70,000 people took part in large-scale anti-war demonstrations. The demonstrators heard pleas for an end to the bombing of North Vietnam and for a serious commitment to negotiations, in response to the negotiation offers from North Vietnam and UN efforts to settle the war. To be more precise, this is what they heard if they heard anything at all. On the Boston Common, for example, they heard not a word from the speakers, who were drowned out by hecklers and counter-demonstrators.

On the Senate floor, Senator Mansfield denounced the "sense of utter irresponsibility" shown by the demonstrators, while Everett Dirksen said the demonstrations were "enough to make any person loyal to his country weep." Richard Nixon wrote, in a letter to *The New York Times,* that ". . . victory for the Viet Cong . . . would mean ultimately the destruction of freedom of speech for all men for all time not only in Asia but in the United States as well"—nothing less.

In a sense, Senator Mansfield was right in speaking of the sense of utter irresponsibility shown by demonstrators. They should have been demanding not an end to the bombing of North Vietnam and negotiations, but a complete and immediate withdrawal of all American troops and materiel—

an end to any forceful interference in the internal affairs of Vietnam or any other nation. They should have been demanding not merely that the US adhere to international law and its own treaty obligations—thus removing itself forthwith from Vietnam; but they should also have exercised their right and duty to resist the violence of the State, which was as vicious in practice as it was illegal in principle.

In October 1967, there were, once again, mass demonstrations against the war, this time in Washington and at the Pentagon. A few months earlier, still larger, though less militant, demonstrations had taken place in New York. The Têt offensive, shortly after, revealed that American military strategy was "foolish to the point of insanity."[1] It also revealed to the public that government propaganda was either an illusion or a fraud. Moreover, an international monetary crisis threatened, attributable in part to Vietnam.

In retrospect, it seems possible that the war could have been ended if popular pressure had been maintained. But many radicals felt that the war was over, that it had become, in any case, a "liberal issue," and they turned to other concerns. Those who had demanded no more than an end to the bombing of North Vietnam and a commitment to negotiations saw their demands being realized, and lapsed into silence.

These demands, however, had always been beside the point. As to negotiations, there is, in fact, very little to negotiate. As long as an American army of occupation remains in Vietnam, the war will continue. Withdrawal of American troops must be a unilateral act, as the invasion of Vietnam by the American government was a unilateral act in the first place. Those who had been calling for "negotiations now" were deluding themselves and others, just as those who now call for a cease-fire that will leave an American expeditionary force in Vietnam are not facing reality.

As to the bombing of North Vietnam, this had always been a side-show, in large measure a propaganda cover for the American invasion of the South. The US government could not admit that it was invading South Vietnam to protect from its own population a government that we had installed. Therefore it was rescuing the South Vietnamese from "aggression." But then surely it must strike at the "source of aggression." Hence the bombing of North Vietnam. This, at least, seems the most rational explanation for the bombing of North Vietnam in February 1965, at a time when no North Vietnamese troops were in the South, so far as was known, and there was a bare trickle of supplies.

To be sure, those who are "in the know" have different explanations for the bombing of North Vietnam. Consider, for example, the explanation offered by Sir Robert Thompson, the British counter-insurgency expert who has been for many years a close adviser of the American army in South Vietnam—a man who is, incidentally, much admired by American social scientists who like to consider themselves "tough-minded, hard-nosed realists," no doubt because of his utter contempt for democracy and his relatively pure colonialist attitudes. In the British newspaper *The Guardian,* May 19, 1969, his views are explained as follows:

> He also condemns the bombing of the North. The US Air Force in 1965 was having great budgetary problems, because the army was the only one that had a war on its hands and was thus getting all the money. "So the Air Force had to get in, and you had the bombing of North Vietnam . . . the budgetary problems of the Air Force were then solved."

In his *No Exit From Vietnam* (1969), he explains more graphically the attractiveness of air power:

> One can so easily imagine the Commander of the Strategic Air Command striding up and down his operations room wondering how he could get in on the act. With all that power available and an enormous investment doing nothing, it is not surprising that reasons and means had to be found for their engagement. The war was therefore waged in a manner which enabled this massive air armada to be used round the clock. . . . In this way the war could be fought as an American war without the previous frustrations of cooperating with the Vietnamese.

Or consider the explanation for the bombing of the North offered by Adam Yarmolinsky, Principal Deputy Assistant Secretary of Defense for International Security Affairs, 1965–66, previous Special Assistant to the Secretary of Defense. According to his analysis, the strategic bombing of North Vietnam "produced no military advantages except for its putative favorable impact on morale in the south. But [this step] was taken, at least in part, because it was one of the things that the US military forces were best prepared to do."[2]

So North Vietnam was flattened and impelled to send troops to the South, as it did a few months after the bombing began, if the Department of Defense can be believed.

Since the bombing of North Vietnam "produced no military advantages" and was extremely costly, it could be stopped with little difficulty and little effect on the American war in South Vietnam. And so it was, in two steps: on April 1, 1968, when the regular bombing was restricted to the southern part of North Vietnam, and on November 1, when it was halted. At the same time, the total American bombing, now restricted to Laos and South Vietnam, was increased in April and increased again in November. By March 1969 the total level of bombardment had reached 130,000 tons a month—nearly two Hiroshimas a week in South Vietnam and Laos, defenseless countries. And Melvin Laird's projection for the next twelve to eighteen months was the same.[3] The redistribution (and intensification) of bombing and the largely empty negotiations stilled domestic protest for a time and permitted the war to go on as before.

We can now look back over the failure of the "peace movement" to sustain and intensify its protest over the past four years. By now, defoliation has been carried out over an area the size of Massachusetts, with what effect no one has any real idea. The bombardment of Vietnam far exceeds the bombardment of Korea or anything in World War II. The number of Vietnamese killed or driven from their homes cannot be seriously estimated.

It is important to understand that the massacre of the rural population of Vietnam and their forced evacuation is not an accidental by-product of the war. Rather it is of the very essence of American strategy. The theory behind it has been explained with great clarity and explicitness, for example, by Professor Samuel Huntington, Chairman of the Government Department at Harvard and at the time (1968) Chairman of the Council on Vietnamese Studies of the Southeast Asia Development Advisory Group, in effect the State Department task force on Vietnam. Writing in *Foreign Affairs,* he explains that the Viet Cong is "a powerful force which cannot be dislodged from its constituency so long as the constituency continues to exist." The conclusion is obvious, and he does not shrink from it. We can ensure that the constituency ceases to exist by "direct application of mechanical and conventional power . . . on such a massive scale as to produce a massive migration from countryside to city," where the Viet Cong con-

(Photo by Joseph W. Carey, BBM.)

stituency—the rural population—can, it is hoped, be controlled in refugee camps and suburban slums around Saigon.

Technically, the process is known as "urbanization" or "modernization." It is described, with the proper contempt, by Daniel Ellsberg, a Department of Defense consultant on pacification in South Vietnam, who concludes, from his extensive on-the-spot observations, that "we have, of course, demolished the society of Vietnam," that "the bombing of the South has gone on long enough to disrupt the society of South Vietnam enormously and probably permanently"; he speaks of the "people who have been driven to Saigon by what Huntington regards as our 'modernizing instruments' in Vietnam, bombs and artillery."[4] Reporters have long been aware of the nature of these tactics, aware that "by now the sheer weight of years of firepower, massive sweeps, and grand forced population shifts have reduced the population base of the NLF . . ."[5] so that conceivably, by brute force, we may still hope to "win."

One thing is clear: so long as an organized social life can be maintained in South Vietnam, the NLF will be a powerful, probably dominant, force. This is the dilemma which has always plagued American policy, and which has made it impossible for us to permit even the most rudimentary democratic institutions in South Vietnam. For these reasons we have been forced to the solution outlined by Professor Huntington: to crush the people's war, we must eliminate the people.

A second thing is tolerably clear: there has been no modification in this policy. Once again, as two years ago, there is mounting popular protest against the war. Once again, a tactical adjustment is being devised that will permit Washington to pursue its dual goal, to pacify the people of South Vietnam while pacifying the American people also. The first of these tasks has not been accomplished too well. The second, to our shame, has been managed quite successfully, for the most part. Now, we hear that the burden of fighting the war is to be shifted away from the American infantry to the B-52s and fighter-bombers and a mercenary force of Vietnamese. Only a token force of between 200,000 and 300,000 men, backed by the Pacific Naval and Air command, will be retained indefinitely, to ensure that the Vietnamese have the right of self-determination.

At a recent press conference, Averell Harriman explained that the North Vietnamese cannot believe that we really intend to abandon the huge military bases we have constructed in Vietnam, such as the one at Cam Ranh Bay (*Village Voice*, Nov. 27). Knowledgeable American observers have found it equally difficult to believe this. For example, as long ago as August 27, 1965, James Reston wrote in the *Times:*

> US bases and supply areas are being constructed on a scale far larger than is necessary to care for the present level of American forces . . . in fact, the US base at Cam Ranh . . . is being developed

> into another Okinawa, not merely for the purposes of this war, but as a major power complex from which American officials hope a wider alliance of Asian nations, with the help of the US, will eventually be able to contain the expansion of China.

The phrase "contain the expansion of China" must be understood as code for the unpronounceable expression: "repress movements for national independence and social reconstruction in Southeast Asia."

Premier Eisaku Sato, in a speech described by American officials as part of a joint Japanese-American policy statement, announced that we are entering a "new Pacific age" in which "a new order will be created by Japan and the United States" (*New York Times*, Nov. 22, 1969). His words, one must assume, were chosen advisedly. To perpetuate this new order we will need military bases such as that at Cam Ranh Bay, which can play the role of the Canal Zone in the Western Hemisphere. There we can base our own forces and train those of our loyal dependencies.

We will no doubt soon proceed to construct an "Inter-Asian" army that can protect helpless governments from their own populations, much as the Brazilians were called in to legitimize our Dominican intervention. Where popular rebellion is in progress, these forces can gain valuable experience. Thus a senior American officer at Camp Bearcat in South Vietnam, where Thai units are based, explains that "they are infusing their army with experience they could never get in their own homeland. . . . They are coordinating their own piece of real estate." And a Thai colonel adds: "If my country ever has the same subversion, I'll have to fight there. I want to practice here" (*New York Times*, December 3). Surely Reston was right in 1965 in speculating about our long-range plans for the South Vietnamese bases, from which our "token force" of a quarter of a million men will operate in the Seventies.*

Who can complain about a quarter of a million men, a force that can be compared, let us say, with the Japanese army of 160,000 which invaded North China in 1937, in an act of aggression that scandalized the civilized world and set the stage for the Pacific phase of World War II? In fact, counter-insurgency experts like Sir Robert Thompson have long argued that

*On December 10, 1969, after this article was written, Reston returned to the question of Cam Ranh Bay, stating that it was now "an air and naval base which is the best in Asia," and that it has been a "fundamental question throughout the Paris negotiations" whether the US is willing to abandon it "and many other modern military bases." He raises the question whether the US would withdraw all troops or only all "combat forces," a plan which "could leave a couple of hundred thousand Americans in Vietnam to maintain and fly the planes and helicopter gunships and continue to train and supply and help direct the Vietnamese."

There is no indication of any serious intention to withdraw all forces or to abandon the bases. As Joseph Kraft has reported, the American refusal to commit itself to the principle of complete withdrawal is one of the factors blocking progress in Paris.

the American forces were far too large to be effective, and have advocated a "low-cost, long-haul strategy" of a sort which will now very likely be adopted by the Nixon administration, if, once again, the American people will trust their leaders and settle into passivity.

As American combat troops are withdrawn, their place, it is hoped, will be taken by a more effective force of Vietnamese—just as Czechoslovakia is controlled, it is reported, by fewer than 100,000 Russian troops. Meanwhile, the war will no doubt be escalated technologically. It will become more "capital intensive."[6] Some of the prospects were revealed in a speech by Chief of Staff William Westmoreland, reported in the *Christian Science Monitor* (October 25-7) under the heading: "Technologically the Vietnam war has been a great success." General Westmoreland "sees machines carrying more and more of the burden." He says:

> I see an army built into and around an integrated area control system that exploits the advanced technology of communications, sensors, fire direction, and the required automatic data processing—a system that is sensitive to the dynamics of the ever-changing battlefield—a system that materially assists the tactical commander in making sound and timely decisions.

Further details are presented by Leonard Sullivan, Deputy Director of Research and Development for South East Asian Matters:[7]

> These developments open up some very exciting horizons as to what we can do five or ten years from now: When one realizes that we can detect anything that perspires, moves, carries metal, makes a noise, or is hotter or colder than its surroundings, one begins to see the potential. This is the beginning of instrumentation of the entire battlefield. Eventually, we will be able to tell when anybody shoots, what he is shooting at, and where he was shooting from. You begin to get a "Year 2000" vision of an electronic map with little lights that flash for different kinds of activity. This is what we require for this "porous" war, where the friendly and the enemy are all mixed together.

Note the time scale that is projected for Vietnam. News reports reveal some of the early stages of these exciting developments. The *Times*, November 22, reports a plan to use remote-controlled unmanned aircraft as supply transports for combat areas. On October 1, the *Times* explains that:

> The landscape of Vietnam and the border regions are studded with electronic sensors that beep information into the banks of computers. Radar, cameras, infrared detectors and a growing array of more exot-

> ic devices contribute to the mass of information. Not long ago reconnaissance planes began carrying television cameras.

The data go into the Combined Intelligence Center near Tansonnhut Air Base: "Day and night in its antiseptic interior a family of blinking, whirring computers devours, digests and spews out a Gargantuan diet of information about the enemy," the better to serve the "conglomerate of allied civil and military organizations that work together to destroy the Vietcong's underground government"—freely admitted to have been the most authentic popular social structure in South Vietnam prior to the American effort to demolish the society of Vietnam. One can understand the gloating of Douglas Pike: "The tactics that delivered victory in the Viet Minh war, however impressive once, had been relegated by science to the military history textbook."[8]

What this means is, to put it simply, that we intend to turn the land of Vietnam into an automated murder machine. The techniques of which Westmoreland, Sullivan, and Pike are so proud are, of course, designed for use against a special kind of enemy: one who is too weak to retaliate, whose land can be occupied. These "Year 2000" devices, which Westmoreland describes as a quantum jump in warfare, are fit only for colonial wars. There is surely an element of lunacy in this technocratic nightmare. And if we are still at all capable of honesty, we will, with little difficulty, identify its antecedents.

Our science may yet succeed in bringing to reality the fears of Bernard Fall—no alarmist, and fundamentally in favor of the war during its early years—who wrote in one of his last essays that "Vietnam as a cultural and historic entity . . . is threatened with extinction as the country literally dies under the blows of the largest military machine ever unleashed on an area of this size." The South Vietnamese minister of information wrote in 1968 that ordinary Vietnamese would continue "to be horrified and embittered at the way the Americans fight their war. . . . Our peasants will remember their cratered rice fields and defoliated forests, devastated by an alien air force that seems at war with the very land of Vietnam."[9]

American reporters have told us the same thing so often that it is almost superfluous to quote. Tom Buckley—to mention only the most recent—describes the delta and the central lowlands:

> . . . bomb craters beyond counting, the dead gray and black fields, that have been defoliated and scorched by napalm, land that has been plowed flat to destroy Vietcong hiding places. And everywhere can be seen the piles of ashes forming the outlines of huts and houses, to show where hamlets once stood.[10]

The truth about defoliants is only beginning to emerge, with the discovery that one of the two primary agents used is "potentially dangerous, but needing further study" while the other causes cancer and birth defects, and probably mental retardation. Both will continue to be used in Vietnam against enemy "training and regroupment centers"—i.e., anywhere we please, throughout the countryside.[11]

Of course it may be argued that the American government did not know, in 1961, that these agents were so dangerous. That is true. It was merely an experiment. Virtually nothing was known about what the effects might be. Perhaps there would be no ill effects, or perhaps—at the other extreme—Vietnam would become unfit for human life, or a race of mutants and mental retardates would be created. How could we know, without trying? In such ways "the tactics that delivered victory in the Viet Minh war, however impressive once, had been relegated by science to the military history textbook."

• • • • •

. . . Americans know virtually nothing about the bombing of South Vietnam. To my knowledge, there has been only one pro-Western correspondent who has spent time in the liberated zones of South Vietnam, Katsuichi Honda—and I am sure that his reports in *Asahi* in the fall of 1967 are known to very few Americans.[12] He describes, for example, the incessant attacks on undefended villages by gunboats in the Mekong river and by helicopter gunships "firing away at random at farmhouses":

> They seemed to fire whimsically and in passing even though they were not being shot at from the ground nor could they identify the people as NLF. They did it impulsively for fun, using the farmers for targets as if in a hunting mood. They are hunting Asians. . . . This whimsical firing would explain the reason why the surgical wards in every hospital in the towns of the Mekong delta were full of wounded.

He is speaking, notice, of the Mekong Delta, where few North Vietnamese soldiers were identified until several months after the Têt offensive; where, according to American intelligence, there were 800 North Vietnamese troops before last summer;[13] and, which contained some 40 percent of the population of South Vietnam prior to the American assault.

Occasionally such material finds its way to the American press. Consider again the Mekong Delta. "In March [1969] alone, the United States Ninth Infantry Division reported that it killed 3,504 Vietcong troops and sympathizers in the northern delta [and] senior officers confidently forecast that they will continue to kill at least 100 a day well into the summer." The "conflagration . . . is tearing the social fabric apart." In "free-fire zones, the Americans could bring to bear at any time the enormous firepower available from helicopter gunships, bombers and artillery . . . fighter-bombers and artillery pound the enemy positions into the gray porridge that the green delta land becomes when pulverized by high explosives."[14]

Apparently the performance of the Ninth Division was not entirely satisfactory, however. ". . . in the Mekong Delta, US military advisers at My Tho told a UPI correspondent, Robert Kaylor, that the government's pacification program was still being hampered by the effects of indiscriminate killing of civilians by US Ninth Infantry Division troops recently withdrawn from the area. 'You can't exactly expect people who have had parts of their family blown away by the Ninth to be wholeheartedly on our side,' said the US source, a member of a pacification team."[15]

In the *Monitor,* October 14 [1969], there is a front page story reviewing such efforts. It explains that "the proportion of the country 'pacified' has risen with the flow of peasants to resettlement and refugee areas," although the Viet Cong "currently are intensifying their campaign to drive peasants back to their home areas where [they] have a better chance of controlling them." The picture is clear. We, in our magnanimity, are using our modernizing instruments, bombs and artillery, to lead the suffering peasants to the promised land of resettlement and refugee areas, while the ferocious Viet Cong—mere "village thugs," as the MIT political scientist, Ithiel Pool, explains in the journal of the Gandhi Peace Foundation—cruelly drive them back to their homes. The *Monitor* article also notes that "Despite years of thought and effort, officials here are still not agreed on how best to pacify a troubled land. In those years, pacification has advanced from being a theoretical ideal—though inconvenient—to the more important but second-class status of being 'the other war' "—and a proper theoretical exercise for American scientists and scholars."

The New York Times, September 24, presents an example of how pacification proceeds. Northwest of Saigon, 700 soldiers encircled a village, killing twenty-two and arresting fifty-three. It was the fourth such operation in this village in fifteen months. As for the villagers: "The Vietcong are everywhere, they say, and will be back when the Americans leave." An American junior officer, looking at the deserted central market, had this to say: "They say this village is 80 percent VC supporters. By the time we finish this it will be 95 percent." Such reports are hardly more newsworthy than a small item of September 27 which notes "that United States Army helicopter gunships mistakenly attacked a group of Vietnamese civilians 25 miles west of Tamky Tuesday, killing 14 civilians . . . United States helicopter gunships killed 7 unarmed civilians and wounded 17 others in a similar incident Sept. 16 in the Mekong delta." It is not easy to avoid such accidents as we try to ensure that the Viet Cong constituency ceases to exist.

In *Look* magazine, November 18, Foreign Editor Robert Moskin describes his visit to a refugee camp, which "tells part of the story of Vietnam's hopelessness." Its 3,125 refugees (240 men) were transferred to this "desolate sand-dune camp" in a military sweep last summer from an island that was regarded as a VC stronghold: "The rest of the men are still hiding with the VC in the tall grass." This is in Quang Nam province,

Concertina wire surrounding a Vietnamese orphanage. The beer cans are filled with pebbles to warn of entry. *(Photo by Robert C. Scheu, Photon West.)*

where even the American officials in charge admit that the battle was lost "to Viet-Cong forces recruited for the most part from within the province."[16] With an honesty that others would do well to emulate, Moskin states that in Vietnam "America's historic westward-driving wave has crested."

With justice, a staff major [of the Americal Division in Chulai] said: "We are at war with the 10-year-old children. It may not be humanitarian, but that's what it's like."[17]

And now there is Song My—"Pinkville." More than two decades of indoctrination and counter-revolutionary interventions have created the possibility of a name like "Pinkville"—and the acts that may be done in a place so named. Orville and Jonathan Schell have pointed out[18] what any literate person should realize, that this was no isolated atrocity, but the logical consequence of a virtual war of extermination directed against helpless peasants: "enemies," "reds," "dinks." But there are, perhaps, still deeper roots. Some time ago, I read with a slight shock the statement by Eqbal Ahmad that "America has institutionalized even its genocide," referring to the fact that the extermination of the Indians "has become the object of public entertainment and children's games."[19] Shortly after, I was thumbing through my daughter's fourth-grade social science reader.[20] The protagonist, Robert, is told the story of the extermination of the Pequot tribe by Captain John Mason:

> His little army attacked in the morning before it was light and took the Pequots by surprise. The soldiers broke down the stockade with their axes, rushed inside, and set fire to the wigwams. They killed nearly all the braves, squaws, and children, and burned their corn and other food. There were no Pequots left to make more trouble. When the other Indian tribes saw what good fighters the white men were, they kept the peace for many years.
>
> "I wish I were a man and had been there," thought Robert.

Nowhere does Robert express, or hear, second thoughts about the matter. The text omits some other pertinent remarks: for example, by Cotton Mather, who said that "It was supposed that no less than six hundred Pequot souls were brought down to hell that day."[21] Is it an exaggeration to suggest that our history of extermination and racism is reaching its climax in Vietnam today? It is not a question that Americans can easily put aside.

Notes

[1]Assistant Secretary of Defense Paul Warnke—as quoted by Townsend Hoopes, see *New York Times*, Sept. 28, 1969.

[2]*No More Vietnams?*, R. Pfeffer, ed., Harper & Row, 1968.

[3]For detailed analysis based largely on Defense Department sources, see Gabriel Kolko, *London Bulletin*, August, 1969.

[4]*No More Vietnams?* For further discussion, see my article in *The New York Review*, Jan. 2, 1969.

[5]Elizabeth Pond, *Christian Science Monitor*, Nov. 8, 1969.

[6]In the apt phrase of E. Herman and R. Duboff, "How to coo like a dove while fighting to win," pamphlet of Philadelphia SANE, 20 S. 12th St., Phila. 19107.

[7]*Congressional Record*, Aug. 11, 1969. Cited in the *Bulletin of Concerned Asian Scholars*, Oct., 1969 (1737 Cambridge St., Cambridge, Mass.—an important journal for those concerned with Asian affairs).

[8]*War, Peace, and the Viet Cong*, MIT, 1969. He estimates that in 1963 "perhaps half the population of South Vietnam at least tacitly supported the NLF." The same estimate was given by the US Mission in 1962. Elsewhere, he has explained that in late 1964 it was impossible to consider an apparently genuine offer of a coalition government, because there was no force that could compete politically with the Viet Cong, with the possible exception of the Buddhists, who were not long after suppressed as a political force by Marshal Ky's American-backed storm troopers. The same difficulty has been noted, repeatedly, by spokesmen for the American and Saigon governments and reporters. For some examples, see Herman and Duboff, *op. cit.*, or my *American Power and the New Mandarins*, Pantheon, 1969, chapter 3.

[9]*New York Times*, June 11, 1968.

[10]*New York Times Magazine*, November 23, 1969.

[11]See Washington *Post,* Oct. 31; Los Angeles *Times,* Oct. 31; New York *Post,* Nov. 4; *Science,* Nov. 7. A Vietnamese student in the United States, Ngo Vinh Long, has summarized much of what is known, including his personal experience from 1959-1963 when he visited "virtually every hamlet and village in the country" as a military map maker, in *Thoi-Bao Ga,* Nov. 1969, 76a Pleasant St., Cambridge, Mass., a monthly publication of Vietnamese students in the United States. He describes how defoliation has been used since 1961 to drive peasants into government controlled camps, and from his own experience and published records in Vietnam, he records some of the effects: starvation, death, hideously deformed babies. He quotes the head of the Agronomy Section of the Japan Science Council who claims that by 1967 about half the arable land had been seriously affected. For American estimates, see the report of the Daddario subcommittee of the House committee on Science and Astronautics, Aug. 8, 1969. They estimate the total area sprayed through 1968 as 6,600 square miles (extrapolating through 1969 the figure would reach about 8,600 square miles, about 60 percent of this respraying—over 10 percent of it crop destruction).

[12]They have appeared in English, and can be obtained from the Committee for the English publication of "Vietnam—a voice from the villages," c/o Mrs. Reiko Ishida, 2-13-7, Nishikata, Bunyo-ku, Tokyo.

[13]"Before this summer, the enemy in the delta consisted mostly of indigenous Vietcong units and guerrillas, many of whom worked during the day in the rice fields and fought at night. The only North Vietnamese were troops and officers who led some of the guerrilla units. They numbered about 800 as against an estimated total of 49,000 Vietcong soldiers and support troops." *New York Times,* September 15, 1969. On Sept. 16, 1969, the *Times* reports that "for the first time in the war, a regular North Vietnamese army unit, the 18B Regiment, had attacked in the delta."

[14]*New York Times,* Peter Arnett, April 15, 1969. Arnett claims that only 90 percent of the enemy forces of 40,000 are recruited locally, giving a far higher estimate of North Vietnamese than the intelligence reports cited above, or others: e.g., *Monitor,* Sept. 16, which reports that in the early fall of 1969 "North Vietnamese troops in the delta doubled in number, to between 2,000 and 3,000 men."

[15]Boston *Globe,* Dec. 1.

[16]William Nighswonger, *Rural Pacification in Vietnam,* Praeger, 1967.

[17]Henry Kamm, *New York Times,* Dec. 1.

[18]*New York Times,* Nov. 26.

[19]In *No More Vietnams?* On the widely noted analogy between Vietnam and the Indian wars see my *American Power and the New Mandarins,* chapter 3, note 42.

[20]Harold B. Clifford, *Exploring New England,* New Unified Social Studies, Chicago: Follett Publishing Co., 1961.

[21]See Howard Zinn, "Violence and social change," Boston University *Graduate Journal,* Fall, 1968. When disease decimated the Indians, Mather said: "The woods were almost cleared of those pernicious creatures, to make room for a better growth."

Noam Chomsky, professor at the Massachusetts Institute of Technology, is well-known in the fields of speech and linguistics, as well as for his activism in the U.S. peace movement. His recent book American Power and the New Mandarins *examines the role liberal social science has played in the Cold War.*

On Genocide

Jean-Paul Sartre

The word "genocide" is relatively new. It was coined by the jurist Raphael Lemkin between the two world wars. But the fact of genocide is as old as humanity. To this day there has been no society protected by its structure from committing that crime. Every case of genocide is a product of history and bears the stamp of the society which has given birth to it. The one we have before us for judgment is the act of the greatest capitalist power in the world today. It is as such that we must try to analyze it—in other words, as the simultaneous expression of the economic infrastructure of that power, its political objectives and the contradictions of its present situation.

In particular, we must try to understand the genocidal intent in the war which the American government is waging against Vietnam, for Article 2 of the 1948 Geneva Convention defines genocide on the basis of intent; the Convention was tacitly referring to memories which were still fresh. Hitler had proclaimed it his deliberate intent to exterminate the Jews. He made genocide a political means and did not hide it. A Jew had to be put to death, whoever he was, not for having been caught carrying a weapon or for having joined a resistance movement, but simply *because he was a Jew*. The American government has avoided making such clear statements. It has even claimed that it was answering the call of its allies, the South Vietnamese, who had been attacked by the communists. Is it possible for us, by studying the facts objectively, to discover implicit in them such a genocidal intention? And after such an investigation, can we say that the armed forces of the United States are killing Vietnamese in Vietnam for the simple reason that they are Vietnamese?

This is something which can only be established after an historical examination: the structure of war changes right along with the infrastructures of society. Between 1860 and the present day, the meaning and the objectives of military conflicts have changed profoundly, the final stage of this metamorphosis being precisely the "war of example" which the United States is waging in Vietnam.

In 1856, there was a convention for the protection of the property of neutrals; 1864, Geneva: protection for the wounded; 1899, 1907, The Hague: two conferences which attempted to make rules for war. It is no accident that jurists and governments were multiplying their efforts to "humanize war" on the very eve of the two most frightful massacres that mankind has ever known. Vladimir Dedijer has shown very effectively in his

Reprinted from *Ramparts*, February 1968.

study "On Military Conventions" that the capitalist societies during this same period were giving birth to the monster of total war in which they express their true nature. He attributes this phenomenon to the following:

1. The competition between industrial nations fighting for new markets produces a permanent antagonism which is expressed in ideology and in practice by what is known as "bourgeois nationalism."

2. The development of industry, which is the source of this hostility, provides the means of resolving it to the advantage of one of the competitors, through the production of more and more *massively* destructive weapons. The consequence of this development is that it becomes increasingly difficult to make any distinction between the front and behind the lines, between the civilian population and the soldiers.

3. At the same time, new military objectives—the factories—arise near the towns. And even when they are not producing materiel directly for the armies, they maintain, at least to some extent, the economic strength of the country. It is precisely this strength that the enemy aims to destroy: this is at once the aim of war and the means to that end.

4. The consequence of this is that everyone is mobilized: the peasant fights at the front, the worker fights behind the lines, the peasant women take over for their husbands in the fields. This *total* struggle of nation against nation tends to make the worker a soldier too, since in the last analysis the power which is economically stronger is more likely to win.

5. The democratic facade of the bourgeois nations and the emancipation of the working class have led to the participation of the masses in politics. The masses have no control at all over government decisions, but the middle classes imagine that by voting they exercise some kind of remote control. Except in cases of defensive wars, the working classes are torn between their desire for peace and the nationalism which has been instilled in them. Thus war, seen in a new light and distorted by propaganda, becomes the ethical decision of the whole community. All the citizens of each warring nation (or almost all, after they have been manipulated) are the enemies of all those of the other country. War has become absolutely total.

6. These same societies, as they continue their technological expansion, continue to extend the scope of their competition by increasing communications. The famous "One World" of the Americans was already in existence by the end of the 19th century when Argentine wheat dealt a final blow to English agriculture. Total war is no longer only between all members of one national community and all those of another: it is also total because it will very likely set the whole world up in flames.

Thus, war between the bourgeois nations—of which the 1914 war was the first example but which had threatened Europe since 1900—is not the "invention" of one man or one government, but simply a necessity for those who, since the beginning of the century, have sought to "extend politics by other means." The option is clear: either *no* war or *that* kind of total war. Our fathers fought that kind of war. And the governments who saw it coming, with neither the intelligence nor the courage to stop it, were wasting their time and the time of the jurists when they stupidly tried to "humanize" it.

Nevertheless, during the First World War a genocidal intent appeared only sporadically. As in previous centuries, the essential aim was to crush the military power of the enemy and only secondarily to ruin his economy. But even though there was no longer any clear distinction between civilians and soldiers, it was still only rarely (except for a few terrorist raids) that the civilian population was expressly made a target. Moreover, the belligerent nations (or at least those who were doing the fighting) were industrial powers. This made for a certain initial balance: against the possibility of any real extermination each side had its own deterrent force—namely the power of applying the law of "an eye for an eye." This explains why, in the midst of the carnage, a kind of prudence was maintained.

However, since 1830, throughout the last century and continuing to this very day, there have been countless acts of genocide whose causes are likewise to be found in the structure of capitalist societies. To export their products and their capital, the great powers, particularly England and France, set up colonial empires. The name "overseas possessions" given by the French to their conquests indicates clearly that they had been able to acquire them only by wars of aggression. The adversary was sought out in his own territory, in Africa and Asia, in the underdeveloped countries, and far from waging "total war" (which would have required an initial balance of forces), the colonial powers, because of their overwhelming superiority of firepower, found it necessary to commit only an expeditionary force. Victory was easy, at least in conventional military terms. But since this blatant aggression kindled the hatred of the civilian population, and since civilians were potentially rebels and soldiers, the colonial troops maintained their authority by terror—by perpetual massacre. These massacres were genocidal in character: they aimed at the destruction of "a part of an ethnic, national, or religious group" in order to terrorize the remainder and to wrench apart the indigenous society.

After the bloodbath of conquest in Algeria during the last century, the French imposed the *Code Civil*, with its middle-class conceptions of property and inheritance, on a tribal society where each community held land in common. Thus they systematically destroyed the economic infrastructure of the country, and tribes of peasants soon saw their lands fall into the hands of French speculators. Indeed, colonization is not a matter of mere conquest as was the German annexation of Alsace-Lorraine; it is by its very nature an act of cultural genocide. Colonization cannot take place without systematically liquidating all the characteristics of the native society—and simultaneously refusing to integrate the natives into the mother country and denying them access to its advantages. Colonialism is, after all, an economic system: the colony sells its raw materials and agricultural products at a reduced price to the colonizing power. The latter, in return, sells its manufactured goods to the colony at world market prices. This curious system of trade is only possible if there is a colonial subproletariat which can be forced to work for starvation wages. For the subject people this inevitably means the extinction of their national character, culture, customs, sometimes even language. They live in their underworld of misery like dark phantoms ceaselessly reminded of their subhumanity.

However, their value as an almost unpaid labor force protects them, to a certain extent, against physical genocide. The Nuremberg Tribunal was still fresh in people's minds when the French massacred 45,000 Algerians at Setif, as an "example." But this sort of thing was so commonplace that no one even thought to condemn the French government in the same terms as they did the Nazis.

But this "deliberate destruction of a part of a national group" could not be carried out any more extensively without harming the interests of the French settlers. By exterminating the subproletariat, they would have exterminated themselves as settlers. This explains the contradictory attitude of these *pieds-noirs* during the Algerian war: they urged the Army to commit massacres, and more than one of them dreamed of total genocide. At the same time they attempted to compel the Algerians to "fraternize" with them. It is because France could neither liquidate the Algerian people nor integrate them with the French that it lost the Algerian war.

These observations enable us to understand how the structure of colonial wars underwent a transformation after the end of the Second World War. For it was at about this time that the colonial peoples, enlightened by that conflict and its impact on the "empires," and later by the victory of Mao Tse-tung, resolved to regain their national independence. The characteristics of the struggle were determined from the beginning: the colonialists had the superiority in weapons, the indigenous population the advantage of numbers. Even in Algeria—a colony where there was settlement as much as there was exploitation—the proportion of *colons* to natives was one to nine. During the two world wars, many of the colonial peoples had been trained as soldiers and had become experienced fighters. However, the short supply and poor quality of their arms—at least in the beginning—kept the number of fighting units low. These objective conditions dictated their strategy, too: terrorism, ambushes, harassing the enemy, extreme mobility of the combat groups which had to strike unexpectedly and disappear at once. This was made possible only by the support of the entire population. Hence the famous symbiosis between the liberation forces and the masses of people: the former everywhere organizing agrarian reforms, political organs and education; the latter supporting, feeding and hiding the soldiers of the army of liberation, and replenishing its ranks with their sons.

It is no accident that people's war, with its principles, its strategy, its tactics and its theoreticians, appeared at the very moment that the industrial powers pushed total war to the ultimate by the industrial production of atomic fission. Nor is it any accident that it brought about the destruction of colonialism. The contradiction which led to the victory of the FLN in Algeria was characteristic of that time; people's war sounded the death-knell of conventional warfare at exactly the same moment as the hydrogen bomb. Against partisans supported by the entire population, the colonial armies were helpless. They had only one way of escaping this demoralizing harassment which threatened to culminate in a Dien Bien Phu, and that was to "empty the sea of its water"—i.e., the civilian population. And, in fact, the colonial soldiers soon learned that their most redoubtable foes were the silent, stubborn peasants who, just one kilometer from the scene of the ambush which had wiped out a regiment, knew nothing, had seen nothing. And since it was the unity of an entire people which held the conventional army at bay, the only anti-guerrilla strategy which could work was the destruction of this people, in other words, of civilians, of women and children.

Torture and genocide: that was the answer of the colonial powers to the revolt of the subject peoples. And that answer, as we know, was worthless unless it was thorough and total. The populace—resolute, united by the politicized and fierce partisan army—was no longer to be cowed as in the good old days of colonialism, by an "admonitory" massacre which was supposed to serve "as an example." On the contrary, this only augmented the people's hate. Thus it was no longer a question of intimidating the populace, but rather of physically liquidating it. And since that was not possible without concurrently liquidating the colonial economy and the whole colonial system, the settlers panicked, the colonial powers got tired of pouring men and money into an interminable conflict, the mass of the people in the mother country opposed the continuation of an inhuman war, and the colonies became sovereign states.

There have been cases, however, in which the genocidal response to people's war is not checked by infrastructural contradictions. Then total genocide emerges as the absolute basis of an anti-guerrilla strategy. And under certain conditions it even emerges as the explicit objective—sought either immediately or by degrees. This is precisely what is happening in the Vietnam war. We are dealing here with a new stage in the development of imperialism, a stage usually called neo-colonialism because it is characterized by aggression against a former colony which has already gained its independence, with the aim of subjugating it anew to colonial rule. With the beginning of independence, the neo-colonialists take care to finance a *putsch* or *coup d'état* so that the new heads of state do not represent the interests of the masses but those of a narrow privileged strata, and, consequently, of foreign capital.

Ngo Dinh Diem appeared—hand-picked, maintained and armed by the

United States. He proclaimed his decision to reject the Geneva Agreements and to constitute the Vietnamese territory to the south of the 17th parallel as an independent state. What followed was the necessary consequence of these premises: a police force and an army were created to hunt down people who had fought against the French, and who now felt thwarted of their victory, a sentiment which automatically marked them as enemies of the new regime. In short, it was the reign of terror which provoked a new uprising in the South and rekindled the people's war.

Did the United States ever imagine that Diem could nip the revolt in the bud? In any event, they lost no time in sending in experts and then troops, and then they were involved in the conflict up to their necks. And we find once again almost the same pattern of war as the one that Ho Chi Minh fought against the French, except that at first the American government declared that it was only sending its troops out of generosity, to fulfill its obligations to an ally.

That is the outward appearance. But looking deeper, these two successive wars are essentially different in character: the United States, unlike France, has no economic interests in Vietnam. American firms have made some investments, but not so much that they couldn't be sacrificed, if necessary, without troubling the American nation as a whole or really hurting the monopolies. Moreover, since the U.S. government is not waging the war for reasons of a *directly* economic nature, there is nothing to stop it from ending the war by the ultimate tactic—in other words, by genocide. This is not to say that there is proof that the U.S. does in fact envision genocide, but simply that nothing prevents the U.S. from envisaging it.

In fact, according to the Americans themselves, the conflict has two objectives. Just recently, Dean Rusk stated: "We are defending ourselves." It is no longer Diem, the ally whom the Americans are generously helping out: it is the United States itself which is in danger in Saigon. Obviously, this means that the first objective is a military one: to encircle Communist China. Therefore, the United States will not let Southeast Asia escape. It has put its men in power in Thailand, it controls two-thirds of Laos and threatens to invade Cambodia. But these conquests will be hollow if it finds itself confronted by a free and unified Vietnam with 32 million inhabitants. That is why the military leaders like to talk in terms of "key positions." That is why Dean Rusk says, with unintentional humor, that the armed forces of the United States are fighting in Vietnam "in order to avoid a third world war." Either this phrase is meaningless, or else it must be taken to mean: "in order to *win* this third conflict." In short, the first objective is dictated by the necessity of establishing a Pacific line of defense, something which is necessary only in the context of the general policies of imperialism.

The second objective is an economic one. In October 1966, General Westmoreland defined it as follows: "We are fighting the war in Vietnam to show that guerrilla warfare does not pay." To show whom? The Vietnamese? That would be very surprising. Must so many human lives and so much money be wasted merely to teach a lesson to a nation of poor peasants thousands of miles from San Francisco? And, in particular, what need was there to attack them, provoke them into fighting and subsequently to go about crushing them, when the big American companies have only negligible interests in Vietnam? Westmoreland's statement, like Rusk's, has to be filled in. The Americans want to show others that guerrilla war does not pay: they want to show all the oppressed and exploited nations that might be tempted to shake off the American yoke by launching a people's war, at first against their own pseudo-governments, the compradors and the army, then against the U.S. "Special Forces," and finally against the GIs. In short, they want to show Latin America first of all, and more generally, all of the Third World. To Che Guevara who said, "We need several Vietnams," the American government answers, "They will all be crushed the way we are crushing the first."

In other words, this war has above all an admonitory value, as an example for three and perhaps four continents. (After all, Greece is a peasant nation too. A dictatorship has just been set up there; it is good to give the Greeks a warning: submit or face extermination.) This genocidal example is addressed to the whole of humanity. By means of this warning, six per cent of mankind hopes to succeed in controlling the other 94 per cent at a reasonably low cost in money and effort. Of course it would be preferable, for propaganda purposes, if the Vietnamese would submit before being exterminated. But it is not certain that the situation wouldn't be clearer if Vietnam *were* wiped off the map. Otherwise someone might think that Vietnam's submission had been attributable to some *avoidable* weakness. But if these peasants do not weaken for an instant, and if the price they pay for their heroism is *inevitable* death, the guerrillas of the future will be all the more discouraged.

At this point in our demonstration, three facts are established: (1) What the U.S. government wants is to have a base against China and to set an example. (2) The first objective *can* be achieved, without any difficulty (except, of course, for the resistance of the Vietnamese), by wiping out a whole people and imposing the Pax Americana on an uninhabited Vietnam. (3) To achieve the second, the U.S. *must* carry out, at least in part, this extermination.

The declarations of American statesmen are not as candid as Hitler's were in his day. But candor is not essential to us here. It is enough that the facts speak; the speeches which come with them are believed only by the American people. The rest of the world understands well enough: governments which are the friends of the United States keep silent; the others denounce this genocide. The Americans try to reply that these unproved accusations only show these governments' partiality. "In fact," the American government says, "all we have ever done is to offer the Vietnamese, North and South, the option of ceasing their aggression or being crushed." It is scarcely necessary to mention that this offer is absurd, since it is the Americans who commit the aggression and consequently they are the only ones who can put an end to it. But this absurdity is not undeliberate: the Americans are ingeniously formulating, without appearing to do so, a demand which the Vietnamese cannot satisfy. They do offer an alternative: Declare you are beaten or we will bomb you back to the stone age. But the fact remains that the second term of this alternative is genocide. They have said: "genocide, yes, but *conditional* genocide." Is this juridically valid? Is it even conceivable?

If the proposition made any juridical sense at all, the U.S. government might narrowly escape the accusation of genocide. But the 1948 Convention leaves no such loopholes: an act of genocide, especially if it is carried out over a period of several years, is no less genocide for being blackmail. The perpetrator may declare he will stop if the victim gives in; this is still —without any juridical doubt whatsoever—a genocide. And this is all the more true when, as is the case here, a good part of the group has been annihilated to force the rest to give in.

But let us look at this more closely and examine the nature of the two terms of the alternative. In the South, the choice is the following: villages burned, the populace subjected to massive bombing, livestock shot, vegetation destroyed by defoliants, crops ruined by toxic aerosols, and everywhere indiscriminate shooting, murder, rape and looting. This is genocide in the strictest sense: massive extermination. The other option: what is *it?* What are the Vietnamese people supposed to do to escape this horrible death? Join the armed forces of Saigon or be enclosed in strategic or today's "New Life" hamlets, two names for the same concentration camps?

We know about these camps from numerous witnesses. They are fenced in by barbed wire. Even the most elementary needs are denied: there is malnutrition and a total lack of hygiene. The prisoners are heaped together in small tents or sheds. The social structure is destroyed. Husbands are separated from their wives, mothers from their children; family life, so important to the Vietnamese, no longer exists. As families are split up, the birth rate falls; any possibility of religious or cultural life is suppressed; even work—the work which might permit people to maintain themselves and their families—is refused them. These unfortunate people are not even slaves (slavery did not prevent the Negroes in the United States from developing a rich culture); they are reduced to a living heap of vegetable existence. When, sometimes, a fragmented family group is freed—children with an elder sister or a young mother—it goes to swell the ranks of the subproletariat in the big cities; the elder sister or the mother, with no job and mouths to feed, reaches the last stage of her degradation in prostituting herself to the GIs.

Refugee camp in South Vietnam. *(Photo by Orville Schell.)*

The camps I describe are but another kind of genocide, equally condemned by the 1948 Convention:

"Causing serious bodily or mental harm to members of the group.

"Deliberately inflicting on the group conditions of life calculated to bring about its physical destruction in whole or in part.

"Imposing measures intended to prevent births within the group.

"Forcibly transferring children of the group to another group."

In other words, it is not true that the choice is between death or submission. For submission, in those circumstances, is submission to genocide. Let us say that a choice must be made between a violent and immediate death and a slow death from mental and physical degradation. Or, if you prefer, *there is no choice at all.*

Is it any different for the North?

One choice is *extermination.* Not just the daily risk of death, but the systematic destruction of the economic base of the country: from the dikes to the factories, nothing will be left standing. Deliberate attacks against civilians and, in particular, the rural population. Systematic destruction of hospitals, schools and places of worship. An all-out campaign to destroy the achievements of 20 years of socialism. The purpose may be only to intimidate the populace. But this can only be achieved by the daily extermination of an ever larger part of the group. So this intimidation itself in its psycho-social consequence is a genocide. Among the children in particular it must be engendering psychological disorders which will for years, if not permanently, "cause serious . . . mental harm."

The other choice is *capitulation.* This means that the North Vietnamese must declare themselves ready to stand by and watch while their country is divided and the Americans impose a direct or indirect dictatorship on their compatriots, in fact on members of their own families from whom the war has separated them. And would this intolerable humiliation bring an end to the war? This is far from certain. The National Liberation Front and the Democratic Republic of Vietnam, although fraternally united, have different strategies and tactics because their war situations are different. If the NLF continued the struggle, American bombs would go on blasting the DRV whether it capitulated or not.

If the war were to cease, the United States—according to official statements—would feel very generously inclined to help in the reconstruction of the DRV, and we know exactly what this means. It means that the United States would destroy, through private investments and conditional loans, the whole economic base of socialism. And this too is genocide. They would be splitting a sovereign country in half, occupying one of the halves by a reign of terror and keeping the other half under control by economic pressure. The "national group" Vietnam would not be physically eliminated, yet it would no longer exist. Economically, politically and culturally it would be suppressed.

In the North as in the South, the choice is only between two types of liquidation: collective death or dismemberment. The American government has had ample opportunity to test the resistance of the NLF and the DRV: by now it knows that only total destruction will be effective. The Front is stronger than ever; North Vietnam is unshakable. For this very reason, the calculated extermination of the Vietnamese people cannot really be intended to make them capitulate. The Americans offer them a *paix des braves* knowing full well that they will not accept it. And this phony alternative hides the true goal of imperialism, which is to reach, step by step, the highest stage of escalation—total genocide.

Of course, the United States government *could have* tried to reach this stage in one jump and wipe out Vietnam in a *Blitzkrieg* against the whole country. But this extermination first required setting up complicated installations—for instance, creating and maintaining air bases in Thailand which would shorten the bombing runs by 3000 miles.

Meanwhile, the major *purpose* of "escalation" was, and still is, to prepare international opinion for genocide. From this point of view, Americans have succeeded only too well. The repeated and systematic bombings of populated areas of Haiphong and Hanoi, which two years ago would have raised violent protests in Europe, occur today in a climate of general indifference resulting perhaps more from catatonia than from apathy. The tactic has borne its fruit: public opinion now sees escalation as a slowly and continuously increasing pressure to bargain, while in reality it is the preparation of minds for the final genocide. Is such a genocide possible? No. But that is due to the Vietnamese and the Vietnamese alone; to their courage, and to the remarkable efficiency of their organization. As for the United States government, it cannot be absolved of its crime just because its victim has enough intelligence and enough heroism to limit its effects.

We may conclude that in the face of a people's war (the characteristic product of our times, the answer to imperialism and the demand for sovereignty of a people conscious of its unity) there are two possible responses: either the aggressor withdraws, he acknowledges that a whole nation confronts him, and he makes peace; or else he recognizes the inefficacy of conventional strategy, and, if he can do so without jeopardizing his interests, he resorts to extermination pure and simple. There is no third alternative, but making peace is still at least *possible*.

But as the armed forces of the U.S.A. entrench themselves firmly in Vietnam, as they intensify the bombing and the massacres, as they try to bring Laos under their control, as they plan the invasion of Cambodia, there is less and less doubt that the government of the United States, despite its hypocritical denials, has chosen genocide.

The genocidal intent is implicit in the facts. It is necessarily premeditated. Perhaps in bygone times, in the midst of tribal wars, acts of genocide were perpetrated on the spur of the moment in fits of passion. But the anti-guerrilla genocide which our times have produced requires organization, military bases, a structure of accomplices, budget appropriations. Therefore, its authors must meditate and plan out their act. Does this mean that they are thoroughly conscious of their intentions? It is impossible to decide. We would have to plumb the depths of their consciences—and the Puritan bad faith of Americans works wonders.

There are probably people in the State Department who have become so used to fooling themselves that they still think they are working for the good of the Vietnamese people. However, we may only surmise that there are fewer and fewer of these hypocritical innocents after the recent statements of their spokesmen: "We are defending ourselves; even if the Saigon government begged us, we would not leave Vietnam, etc., etc." At any rate, we don't have to concern ourselves with this psychological hide-and-seek. The truth is apparent *on the battlefield* in the racism of the American soldiers.

This racism—anti-black, anti-Asiatic, anti-Mexican—is a basic American attitude with deep historical roots and which existed, latently and overtly, well before the Vietnamese conflict. One proof of this is that the United States government refused to ratify the Genocide Convention. This doesn't mean that in 1948 the U.S. intended to exterminate a people; what it does mean—according to the statements of the U.S. Senate—is that the Convention would conflict with the laws of several states; in other words, the current policymakers enjoy a free hand in Vietnam because their predecessors catered to the anti-black racism of Southern whites. In any case, since 1966, the racism of Yankee soldiers, from Saigon to the 17th parallel, has become more and more marked. Young American men use torture (even including the "field telephone treatment"*), they shoot unarmed women for nothing more than target practice, they kick wounded Vietnamese in the genitals, they cut ears off dead men to take home for trophies. Officers are the worst: a general boasted of hunting "VCs" from his helicopter and gunning them down in the rice paddies. Obviously, these were not NLF soldiers who knew how to defend themselves; they were peasants tending their rice. In the confused minds of the American soldiers, "Viet Cong" and "Vietnamese" tend increasingly to blend into one another. They often say themselves, "The only good Vietnamese is a dead Vietnamese," or what amounts to the same thing, "A dead Vietnamese is a Viet Cong."

For example: south of the 17th parallel, peasants prepare to harvest their rice. American soldiers arrive on the scene, set fire to their houses and want to transfer them to a strategic hamlet. The peasants protest. What else can they do, bare-handed against these Martians? They say:

*The portable generator for a field telephone is used as an instrument for interrogation by hitching the two lead wires to the victim's genitals and turning the handle. (*Editor's note.*)

"The quality of the rice is good: we want to stay to eat our rice." Nothing more. But this is enough to irritate the young Yankees: "It's the Viet Cong who put that into your head; they are the ones who have taught you to resist." These soldiers are so misled that they take the feeble protests which their own violence has aroused for "subversive" resistance. At the outset, they were probably disappointed: they came to save Vietnam from "communist aggressors." But they soon had to realize that the Vietnamese did not want them. Their attractive role as liberators changed to that of occupation troops. For the soldiers it was the first glimmering of consciousness: "We are unwanted, we have no business here." But they go no further. They simply tell themselves that a Vietnamese is by definition suspect.

And from the neo-colonialists' point of view, this is true. They vaguely understand that in a people's war, civilians are the only visible enemies. Their frustration turns to hatred of the Vietnamese; racism takes it from there. The soldiers discover with a savage joy that they are there to kill the Vietnamese they had been pretending to save. All of them are potential communists, as proved by the fact that they hate Americans.

Now we recognize in those dark and misled souls the truth of the

(Photo by Robert C. Scheu, Photon West.)

Vietnam war: it meets all of Hitler's specifications. Hitler killed the Jews because they were Jews. The armed forces of the United States torture and kill men, women and children in Vietnam merely *because they are Vietnamese.* Whatever lies or euphemisms the government may think up, the spirit of genocide is in the minds of the soldiers. This is their way of living out the genocidal situation into which their government has thrown them. As Peter Martinson, a 23-year-old student who had "interrogated" prisoners for ten months and could scarcely live with his memories, said: "I am a middle-class American. I look like any other student, yet somehow I am a war criminal." And he was right when he added: "Anyone in my place would have acted as I did." His only mistake was to attribute his degrading crimes to the influence of war *in general.*

No, it is not war in the abstract: it is the greatest power on earth against a poor peasant people. Those who fight it are *living out* the only possible relationship between an over-industrialized country and an underdeveloped country, that is to say, a genocidal relationship implemented through racism—the only relationship, short of picking up and pulling out.

Total war presupposes a certain balance of forces, a certain reciprocity. Colonial wars were not reciprocal, but the interests of the colonialists limited the scope of genocide. The present genocide, the end result of the unequal development of societies, is total war waged to the limit by one side, without the slightest reciprocity.

The American government is not guilty of inventing modern genocide, or even of having chosen it from other possible and effective measures against guerrilla warfare. It is not guilty, for example, of having preferred genocide for strategic and economic reasons. Indeed, genocide presents itself as the *only possible reaction* to the rising of a whole people against its oppressors.

The American government is guilty of having preferred, and of still preferring, a policy of war and aggression aimed at total genocide to a policy of peace, the only policy which can really replace the former. A policy of peace would necessarily have required a reconsideration of the objectives imposed on that government by the large imperialist companies through the intermediary of their pressure groups. America is guilty of continuing and intensifying the war despite the fact that every day its leaders realize more acutely, from the reports of the military commanders, that the only way to win is "to free Vietnam of all the Vietnamese." The government is guilty—despite the lessons it has been taught by this unique, unbearable experience—of proceeding at every moment a little further along a path which leads it to the point of no return. And it is guilty—according to its own admissions—of consciously carrying out this admonitory war in order to use genocide as a challenge and a threat to all peoples of the world.

We have seen that one of the features of total war has been the growing scope and efficiency of communication. As early as 1914, war could no longer be "localized." It had to spread throughout the whole world. In 1967, this process is being intensified. The ties of the "One World," on which the United States wants to impose its hegemony, have grown tighter and tighter. For this reason, as the American government very well knows, the current genocide is conceived as an answer to people's war and perpetrated in Vietnam not against the Vietnamese alone, but against humanity.

When a peasant falls in his rice paddy, mowed down by a machine gun, every one of us is hit. The Vietnamese fight for all men and the American forces against all. Neither figuratively nor abstractly. And not only because genocide would be a crime universally condemned by international law, but because little by little the whole human race is being subjected to this genocidal blackmail piled on top of atomic blackmail, that is, to absolute, total war. This crime, carried out every day before the eyes of the world, renders all who do not denounce it accomplices of those who commit it, so that we are being degraded today for our future enslavement.

In this sense imperialist genocide can only become more complete. The group which the United States wants to intimidate and terrorize by way of the Vietnamese nation is the human group in its entirety.

French philosopher and writer Jean-Paul Sartre has been speaking out in opposition to the war since the early '50s. In 1967 he was a member of Bertrand Russell's War Crimes Tribunal, for which he and Russell were severely criticized by the American press.

Reports from North Vietnam

Richard Gott

Life Returns to a Battered Land

The priorities here in North Vietnam are still roads and agriculture, as they have been ever since the bombing stopped in 1968. The ruined towns have been left almost untouched. Most reconstruction work seems to consist of clearing ruins, piling up bricks, rebuilding administrative blocks, and

Reprinted by permission from the *Manchester Guardian Weekly*, February 28, March 7, and March 14, 1970.

providing a few amenities like the post office or the cinema. But a good number of private enterprise wattle and daub houses are going up, often erected within a still-standing shell of brick or concrete. Painted up and thatched with rice straw, they make what seem to be destined to be permanent homes for many years to come.

Also being constructed, possibly with more official sanction, are long low huts with a wooden framework and walls of rush matting, roofed with straw or sometimes with tiles. The materials are primitive but the construction workmanlike—a far cry from the amateur makeshift shanty towns of Latin America, or indeed most of Asia.

Nor is all desolation. Even in the worst-destroyed urban area trees survive and vegetation returns. This is not the wilderness taking over, for it is carefully controlled. Often amid the ruins one finds bright vegetable plots with cabbages, cauliflowers, lettuces, and sweet potatoes. The soil is so fertile that they grow to huge sizes. These allotments are encouraged in order to help provide food for the town.

On the road south, particularly in the Fourth Zone, one often passes road gangs at work, usually teenage girls from volunteer brigades. (The volunteering is fairly genuine and although the work is hard—and was unimaginably dangerous during the bombing—joining a road gang is one of the quickest ways out of the claustrophobic atmosphere of the village.)

On the main roads in the South much of the basic repair work has been done. The current task is to widen the shoulders so that the motorized traffic becomes less tangled up with the almost permanent ribbon of buffaloes, bicycles, and market women who clip along at a fair trot under the weight of their double baskets, hung from the shoulder on a bamboo pole. The girls working on the road seemed a cheery crowd and showed eager interest when I stopped to take photographs and to ask about their backgrounds and future ambitions. (Most were local and wanted to go to the university.) They were operating a human chain, carrying earth from the fields to the road and then beating it down with wooden weights.

Older women put turf along the sides of the road—built up on a dike—to keep it in place. With many people working, progress is rapid. But in one of the four southern provinces there are more than a thousand kilometers of road to be repaired and over 100 bridges to be replaced. They hoped to be able to complete the tarmac surfacing and the bridge renewal on at least one North-South road by the end of 1970.

Once these roads are finished it may be possible to divert those labor gangs to rebuilding factories and towns. Virtually all Vietnamese achievements since 1954 have been destroyed or rendered useless. The French withdrew in that year taking everything with them, prophesying economic ruin, and hoping that the economic collapse of Vietnam would provide a suitably edifying warning to French Africa. Russia, China, and Eastern Europe leapt in to help build North Vietnam into a showcase of socialism in Asia. Together with the Vietnamese they made a good job of it. Factories were tailored to Vietnamese needs—power stations, rice mills, paper plants, bicycle assembly shops, printing presses, machine tools. Nothing fancy and nothing extra, but adequate to a country of peasants almost entirely lacking in modern skills. More than 10 years of this costly endeavor now lies in ruins—sagging concrete beams and roofs open to the sky.

The Vietnamese have immense reserves of optimism. Rather than dwelling on the big factories that have been destroyed, they point to the small ones that were dispersed, and survived. "More important," I was told, "is the fact that the technicians survive. That's what we really lacked before. Their experience has survived the bombs."

Vietnamese optimism about the future is based, too, on the hope that their socialist allies will be prepared to do again at least as much as they did from 1954 on. The director of the Historical Museum told me of how Ho Chi Minh had rung him up when the bombing began and said, "Our friends will help us if a factory is bombed, but they cannot help if the museum is destroyed. Evacuate things immediately."

The optimism is probably well-founded. I did not find the Russians nearly so hostile to the Vietnamese as I had expected to. Although there is a certain amount of non-comprehension on both sides, I was left with the impression that the Russians are as involved now in Vietnam, both materially and emotionally, as they've ever been.

The Sino-Soviet split, which distressed Ho Chi Minh so much, has paradoxically worked to the advantage of the Vietnamese. It gives them far more independence than they've ever had before, and although they permanently walk a tightrope, they now run less risk of the two countries ganging up on them to demand a tactical pullback—as happened essentially in 1954. Outside assistance still comes chiefly from Russia and Eastern Europe, but a certain amount of "intermediate technology"—small hydro-electric plants for agricultural use and the like—comes from China.

The geographic dispersal of industry—speeded up in wartime—had begun before 1965. The Government's policy, itself inherited from the French, was to spread small industry to provincial towns and to try to avoid turning the Hanoi-Haiphong-Honggai area into an industrial and commercial complex. Thus smaller towns like Nam Dinh and Vinh had a fairly substantial industrial base as well. But virtually everything that remained in these towns was smashed, and for the moment the country survives on the machinery that was evacuated into villages and caves, on patched power stations and small generators. The centers of Hanoi and Haiphong were relatively untouched, but the eastern entrance to Hanoi, where a string of factories line the road, was heavily bombed.

The intention now is to make each province as self-supporting as possible—except perhaps in rice. Already there are small workshops out in the countryside—really too small to be dignified with the name of factory

—with machine tools (made in Hanoi) and forges producing simple agricultural machinery: threshers, huskers, and small carts.

I visited several of these evacuated machine shops hidden away in different parts of the country, sometimes in a cave or sheltered by high mountains, sometimes harbored in an ordinary village—literally a "cottage" industry. The people on the spot are anxious to go back to their ruined towns to rebuild them, but one notes a reluctance in Hanoi to hurry this process. "There is no specific reason why we should recentralize industry," I was told. "It depends on each case. If it's all right where it is then it will stay. Otherwise it might be moved." A printing shop I saw hidden away in a delightful village close to a bombed town looked as though it would be left there. But the director of a machine shop making threshers in a village far from anywhere in an area where road communications had been badly affected by bombing was anxious to go somewhere more accessible.

The rebuilding of the towns still seems a very long way off. A journalist on a local paper explained: "Our problem is not reconstruction, but to improve the living conditions of the peasants and to increase production. If we can do this, then we can start on reconstruction. Of course we want to rebuild our provincial capital. We have a plan. But we don't want to build something that will only last a few years. We want to build for the future."

I heard the same story from the director of a State farm growing tea. "We have a plan for when the war ends. More houses, a cinema, a theater, improvements to the school. But first we must increase the acreage." And a province chief told me, "We have a plan for the future, but it is a plan only. The US planes may renew their destruction."

This latter excuse, while apparently prevalent last year, no longer seems to be taken very seriously. But the delay in reconstruction must have some reason and possibly reflects some internal disagreements about the relative priority to be given to agriculture and industry. On the face of it there is unity. "We don't want any spinning-wheel socialism here," I was told by a party secretary. "To create socialism you need heavy industry." Everyone seems agreed on this. On the other hand, no one wants to interfere with the agricultural cooperatives, which are considered to be working well even though they absorb far too much labor.

The Vietnamese were somewhat reluctant to talk about reconstruction and possible aid from the West. It is a sensitive political subject since an overeager desire to reconstruct might be read as a decline in "fighting spirit." But the Swedish mission in Hanoi, discussing the details of future post-war international cooperation, told me that they had had no difficulty in discussing quite concrete projects with the Vietnamese. The Swedes hope to be able to set up some sort of agency, trusted by the Vietnamese, that would be able to channel Western aid into Vietnam—initially perhaps from Sweden, France, and Japan. The French have already sent a commercial secretary to bolster up their massive mission here. Even the Danish

Ambassador to Peking recently paid a fleeting visit. Britain, as usual, is uninterested. But it would be sad if the horror aroused in the world by the bombing of Vietnam were not at some stage to be translated into action to help the Vietnamese recover.

Precision Bombing Not Very Precise

The Fourth Zone of North Vietnam—the four provinces south of the 19th Parallel that the Americans call "the panhandle"—has had more bombs dropped on it than any other area in the history of the world. It looks like it; though today, rather more than a year since the bombing stopped, lush vegetation is beginning to hide some of the worst scars.

But even if the inhabitants, about 20 per cent of North Vietnam's population of 20 million, wished to forget the war, the pounding by American bombers of the mountainous areas of neighboring Laos—which reverberates daily through the Fourth Zone—is a constant reminder that the war is not over. Vietnam's problem is not solely one of reconstruction.

During a five-week visit to North Vietnam I have been able to drive as far South as the 18th Parallel and to spend some days in the province of Hatinh. This area, where the bombing redoubled its intensity in 1968, is still a shattering sight. Sometimes, bouncing along in an old Russian jeep, I would look out and see a perfectly normal landscape of women planting rice and boys on the backs of buffaloes. This place, I would mentally note, has been left alone; I must be careful not to exaggerate.

Then, round the next corner would come a broken bridge, a burnt-out house, a cratered rice field or a string of twisted railway trucks. Some valleys are almost showpieces of destruction, the hillsides deeply scored and the floor barren and deserted. Only an occasional small ridge indicates where once was a rice field.

Much of the bombing north of Vinh concentrated on the areas where road and railway ran in harness. With a bridge as well, all havoc was let loose. In underdeveloped countries people like to live near roads and rivers and railways. Inevitably they concentrate near bridges. We shall never know how many people were killed, but the authorities appear to have been tireless in organizing the evacuation and probably most of the houses by bridges were empty when the bombs fell.

One village I visited near a main road had moved the inhabitants out of the hamlets nearest the road and billeted them on those farther away. But the bombing was normally very wide of the mark—even on the best days an error of 400 yards seems to have been regarded by the Americans as a good average. Sheer tonnage, however, told in the end. Every major bridge, except that at Ham Rong, was destroyed. And they are big affairs, often huge girder bridges swung from five or six stone pillars.

I counted more than twenty large ones on my 200-mile journey south from Hanoi; the small ones were too many to count. The Ham Rong bridge, a battered wrecked piece of engineering which somehow managed to hold together, apparently accounted for the loss of 99 American planes. It has become, for the Vietnamese, their symbol of successful resistance.

On the road south from Hanoi one passes first through the town of Phuly. Harrison Salisbury of the *New York Times* saw its remains early in 1967. It has been bombed repeatedly since. Largely built after 1954, its misfortune was to have the river on one side, the railway on the other and Route No. 1 running through the middle. A tempting target. Formerly a town of more than 10,000, it has been leveled, obliterated, razed to the ground. My interpreter knew these phrases, and when he used them in conversation in Hanoi, I hadn't really believed that he understood their literal meaning. But his English was exact.

At Phuly the railway turns southeast to the textile town of Nam Dinh, North Vietnam's fourth largest urban center. Here fifty workers were killed at a weaving factory while changing shifts. At least half the town has been destroyed. Three and four storey houses have been swept away, their size only indicated by the neat piles of brick recovered from the rubble, and the occasional shell left standing. Here there is a church with a hole knocked in its side and an intact madonna surveying the desolate scene, as in the famous photograph of Dresden.

Farther south again, at Ninh Binh, where the railway rejoins the road, the scenes of destruction are the same though on a smaller scale. At Thanh Hoa, an engineering plant, a fertilizer factory, a power station, and a rice mill proved irresistible to the bombers, smashing not only the basis of an industry geared principally to agricultural development, but also the houses of the workers, in a town which once held 60,000.

The list is endless. Vinh, a major industrial city and port—the third largest town in North Vietnam after Hanoi and Haiphong—wholly destroyed. Or the small town of Hatinh, which once housed 12,000. To judge from a few remaining facades, it was once a rather pretty colonial town.

It had paved streets, and, more unusual, paved pavements. A church, a pagoda, a new hospital with 200 beds, an agricultural implements workshop, a small power station for the needs of the town and to assist the rural electrification program. All gone. These were not towns I was specially taken to see. They just happened to be on the road south.

They did take me, at my request, to the Dong Loc crossroads, one of the principal areas where the Americans concentrated their bombs after March, 1968, and destined to become famous in the annals of aerial bombardment. During the four years' bombing, over 40,000 bombs were dropped here, and the figure is easy to believe. More incredible still is that 50 per cent of all the bombs dropped on this area fell during the limited bombing period in 1968.

Perhaps more extraordinary than anything is that in spite of all this destruction, the roads to the South were kept open. "Infiltration" actually increased. Heavy bombardment could not prevent the small quantity of supplies needed by the South from getting through. Nor did it affect the determination of the Vietnamese to continue the war. "What did you feel when the bombing finally stopped?" I asked the man responsible for keeping the roads open in one of the Fourth Zone provinces. He replied quite simply, without a propaganda flourish, "I knew we had to do two things: to try to supply more men and goods to our Southern people, and to rebuild the roads and bridges."

The results of the bombing in this southern area of North Vietnam must throw serious doubts on the advantages of air superiority, and by implication on the effectiveness of the continuing air war in the South and in Laos. From what I have seen, there is clearly no such thing as precision bombing. Even against very lightly defended targets, a vast quantity of bombs had to be dropped over a very wide area.

This is not to deny that the bombing of the North has done very great damage. Vietnam has not been bombed back into the Stone Age, but a promising underdeveloped country that was pushing its way through the middle of the nineteenth century, has been forcibly smashed back into the eighteenth. The only result of this unpleasant experiment has been to prove the very definite limitations in warfare of air superiority. They were known already.

Peasants and Revolution

To anyone familiar with the underdeveloped rural areas of the world, especially in Latin America, North Vietnam is by no means an abjectly poor country. The population is poor, of course, but there is no "misery" —that appalling hopeless poverty one encounters too often in the Third World.

Of course, there are inequalities. Hanoi is better off than the countryside. The delta areas are richer than the "panhandle." The mountainous regions have less pressure of population. But by getting rid of the rich, and avoiding extremes of poverty, Vietnam gives the impression of a prospering, cohesive society, unique in the underdeveloped world.

The pattern and details of village life remain as they have been for centuries. "Communism" merely provides a new economic framework which is better able to provide continuity than the old landlord system. Essentially the village stays the same in a changing environment.

Vietnam, even before the arrival of the French, had become about as advanced as a primitive peasant society can be. Brick and bamboo for houses, metal-tipped ploughs and buffaloes for ploughing, reeds and straw for thatch and bedding, cotton and silk for clothes, to a casual observer the Vietnamese village must have been not without charm.

The major snags to this primitive way of life were a social and economic system that denied to a high proportion of peasant families the fruits of their work; insanitary conditions, resulting from a lack of very elementary rules of hygiene, and leading to a high infant death rate and not infrequent epidemics; the inability of the system to cope with such recurrent themes as crop failure and floods which brought famine in their train, and, lastly, illiteracy and lack of contact with the outside world.

In addition, there was a limit under the old system to the productive capacity of the land and its ability to feed a growing population. Early death, emigration, and periodic famine and epidemic syphoned off the surplus population and enabled village society to maintain its age-old existence virtually unchanged. Even when the French arrived, the initial result of colonial rule was merely to reinforce the archaic mandarin/landlord structure in the countryside that had survived so well.

Later of course the economic impact of colonial rule was to become more severe. The Great Depression had a disastrous effect on the extremities of empire. The primarily peasant economy of Vietnam found itself subject to pressures that it could not contain. Thus Ho Chi Minh's Communist Party was born in 1930 into a period of major unrest, which culminated in the famine of 1944–5 in which two million Vietnamese are believed to have died. This complete breakdown of the old system, such that minor misery became mass starvation, appears to have created a situation in which revolution was possible, though it took nearly 10 years of war—from 1946 to 1954—before the revolution could be carried through, and then it was only in the north of the country.

Clearly Vietnam has had a revolution, but what it consists of and who carried it out and why, still remains much of a mystery. I traveled round the country asking old villagers what they could remember of the past, and the thing that emerges most clearly is the lack of evidence that the peasantry in general was raring to have a go at the landlords, even though their former living and working conditions were barely supportable. One old revolutionary peasant leader in his seventies explained to me that "it was not too difficult to make the people understand that they were being exploited. The problem was to persuade the peasants to struggle." Nearly all those I talked to referred to the landlords' "grip on the minds of the people."

One old man in a southern province came out specially on his bicycle to where I was staying, to talk about his personal experience of stirring up the peasants: "When a landlord passed in the road, the peasants used to fold their arms and bow. Not until we had land reform could we get rid of the influence of the landlords. This was our greatest difficulty. Vietnamese peasants lived under feudal lords for thousands of years. They were psychologically subservient to landlords. Whenever they wanted to do anything, they felt they ought to ask the landlord first. Basically, peasants have a very conservative attitude and are very mean. They have to be educated. This was the biggest problem."

This, of course, is not the whole story. There were peasant revolts in the colonial period, and I did find one village where they admitted that the peasants had seized the land of a dead landlord before the land reform was authorized. But with the exception of a revolt in 1930, the Communist Party itself seems to have steered well clear of insurrectionary movements.

"Did you kill the mandarins?" I asked one old revolutionary in the delta, and got back a very stern reply: "In the 1930s those villages with a party cadre obeyed the rule of the party not to kill mandarins. But those without a cadre also organized protest meetings. Sometimes they killed mandarins and cut their ears off." Communists have a traditional dislike of things getting out of control, and Ho Chi Minh himself underlined on the eve of land reform that "spontaneous agitation must be avoided absolutely."

But a revolutionary process, once begun, is rarely held in check by party cadres—perhaps fortunately. The land reform in North Vietnam, when it finally came after 1954, was a chaotic affair, with thousands of people using the opportunity to pay off old scores. But out of the chaos emerged an entirely new social and economic pattern in the countryside. On its stability and efficiency the whole future of the revolution depends.

Basically what has changed are the disadvantages that made former village society very far from utopian; that is to say, insanitary conditions, lack of security against disaster, and cultural isolation. By tackling these problems, the Government can justly claim to have vastly improved the material conditions of life. Doctors, clinics, and elementary hygiene precautions have significantly changed the old cycle of birth, disease, and death.

Receptiveness to new ideas is perhaps one of the most important changes. The use of compost, better seeds, deeper ploughing, combined with more advanced methods of irrigation, plus electrification, all have their corollary in increased production. The peasant still works as hard as he always did, but he sees better results for his labor. Not only is sufficient food available for all, but he also has some personal advantages in the shape of a bicycle, a mackintosh cape, a thermos and a mosquito net, and, if he's lucky, a transistor. Clothing, too, is adequate, if not abundant. Reflecting the changes are the new, large rice-fields of the cooperative and the new trees built along the dikes—"at the command of our beloved President Ho Chi Minh"—subtly transforming a landscape which had otherwise remained the same for centuries.

The most important change of all is in the peasants themselves. It would be hard to find now a more purposeful or determined people. There is none of that awful cringing deference that you encounter among Latin American peasants—who remain beaten into apathy by centuries of landlord oppression. The departure of the landlords has lifted a yoke from the peasantry and liberated an almost unprecedentedly powerful force.

But will some profounder change in village society be needed before Vietnam can move into a new stage of development? Traditionally Communist regimes—or indeed most regimes hellbent on industrialization—ride roughshod over the peasantry. Must Vietnam follow this path, seizing the peasants' surplus to rebuild the shattered steelworks? The present system, I suspect, leaves the peasant with too much economic power vis-a-vis the central government. More than 90 per cent of Vietnam's villages were formed into cooperatives 10 years ago. At present they run themselves and are not overly dependent on "advice" from outside.

Were the Government to wish to extract more from the countryside, stronger political control would need to be enforced. A man running a State Farm, which are still a minute proportion of the total, told me they were the wave of the future and that it was silly to be romantic about the cooperatives and the intrinsic value of the Vietnamese village as a social entity: "The mentality of the peasant is changing much too fast for that."

In wartime nothing drastic is likely to be decided, but the stated policy of trying to reduce the labor force in the cooperatives by one third within five years must inevitably alter the character of village life in a significant fashion.

Hanoi Getting Back to Normal

The most curious aspect of North Vietnam is that one can quite easily forget that it is a country still at war. On arrival I studiously noted down anything that might indicate that there was a war on—the air-raid shelters by the lake in Hanoi, the famous concrete boltholes in the pavement, camouflaged helmets and denims, Russian jeeps and the occasional convoy, and the ubiquitous slogans urging the population on to greater efforts to help their Southern "kith and kin."

Later, getting used to the atmosphere, I came to feel that, in Hanoi at any rate, life was back to normal—certainly as normal as it can ever have been in the last thirty years. There are soldiers around, but so there are in most underdeveloped countries nowadays. Here they look as if they wear their army denims to save their ordinary clothes.

I found it totally impossible to substantiate the claims made by some diplomats that you notice a dearth of young men in Vietnam—either in Hanoi or in the countryside. The faces of the Vietnamese bear few traces of age—they often have jet black hair till their sixties—and I could never guess it anywhere near correctly. My impression is that the impact of North Vietnam's manpower loss has been vastly exaggerated.

In every village I inquired what percentage of their young people were called up for national service. The answers varied from 40 per cent of the 18-22 age-group in the heavily populated Red River delta area to a mere 20 per cent in the mountainous provinces. This hardly seems an exorbitant figure, especially if it is recalled that national service includes those who go to road gangs and higher education as well as the army.

But there is a very definite atmosphere of "après-guerre." People invariably talk about the war beginning in 1965 with the bombing, the unspoken assumption being that it ended when the bombing stopped in 1968. The absence of air-raids and the relaxation on rationing contribute to this.

Rationing still exists in Vietnam and will obviously continue for a long time. The rice ration has gone up in the past year from 26 to 34 pounds

North Vietnamese women's militia in training with rifles slung over their shoulders. *(Wide World.)*

per person per month. Even before 1965 rice, meat and textiles were rationed, as perhaps they must always be in a poor country struggling to impose equality. During the bombing, sugar, eggs and fish sauce were added to the list. Soap, fish, salt and cigarettes are unrationed, while butter, milk and cheese are virtually unobtainable.

Rationing depends to some extent on the nature of the work. Brainworkers get more sugar, manual workers get more meat. This means pork. Beef or buffalo is rare.

I was in Hanoi for the Têt celebrations a few weeks ago, and food and amusement on this occasion were abundant. In addition to the traditional cakes and sticky rice, you could throw missiles at President Nixon at makeshift pavement coconut shies. The Government stores too were fuller than usual and small coffee and patisserie shops suddenly sprang up for the festival.

Clearly for most of the population, the heroic period of the war is over, and at the vast new military exhibition on the outskirts of Hanoi, the exploits of the "Second Resistance War," as it is called, are remembered. Huge working models display the defense system of Hanoi.

Although they've opened their War Museum before the war is over, North Vietnam's leaders do not forget for a moment the existence of a war, both in South Vietnam and Laos. The old people running the country and the Party could not possibly forget.

Nor is the war in the South unpopular. There was always a louder clap for the spokesman from the Provisional Revolutionary Government than for anyone else. Literacy has brought the Government's nationalistic policies a larger and more appreciative audience. In addition I was struck by the number of Southerners one meets. A high proportion of these were party cadres, and this must provide additional pressure on the Government to continue the war. They have a genuine longing to return South.

I was left eventually with the impression that the principal aim of the Government remains what it always has been: to get rid of the Americans and to reunify the country under Communist leadership. The present leadership—currently dominated by Le Duan, the Party Secretary—has inherited this policy from Ho Chi Minh, and about this basic aim there is no possibility of negotiation whatever. To give way on this point would be tantamount to suggesting that the Communist movement founded and led by Ho Chi Minh was not the legitimate government of Vietnam and the heir to Vietnam's nationalist tradition. It would seriously undermine the mystique the regime has created, and which now sustains it.

This basic aim apart, everything else, including the timetable, is negotiable. The Government, after all, is largely formed of Communists of the old school—dogmatic but also highly disciplined and ultimately flexible, by no means adventurous, realists rather than romantics. Their present policy is to sit it out. There will be no repeat performance of initiatives like the Têt offensive unless there is fresh American escalation.

The Vietnamese believe themselves to be wholly in command of the situation. Though immensely depressed by the realization that a long war is the only strategy, they clearly feel that they can cope with any setbacks in the South, and that their superior "base" position gives them a long-term advantage over the Americans. North Vietnam has been badly smashed about physically, but it has not suffered the spiritual ravages that have affected the United States.

My impression was that few were optimistic about a breakthrough in the short-term. "We are making efforts on all fronts," the representative in Hanoi of the Provisional Revolutionary Government (of South Vietnam) explained. "But things are very difficult. We are prepared for a long and hard war. We have always had to be prepared for this. But as the Americans gradually go, the position will change. They'd have to send a lot more troops if they wanted to restore the status quo—at least 800,000."

Although, as I have suggested, the ultimate aim of the North Vietnamese is a reunited Communist Vietnam, the position of the PRG is of course very different. "Post-war South Vietnam will not be able to suddenly cut its links with the West," I was told by the PRG representative. "All its imports come from the West. That's why we have a completely different line from North Vietnam. We seek relations with all countries—Communist, capitalist, and the Third World."

It is also true that in the liberated areas of South Vietnam, the PRG is not following the same policies as operate in the North. For example, the land-reform in the South does not involve total confiscation of the land. The old landlords are left with a few hectares. I asked whether this created problems of continuing social dominance by the landlord—a phenomenon that often occurs with partial land reforms—but was told that so far the PRG was satisfied with the results of the reform.

The PRG representative also analyzed the difficulty of securing support in the towns. "In South Vietnam," he explained, "the Americans have tried to create a class strong enough to confront us. There are more rich people in the South than there were before, but they have not made money from industry but from imports. They have grown wealthy solely as a result of United States aid. With a hundred thousand American soldiers permanently stationed in Saigon, the influx of dollars is enormous—quite apart from what is being spent in the rest of the country. But once aid diminishes or the war ends, this rich privilege will collapse.

"Already the writing is on the wall. The Americans don't dare create industry because they know that sooner or later it will be in the hands of the PRG. The rich are already beginning to move their money out to foreign banks. They are frightened at the prospect of an American withdrawal. They reason that the Americans will have to leave, both because of military failure and because of problems at home. Once the Americans go, there won't be so much money available. That's why they put pressure on the Americans to stay."

I also asked him about the possibility of massacres in the South after the Americans leave. It was a difficult question to ask of such a civilized man as we sat drinking tea, especially after the events of Song My. He replied formally: "Our policy is one of national reconciliation. We have never envisaged reprisals against those who supported the Americans."

I had little success in North Vietnam, obviously, in probing the secrets of military strategy or the post-war objectives of the army. As in most parts of the world, the army is a law unto itself. But two things stand out. First, the enormous efficiency with which bridges were rebuilt and roads kept open during the bombing, suggests that the same pattern can be repeated in the South. Secondly, at no stage did I get the feeling that the war was regarded in any way as intolerable. The Vietnamese support for the Pathet Lao in Laos—a secondary field of operations—indicates that the South by no means absorbs all the country's energies.

The Lessons to Learn from North Vietnam

Very early in the morning on the first day after Têt, Tram Duy Hung, the mayor of Hanoi, could be seen trundling a barrowful of cement across a building site. There were short speeches, dutiful attendance by a few Chinese and Cubans, and the entire East European press corps, and an atmosphere of faint hilarity. But this was not at all a ceremonial occasion.

A hundred and fifty party workers and bureaucrats were putting in the first of their fifteen days a year of "Socialist labor." Their task was to dig foundations and make concrete panels for the 10,000 prefabricated houses that the Hanoi council hopes to have built by the end of the year. And they were really working. There was the stout manager of my hotel, digging away like a demon, and an old lawyer poking cement into its frame with the concentration that he usually reserved for denouncing American war crimes.

This is not yet the "voluntary work" of Cuba, that sends office workers to the fields for anything up to one week in the month: nor is it the Chinese system of sending intellectuals to remote villages to take lessons in humility. But, like everything in Vietnam, it is a compromise.

"We don't want to use the phrase 'Vietnamese socialism,' " I was told by To Huu, a poet and member of the party secretariat. "There will never be a 'Vietnamese way.' We don't want to invent a new doctrine. There are already too many 'isms.' Marxism-Leninism is quite sufficient. Applying it to the specific conditions of the country is all we try to do."

Russian in style, Chinese in action, there is nevertheless something rather special about Vietnam which differentiates it from other Communist countries, and I attribute this largely to the regime's isolation. Hanoi is one of the most shut-off places that exists. Though it has made a profound impact on the history of the world, the world, one feels, has left Hanoi virtually untouched—except in the sense that bombs have occasionally smashed and violated it.

It is difficult enough to get to: two planes a week from China; Aeroflot once a fortnight from Moscow; and an irregular weekly service run by the International Control Commission from Saigon and Vientiane. Visas for Westerners are few and far between. I first applied in 1966, receiving it only last month.

Prolonged isolation seems to have left the Vietnamese largely unaware that their war of liberation has upset the entire global equilibrium. And they often seem unaware of their own very real successes: the most impressive being the achievement of social justice and a sense of human dignity in the countryside at a lower cost than is usual with revolutionary regimes. The existence of the South, where recalcitrant landlords could disappear too, has of course contributed to the blandness of the revolution.

Isolation has also meant that North Vietnam, ideologically speaking, is tremendously out of date. The powerful currents that have shaken up the Communist world since the death of Stalin seem to have passed them by. Vietnam reminds one of the early days of Communist revolution, when the first flush of enthusiasm had not yet been wiped from the convert's brow. The posters and the art recall the most heroic phases of Russia's revolution, and even the workers, pedaling to work in their peaked caps and blue serge jackets, look as though they come from a vintage film of the 1920s.

Sometimes I felt that I had traveled back in time to the days of the Comintern, when all was ostensibly sweetness and light among the Communist fraternity. One tends to forget, nearly fourteen years after Khrushchev's epoch-ending speech, that pockets of Stalinism still exist in forgotten parts of the world. In the context of Vietnam, "Stalinist" hardly seems a very useful adjective, unless one can put aside for a moment the pejorative meaning of the word. There was a time when Stalin's Russia seemed to many people, however mistakenly, a beacon in a dark and ugly world. For some (many of whom later became ardent cold warriors), it was a utopian, optimistic spring.

Today, North Vietnam retains some of that joyous, youthful optimism, and seems to have managed to survive so far without the drastic purges and slaughtered kulaks of the Soviet Union. Anyone brought up on Khrushchev's 1956 speech could hardly be naive enough to state in 1970 that he had seen the future and it worked. But the Vietnamese have not done so badly.

To try to discover more about the Vietnamese attitude toward Stalin, I eventually plucked up courage and asked To Huu how he could explain it. "Quite frankly," he told me. "Stalin was one of our benefactors. He knew how to apply Leninism to the construction of socialism in the Soviet Union, and thanks to his conduct of the national defense against fascism, we now have all the Socialist countries of Eastern Europe.

"Our Socialist friends say that he committed errors. Perhaps he did, but not toward us. And beside his great actions, these were small. He was a great Socialist, a great Leninist, and a great man, but we do not believe there is any point in getting involved in useless discussions about this. He was not a new Lenin, but a great disciple of Lenin's. Perhaps the best. History will judge."

Vietnamese enthusiasm for Stalin, however, does not necessarily line them up with the Chinese. My impression was that Vietnam feels the need to keep its distance from China. Nor is it just a nostalgic backward look over the shoulder. It is also a weapon to be used in the constant struggle to ensure that the solidarity of the Socialist countries in their fight is not just a slogan. In December, on the ninetieth anniversary of Stalin's birthday, "Nhan Dan" carried a leading article on the theme that "Stalin's services and work have not lost their lustre." It contained a charming reminder to the Russians, and perhaps to the North Vietnamese themselves, not to forget that the end of the bombing did not mean the end of the war:

"We will forever remember the famous appeal of Stalin, which had wide repercussions in the West right after the October revolution: 'Don't forget the East.' As President Ho Chi Minh pointed out, this appeal reminded the Russian people who had just won a victory, and the international proletariat, that they must closely link their struggle to that of the oppressed peoples in Asia against the common enemy—imperialism." The need for this reminder, the Vietnamese clearly feel, has not diminished with the years.

My two personal conclusions about Vietnam are that, first, the West has underestimated the speed at which an underdeveloped country and people can "stand up"—to use Mao's phrase. And secondly, the West has overestimated the possibilities of revolution in the Third World. In a recent book, a former American Secretary of the Air Force writes that "Oriental resignation" and "abundant coolie labor" were responsible for foiling America's bombing strategy.

No one who has been to North Vietnam could conceivably use the words "resignation" or "coolie" to refer to its population. The whole idea that there is some kind of traditionally dumb labor force that can be turned to any task by harsh and insensitive overseers is wholly mistaken. I never met a single person who did not look as though he knew exactly what he was doing and why he was doing it. It would be hard to imagine a population more highly motivated, with the possible and significant exception of the United States.

In all my dealings with the Vietnamese not once did they fail to keep an appointment. They were invariably punctual. In the countryside or in factories, workers showed no signs of being under any form of coercion, psychological or otherwise. They looked as though they knew there was a job to be done, and they got on with it accordingly.

Their general attitude was more comparable to that of people in a highly industrialized country than to the traditional image Westerners have of Asians, sunk in the "Oriental" apathy of centuries. There are many problems in North Vietnam; insofar as they are being overcome it is because the revolution has turned "resigned Oriental coolies" into alert and motivated human beings.

For some reason Western governments and their adherents became converts to Guevaraism during the 1960s, believing that the injection of a few guerrilla fighters into peasant areas would automatically spark off revolution unless hastily smothered with rural development teams and counter-insurgency experts. Yet the belief that if Vietnam "falls" a score of guerrilla groups in neighboring countries will be able to seize power is a theory as absurd as it is pervasive.

The recent history of Vietnam and its revolution seems to suggest that it is by no means easy "to create two, three, many Vietnams"—as Guevara himself phrased it. Revolutions are not like ripe fruit on trees to be plucked by any passing guerrilla fighter. They mature slowly over centuries and ripen in the fierce heat of famine, plague, war, and economic disaster. We tend to see the victory over guerrillas in the Philippines and Malaya as being due to the skill of counter-guerrilla forces. It may equally have arisen from a lack of revolutionary content in the social and economic situation of those countries. This is the lesson that should be learnt from Vietnam.

In 1970 Richard Gott was the first British journalist from a national newspaper to visit North Vietnam since 1965. This series of articles was written from Hanoi.

Notes on the Cultural Life of the Democratic Republic of Vietnam

Peter Weiss

We visited the Democratic Republic of Vietnam from May 14, 1968, to June 21, 1968, and thus had the opportunity to get to know some of the provinces of the Red River Delta region, the coal province of Quangninh, the cities of Hanoi and Haiphong, and bombed regions south of the nineteenth parallel. . . . Here an attempt will be made to answer the following questions.

How is it possible for this population, today in the third generation, to withstand an attack that, in its totality, has already far exceeded the destructive action of World War II? How is it possible for the people of North Vietnam, and with them the people of the National Liberation Front in the South, not only to endure this destruction but, beyond that, to launch a successful counteroffensive against the world's strongest military power? What is it that enables this nation, in spite of the fact that all its edifices have been demolished, to maintain its production and its social unity?

Through numerous contacts and conversations, the people's characteristics and their historical, social, and political perspectives became clear and provided material for explaining why aggression by an imperialist technocracy, by the world of the rich, against this small agrarian state, representative of the poor people of the world, must prove unavailing.

Origins of Vietnamese Culture

French colonialism tried to minimize the value of Vietnamese poetry. As part of their plan to undo the people, the European rulers disputed the existence of a national epic tradition in this country. Their historians reduced legendary heroes to the status of village sprites; with the help of the mandarins they tried to reduce the hold of these exemplary folk heroes upon the minds of the people. Shamans and soothsayers flourished in the disunity, and together with them the Catholic missionaries did their best to destroy cultural values and advance superstition.

The goal of the program of enlightenment carried out after the revolution by scholarly cadres was to eliminate the residual influence of the medicine men and, in the villages, to awaken original cultural customs and forms of artistic expression grown dormant.

To be sure, during colonial times isolated missionaries and researchers had recorded the customs and rituals of the country, and had also made some collections of legends and fairy tales, though without understanding the background and meaning of this evidence of the past. For the most part peasant folklore was attributed to Chinese influence.

The strengthening of national traditions, the emphasis on a strong consciousness of self—things we are rather skeptical about because of our own experience—have great meaning for the Vietnamese struggle. The historical picture had to be revised to make a politically directed defense possible. This impoverished colonial country, to which all rights had been denied, had to develop, without any great powers to help it, means of ensuring unity and resolution against superior opponents: France, Japan, the United States. At first Vietnam had nothing to depend on but this thought of a common identity. In its *national war of liberation*—which is setting an example for other similarly colonialized or suppressed and exploited peoples of the Third World—Vietnam found an important weapon in the power of inner conviction. Without developing a consciousness of fighting to build up its own nation, this underdeveloped country would not have succeeded in standing up to the strongest and most cynical of opponents.

This seeking out of its own history, this investigation of the remote past, is part of the process of rebirth with which revolutionary activity began. When the scholars and politicians of Vietnam emphasize and endorse the peculiarities of their culture against alien influences and overlays, they are merely doing belatedly what Western nations did long ago. However, simultaneously with this kind of building process a socialist system with an international outlook is concomitantly being erected, thus eliminating chauvinistic elements. The discovery of a history of cultural development, the knowledge of historic heroes and battles, the demonstration of the tenacity that the masses of people again and again displayed in rising up against intruders, all these things foreshadow the endurance that is the hallmark of current actions.

The Early History of Vietnam

In times of peril the peasant population embodied the strength of the country. If peace seemed to be secured, the interests of the ruling class returned to the fore. While the nobility assimilated the language and writing, the scholarly pursuits, arts, and philosophies of the Middle Kingdom, the common people in the villages retained their own customs and language. Even when they were economically exploiting the labor power of the peasant to the limit, still the ruling class did not succeed in influencing the life of the villages. Their intellectual influence, as the saying has it, extended no farther than the village hedge.

The preoccupations of the rulers were accumulating riches and pursuing internecine struggles for influence and power; but unity was the mark of the peasant's life. And as the peasants repelled the armies from the north, as they rebelled against the enemy's occupation troops, they likewise turned against their own masters when oppression became intolerable. It was always the peasants, in their striving for justice, who gradually forced social changes in their country.

The Peasant Revolts

Accounts in Vietnamese history of the ceaseless struggle against enemy conquerors and domestic oppressors, and likewise of the preservation of national identity and continuity throughout these times of strife, always have the same perspective as the current situation. Descriptions of ancient wars have immediate parallels in the modern conflict with France and the United States. Behind the great Chinese armies, the fleet of junks, stand the French colonial troops, the American invasion host and the Seventh

Fleet. When the historians trace back the history of Vietnam they clarify the present situation for us. When they speak of historical victories they imply their present confidence in victory.

Beginnings of a Modern Literature

But everything that was built up by the revolutionaries has now been laid waste by the enemy. A new strategy, a reorganization of social and economic life, has had to be put into effect. Older people also know that it is not enough to decentralize industry and the school system, to conceal new workshops, factories, scientific centers, hospitals, and dressing stations in the jungle, in caves, and under the ground; literature, art, music, and the theater must simultaneously be kept alive, with intellectual activity encouraged everywhere. They know that the strength to resist is possible only when the struggle to maintain cultural values is carried on together with the military effort.

Dang Thai Mai [president of the Writers' Association] says: "If we think of the transformations that people underwent in the course of the few months after the revolution, if we consider the accomplishments which people are capable of, people who shortly before were still merely enduring in deepest degradation, how great is the contrast with Saigon, that city in which an even more powerful enemy uses corruption and spiritual terror as the weapons of his oppression."

Nguyen Dinh Thi [writer in the people's army]

"Many people who had learned to read and write as adults and who were not well acquainted with foreign words thought when they heard the term 'individualist' that it meant 'cannibal.' They associated the unintelligible concept of individualism with something dangerous, with the cannibalistic. They themselves had never had time to feel unique or singular. They shared work together, lived together, and since time immemorial had made common cause against natural catastrophe and enemy attack. A joy, a sorrow, a difficulty, had seldom been experienced alone; as a rule many shared in it. They all know what sharing means, without much being said about it. Denial, endless toil, the death of a loved one: every one of them has been equally subject to these things. And leave-taking, waiting: to be able to live at all we have to learn to wait for each other.

"Descriptions of loneliness, of having no way out, of not belonging, of personal disappointment, these matters are not relevant. The question is, rather, 'How can so and so be helped in his difficult situation?' Or 'How was this fear overcome, how was that piece of work mastered?' Or one might ask: 'Did he bear up in the face of danger?' And when inquiry is made about some individual case, the question is: 'Did he set an example?' Or 'Did he do what was asked of him?' And if he failed: 'What were the reasons for his failure and how is it to be avoided in the future?' The great

A dance entitled "In celebration of President Ho Chi Minh's birthday" performed by the Art Ensemble of the General Logistics Department in North Vietnam. The banner reads: FORWARD! TOTAL VICTORY IS CERTAIN FOR OUR ARMY.

threat is still at hand. The enemy's attacks ceaselessly menace everyone's existence. His gigantic superiority. Each month the tonnage of bombs dropped increases. It is possible that even the last two cities, Hanoi and Haiphong, will yet be destroyed. Against this are pitted values superior to the instruments of destruction. Concurrent with the military struggle—the only struggle that the enemy understands and in which he must be defeated—is the other struggle: the struggle for truth, for education, for social reform. That there is no feeling of weariness, that never is there a sign of discouragement, this is because there are so many carrying the same load. Confidence is the response to the enemy's nihilism. We talk about building up, not about laying waste.

"As far as my work is concerned, I cannot say that it measures up to the character of a woman I met recently in a village. She had lost two children in the great famine during the Japanese occupation. When the revolution came, she let out only one sigh. Her other children fought against France; another son was killed. She has children in the North and in the South. Now her first grandchild is at the front. She has raised children and grandchildren. She is too old now to work in the rice fields, yet she still works at home, cooks, takes care of the smallest children. She has never stopped working. These are our readers. What can we give them? They are the ones who are giving *us* strength.

"We call these old women Mother, Grandma. They call us Son, Brother.

"Even the district chairman, or some minister from Hanoi, when he is visiting a village calls them Mother or Grandma. Anyone disrespectful of an old person is despised. One of the cruelest weapons of the enemy in the South is to tear families apart, separate children from parents, take the husband away from his wife by force. Thus they try to extirpate culture at its deepest root.

"We often talk about our profession. For months, years on end we live in the jungle, sharing each potato, each bit of manioc. So, too, do we share literature with each other. Personal means of expression, the search for the new, the unique, all this is subordinated to the necessity of speaking as simply and directly as possible. Power lies in the masses. The peasants and industrial workers judge what you write. They check on your words. If they are true, if they describe events precisely, the conditions of life in the country, if they offer clear examples of the common effort, if they find a way to express the resistance, the hopes, the cares, the plans for the future in which all share, then they listen to you as no reading public ever has before. If you do not find this kind of language, you might as well be mute.

"After the truce of 1954 we called on the soldiers to write down their memories of the war years. We wanted to stimulate their powers of expression. We received over 10,000 replies. Many writers were so talented that they were encouraged to continue. A number of them who began writing at that time are well-known authors today.

"Today, more than anything, short stories are being written. The great novel, the novel that gives a panoramic view of the whole revolutionary period, is not yet on the scene. Measured against world literature we have no daring works. These peasants and soldiers, these self-taught people, are not trying to change literature by experimenting with the use of language. What they want to do is change the reader, their own world.

"For us a book is a weapon. Our readers know how to use a jungle knife, a hand grenade. They want to have the same trust in what a book says as in their weapons. Writing must support them and strengthen them, must offer them explanations, a point of view. We have founded no literary school. We have no time for experimenting with form, with visionary new literary creations.

"We asked ourselves whether our attempt to make our literature easily understood, to limit it to the everyday, the familiar, must not have a leveling effect. We took into account the fact that a limitation of fantasy could act as a curb on the widening of consciousness.

"Yet for the time being all that we have is the battlefield. With us everything has to do with realistic action. At the present time we need, above all, descriptions of the situation as it exists. We try to analyze events. Insofar as we make clear what is happening within people, show how they are holding firm, what they are accomplishing, we contribute to a strengthening of the power to resist. It is natural that from time to time the toil, the pain of losing some member of the family, the never-ending pressure of destruction, should overshadow hope. It would be inhuman to suppose that deprivations continuing year after year would leave no mark. Our consciousness for the time being is satisfied with a clear presentation of the perspectives of the people's war. We remind people of the indignities of colonialism, of the gigantic efforts which led to revolution, of the successes achieved during the years of construction. Our literature holds fast, it affirms. It assimilates the difficult experiences since the bombing attacks. Literature absorbs what the people have accumulated by way of thinking power and self-control.

"Since the people never had an opportunity to come to terms with the differential problems of modern art, we use a mode of expression understood by all. We have not abandoned artistic form or carefully thought-out composition, for these can be incidentally appreciated. Yet we do not make use of our documentations for their own sake. Aesthetics interests us only as a means of advancing elucidation. Our literature is intended to be political, to have a practical application.

"We write wherever we may be, on whatever part of the front we may happen to be. Our manuscripts are tiny scraps of paper that we carry in the pockets of our uniforms. We are ants, moles.

"Our books sell out quickly. We can't keep up with the readers' needs; 10,000, 20,000 copies of a book are sold within a week. We can't print larger editions because of the paper shortage. Only occasionally is a book printed in a 50,000-copy edition, like . . . a To Huu poetry collection.

"We writers have also discussed the nationalist content of various forms of artistic expression. We have debated whether the strong nationalistic tone of the war of liberation may be clouding the meaning of proletarian internationalism.

"I would like to reply to this question this way: Vietnam is a scrap of land among the great powers. Our nationalist struggle has had to prove itself for thousands of years. Without patriotism we could never have freed ourselves from slavery. Half of our country is still in the enemy's hands. We enjoy the respect and assistance of the socialist countries. Yet within socialism there are great ideological arguments. There are different opinions about the conduct of the world revolution. In Europe, in Latin America, Africa, Asia, and in the United States special theories and practices are being developed for the class war. There is no common strategy at this present stage of history. We proceed according to the experience accumulated in our own country. We started the revolution strictly on our own, without any help whatsoever from the outside. It is the people themselves who, almost 25 years after the revolutionary victory, are defending this country against those who would destroy the foundations of our socialist state. We can thank a tradition going back to the peasant uprisings of earlier centuries for whatever strength and endurance we have been able to muster. We call this war a *national* war of liberation because our struggle is in its military phase. Yet while we are strengthening our position in this nationalist struggle, we still continue our analysis of the conflicts within socialism and determine the position that Vietnam must take in the international resistance to imperialism."

Raw Material for a Poem by To Huu [party secretary and leading poet]

"Art cannot be regulated by one single decision.

"During the last twenty years we have tried in our writings to bring to light the thought and poetry of the people, for in the people is found our democratic tradition, beneath the overlay of the culture of the privileged classes.

"In our political effort we have succeeded in assimilating this democratic idiom. In literary work we have only partially succeeded. Art and literature progress more slowly than politics. Our political and military weapons are superior to our poems in swiftness and striking power.

"The fighter planes in the sky drown out our words.

"On this account our tradition of resistance still finds strongest expression in the salvos of our cannon and in our fighting men.

"There is trust in the rifle, the cannon, the hand grenade. Our words carry elements of uncertainty. Our military operations are precisely synchronized, one after the other. Our writing is a slow circling about, a listening, an answering, as on the Hat Cheo stage [ancient Vietnamese dramatic form].

"We speak the language of the peasants. A language rich in invention but quite limited.

"We live far from the advanced world. There are many things we understand only imperfectly. We do not know how life is in the developed countries. We do not know what the conditions are there for the struggle.

"Being situated far from the advanced world there is only one possibility for us. The possibility of using force.

"For us there is no path through legalism. We began the struggle in extreme degradation. From degradation we have progressed to poverty. From poverty we are working out for ourselves the basic values of existence. There is much we do not understand.

"We do not understand those who measure everything in terms of money.

"We ask ourselves, what else do they have besides money when they come parachuting down on our country?

"Our struggle is different from the one in the Soviet Union, different from the one in China, in Cuba. Before us lies the Pacific Ocean, and its name is betrayal. From it comes everything that threatens us, all our pain.

"Behind us, the mountains. Here we must live, between sea and mountains. Here we must hold fast, for us there is no long march; we must cling to our own soil.

"We have not laid siege to the cities from the countryside. We have used the strength of the cities. The peasants' struggle has been united with the workers' armed resistance in the cities.

"In Cuba the suffering of the people was the same as our suffering. Yet there the historical process preceding the revolution was much shorter, smaller. We love Cuba very much, in her hour of danger.

"We talk a lot about patriotism. But what we are fighting for is the small man's patriotism, local patriotism. We don't ever forget that in this war for unity the workers' parties of the world are at stake.

"While we are fighting we always keep in mind this great latent strength. We think of the workers, peasants, students, intellectuals of Europe and America. We had to wait for five years before the people of South Vietnam had grasped the situation and started to counterattack. In the other lands of East Asia the conditions for revolutionary struggle have now been created.

"Laos, Thailand, Cambodia will go the same way as Vietnam. The Indonesian people will also make a start toward freedom.

"When the fighting is over we will get on with the work of construction that we started a decade and a half ago.

"In our preparations we think of the South. In the South the poisoning of souls is worse than the physical dying.

"Women in the South are forced to trample in the dirt the rights they have fought for.

"Young people are again being forced to do slavish things.

"Yet we know from experience that when the revolution comes, the old and the corrupt quickly disappear, often without a sign or sound.

"We see it every day: many who had just been living in terror become fighters.

"Their faces change.

"The faces of the women in the North are likewise marked by deprivation. They work hard, sleep little. And marked, too, are the faces of the young soldiers, the pioneers. And yet they mirror strength and confidence. They are masters of their own lives.

"Their sisters and brothers in the South: someday they, too, will be entitled to rule their own land.

"Someday the present struggle shall grow into peaceful activity. Needs for material goods will arise. Yet these wishes must never get the upper hand over the thinking, the ideological life.

"If we do not preserve the values of this genuine freedom, then the hard-won achievements of the revolution will have been in vain.

"When there are cities again, electric light, a tablecloth on the table, our resistance must be continued; we have to keep on growing, we must not sink back into quiescence.

"Every day of repose is dangerous.

"The rebuilding of our unspeakably ravaged land will require the efforts of all living generations.

"A pause.

"A moment of relaxation.

"A legitimate wish.

"But the enemy is not yet beaten.

"It will be a long time before he is beaten.

"We say to them who rise up against the reactionary regimes in their countries: 'You are the majority.'

"When you are in possession of the truth, then you are the majority."

Afterword

The cultural life of Vietnam provides the basis for the people's unbroken will to resist. Yet this intellectual activity, which now has become a collective possession, must be seen as working in concert with everyday activities—activities marked by discipline, loyalty, and political conviction—aimed at the maintenance of production and defense against the enemy. Behind every cultural activity stands the bombing war, with its devastating consequences. Every cultural expression, whether it is concerned with historical traditions, the origins of art, the forms of literature and theater, the work of acting groups, or the development of a national personality, immediately points to the war that is being carried on in both North and South, in the effort to hold the initiative until the enemy of Vietnam has departed.

A poem, a picture, a theater piece, an ideological discussion, an hour of instruction, the results of a piece of research, all are equally valuable constituent parts of a common line of defense, along which, at other points, are field hospitals, artillery emplacements, agricultural collectives, workshops, or supply columns. A success in the artistic, scientific, or educational areas is always seen as a victory over the aggressor who wants to destroy the social foundations of Vietnam. And in each particular of the victory the power to endure is witnessed anew, the power to bear up against deprivation, suffering, destruction, and death.

In response to the widespread physical destruction, new industries, universities, and other decentralized institutions have been reestablished, hidden away in jungles and caves, and substitutes have been provided for every bombed-out street and dike. Maintaining the country, an effort separately pursued by each province, providing roads, education, care of the sick and wounded, work in the fields, troop replacements, assistance sent to the South, all this goes on in the bombed regions, however much hindered and imperiled. The tonnage of bombs dropped contradicts the cynical claims that, in view of the fact that production and a cultural life are being maintained in North Vietnam, you cannot speak of total war and genocide. The intention of the United States is clear. It has not been realized, however, since ways and means have been found to counter it.

Peter Weiss, author of Marat/Sade *and* The Investigation, *is a German playwright, novelist, poet, and film-maker. These excerpts are from his book* Notes on the Cultural Life of the Democratic Republic of North Vietnam, *which was written after extensive travel and study in that country.*

The NLF Asks the American Left: "Where are you now that we *really* need you?"

Franz Schurmann

Late in April of this year [1969], I began to receive urgent messages from the Swedish International Liaison Committee asking me to attend an "emergency action conference" on Vietnam from May 16 to 18. Like others invited, I hesitated. Stockholm was too far; there was no money to pay the expensive air fare; what could a conference possibly accomplish? And, why an "*emergency action* conference"? Although I knew in my mind that the war was still raging and Nixon was determined to keep a grip on South Vietnam, all the talk about negotiation made me think that this might, after all, be the last act of the drama. In fact, the days spent in Stockholm, particularly with the Vietnamese, were so pleasant that it was hard to think of the war. I have never met anyone who looked less martial than the Vietnamese of the NLF and the DRV (Democratic Republic of Vietnam), although many of them had years of guerrilla fighting behind them. The Vietnamese asked nothing from the Americans except support for their ten-point proposal, nor did they talk much about the horrors of the war.

When I returned to Berkeley, the city was under military occupation. The memory of Stockholm faded rapidly under the impact of Reagan and Madigan's little counterinsurgency. Only now, in London, have the reasons for the emergency action conference become clear to me. Today's Paris *Herald Tribune* (June 5) reports that May set a record for B-52 raids over South Vietnam. The Quaker White Paper of May 5 said in its typically quiet way: "The cumulative result of U.S. involvement borders not on Vietnam's salvation, but on its death." America, repeatedly denied victory, now has chosen the ultimate solution—the destruction of South Vietnam.

I still do not fully understand why there was no sense of crisis at Stock-

Reprinted from *Ramparts*, August 1969.

holm. In particular, I do not understand why the Vietnamese, who came in strength from Paris, Hanoi, and the jungles of South Vietnam, did not inject a sense of urgency into the meetings. Yet I should have been prepared for this sense of calm since I had had a similar experience in Hanoi. I had expected to see the population there tense and constantly fearful of American raids. Instead, I saw people going about their business, moving fast only when the air raid alerts sounded. At times North Vietnam seemed like a land at peace, but everywhere one could see the ruins and, on occasion, hear the Shrike missiles exploding in populated areas. When I asked the Vietnamese about this calm, they said that they would never allow the U.S. Air Force to dominate their lives, no matter how terrible the bombing. These are the people whose will the Pentagon intends to break by its bombing. Again, in Stockholm I expected to find Vietnamese as victims of American terror and instead found people of extraordinary humanity, the last people one could consider "victims."

The Vietnamese came to Stockholm in full strength. While, with their usual politeness, they spoke with all who came, for obvious reasons they gave particular attention to the Americans. I spent three evenings with them—Friday, Saturday, and Sunday, the days of the conference. All the meetings were held in private homes; the first was held with all the Americans present, and the others with smaller groups to permit better discussion. The CIA's bugging devices picked up conversation which must be puzzling to the analysts in Langley. Much of it was an exchange of personal experiences. The Americans talked of the anti-war movement, student protest, the struggle against the military-industrial complex. The Vietnamese spoke about the NLF's ten-point proposal.

The Vietnamese knew that all the Americans present had political attitudes which went far beyond support of the Vietnamese. We were for a dismantling of the American Empire and its genocidal war machine, and for a radical transformation of American society. Even before the ten points were announced, we were for the unconditional withdrawal of all American and satellite troops from Vietnam, for the abandonment of the Saigon dictatorship, and for an end to the war of destruction. We did not have to come to Stockholm to say that. But as we talked during the first two evenings and later at a Chinese restaurant, I realized that the Vietnamese above all wanted to see and hear those Americans who had struggled for their cause since the inception of large-scale American aggression against Vietnam. Over the years, bonds of friendship had grown between Vietnamese and Americans. The Vietnamese wanted to be sure those bonds still existed. To many Americans that may sound like a naive and/or phony reason, but it springs directly from a way of acting which has given the Vietnamese the strength to resist the most powerful nation in the world. They long ago discovered the truth that a movement is people directly relating to each other in terms of a common cause.

The Vietnamese believe that ideas and influences are transmitted mainly through personal contact. This may be because of their Confucian tradition, but more likely it has grown out of generations of experience in politics and war. What is a guerrilla war but networks of human bonds? In his book *The Viet Cong,* former USIA official Douglas Pike presents a picture of the Viet Cong as a kind of organizational weapon where men are manipulated by ideology, indoctrination, command, coercion, terror, etc. In the fashion of political scientists, he makes the war appear very abstract. And indeed for the Americans, the Vietnam war is abstract—except for those sacrificed on the innumerable "hamburger hills" of Vietnam. The B-52 pilot drops his load on something below and heads back to his officers' club in Thailand. But that abstractness is essential to the way the United States has chosen to fight the war. The Vietnam war has become genocidal through technology, which breaks all direct links between the makers and users of weapons and those whom they kill. The organization-man portrayal of the Viet Cong makes it easier to destroy him from afar. But those who are most dehumanized by this kind of war are the Americans, not the Vietnamese.

But militarists in Vietnam and fascists in our own police forces are not the only ones who act in terms of abstractions. We on the left also speak abstractly about "the movement," "the system," "the struggle." At the Stockholm conference we tried to reassure the Vietnamese that, even though the left no longer makes Vietnam its central issue, the wave of disruption in the United States is raising the social cost of the war for Nixon, thus contributing directly to its ending. Everyone is against the war now—except for the militarists who have a vested interest in it. We explained that Vietnam has now become a liberal's issue, and so the left has moved toward fighting the system directly: attacking the military-industrial complex, striking at institutional racism—in general, pulling out the seams of the system.

While appreciating this analysis, the Vietnamese asked numerous questions about specific anti-war actions: Are draftees and soldiers still refusing to fight in Vietnam? Who is writing and demonstrating against the war? What do people say about the NLF? (They still joked about "the faceless Viet Cong.") It was not enough for them that half our Congress demands an end to the war, that public opinion wants the U.S. out of Vietnam, that the stock market has shown its most consistent pattern in years in reacting to peace or escalation news about Vietnam. They did not come to hear those analyses which they already knew from the American mass media. They came to ask the Americans to support them, the National Front for the Liberation of South Vietnam.

Representatives from 53 countries and territories attended the conference. Gunnar Myrdal gave the opening speech, and Bertil Svahnstrom of the International Liaison Committee chaired the first session. But the key speeches were by Mrs. Nguyen Thu Binh, Nguyen Minh Vy, and Noam Chomsky. Mrs. Binh, speaking as a leader of a movement which in years of struggle has acquired a political and moral identity, told of the cruelties of the war and of the negotiations at Paris. Chomsky spoke as an individual, as did most of the other Americans, including Gabriel Kolko and Carleton Goodlett. He represented no movement, only his own moving record of thought and action in the struggle against American imperialism and militarism.

In the subsequent private meetings with the Vietnamese, we again spoke as individuals and they as members of a movement. There was some bickering among us, which distressed the Vietnamese, but what bothered them most was the egotism of the American "movement," its inability to unite around the issue of the war and the NLF's struggle. They know that American society is in a revolutionary upheaval, that the left has transcending domestic issues to deal with (like ghetto oppression, people's parks, police terror). They do not expect us to abandon these issues. But they believe fervently that the war and the struggle of the NLF is the paramount issue now facing the left throughout the world, and that the left can at least be temporarily united around that issue.

The Stockholm conference began on May 16, two days after Nixon's speech on Vietnam. Naturally that speech, and the ten-point proposal which the NLF had made some days before, were chief topics of conversation at Stockholm. The Vietnamese made few concrete references to the Paris negotiations, but Nguyen Minh Vy of the DRV delegation said, "The war is cruel but even more cruel are the negotiations at Paris." Mrs. Binh said the same. For the American negotiators at Paris, the discussions are a game to be played with all the adroitness they can muster; after the sessions are over, they can go on to their cocktail parties. For the Vietnamese, the Paris negotiations are part of the struggle which their compatriots are waging in South Vietnam. The NLF made it clear that the ten-point proposal was as far as they would go; some within their own ranks apparently believed that it had already gone too far.

The American position, as well as one can judge it, is that there must be "mutual withdrawal" of all "non-South Vietnamese" forces from South Vietnam *before* elections can be held. Naturally, the Americans have been vague about the exact role of the Thieu-Ky regime (which apparently has disquieted "President" Thieu). In Stockholm, we heard the NLF's first reactions to Nixon's proposals. Mrs. Binh, speaking with vehemence, stated three points summarizing the NLF reaction: (1) that the NLF would never agree to mutual withdrawal; (2) that the United States was as committed as before to the Thieu-Ky-Huong regime; and (3) that the United States was intensifying rather than de-escalating the war in South Vietnam. Her anger was greatest when she said that Nixon's proposals for mutual withdrawal were a "maneuver" to get Vietnamese to fight Vietnamese under the command of the Americans.

Washington's real attitude appears to be: any organized enemy forces are "North Vietnamese"; guerrilla units are "South Vietnamese." But since the guerrillas are by now a well organized fighting force, accepting the American definition of "non-South Vietnamese" would probably mean that, under mutual withdrawal, virtually all NLF fighting forces must withdraw from South Vietnam. If the Americans and their satellites also withdraw, then this leaves the ARVNs (troops of the Army of the Republic of Vietnam) alone as a military force in South Vietnam. No matter how dispirited, fearful and ineffective a fighting force the ARVNs are, they could probably muster enough strength to extend their control over the war-devastated countryside once the NLF had withdrawn. Mutual withdrawal sounds so reasonable. What it really means is a call to the Vietnamese to lay down their arms and surrender.

On the other hand, the NLF's proposal to let the Vietnamese parties themselves settle the problem of their own armed forces in South Vietnam means automatic victory for the NLF. Despite their million-man army, the ARVN would collapse once American support was withdrawn. News media sympathetic to Washington have tried their best recently to portray the ARVNs in a favorable light (maybe if they are able to shoulder the burden, U.S. troops can be withdrawn!); but the true picture has not changed for the last decade and a half. The United States still has not learned that the Vietnamese can be the bravest and toughest people in the world if they

(Photo by Paul Avery, Empire.)

fight for their own country, but if asked to shed their blood for a foreign ruler, they are the worst of troops.

The ten-point proposal of the NLF can be stated as three basic demands: (1) the United States must begin the process of withdrawal of its troops from South Vietnam; (2) it must agree to the establishment of a coalition government to replace the present client regime of Thieu, Ky, and Huong; and (3) it must unequivocally de-escalate the war. While the first and third points have been consistently demanded by the NLF, the acquiescence in a coalition government is a new approach. Washington, knowing how much it has contributed to destroying the indigenous political movements of the South Vietnamese cities (notably Buddhist), fears that any coalition government will just be a prelude to the NLF taking power when U.S. forces leave. That fear is probably justified. On the other hand, the NLF, despite the fact that it is already a coalition (something often conveniently overlooked in the West), has been predominantly a movement of the peasantry. To govern effectively in a new South Vietnam, it must have the support of broad urban political elements which, in the past, have expressed themselves in the Buddhist and student movements. The social and political realities of South Vietnam will probably make a coalition government of various moderate and radical tendencies the only possible form of government in that country.

Nixon's speech seemed to have been a rejoinder to the NLF's ten-point proposal; indeed, he proposed eight points of his own for discussion at Paris. The tone was symbolized by one key sentence: ". . . we have to demonstrate . . . that confrontation with the United States is costly and unrewarding." Nixon says clearly that the United States cannot afford to lose any war. That means it cannot afford to lose the war in Vietnam. The Vietnamese have many times offered to let the United States depart from South Vietnam with honor. But Nixon stated with crystal clarity that the U.S. will not accept any disguised defeat. He said: "If we simply abandon our effort in Vietnam, the cause of peace might not survive the damage that would be done to other nations' confidence in our reliability." The same statements have been made by America's rulers ever since the beginning of the Cold War. An American defeat will start the dominoes falling . . .

Participants in the Stockholm conference pointed out what many newspapers in the United States have noted: that the war has been greatly escalated since the Nixon Administration came into power. B-52 raids are raining destruction on South Vietnam on a scale unprecedented in any previous war. Kolko noted that in the first nine months of 1968 two million craters, 15 by 23 feet, had been inflicted on South Vietnam by B-52's. I. F. Stone, in his May 19, 1969 newsletter, reported that in January 1969, B-52's dropped 129,700 tons of bombs on South Vietnam, the highest monthly tonnage since the air war began; at that rate, the number of craters in 1969 will be double that of the previous year. U.S.-initiated ground combat actions in 1969 have greatly increased over 1968.

Although not immediately apparent in the midst of the bland verbiage, Nixon's answer to the NLF demand for de-escalation of the war was clear —step up the war as much as possible, but quietly. That pleased the militarists. But Nixon knows well the limitations of American power in Vietnam. He knows that the "galloping optimism" of the last months of 1968 was smashed by the post-Têt offensive of the NLF. U.S. casualty figures once again rose dramatically, and U.S forces were once again put on the defensive. He knows that victory cannot be won on the battlefield. Mrs. Binh's first reaction to Nixon's proposals was to label them a "maneuver." Maneuver—the word cropped up again and again in the Stockholm meetings. The Vietnamese said repeatedly and persuasively that Nixon's goals in South Vietnam had not changed from those of his predecessors— to keep South Vietnam under American control and maintain a Saigon puppet government in power. Only the means have changed.

If Nixon remains as determined to secure a military victory in South Vietnam as he indicated in his speech, then the rain of destruction will continue to pour down over the Vietnamese. And as the war becomes more technological, it becomes more genocidal. Nixon's adroit maneuvering makes it difficult to realize this, and rearouses hopes that the end of the war may be just around the corner. In fact, four million people (one-third the rural population of South Vietnam) have been driven off the land and into the cities by American bombing. Saigon has become the most densely populated city in the world. The killing, bombing, starvation, and disease exceed that caused by the Germans in World War II.

How can one explain to the Vietnamese that the revolutionary action of setting up a "people's park" is linked to their struggle for survival and victory? That is what we, individuals from the American left, tried again and again to explain in Stockholm. The American left's response to the war is an escalating series of guerrilla-type actions directed against the system. None by itself produces many tangible results, but together they are opening up the festering sores of American society. Vietnam was a powerful catalyst in the creation of revolutionary currents in America. But the Vietnamese want to know how this relates to Vietnam, how it helps bring an end to the genocide being practiced on their people.

I think there is a major error of thought which the left has made concerning Vietnam, particularly the ideologically inclined left: it has refused to believe that Vietnam is really a critical issue for the American ruling class. Accepting conventional Marxist interpretations of imperialism, it assumed that the Vietnam war was fought for the defense of imperialist economic and political interests. Believing in the rationality of the ruling class, it further assumed that once the short-term economic utility of that war diminished, the ruling class would order the government to terminate it; after all, the state is but the instrument of the ruling class. There is an element of truth in this. As the balance of payment crisis has worsened and inflation has threatened to get out of control, businessmen have pressed for a termination of the war. But even if Eisenhower believed that Vietnam had to be held for its raw materials, this (along with any other economic reasons motivating Kennedy and Johnson) has declined as a rationale for the war. At this point there really is no economic rationale to explain the genocide in Vietnam.

There is, however, one key issue in the Vietnam war, present from the beginning, which has not assumed overriding importance: does America have the power to destroy a popular revolution? Ever since World War I, America has lived with periodic outbursts of paranoia that darker, poorer hordes would burst forth from the recesses of the Eastern Hemisphere and overwhelm God's chosen country. Paradoxically, they thought the Germans in World War I were part of that threatening wave. They called the Germans "Huns," "Teutono-orientals." Then, after the war, the "yellow hordes" became "red" as revolution appeared to be spreading from Moscow. During the years of the liberals' reign, beginning with FDR, a new confidence emerged that, perhaps after all, the dark peoples could be converted to light, and there was even hope that "red" could become "pink" and eventually "white." But when the period of docile decolonization was followed by social revolutions in the poor countries (Cuba and Vietnam being the most threatening), the old paranoia began to revive. Now social insurgency has spread even to the advanced capitalist countries, in the form of minority revolts and student movements. There is no sign that this wave of insurgency will diminish. As the poor countries become poorer and military dictatorships impose tighter grips on them, the pressures of revolution rise. As cities and universities continue to decay in the advanced countries, fuel for new insurgencies is created.

Americans have seen the Vietnamese mount effective resistance against the most powerful nation in the world. They have seen that insurgency grows from rebellion to revolution to organized military action on a large scale. They have seen their own capabilities, particularly in the area of manpower, diminish. Their last weapon is technology, particularly airpower. If they cannot win or at least achieve decisive advantage against the Vietnamese through technology, then *what will they do when other Vietnams erupt?*

The Vietnamese believe that the Vietnam war is the paramount issue facing the left. The Pentagon similarly believes that the test of technological counterinsurgency in Vietnam is critical for America's defense in the future. It would like to continue that test without arousing further antagonism: lower the costs in men, money and matériel; avoid antagonizing people by keeping silent about the destruction; allow Nixon to maneuver in Paris and elsewhere. Vietnam may not be a critical issue for America's businessmen, but it is *the* critical issue for the Pentagon. Never since the end of World War II has the Pentagon been subject to such pressures as now. Never has the opposition to the Vietnam war been as great. The only criterion for the effectiveness of that opposition is whether the scale of warfare in Vietnam goes down. Needless to say, once the genocide has been completed, opposition becomes irrelevant.

A few years ago, the government and its academic apologists told the

American people that Vietnam was a testing ground for Mao Tse-tung's theory of national liberation movements. Therefore, America had to prove to the Chinese and to any potential national liberation movements that America was no "paper tiger," that it could defeat them. Nothing has changed but the means in the Pentagon's determination to win that test. But the change in means is not just a tactical shift. In the course of the war, the Pentagon has discovered a basic strategic reality which not only has made a change in tactics imperative, but has also intensified the necessity of winning the "test." That reality is the incapacity of the United States to rely on manpower, its own or that of its satellites, to crush popular revolution. The current decisive shift to reliance on technology rather than on men marks a major characteristic of Nixon's general military policy.

In 1959, Maxwell Taylor of the U.S. Army (later Kennedy's Chairman of the Joint Chiefs of Staff and then ambassador to Saigon) wrote a book, *The Uncertain Trumpet,* in which he advocated a greater buildup in conventional warfare capabilities to meet "limited war" situations. He argued, as did Kennedy, that Dullesian doctrines of massive retaliation were, in effect, paper tigers. The United States, even with massive nuclear superiority, would not start a nuclear war, and this would leave the communists and other troublemakers free to wage brushfire wars with impunity. Taylor advocated a large-scale buildup of the U.S. Army to meet such challenges, and Kennedy supplemented that with his notions of counterinsurgency. Both notions depended on the availability of manpower, American and foreign, to fight such brushfire wars.

During the years 1964 to 1966, Dean Rusk flew around the world urging America's Asian and European allies to send troops to Vietnam. Some were sent, but in numbers so small that the euphemism "allies" could not disguise the overwhelmingly American character of the intervention. As protest of the war grew in the United States, draft resistance and then resistance within the Army itself intensified. In Vietnam, less than one-fifth of the half million American troops there take part in combat, the low ratio being due to the high support ratio of the American armed forces. Although Americans in combat acquit themselves bravely, as we saw recently in the "Hamburger Hill" operation, America's combat effectives are few in number, and getting fewer all the time. Vietnam has demonstrated America's incapacity to mobilize large numbers of its own or other countries' men to fight its imperial wars. On the other hand, the Vietnamese have shown an extraordinary capacity to recruit new soldiers to their cause from among the population. No man can be coerced into fighting as bravely and efficiently as do the Vietnamese in the NLF. The pathetic ARVNs are a supreme example of the kind of soldiers created by coercion and forced drafting. The war has, in fact, become a testing ground of a major Chinese proposition of guerrilla war—that men are more important than weapons. The war, under Nixon, is becoming one of men (Vietnamese) against weapons (American).

The sophisticated and diversified use of air power has become the chief

American weapon in Vietnam (well described in Gabriel Bonnet's recent book, *La Guerre Revolutionnaire du Vietnam*). Fighter aircraft and B-52's have virtually replaced artillery; in fact, they have almost replaced troops as the chief instruments for destroying enemy units. Westmoreland used troops to make contact with the enemy, then withdrew them and called in planes and artillery to decimate the enemy units. Helicopters have been used in the most varied of ways. Of considerable importance to potential counterinsurgency in other countries is the use of helicopter gunships to attack urban insurgents, as could be seen on American television screens during last year's Têt Offensive. But the most important aerial weapon remains saturation bombing by B-52's of virtually the entire rural area of South Vietnam (supplemented by defoliation and crop destruction). That bombing is designed to empty the "ocean" in order to deprive the "fish" of water.

Can the Vietnamese survive and win in the face of this holocaust? If they do, then it will be in the same way they have survived and won during the past years. The U.S. government and its academic helpers have published many studies of what makes the Viet Cong fight, some of which have even been informative. But the left has shown amazingly little interest in the Vietnamese as a people, and that interest has even been declining in recent months. Ho Chi Minh is a familiar and revered figure, but beyond him the Vietnamese remain abstract. Few on the left listen to Vietnamese music; some have laughed at the clumsiness of Vietnamese films. In fact, the only films on Vietnam which have made an impression have been those made by Americans, Frenchmen, or Cubans. Perhaps the Vietnamese are too remote culturally for Westerners to understand, and so have been relegated to that general category of strange Asians, worthy of respect but inscrutable. Compared to the massive amount of literature about Cuba, there is little left literature on Vietnam (as distinct from the Vietnam war).

South Vietnamese Funeral. *(Photo by Joseph W. Carey, BBM.)*

Cuba is closer to the Western experience. Much of its music is North American, and even "Guantanamera" can be sung. Che Guevara is a more real figure to Americans than is Ho Chi Minh. In the 1930's, Spain became a reality to the left, as a people, a culture, a struggle. Not so in the case of Vietnam. For the left as for much of the rest of America, the Vietnamese are still "faceless."

All this would not matter in ordinary times, for no people has any obligation to understand and feel the culture of another. But today we are not just witnessing the agony of the Vietnamese; we must realize that if they should be crushed, so will popular revolutions elsewhere. If the Pentagon wins its test of technological counterinsurgency, it will pass on its weapons and experiences to the forces of law and order for use on protesters and rebels in America itself. (Indeed it already has.) The left in many parts of the world may soon have to learn to survive the forces of repression as the Vietnamese have learned. But no amount of organizational studies of the Viet Cong will ever reveal the sources of their strength. The more one looks at the ideology and organization of the Vietnamese, the less convincing they are as factors in this strength. Perhaps the secret lies in what Mao Tse-tung calls "spirit." But "spirit" means nothing to the practical American mind.

I do not know if that spirit of love of country and people I saw in North Vietnam last year and again in Stockholm was the same years ago. I suspect it was there in a general way, but the Vietnamese movement in its earlier stages put great stress on ideology and organization. As the horrors of the war intensified, maybe to the surprise of the Vietnamese themselves, the sentiments of patriotism became more and more apparent. They began to see that their soldiers fought, not because of ideology and organization, but because of deeper sentiments. As those sentiments became more important, so did the humanization of the movement, and that humanization became the greatest source of its strength. Ironically, the impersonal technological monster which is the U.S. Air Force can take the credit for having helped give the Vietnamese their present endurance and power.

To "remember Vietnam" is not just an obligation of the left to continue the pressure to end the war and save Vietnam from genocide. By making the Vietnamese and not just the Vietnam war real, the left may discover that its own ability as revolutionaries to love America will give it a source of strength and solidarity it does not have now where each does his own thing. Even more, the portrayal of the Vietnamese as a real people may finally make the American people aware that there is only one meaningful political force in South Vietnam—the National Front for the Liberation of South Vietnam.

The war is going to enter a critical phase this summer. Nixon has announced some future withdrawals of American troops from South Vietnam, and "President" Thieu will happily express his agreement to hold elections. Like Laird's famous ten per cent budget cuts in B-52 raids, the Nixon-Thieu maneuvers will probably be accompanied by an intensification of the war, particularly of airborne destruction. New records in monthly bomb tonnage dropped will be achieved. If the substitution of air power for men can keep casualties down and, with the resulting withdrawal of troops, cut costs, and if the sleight-of-hand can kindle hope that something may be moving in Paris, then the Pentagon can continue its war until decisive results have been achieved.

The "working group on action" of the Stockholm conference proposed several lines of international action on Vietnam. In the Stockholm tradition, they are circulating a broad international appeal urging American withdrawal from Vietnam and acceptance of the ten-point proposal of the NLF. They urged demonstrations, meetings, vigils for July 4 and July 20 (July 20 is the fifteenth anniversary of Geneva Accords). They called for boycotts of American products, isolation of and protests against American officials, appeals to American military men to refuse to fight in Vietnam. And they recommend that intensive efforts be made to explain the ten-point proposal, and, above all, to make the Vietnamese of the NLF real and visible through the mass media, notably television.

But most important is that in the hundreds of local struggles waged during the summer and autumn, the issue of Vietnam and the Vietnamese be constantly raised. No matter how tired Americans may have become of the war, they must be reminded that the fate of brave Vietnamese will determine what happens to them at home.

Franz Schurmann is a professor of history and sociology at the University of California at Berkeley. He is the author of Ideology and Organization in Communist China *(University of California Press) and co-author of* The China Reader *(Vintage), and of* The Politics of Escalation in Vietnam *(Fawcett).*

---

chapter two

LAOS AND CAMBODIA

At the same time that American commitments were openly growing in Vietnam, the United States government was carrying out a secret war in Laos and working to subvert Cambodian sovereignty and neutrality. Although Americans heard only about Vietnam, U.S. policymakers have always known that the Vietnam war involved all of Indochina. Initially, the U.S. backed the French in their colonial war in Indochina because it was against the indigenous communist movement, which had successfully taken power in Vietnam after the Japanese defeat in World War II. When the French were expelled by the Viet Minh and the Pathet Lao, the U.S. began to work systematically to undermine the neutrality of Laos, Cambodia, and Vietnam. While the U.S. was officially pledging noninterference with implementation of the 1954 Geneva Agreements, Secretary of State John Foster Dulles was organizing the Southeast Asia Treaty Organization (SEATO) in order to extend American hegemony to Indochina.

David Horowitz maintains that SEATO was created to counter the Geneva Agreements by forcing the neutral Indochinese states under the "protection" of the anti-communist SEATO nations. The primary purpose of SEATO was to open the way for U.S. intervention in Southeast Asian countries to prevent their supposed subversion by the indigenous populations, rather than to protect those countries from foreign aggression.

In Laos, as shown by both Horowitz and Banning Garrett, Prince Souvanna Phouma was not as willing as Diem to become an American puppet and pursue the anti-communist civil war. But with the U.S. Central Intelligence Agency's subversion of the Royal Lao Government administration and army, and the creation of a Laotian elite and economy completely dependent on American aid, the United States was finally able to undermine the neutralist position of Laos. The result was that the U.S. was able to establish forward bases in Laos for attacking Vietnam and menacing China and succeeded in forcing Souvanna Phouma to pursue the American plan of exterminating the Pathet Lao.

The United States has justified its actions in Laos by claiming North Vietnamese invasion. These unsubstantiated claims, Garrett maintains, were used by the Laotian right wing and the CIA to undermine neutralist attempts to integrate the Pathet Lao into the government, as called for by the Geneva Agreements of 1954 and 1962. It is true that the Pathet Lao have received aid and advisors from North Vietnam; however, the presence of North Vietnamese troops in Laos has come in response to the U.S. intervention and escalation, particularly President Nixon's escalation of the bombing.

The Pathet Lao, Garrett argues, is a strong revolutionary movement which is radically altering Laotian society. In their liberated zones they have built upon traditional Laotian culture to create new modes of production and organization. The United States policy, however, has been to attack the very foundation of Pathet Lao society and attempt to destroy it with massive bombing. This policy of forced urbanization—using bombs to force the surviving population into a few cities or controlled rural areas—has produced nearly 800,000 refugees, more than a quarter of the total population of Laos. But, as in Vietnam, the American escalation, instead of destroying the enemy, has increased their determination to fight back.

Prince Sihanouk of Cambodia was not so easily undone as Souvanna Phouma. The U.S. tried to subvert his independence after the Geneva Agreements in two ways—first, by giving Cambodia military and economic aid and trying to win over members of the elite, as had been done in Vietnam and Laos, and, second, in the late fifties, when it was clear that Sihanouk would not be dominated, by having the CIA sponsor a right wing guerrilla group, the Khmer Serai, which attempted on numerous occasions to overthrow Sihanouk. In 1963, in fact, after the exposure of a Khmer Serai plot, Sihanouk terminated U.S. aid; however, the United States' friends within the Cambodian elite and the Khmer Serai were finally successful in the March 1970 coup. Although prior to the coup Sihanouk's position in Cambodia had become increasingly tenuous for domestic reasons, it was U.S. pressure which toppled the last domino in Indochina. Sihanouk has now joined his former left wing guerrilla antagonists, the Khmer Rouge, and is head of the National United Front of Cambodia, a broad coalition of Cambodians backed by the Vietnamese, which is fighting to liberate Cambodia. According to Garrett's analysis, the NUF is fighting a protracted war: their strategy is to organize and consolidate a revolutionary movement and army in the countryside, culminating in taking the capital and toppling the U.S. backed Lon Nol government.

Revisionist Tales of Negotiations with the Communists

David Horowitz

Diplomacy—to revise an old saying—is only the continuation of war by other means. Far from providing a machinery to resolve conflicts in any final sense, negotiations can be seen at best as attempts to register and define a new status quo which, it is hoped, will provide a more stable (and peaceful) framework for contending forces. In the midst of a global revolutionary epoch like the present one, where the overarching framework of international politics is a Cold War, no status quo is ultimately stable, and hence negotiations more than ever appear as attempts to win at the conference table the war aims that have been foregone on the battlefield. At the very least the contending parties hope to use the compromise formula arrived at through negotiations as a vantage point from which to launch the next phase of the continuing struggle. This accounts for the trail of broken agreements that litter the field of contemporary diplomatic history. For when one party to an agreement feels the balance of power shifting in its favor—whether in the local or global sphere—it will be sorely tempted to abandon the old framework and to seek by force to fashion a new, more favorable, status quo.

Now, once again, America's cold warriors are sitting down with the communists to attempt to move a conflict off the battleground of open warfare and onto the plane of diplomatic negotiation. Once again, moreover, a large segment of the American press is running through its orthodox version of Cold War history to discredit the negotiations: the "record" shows that you can't trust the communists (look at Yalta); that the Reds are devious and dilatory (look at Korea); and that they will never keep their word (look at the Geneva Accords on Vietnam and Laos). One might well ask why U.S. statesmen (always pictured as implausibly noble, forbearing and mild—even the Johnson administration has been unable to mar that image) bother to come to these meetings in the first place. Averell Harriman, in particular, should know better—he has been to so many of them.

But there is another history which, in the wake of the devastation of Vietnam, Americans are slowly beginning to perceive. This history shows that America, like any nation, negotiates to maintain the aims and posture of its overall strategy, and that, as an expansionist power which has risen to unprecedented heights of global predominance in the post-war years,

Reprinted from *Ramparts,* June 29, 1968.

America itself has shown very little compunction about the international agreements and norms which it has found necessary to trample in its path.

If one were to set about systematically to invent an historical episode to show that the United States in its dealings with the communists has no regard for international agreements and peace settlements and that its official rhetoric about free elections is just so much dust thrown into the eyes of the naive and unwary, one could hardly surpass the actual sequence of events surrounding the Geneva settlement of 1954. These events are well-known and require only the briefest recounting. As the Geneva meeting became a reality, Washington sought by every means possible to obstruct and destroy its work, first by seeking to organize an Anglo-American nuclear attack and military intervention in Vietnam (with a possible thrust against the Chinese), and then by setting up an organizational framework (SEATO) and an on-the-scene instrument (Ngo Dinh Diem) to undermine whatever peace settlement was reached.

The settlement itself was notable chiefly for the mammoth concessions wrung from the Viet Minh, represented by Pham Van Dong, the present premier of the Democratic Republic of Vietnam. The Viet Minh entered the conference with three-quarters of Vietnam under its control; a war-weary, economically drained and thoroughly demoralized France clung to the remainder. However, the Vietnamese were well aware of the possibility of an American intervention and/or nuclear assault on their country, and for this reason, probably as much as any other, they decided to go to the conference table.

In brief, the Viet Minh agreed to a temporary division of the country at the 17th parallel, while internationally supervised free elections were to be organized to decide what regime was to be the legitimate sovereignty in all Vietnam. The United States declared explicitly at Geneva that it would not seek to undermine these agreements and that it was committed to the principle of holding internationally-supervised elections to reunite divided countries like Vietnam. The Viet Minh accordingly laid down its arms in the South, and Washington's agent Ngo Dinh Diem went into action.

With massive American support, Diem moved swiftly to crush all opposition groups, and with the aid of the CIA and Michigan State University [see *Ramparts* magazine, April 1965] he imposed a totalitarian police state on South Vietnam.

In June 1955, one year after the Geneva Conference, Diem announced that he would not honor the Geneva Accords on unification elections. Shortly thereafter, the paymaster of the Diem regime in the person of Secretary of State Dulles gave public support to Diem's pronouncement. With these declarations, the Geneva Accords expired.

The Geneva Accords offered no more protection to Laos against American Cold War policies than they had offered to Vietnam. The agreements had included a formula for the neutralization of Laos, which had been the scene of a national guerrilla struggle parallel to that of the Viet Minh's (though less successful). But the United States' decision to under-

Aerial view of paddy fields in Mekong Delta. *(© Phillip Jones Griffiths, Magnum.)*

mine the Geneva Accords with respect to Vietnam *ipso facto* determined its policy towards the future neutralist regime in neighboring Laos.

Dulles' objective was to make Laos, like South Vietnam, a protectorate of the newly-organized Southeast Asia Treaty Organization. Unlike Diem, however, Premier Souvanna Phouma could not be counted on to request American military assistance under Article IV of the Southeast Asia Collective Defense Treaty. Indeed, he immediately incurred American displeasure by working systematically to achieve the neutral coalition government that had been intended for his country by the 1954 agreements. However, Souvanna made the error of trying to found his neutralist regime on a vastly expanded Laotian Army built with U.S. aid and including a U.S. Military Assistance Advisory Group disguised as a "Programs Evaluation Office." The result was a massive intrusion of U.S. aid ($150 for every inhabitant by the end of 1960, almost double the previous Laotian per capita annual income) which not only wrecked the economy but rendered it completely dependent on U.S. support.

In May 1958, elections were held in which the procommunist Pathet Lao won nine of the 21 seats contested (the full Assembly consisted of 59 members). This kind of free election result was quite unacceptable to the United States, whose ambassador admitted that he had "struggled for 16 months to prevent a coalition." Accordingly, the CIA went into action and set up a Committee for the Defense of the National Interest which was able to defeat Souvanna on a vote of confidence after the U.S. withheld its monthly aid payment. (This episode was reported on July 23, 1958, in a two-inch story in the "authoritative" *New York Times* which noted that Souvanna had resigned "because he said he had lost faith in the Pathet Lao.")

In May 1959, the new premier, Phoui, attacked the Pathet Lao shortly after he had renounced the Geneva agreements altogether, to the State Department's immense satisfaction. However, the CIA had brought its own man, Phoumi Nosavan, back to Laos from France to head the Committee for the Defense of the National Interest. On December 31, 1959, Phoumi overthrew Phoui. Phoumi then eliminated the Pathet Lao through an election which the *New York Times* called "orderly," but which was so flagrantly rigged that it offended even his CIA advisors. But this shift in power to a right-wing clique of officers without popular support only resulted in chaos: a counter-coup by "neutralist" paratrooper Captain Kong Le restored Souvanna; in December 1960, the United States again withheld its aid; Phoumi went back to his CIA patrons; and there were two Laotian governments in open warfare (both using U.S. material) in the outskirts of the capital city of Vientiane. At first each of the factions (Souvanna's and Phoumi's) had strong support among U.S. officials, but in the end the neutralists were forced to depend on the support of the Pathet Lao, Hanoi, and a Soviet airlift, while Phoumi's men were directing shells onto Vientiane from U.S. positions in Thailand across the river. Just before handing the whole mess over to Kennedy, Eisenhower armed Phoumi with six AT-6 fighter-bombers equipped with rockets and bombs. A direct military confrontation between the United States and the Soviet Union had become a real possibility.

Kennedy's first major foreign policy decision was to cut his losses in Laos. He rejected proposals for the direct interposition of American troops after the Joint Chiefs opposed a limited intervention that was not backed by an ultimate commitment to use nuclear power. This meant that he had to struggle back towards the 1954 formulas of neutrality, coalition and the exclusion of foreign troops which the United States had worked so hard to subvert. Simultaneously, however, Kennedy rejected the idea of a renegotiated neutral settlement for South Vietnam, fearing that he would be charged with creating a domino situation, producing one neutral state after another. At first the communists held out for a conference to neutralize South Vietnam as well, but in the end they yielded and the 14 nations reassembled in Geneva to endorse the Laos agreements of July 23, 1962.

With American escalation proceeding full speed next door in Vietnam, the breakdown of the Laos agreements was both inevitable and two-sided. Souvanna himself observed that there would be no peace in Laos until the war was ended.

In April 1963, the fighting in Laos resumed between neutralists and Pathet Lao when the "left-leaning" neutralist Foreign Minister Quinim Pholsena was shot by his "right-leaning" neutralist bodyguard. Washington officials (who had engineered Quinim's fall in 1958) did not appear to be too unhappy at this new threat to the coalition; according to some of them, "The foreign minister was reported to have been using his influence in a move to the left, so that a wide rift was opening within the neutralist ranks." (*New York Times,* April 2, 1963.) Souvanna attempted to restore peace by restoring the coalition; on April 17, 1964, when he finally succeeded in bringing Phoumi and Souphanouvong (leader of the Pathet Lao) to meet him on the Plain of Jars, there were hopes of an early accord to end the civil war. However on April 19, right-wing troops led by Kouprasith Abhay, Phoumi's chief associate in the Vientiane battle of December 1960, seized Vientiane. When the dust settled a month later, Souvanna's neutralist supporters had been "merged" with Phoumi's right-wing factions: the Army was now led by ten generals, of whom nine were right-wing and only one a neutralist.

This sudden and dramatic collapse of Laotian neutralism in May 1964 was followed by renewed fighting over the former neutralist positions on the Plain of Jars and the overt intervention of U.S. Navy jets. When two of these were shot down in early June, USAF F-100's retaliated by shelling the area in what *Aviation Week* magazine pithily observed to be "the first U.S. offensive military action since Korea." Conflict in Laos had again been internationalized, unilaterally, by the United States, and it is not hard to see why. By 1964, counter-insurgency was failing so badly in South Vietnam that even moderates in the Pentagon were calling for a new strategy of attacks against the guerrillas' alleged line of supply, the Ho Chi

Minh Trail. McNamara proposed the exfiltration of South Vietnamese Special Forces into Laos to General Khanh in March 1964; two days later, on March 14, Khanh and Phoumi laid the groundwork for an agreement to station ARVN troops in the Laos panhandle.

One cannot say at this stage whether the Laotian rightists were actually encouraged by their American counterparts to destroy the last chances for a tripartite coalition or whether (as in 1960) they were so emboldened by renewed American support as to go further than their masters had wished. It is clear, however, that Laotian neutralism was no longer compatible with the new expanded strategy evolved by McNamara in 1964 for fighting the Vietnam War—and that when this contradiction became clear, the Geneva agreements of 1962 were as doomed as those which preceded them.

When international politics are cast in purely moral terms (as American publicists are prone to do), the results can only be confusing. Thus, the picture presented here of a generally one-sided U.S. subversion of major agreements with the communists would hardly be credible on such a basis. For example, Stalin was certainly ruthless and perfidious enough toward his own Bolshevik comrades in the '30s to have betrayed Yalta ten times over, if the personal morality of rulers actually played such a decisive role in history. To go a step further, many in the early Cold War years who regarded the U.S. under Roosevelt and Truman as infinitely preferable to Soviet society under Stalin thought at the time that that fact alone was a sufficient basis for understanding the breakdown of the Yalta Accords. In the light of recent historical analyses, however, it is evident that nothing could be further from the truth.

The real key to the international puzzle is not moral abstraction, but concrete power and interest. Nations, as John F. Kennedy once remarked, can be counted on to keep those agreements (and *only* those agreements) which it is in their interest to keep. When a nation seems especially prone to undermine agreements it has made, it is, more likely than not, because the nation is powerful and chafes at the idea of having restraints imposed on its freedom of action (the "arrogance of power" in Senator Fullbright's diagnosis). If the nation also has a rapidly expanding sphere of interest, it will in time almost inevitably see itself "forced" to go beyond negotiated limits. Contrariwise, weak powers (and vis-a-vis the United States, the communist powers—Vietnam in particular—are weak) have a larger stake in preserving those international structures of law which promise to maintain these limits.

Looked at in this perspective, it is evident that the most important East-West agreements since the war, in particular the Yalta and Geneva Accords, were essentially attempts to get the United States to observe some limits to its sphere of influence. But for the entire postwar period, U.S. foreign policy has been launched on a phenomenal course of expansion, with no limit in sight.

As a result, the Monroe Doctrine—laid down unilaterally by the U.S. in

1823 to mark off the Western hemisphere as its preserve—is the one "international" arrangement to which Washington has steadfastly adhered. So long as the United States remained absorbed in its internal expansion westward and was able to operate overseas under the international umbrella of British power, there was no need to go beyond the Doctrine: the U.S. remained "isolationist." But with the break-up of the old colonial empires after the Second World War, all intrinsic constraints to U.S. expansion were removed, and Washington began staking out formal claims to new areas overseas. In order to do this Washington has had to write new versions of the Monroe Doctrine to protect what it defines as its "interests."

Thus the Cold War began with a virtual reiteration of Monroism in the form of a hemispheric defense pact (1945), followed in rapid succession by the Truman Doctrine (1947), the Eisenhower Doctrine (1957) and the Johnson Doctrine (1966), which taken together define the U.S. sphere as the whole world outside the Sino-Soviet bloc, plain and simple.

Never before in history has a power staked out a sphere of influence as extensive as that which the United States has claimed in the postwar period. And never before has the world seen a global police apparatus like the counter-insurgency forces which the U.S. has marshaled in that time.

The Vietnam War represents the attempt of a poor but courageous people to close the door to American expansion in one distant outpost of its new empire. The real question posed by the Paris peace negotiations, therefore, is whether or not the United States is prepared to reconcile itself to such a "withdrawal": whether it will agree to remove from Vietnam its forces and its agents and its bases, and to live up, however belatedly, to its advertised ideals of self-determination and a pluralistic world order.

July 1968

David Horowitz, who is on the editorial board of Ramparts, *is the author of* The Free World Colossus *(Hill & Wang, 1965) and* Empire and Revolution, *and editor of* Corporations and the Cold War *and of* Containment and Revolution. *The author wishes to acknowledge the assistance of Peter Dale Scott in preparing the section on Laos.*

Subversion and Revolution in Laos

Banning Garrett

On March 11, 1968, Pathet Lao troops overran the secret American radar base at Phou Pha Thi along the North Vietnamese border in northeastern Laos. The base had been constructed in late 1964, shortly after the Gulf of Tonkin incident, to guide U.S. aircraft flying from Thailand to their targets in North Vietnam and to release their bomb loads electronically. Pha Thi was also used as a base for rescue helicopters, and according to the *San Francisco Chronicle,* "American Air Force and CIA personnel used the valley landing strip as the base for American-led teams of Meo mercenaries entering North Vietnam on special harassment missions." These teams were also used to attack the Pathet Lao administrative headquarters in Samneua province.

The existence of the base at Pha Thi, besides being a clear violation of the 1962 Geneva Accords on Laos, demonstrates an essential aspect of the war which has long been understood by both sides (if not by the American public): the war in Vietnam and the war in Laos and Cambodia are the same war. They cannot, as some U.S. senators have naively, or deceptively, suggested, be fought or resolved in isolation from one another. As early as 1955, the U.S. was organizing an all-Southeast Asian front against communist revolutions (SEATO). By the late '50s, there were U.S. armed and advised Thai and South Vietnamese troops fighting the Pathet Lao in Laos. For its part, the Pathet Lao had helped the Viet Minh in the struggle against French colonial rule in Indochina, and after the neutralist coalition broke down in Laos in 1958–59, the Pathet Lao once more turned to the North Vietnamese for aid as the U.S. pushed a war of extermination by the Royal Laotian Government (RLG) against the Laotian revolutionaries. While they are fighting for a revolution within the context of Laotian society, then, the Pathet Lao have historically also been engaged in an Indochina-wide struggle, by virtue of the very scale on which the war against them has been fought.

The U.S. has consistently justified its actions in Indochina by saying that it was defending Laos and South Vietnam from North Vietnamese aggression. This argument has no more validity in respect to Laos than it does to South Vietnam. The Pathet Lao (officially the Neo Lao Hak Sat after 1955) is an indigenous revolutionary movement and North Vietnamese aid to the Pathet Lao has been in direct response to American intervention in

Reprinted from *Ramparts,* June 1970; revised and updated.

the Laotian civil war. Indeed, the real subversion in Laos has been the virtually complete take-over by the CIA of the Laotian government administration and army and the creation of an economy which is almost totally dependent on United States aid.

A Revolution Is Born

In Laos as in Vietnam, an anti-French independence movement emerged immediately after the surrender of the Japanese, who had occupied Indochina during World War II. In coordination with similar moves in Cambodia and Vietnam, the Laotian resistance seized power in one provincial capital after another, starting in Vientiane. On September 1, 1945, Prince Phetsarath proclaimed the rupture of ties with France and declared the independent kingdom of Luang Prabang. He appointed a provisional national assembly, and an independent and unified Laos had a short-lived nominal existence.

On September 17, however, the King of Laos announced the continuance of the French protectorate, dismissing Phetsarath, who then set up a provisional government of Lao Issara (Free Laos), in which Souvanna Phouma—later to lead the "neutralists"—and Souphanouvong—later to lead the Pathet Lao—held important posts. Unwilling to lose their holdings in Indochina, the French began working their way up from the south (the Allies having agreed to let the Kuomintang occupy northern Indochina), decimating the Lao Issara troops and forcing the provisional government into exile in Bangkok. The French then resumed control of Laos and began to reorganize the Laotian units of the French army, instituting a draft of Laotians to aid the French in their fight against the Viet Minh.

Souphanouvong, Souvanna Phouma and Phetsarath were all brothers (Souphanouvong a half-brother of the others), and they had all received engineering degrees in France. Phetsarath represented the royalist, more traditionalist ideology and interests in Laos. Souvanna Phouma was the republican, the neutralist; and Souphanouvong was already a leftist.

Souphanouvong, future leader of the Pathet Lao, had been in France during the Popular Front in 1937, and had been in contact with "progressive" intellectuals and leaders of the working class. When he returned to Laos in 1938, he was appointed to the Public Works Department of the French administration. He spent most of the years from 1938 to 1945 building bridges throughout Indochina. Through his job, he contacted many leaders of the rural tribes and gained extensive knowledge of the topography of Laos. It is not surprising, therefore, that Souphanouvong had a broad Indochinese, rather than narrowly Laotian, view of the anti-colonial struggle. Unlike the neutralists and royalists, he felt that true Laotian independence was inseparable from the elimination of French control in all Indochina and that it was inconsistent to allow the French to use Laos as a staging area for attacks on the Viet Minh, using Lao troops.

In September 1947, Souphanouvong "presided over a conference held in Udorn, Thailand (presently a U.S. Air Force base), and attended by delegates of the communist parties of Indonesia, Malaya and Burma, by representatives of the Lao Issara, the Khmer Issarak (Cambodian Freedom Movement) and the Viet Minh." Thus, at an early date, Southeast Asians were organizing a united front against Western imperialism.

When the French signed a limited agreement for Laotian independence within the French Union and the Lao Issara dissolved, Souphanouvong left for the hills and began to organize a resistance movement, culminating in the formation of the Pathet Lao on August 13, 1950.

In 1951, the Viet Minh, the Pathet Lao and the Khmer Issarak met and agreed to coordinate their fight against the French. Troops of the Viet Minh and the Pathet Lao fought together in Laos in 1953, and in preparation for Dien Bien Phu in 1954.

The Revolution Is National and Social

Organized as an independence movement against the French attempt to re-establish their Indochinese empire, the Pathet Lao was also a revolutionary movement against the quasi-feudal structure of Laotian society, which had been reinforced by French rule. Like "protracted war" in China and Vietnam, the struggle in Laos has meant a continuous revolution in Laotian society.

Prior to the national organization of the Pathet Lao, most peasants did not even know they were "Laotians," nor did they share common ethnic backgrounds and languages. (In Houa Khong province, for example, there are 35 ethnically different groups.) Other than forays by Royal Laotian Government troops, tax collectors (recently the RLG has given up attempting to collect taxes, with the U.S. defraying the cost) and opium traders (to whom the mountain tribesmen sold their crops), the peasant has had little contact with the outside world. (In one area where a study was done in 1966, most of the people did not know who Souvanna Phouma, the Laotian head of state, was.) Laotian peasant communities are extremely isolated not only from the central government but from one another, and have a long history of tribal wars.

It is in this milieu that the Pathet Lao has tried to create a sense of national identity, of inter-tribal cooperation and communication, and of the solidarity of Indochinese peoples in the struggle against the U.S.

As in Vietnam, one of the first acts of the Pathet Lao was to remove RLG-appointed village headmen and to secure, in accordance with custom, the election of sympathetic but popular leaders. Pathet Lao cadres live and work in the villages with the people, in contrast to the government agents who used to come through, commandeering "the best girls, the best pigs, and the best chickens," and conscripting labor for their personal use.

According to an unpublished report by an AID (Agency for International Development) official on the Pathet Lao in Xieng Khouang

Province, the Pathet Lao cadres are encouraged to practice the "four togethers": eat together, work together, discuss together, and assist each other together. The cadre is in the middle of a conflict situation, partially stimulated by his own role, and therefore he may be considered intimidating or coercive by some of the villagers, who see change as threatening. But his success as a cadre is based on his ability to work closely with the people, to win their respect, and to stimulate and direct class and generational conflicts. Unlike the RLG agent, the Pathet Lao cadre cannot establish control of a village by force, for his purpose is not to gain passive acquiescence of the villagers to the status quo, but rather to stimulate radical change and, as necessitated over the past few years, to persuade the people to make tremendous sacrifices in the revolutionary war.

The party emphasizes the youth, both men and women, not only because they are the future of the revolution, but also because they are more flexible and more open to radical change, in themselves as well as in their society. The Pathet Lao are trying to stimulate fundamental changes in individual consciousness: people are encouraged to adopt ideas on the basis of persuasion, rational discussion, and individual choice, rather than on the basis of traditional authority. Reportedly, people are to be convinced, not coerced, and should genuinely believe in what they are doing. Education serves the dual purposes of introducing new ideas and techniques, and of introducing new modes of thought and action, such as a "rationalistic" or "scientific" attitude toward problems and traditions, and personal responsibility for realizing social goals and values. These new modes and ideas are understandably more easily adopted by the young than by older people. Not surprisingly the conflict between generations is heightened as the youth learn to question traditional values and modes of behavior and learn to work in new types of organizations outside the traditional family.

Almost everyone, however, is expected to learn to read, which includes previously illiterate adults (especially among the minority tribes, as the RLG had forbidden education in any of the minority tribal languages). The Pathet Lao have developed textbooks in minority languages and an extensive system of education, culminating in university work in either North Vietnam or China. There are several secondary schools per province, and some 10,000 to 20,000 students are enrolled in Sithone Kommadam University, in Son Tay, North Vietnam. Significantly, students, particularly those in training to become teachers, spend much of their time tending crops and animals for their schools. Traditionally, in Laos students wore suits, attended schools in the urban areas, and expected to return to prestigious jobs with "white-collar" status, never to participate in manual labor. The Pathet Lao teachers, however, are expected to return to the villages and live and work with the people. Like the Chinese Communists, the Pathet Lao seem concerned about the possible development of a class division based on differences of mental and manual labor, with the mental laborers dominating.

The Pathet Lao have been gradually equalizing wealth through progressive taxation while at the same time developing the economy. They have created a system of state-run stores, with many rationed items, some of which are imported from North Vietnam. "Conspicuous waste," such as extravagant weddings or funerals, is strongly discouraged, both as a general measure toward better use of resources, and also because of the general drive to increase production and surplus to support military and other personnel who are unable to engage in production. The cadres have also helped to introduce new methods of agriculture and irrigation, while at the same time emphasizing increased community control of resources, such as livestock, in a gradual move toward collectivization.

In an analysis of the economic situation in the liberated areas of Laos, Le Bhinh wrote in the North Vietnamese review, *Nhan Dan,* that:

> The policy of the Laotian Patriotic Front, which is to use agriculture as the basic guideline in building up the economy in liberated areas and expanding production aimed at moving toward self-reliance in food and food supplies, elimination of hunger in ethnic minority areas, progressive improvement of the people's living standards, and serving the war, has produced results in the real-life situation of the people. . . . A major change is taking place: the new way of working is gradually becoming the custom in agricultural production. Countless numbers of peasants have been grouped into united production teams and work teams. . . .

Phoumi Vongvichit, the major theorist of the party's central committee, reports that the people have developed dams and irrigation networks, have restored and improved handicrafts, and have created a light industry with weaving mills, printing presses, drug factories, mechanical work shops, sugar refineries, and potteries. He comments that "these are initial successes worth mentioning in the building of an independent and sovereign economy for the whole country."

In the areas under their control (about two-thirds of the territory and 20 to 30 per cent of the population of three million), the Pathet Lao have open government structures, with a rule-by-committee system. But they have also created government structures in nominally RLG territory. Bernard Fall wrote that, as of 1965, "there existed at least 11 full-fledged PL [Pathet Lao] provincial administrations (out of a total of 16 Laotian provinces), and these successfully overshadowed the legal but ineffective RLG administration."

The exact relationship between the party and local government is not clear. Party cadres are not elected officials and do not have defined administrative powers. Government officials, however, are elected by the people. According to the study by the AID official, "Government officials are chosen almost entirely on the basis of merit, although there seems to be a general preference for the economically deprived villager as opposed to his wealthier counterpart." Furthermore, village and district leaders are "usually chosen by acclamation in a large meeting where the whole 'group' is presented before the villagers. Elections by 'secret ballot' are sometimes held if two men are equally qualified for a position. . . ." One of the functions of the party is to act as a mediator between the people and the government, maintaining both the integrity of the officials and their pursuit of ideological goals. The party apparently has a structure parallel to the government, based in village life, to both stimulate greater revolutionary development and to insure that the government does not lose its link to the village and become another governing bureauracy with no popuar base.

Jacques deCornoy of *Le Monde,* who was behind Pathet Lao lines for 12 days in April 1968, found that the Pathet Lao had built a new social and political organization on the basis of the traditional culture, using such methods as adding new political lyrics to traditional songs, and revolutionary content to traditional dance. In the teacher-training schools, all the most important tribes were represented, and the people were taught both in Lao and in their tribal languages.

The Pathet Lao has been able to unite the different tribal and ethnic groupings in a common struggle, a singular achievement in Laotian history. Traditionally, the ethnic Lao dominated all other minority groups, referring to some of them as the "Kha," or "slave," and using them as such. When the Pathet Lao was organized in August 1950, it included leaders of the various minority tribes, some of whom were chosen as ministers in the resistance government; the original program included equality of races and ethnic groups.

Although the Pathet Lao has membership from all the tribal groups in Laos, including both the Meo and the Lao, the territorial and ethnic configuration of the struggle between the Pathet Lao and the RLG has a continuity with Laotian history. And the allies that each side has sought are based on tradition and on tribal realities. The ethnic Lao population (the base of support for the RLG) is generally settled along the Mekong, on the Thai border—a constantly changing political demarcation that does not correspond to ethnic distribution. There are about seven million Thai Lao across the border from the 800,000 Laotian Lao, and travel across the Mekong to visit relatives is frequent. The minorities which provide the main base for the Pathet Lao are clustered in the hills along the Vietnamese border. Many of these hill tribes spill across the border and have more in common with minorities of Vietnam (particularly North Vietnam) than they do with the Lao.

It may be impossible to resolve this ethnic, geographic and "class" conflict ("class" in that the entire elite is ethnic Lao and has been the socially, politically and economically dominant class, historically as well as presently) in favor of a single, viable Laotian entity. However, the fact that the Pathet Lao have had success in establishing equality and cooperation among the tribal groups indicates that national unity may be possible—if it is achieved within the context of a greater social revolution. The outstanding obstacle, beyond that of culture and tradition, has been the role that

Western forces (first French and now U.S.) have played over the past two decades in inhibiting and distorting political, social and economic development in Laos.

Washington Intervenes

Beginning in the mid-'50s, the political history of Laos has been dominated by America's attempts to establish a government there which would go along with U.S. policy in Indochina and be willing and able to destroy the Pathet Lao. As a result, the Pathet Lao, excluded from effective participation in the government, has been left with no other way to function than insurgency.

By the time of the signing of the Geneva Agreements on July 20, 1954, the Pathet Lao had liberated two-thirds of Laos. Although the Pathet Lao was not officially represented at the Geneva Conference (it was argued that it was a complete fabrication of North Vietnam), it was given two northeastern provinces, Phongsaly and Samneua, as regroupment areas. The conference called for withdrawal of all foreign forces from Laos, and for nationwide elections in 1955. The International Control Commission (ICC) was set up to supervise the implementation of the Geneva Accords, which were designed to integrate the Pathet Lao into the rest of Laotian life, and to neutralize Laos.

Soon after the signing of the Accords, however, U.S. Secretary of State Dulles organized the Southeast Asia Treaty Organization (SEATO), the clear intention of which was not only to prevent future communist revolutions in Laos and South Vietnam but also to "roll back" successful revolutions in China and North Vietnam. As David Horowitz argues, Dulles' objective was to make Laos, like South Vietnam, a protectorate of SEATO. To do this it was necessary not to integrate the Pathet Lao into a coalition government, but to defeat them. Unlike Diem, however, "Premier Souvanna Phouma could not be counted on to request American military assistance under Article IV of the Southeast Asia Collective Defense Treaty. Indeed, he immediately incurred American displeasure by working systematically to achieve the neutral coalition government that had been intended for his country by the 1954 agreements."

The U.S. therefore consciously sought out and backed right-wing elements which were dedicated to wiping out the Pathet Lao rather than to establishing a neutral Laos. (Meanwhile the Pathet Lao had, by November 1954, complied with all the requirements of the Geneva Agreements, including withdrawal of all Viet Minh.) By early July 1955, the U.S. was rearming and expanding the Laotian Army, hoping to achieve a military victory over the Pathet Lao, using U.S. planes for transport of troops and U.S. advisers in the field for an offensive in Samneua and Phongsaly provinces.

It was not until 1957 that the Laotian government, despite overt American and Thai disapproval, agreed on the integration of the Pathet Lao into national life. At that time Souphanouvong and Phoumi Vongvichit of the Pathet Lao became ministers in the coalition government headed by Souvanna Phouma, and the Pathet Lao forces were demobilized. Pathet Lao leaders settled down in Vientiane and organized a political party, the Neo Lao Hak Sat. Elections for an additional 20 parliamentary seats were held in May 1958, and despite U.S. attempts to influence the outcome, the left won 13 of the seats.

The success of the left in the elections so panicked Washington that the U.S. began to engineer a series of events that resulted in a successful coup by the American-groomed cousin of dictator Marshal Sarit of Thailand, General Phoumi Nosavan, bringing to power a right-wing government under Phoui Sananikone that was committed to eliminating the Pathet Lao.

Fabricated reports of North Vietnamese attacks were used by Phoui to obtain emergency dictatorial powers for 12 months. By this time, Phoumi had become the dominant right-wing influence in the Laotian army. In February 1959, the ICC was asked to leave on the grounds that Laos had fulfilled her obligations under the Geneva Agreement, thus paving the way for U.S. intervention. Hugh Toye argues: "It is not hard to imagine how, from the Pathet Lao point of view, it seemed that a dangerous situation was beginning to arise. Their first setback had been the departure of the International Control Commission, one of whose main duties had been to prevent discrimination or reprisals against them. Freed thereafter from international checks, and under increasing pressure from the right, the government had then abandoned the neutral policy of the Vientiane Agreements on the basis of which Samneua and Phongsaly provinces had been handed over by the Pathet Lao. The Pathet Lao then lost their representation in the administration. Finally, all possibility of their working through the Assembly had been deferred by the prime minister's assumption of emergency powers. The Pathet Lao were being forced back into insurgency."

But Phoui made the error of raising the possibility of negotiations with the Pathet Lao, and antagonizing the CIA's protégé, Phoumi. As a result, the CIA backed a successful coup which brought Phoumi and the right wing of the Army to power. Phoumi proceeded to rig the general elections scheduled for April, and to announce that Prince Souphanouvong, who had been arrested on trumped-up charges the previous year, would be publicly tried. (Souphanouvong and 15 other Pathet Lao leaders soon escaped, however, having won over their guards.)

On August 9, 1960, American plans for a solid right-wing regime were once again upset when an unknown paratroop captain, Kong Le, staged a coup in Vientiane. Having been in the field, he knew that the reports of a Viet Minh invasion had been false, and he was aware of the corruption and self-seeking in Vientiane. He announced that he aimed to end the civil war, to remove all foreign troops and to suppress corruption. His intention, essentially, was to return Laos to a neutralist position.

Under the new administration of John F. Kennedy, American policy changed, at least officially, in favor of a neutralist government. Phoumi's position having been weakened after several military fiascos, the three princes reached an agreement to establish a coalition government; Souvanna Phouma, having been assured that the U.S. was only interested in the neutralization of Laos, took office on June 24, 1962. By late July, an agreement had been signed in Geneva. A provisional government of national union had been created which was to consist of seven of Souvanna Phouma's neutralists, four Pathet Lao, four from Phoumi's group and four so-called "Right-wing Neutralists." Once again, integration of the right and left was to be achieved, including the armed forces. American and North Vietnamese forces were to be removed from the country.

The coalition, however, was short-lived. Fighting broke out between the neutralist forces. Several assassinations occurred, including those of two left-wing neutralists in Vientiane in April 1963. The Pathet Lao ministers left for the safety of Pathet Lao headquarters in Khang Khai, and within ten months following the Geneva Agreement, the coalition government had effectively broken up. (The tripartite government officially ended April 24, 1965.)

Souvanna was in the midst of talks with the Pathet Lao over a restoration of the coalition when on April 19, 1964, a group of younger right-wing officers in Vientiane, led by the chief of Phoumi's secret police, arrested him and took control of Vientiane. (The Western powers intervened to secure Souvanna's release.) The coup led to the final disintegration of the neutralist forces, some of whom joined neutralist leader Deuane and the Pathet Lao, with others going to the right. Having lost his base in the army, Souvanna Phouma now agreed to a remodeling of his government, which was unacceptable to the Pathet Lao. On May 17, 1964, he acquiesced in the beginning of U.S. air combat missions over Laos. From this point, many have doubted that Souvanna is his own master.

CIA Uber Alles

Beneath the apparent chaos of coups and power plays over the last 15 years, one consistent pattern of political life in Laos stands out: the subversion by the CIA of the government administration, the domination of the army, and the control by U.S. AID of the entire cash economy of the country.

Although initial aid agreements with Laos were signed in 1950–51 when Laos was still part of the French Union, the first U.S. aid mission in Laos was in 1955, and the Programs Evaluation Office (the first CIA front) was set up in 1958–59. The PEO was the original military aid and advisory group of the U.S. in Laos. It was transformed into the Military Assistance Advisory Group in 1961. By 1962, the U.S. had succeeded in building up a considerable Lao army, with U.S. officers down to the battalion level or even smaller units. After the Geneva Agreements were signed in 1962, all these organizations were consolidated under U.S. AID. (The distinction between CIA and AID has become meaningless with regard to operations and personnel.)

It is always difficult to assess power relations, which usually remain hidden behind formal structures, particularly when information is so scarce and operations so clandestine as in Laos. However, it seems that the CIA has created parallel rule by American "advisers," from top to bottom, both in the Laotian government administration and in the army. Final authority in the military, particularly in the Armée Clandestine, is completely in the hands of the CIA. The Armée Clandestine consists of many units scattered about the country, under the central control of the CIA. The CIA may frequently have difficulty in controlling a particular unit (Vang Pao is known to have embarked on risky military adventures against the advice of the CIA), but ultimate control rests with the Americans, who plan operations, control the supplies of equipment, and have advisers presumably in every unit.

The economic effects of this American intervention have been devastating. As early as 1959, the Senate Congressional Commission Report on aid to Laos stated that "The United States has supported the entire Lao military budget. . . . It is, in fact, virtually supporting the entire economy." In a country of 2.5 to 3 million people, where 90 per cent of the population is peasants living by subsistence farming (at most, 350,000 of the people are even in the cash economy), a few million dollars of aid can maintain the entire economy. Laos has had a consistent import-export deficit of as great as 20 to one (the U.S. effectively pays for at least one-half of the imports), and although before 1953 Laos was a rice producer, by 1955 it had to import 16,000 tons of rice from Thailand, and by 1966, 60,000 tons. (The Muong Sing and Nam Tha rice bowls in northwestern Laos alone could feed most of Laos, but these are under Pathet Lao control and American bombing makes large-scale production impossible.)

Washington and Its Friends

The import program, supported by U.S. aid, has been a lucrative business for the Lao elite since the '50s. The Wall Street Journal wrote in April 1958: "There are from 200 to 300 well-known families in Laos which can secure the maximum of profits in a very great import program"; and more directly to the point: "The political leaders (of the Rightist faction) in Laos are given a number of privileges aimed at maintaining their friendly links with the United States."

This was accomplished when aid to Laos was $30 million, 70 to 80 per cent of which was for military expenditure. The increased aid since then has given the U.S. even more control over the economy. The total amount of U.S. aid disclosed was $480 million for the period 1955–62, and $344 million during 1963–65. Since then, the total AID budget has been about $300 million per year—about $60 million for "technical assistance," the rest classified military expenditures. (This does not include the cost of any U.S. operations, including bombing, which are based in Thailand or South Vietnam. The cost of the bombing alone was about one billion dollars per year by 1970.)

But since the vast majority of the people live outside the cash economy, they cannot be so easily pacified. The peasants and the hill tribes have always been under the domination of the urban elite of Lao, which blocked French attempts at interference with their rule, and have been basically uncooperative with U.S. rural policies. By the time the Kennedy-McNamara pacification ("winning the hearts and minds of the people") program got under way in South Vietnam, the same methods were being applied in Laos. For the AID people were aware that "discontent" in the countryside was the "breeding ground" of communism. So the AID/RDD (Rural Development Division) has become the mediator between the elite (particularly the RLG) and the people. Whereas the RLG used to go on "mopping-up" operations in the countryside (UPI, October 22, 1959), the U.S. has since pushed a more subtle pacification program.

Since the early '60s, the U.S. has created several different modes of "rural development," from village clusters to refugee camps, under the "protection" and "control" of the RLG.

Although there are no reports of barbed wire encased concentration camps in Laos, as there are in Vietnam, it is important to realize that the wrenching of a peasant from his home comes only under the greatest pressure and is totally disorienting. By 1965, there were already between 250,000 and 430,000 refugees in Laos and at present the estimates are 700,000 to 800,000. As in Vietnam, people are "encouraged" to seek the protection of the strategic hamlets by bombing the villages in "enemy" territory. (The answer to peoples' war is to eliminate the people.)

Under the Nixon Administration, depopulation of the Pathet Lao-controlled territory has been stepped up. Virtually all the population in Pathet Lao areas now lives in caves, farming at night. The Pathet Lao, however, have not been wiped out, and their control often extends into nominally RLG areas, where they have created parallel governmental structures which are deeply embedded in the political life of the villages.

Politics on the Royal Laotian Government side, however, has generally taken the form of struggles between a few prominent families who are ethnic Lao elite, a group which has no positive contact with the peasantry. The differences among Laotian groups on the RLG side, then, are not ones of principle, but rather of political power and its spoils—American aid. The Far Eastern Economic Review of June 6, 1968, gives an arresting picture of the situation: "The upper and middle classes have no desire to renounce the standard of living to which many of them, thanks to American aid, have rashly become accustomed. . . . For these *nouveaux riches* there is nothing to beat the status quo. As Prince Boun Oum—Prime Minister of a pro-American government in the Dulles era—is reported to have told his brother when the latter was grumbling that North Vietnamese infiltration had raised the cost of living: 'If we did not have the Viet Minh in our country we would not have a single dollar.' Another rich Lao is said to have remarked that it was far more profitable to have foreign powers quarreling around the country than to attempt any sort of work."

The most important split within the elite is regional—north and south. The "rightists" were grouped mainly in the south; the neutralists, in the northern province of Vientiane. The Lao Issara movement came mainly from the north, and the pro-French forces, who accepted continued French dominance until independence, were from the south, where the French had always had the strongest support in colonial days. In any given region today, the army command is usually based on the most prominent family of the royal household. And in elections of the National Assembly, the prominent family of the region (or the army commander, if there is a difference) completely dominates.

Within this context, we can understand the change in U.S. strategy, from originally backing right-wing General Phoumi Nosavan, to abandoning him. Beginning with Dulles' determination to exterminate the Pathet Lao after the 1954 Geneva Agreements, the U.S. tried to establish in power the right wing under Phoumi Nosavan, and completely override the neutralists, who, under Souvanna Phouma, were willing to accept the integration of the Pathet Lao into the government. This strategy clearly violated the rules of the Lao political game by attempting to give complete dominance to the southern faction over the northern. It was doomed to failure, not only because the Pathet Lao could not be wiped out—particularly by Phoumi's totally incompetent army (or more likely they did not want to kill their brothers, whom they did not consider their enemies) and leadership—but because it could never win the support of the entire elite.

U.S. strategy was then adapted to Lao political realities, on the one hand by securing the economic dependence of the entire elite on U.S. aid, and on the other by moving to eliminate the right as a separate faction and to consolidate rule under Souvanna, who was acceptable to all regions. This could not be done, of course, until after 1962, when a separate Neutralist army that was not subject to U.S. control was eliminated. This U.S. strategy has been effective since 1965, attested to by the abortive coups by Phoumi Nosavan in 1965 and 1966. Regional differences and self-interest continue to be the stuff of Laotian politics.

Therefore, the U.S. has managed to create a politics of stalemate within the elite. On the one hand, the Laotian army is under U.S. control; on the other, the elite is almost completely dependent on U.S. aid, with one significant exception—the opium trade.

The Nixon Strategy

Previous to the consolidation of Souvanna Phouma's rule, without Neutralist troops but with American support, the U.S. countered peace initiatives by Souvanna toward the Pathet Lao by supporting right-wing military coups. With the consolidation of American control over the military, however, and particularly the Meo under Vang Pao, the U.S. has not formally challenged the Souvanna government; it has merely launched aggressive military action which served the same purpose—undermining the potential peace settlements.

The United States consolidated Souvanna Phouma's rule in 1965–66, as the war in Vietnam was being escalated. The level of fighting apparently increased slowly while the U.S. was building up Vang Pao's army for forward actions. At the same time, the bombing turned more and more toward decimation of all Pathet Lao villages. Jacques deCornoy of *Le Monde* reported that by April 1968 all but two of the villages he saw in Samneua province (a Pathet Lao stronghold in the northeast) had been completely destroyed. Roads and bridges were out and the people were living in caves.

Although major battles were fought in the 1967–68 period, the major escalation of the conflict has occurred under Nixon. After the limited bombing halt over North Vietnam on March 31, 1968, the U.S. intensified the bombing of Laos. In November and December of 1968, after the elections and the complete bombing halt of North Vietnam, the bombing was escalated four- and five-fold. By June of 1969 (not February of 1970 as Nixon stated), the U.S. was using B-52s against the Pathet Lao in northeastern Laos, at Muong Soui on the edge of the Plain of Jars (which is about 200 miles from the Ho Chi Minh Trail and has nothing to do with the interdicting of supplies to the NLF). The U.S. bombings were in response to a Pathet Lao retaliatory attack on a major U.S. base in Muong Soui. The Pathet Lao themselves had been responding to a major attack launched against Pathet Lao headquarters at Xieng Khouang in April, when the U.S. leveled the city and Vang Pao's troops walked into an evacuated town, claiming victory.

The Pathet Lao and North Vietnamese evacuated the Plain of Jars (traditionally Pathet Lao territory) in August, and the U.S. bombed it with B-52s after evacuating about 20,000 people from the Plain. (The refugee business is very profitable for the RLG generals, who pilfer from the AID refugee funds—the more refugees they create or "take," the more money they make.) By November the Pathet Lao were returning to the Plain of Jars, and were massively attacked by B-52s in February. But the Pathet Lao and North Vietnamese moved all the way across the Plain and attacked and overran the major American base at Sam Thong, just around a mountain from the formerly secret base at Long Cheng, which is the major base for Vang Pao's Armée Clandestine units, and the major U.S. base for all of Laos. At this writing, that base was still periodically under siege (with massive U.S. air support for the Meos, the Thai mercenaries and the U.S. "advisers" who were trying to hold it). The U.S. has claimed victory (particularly for air power) in the retaking of Sam Thong, although it is more likely the Pathet Lao and North Vietnamese did not try to hold the base, as it would be useless and they would have suffered heavy losses

(Photo by Robert C. Scheu, Photon West.)

from aerial bombardment. After the U.S. invasion of Cambodia, the Pathet Lao liberated the two major American city-bases in Southern Laos, Attopeu and Saravane, thus further pushing the Americans and the RLG up against the Mekong.

The more the U.S. kills the Pathet Lao and destroys their villages and fields, the more dependent they become upon the North Vietnamese, both for supplies and fighting forces. Probably most of the North Vietnamese activity in the country has been in response to the escalation of bombing in Laos (particularly in the northeast) since November of 1968. (By the spring of 1970, the U.S. was bombing Laos at a level of nearly 30,000 sorties per month—a thousand planes per day.) The U.S. has thus created the situation that has brought the North Vietnamese into Laos to defend their allies. And this presence of the North Vietnamese is used to justify the escalation of American activity.

U.S. policy has been to use the Laotian people like currency to buy time for Thailand (so they can "deal with insurgency" and generally consolidate control in Thailand), and to use Laos for fighting the war in Vietnam. The Pathet Lao have had to organize the people in order to survive and fight back. The U.S. bombing has forced some of the peasants to leave Pathet Lao areas. With nowhere to go, they are clustered along the Mekong on the Thai border, and can go no farther. Now the war is coming to them again, giving them and the rest of the peasantry no choice but to fight for survival.

The Laotian war has been a much "cleaner" operation for the U.S. than Vietnam because it has been vastly cheaper and far better planned and has not required American ground forces. The U.S. has successfully gotten Asians to kill Asians in Laos, and has been fighting a war of attrition *against the entire Laotian population.* The fate of Vang Pao and "Pop" Buell's Meos is a case in point: the Meo people are the losers. So far Vang Pao has sustained at least 25,000 losses (although more than half of his forces are Lao Theung, rather than Meo), and countless civilians have been killed or have died of disease. The Meo have been forced by the war from their homes in the hills and are moving into the intolerable valley climates along the Mekong. And they will be victims of Lao racism: they are hated by the Lao and will be very poorly treated by the RLG. The Meo who fought for the CIA (and there are many fighting for the Pathet Lao) are through. The Americans are willing, it seems, to depopulate Laos: the Laotian people, on both sides and in the middle (an increasingly untenable position), are killing each other—and the Americans are pulling the strings.

Banning Garrett is on the staff of the Pacific Studies Center in Palo Alto, California. The Center is a research collective specializing in the social, political, and economic dimensions of American capitalism. Projects range from studies and publications on U.S. involvement in the Third World, multinational corporations, to labor problems and environmental destruction.

The Road to Phnom Penh: Cambodians Take Up The Gun

Banning Garrett

On March 18, 1970, an American-backed military coup overthrew the neutralist government of Prince Norodom Sihanouk, forcing the Cambodian left into all-out insurgency and providing American counterinsurgents with yet another Vietnam. First South Vietnam; then Laos; now Cambodia —American power has finally toppled the last domino in Indochina into communist revolution.

For over a decade, the United States had tried to unseat Sihanouk and replace him with a right-wing regime. Though a conservative in domestic policies, Sihanouk jealously guarded his country's independence, knowing

Reprinted from *Ramparts,* August 1970.

that entangling alliances could only lead Cambodia straight into the Indochina war, and from there into a full-scale revolution of her own. He also knew that if Cambodia ever became a junior partner in America's Asian alliances, she would open herself to the territorial expansion of her traditional enemies, the Thais and the South Vietnamese.

He was right. General Lon Nol, Cambodia's new ruler, has abandoned neutrality. South Vietnam's General Thieu has agreed to occupy Cambodia, defending Lon Nol from the Cambodian people, at least until a successful Cambodianization of the war permits the withdrawal of South Vietnamese combat troops. The Thais have volunteered military aid and their own combat troops. And the Americans, striking from air and land, are turning Cambodia into the newest battlefield in an unending war.

Sihanouk, meanwhile, is now chief of his country's revolutionary movement. "America attracts communism," the former neutralist once explained, "like sugar attracts ants."

Sihanouk first became King of Cambodia in 1941, appointed by the Vichy French, who from the outset of World War II administered the country on behalf of the Japanese. In early 1945, after Vichy fell to the Allies, the Japanese seized direct control of Indochina, made the right-wing collaborator Son Ngoc Thanh premier, and pushed Sihanouk to declare Cambodia independent of French rule. Following the defeat of Japan in World War II, the French returned, jailing Son Ngoc Thanh and forcing Sihanouk to make Cambodia "an autonomous state within the French Union." This effectively reestablished French military and economic control, and gave the French the use of Cambodia and Cambodian troops in their campaign to regain control of Vietnam from the Viet Minh.

In reaction to the French takeover, many of Son Ngoc Thanh's followers fled to Thailand, where they organized a Cambodian independence movement. The new group, the Khmer Issarak, covered the political spectrum from right-wing nationalists to communists, and included ethnic Vietnamese living in Cambodia. By 1953, the anti-French Khmer Issarak, working closely with the Viet Minh, controlled three-fifths of Cambodia.

Sihanouk, his nationalist credentials now in question, began his own "royal crusade for independence." Capitalizing on French fear of the Khmer Serai and the Viet Minh, he skillfully maneuvered the French to back his crusade and, in October 1953, declared the independence of Cambodia.

Sihanouk's success undermined the nationalist position of the Khmer Issarak. Son Ngoc Thanh and a few of his right-wing followers went into exile in Bangkok; the great majority of the Khmer Issarak, including the left, accepted Sihanouk's offer of amnesty and laid down their arms.

Sihanouk then set out to govern Cambodia in classic fashion: balancing right against left, class against class, while maintaining his own position as the indispensable man-in-the-middle. He permitted the communist Pracheachon Party to operate openly. But, stepping down from the throne, he actively campaigned for his own "Buddhist Socialist" Party, the Sangkum, helping it establish exclusive control of the National Assembly. He surrounded himself, both in the Sangkum and in his cabinets, with representatives of the entire span of Cambodian political life, including veterans of the Khmer Issarak. Yet he ran the government as a one-man show, single-handedly making decisions on even the most trivial matters.

Economically, Sihanouk practiced a kind of top-down socialism. But, rather than promoting growth, the profits of state-owned enterprises often ended up in the pockets of Sihanouk's palace cronies. He spoke of industrializing Cambodia, but he was unwilling, probably unable, to attack the large Khmer landowners or the ethnic Chinese and Vietnamese merchants. Balancing in this way, Sihanouk never had any real possibility of moving Cambodia from its subsistence rice economy into the world of modern production. In fact, his methods almost guaranteed the deterioration of economic conditions which contributed heavily to his downfall.

Sihanouk's "socialism" did have its positive effects. The bouncy Prince spent much of his time touring the countryside, inspecting and applauding the installation of mechanical pumps, new dams and canals, and encouraging the creation of agricultural cooperatives and the participation of villagers in voluntary labor schemes to build the many new facilities. In return, the peasants remained loyal to the throne, providing a base of support on which Sihanouk can still depend.

Sihanouk performed his greatest balancing acts, however, when trying to preserve his country's peace and neutrality in the face of America's esca-

Americans entering Cambodia during the 1970 "incursion." *(Photo by Joseph W. Carey, BBM.)*

lating war in Vietnam. For a time he accepted economic and military aid from America—nearly 400 million dollars—which went to subsidize Cambodian imports, fund AID "development" programs, and provide equipment and training for the military. But the Prince also consciously sought aid from other major countries, both communist and non-communist SEATO (Southeast Asia Treaty Organization). He allied with China, but kept sufficient independence so that he was able to cool relations in 1967 when China's Cultural Revolution spread to the youth of Phnom Penh's large Chinese community. He gave the North Vietnamese and NLF free use of Cambodia's border areas, but only in return for their pledge to stay out of his country's internal affairs.

Sihanouk's balancing act simply could not last, however. The war in Vietnam escalated, Cambodia's economy deteriorated, and the man-in-the-middle found it increasingly difficult to play off contending political forces.

From the left, the communist Khmer Rouge began to gain strength. Back in the spring of 1967 a left-wing rebellion broke out in Battambang Province, an area of right-wing terrorism and increasing pressure on the peasants by the landholding elite, government officials and the army. This rebellion marked the Cambodian left's first important military action since they fought with the Viet Minh against the French. Following the Battambang action, several former leaders of the anti-French fight emerged in the leadership of new guerrilla bands.

In response, General Lon Nol, a former Army chief whom Sihanouk had kicked upstairs to the post of Prime Minister, used the Prince's absence from the country to send the army on a search-and-destroy mission against the Khmer Rouge. Sihanouk returned and fired Lon Nol. But to keep things in balance he attacked leftist intellectuals in Phnom Penh and three National Assemblymen as communist conspirators. The three—Hu Nim, Khieu Samphan and Hou Youn—fled from the capital and went to join the Khmer Rouge. In this incident, Sihanouk managed to emerge once again the strong man in the center, but he paid a high price—the beginning of a real communist insurgency in Cambodia.

From that time on, the Khmer Rouge launched guerrilla attacks in most parts of the country. In the fall of 1969, T. D. Allman, writing in *Far Eastern Economic Review,* reported that there were perhaps 3000 Khmer Rouge operating in the countryside, plus a network in the urban centers. Along with peasants, the guerrilla groups included "students, teachers and former French-trained government officers, largely expelled from Phnom Penh in 1967." They were led by Hou Youn and were active, Allman reported, in 15 out of the 19 Cambodian provinces.

The program of the Khmer Rouge was particularly interesting in light of more recent events. Their statements strongly condemned Lon Nol and criticized the army, police extortion and government corruption. Invariably, Lon Nol and his friends were referred to as "American stooges," a distinction the Khmer Rouge never attributed to Sihanouk.

During this same period, another insurgent group emerged, the Khmer Loeu. Hill tribesmen, numbering at most 60,000, the Khmer Loeu live in the remote province of Rattanakiri on the northeast border where Laos, Cambodia and South Vietnam meet. This area, formerly Laotian, has never been under actual Phnom Penh control, and neither the Laotians nor the South Vietnamese have been willing to recognize Cambodia's claim to it. In order to establish their control, Cambodian officials began in 1959 to move ethnic Khmers into the province. The government also tried to relocate the Khmer Loeu into "strategic hamlets" and Cambodianize them, and to parcel out land—through which the Khmer Loeu previously had wandered freely—to Cambodian "colonists" from the lowlands. For more than a thousand years, the hill tribesmen of Southeast Asia have been retreating to more unfavorable land in the face of the advance of the more aggressive Chinese, Vietnamese, Lao, Siamese and Burmese. The Khmer Loeu, like so many of the other minority tribes of the area, were at the end of the road.

In 1968, the Khmer Loeu rebelled. Deserting their villages and moving into the forest, they organized and armed, apparently with the aid of about 50 NLF cadre who speak their language. Their battle, at first simply defensive, was soon to merge with the Indochinese revolution.

Though growing in strength, the Khmer Rouge and Khmer Loeu did not yet pose an immediate revolutionary threat to the government. But their insurgence further polarized the forces which Sihanouk was trying to contain.

The danger from the right was more immediate. Ever since 1958, when the United States grew tired of Sihanouk's neutralism, the CIA had financed and trained the Khmer Serai, a right-wing remnant of the old Khmer Issarak still under the leadership of Son Ngoc Thanh.

In 1959 the Khmer Serai, together with the Thai and South Vietnamese governments, tried unsuccessfully to overthrow Sihanouk. By November 1963 their continued efforts finally led Sihanouk, at great cost to the Cambodian government, to cut off all American foreign aid. In 1966 the Khmer Serai actually declared war on Cambodia, claiming responsibility for incursions across the border. Shortly before the March 1970 coup, they infiltrated the regular Cambodian army to act as a Trojan horse for the CIA.

At the same time, the CIA recruited mercenaries from South Vietnam's million-strong Cambodian minority to fight alongside the Khmer Serai. These mercenaries, the Khmer Krom of Kampuchea (KKK), are extraordinarily vicious. "You know," one of them told J. C. Pomonti of *Le Monde,* "the KKK love to eat the flesh of the Vietnamese. Especially the liver. The liver, that's the best."

Increasingly pressed from both left and right, Sihanouk found less and less room in which to maneuver. The aristocracy, the merchants and the army were all angered because they had lost their traditional share of the financial action; students unable to find jobs and civil servants and intellectuals felt powerless; everyone resented the inefficiency of his one-man rule. Sihanouk's economic schemes, inadequate on paper, were further hampered by his unwillingness to delegate authority and to operate in a consistent fashion. He tried to make too many and too trivial decisions, and his over-all plans were too unstable to allow others to carry out long-range planning.

Finally, in December 1969, the right wing began a concerted drive for power. In order to pay for imports Cambodia was falling deeper and deeper into national debt, and the domestic economy was in sharp decline. Eager to seize the time, rightist businessmen led by Lon Nol and Sirik Matak pushed through the National Assembly, against Sihanouk's will, measures to denationalize banking and the import-export business, bring tax receipts directly into the government treasury instead of into the office of the Chief of State (Sihanouk's office), and shut down the state-run gambling casino, which had long been a source of income for the palace. The United States and the World Bank joined in the push for denationalization, unexpectedly withholding aid even after the July 1969 resumption of U.S.-Cambodian diplomatic relations.

The following month Sihanouk left for France, once again hoping to prove himself the indispensable man. Soon after, Lon Nol stepped up the already existing racist press campaigns against the Vietnamese minority in Cambodia. In early March, the army organized anti-Vietnamese demonstrations in Svay Rieng province. Then, on March 11, 1970, soldiers in civilian dress, reportedly members of the Khmer Serai, led 10,000 demonstrators in an attack on the embassies of the North Vietnamese and the Provisional Revolutionary Government. "The demonstrators—numbering about 10,000—were hardly hostile to the sacking in a country where anti-Vietnamese feeling runs deep," reported Allman, "but the demonstration was hardly spontaneous. Few of the students would have shown up had they not been ordered, and they undoubtedly had no idea that the ultimate result of their demonstration would be the ouster of Sihanouk."

Trying to head off the impending coup, Colonel Oum Mannorine, Sihanouk's brother-in-law, and the pro-Sihanouk police attempted on March 16 to arrest Lon Nol. They failed, and on March 18 Lon Nol and the army took over the government.

It was, as Allman points out, "an upper-class coup, not a revolution."

Only days after the coup, Lon Nol's army killed several hundred unarmed pro-Sihanouk Khmer peasants. By early May the army had also massacred more than 5000 Cambodian Vietnamese, imprisoned nearly 200,000 (60,000 of whom were shipped to Vietnam) and tried, unsuccessfully, to mobilize Khmer villagers for race war against the remaining ethnic Vietnamese. The army launched these attacks more for political than racial reasons: the ethnic Vietnamese in the border area and in the large Vietnamese community showed great sympathy for the NLF. As one

On August 1, 1970, Cambodian-born Vietnamese begin an uncertain voyage to South Vietnam. They are being evacuated by the South Vietnamese Navy in the wake of the Cambodian massacre of Vietnamese in the period following the March 18 coup. *(Photo by Tran Tuong Nhu.)*

assemblyman explained, "Each Vietnamese face could hide a Viet Cong." The massacres of course drove the ethnic Vietnamese, many of them formerly apolitical shopkeepers, sharply to the left.

Lon Nol also brought several thousand Khmer Serai and Khmer Krom into the country, and expects to double the size of his army with 45,000 more U.S.-trained and U.S.-paid Khmer Krom. (U.S. advisers are recruiting additional ethnic Khmers in South Vietnam and Thailand, and will continue to maintain control, even if the U.S. formally withdraws.) In it for the flesh and the money, these mercenaries, along with the Khmer Serai, have been even more intent on looting than is the regular Cambodian army. Even more vicious are the South Vietnamese troops, who, outraged by the massacre of Cambodian Vietnamese, loot the wreckage of the towns they destroy, run the South Vietnamese flag up over occupied buildings, openly demonstrate their contempt for the Cambodians and show little concern for Cambodians caught in crossfires with pro-Sihanouk forces. The paradox is grotesque: the same Vietnamese troops who refuse to fight in their own country are now defending a Cambodian government which massacred their fellow Vietnamese, while they themselves massacre the Khmer people who are fighting to topple that government.

The Americans, if personally less brutal, have produced the most widespread savagery, bringing their "forced urbanization" strategy from Vietnam into Cambodia. As Professor Noam Chomsky explained after returning from a recent trip to Southeast Asia: "It is important to understand that the massacre of the rural population of Vietnam and their forced evacuation is not an accidental by-product of the war. Rather it is of the very essence of American strategy. The theory behind it has been explained with great clarity and explicitness, for example by Professor Samuel Huntington, Chairman of the Government Department at Harvard . . . He explains that the Viet Cong is 'a powerful force which cannot be dislodged from its constituency so long as the constituency continues to exist.' The conclusion is obvious, and he does not shrink from it. We can ensure that the constituency ceases to exist by 'direct application of mechanical and conventional power . . . on such a massive scale as to produce a massive migration from countryside to city' where the Viet Cong constituency—the rural population—can, it is hoped, be controlled in refugee camps and suburban slums around Saigon. . . . Technically, the process is known as 'urbanization' or 'modernization.' " In other words, Chomsky comments, the answer to a people's war is to eliminate the people.

The strategy has one obvious advantage: it requires only enough occupying troops to hold the cities and bomb the countryside. In Laos, with a population of less than three million, the policy of urbanization has produced over 700,000 refugees and, under Nixon, bombing has increased sevenfold, to 27,000 sorties per month. In Cambodia, where the U.S. and its allies are unable to tie down several hundred thousand troops and where the population is already hostile, forced urbanization is perfect—especially since the terrain, unlike that of Laos, is flat and without natural protection from bombing. The saturation bombing that preceded the U.S. invasions (raids of 100 B-52s) may be a portent of things to come. Nixon is clearly in a bind to end the war—one way or another—within the near future. As the Lon Nol regime crumbles further and the anti-American forces gain more control of the countryside, Nixon will be forced to pull out or escalate further.

"Armed struggle, led from the underground, is the only path that will lead our people to victory and will permit its ideals to triumph," urged the deposed Prince Norodom Sihanouk after calling for a National United Front (NUF) to liberate Cambodia. That armed struggle is now under way, led by the still popular Sihanouk and his former Khmer Rouge antagonists, Hu Nim, Khieu Samphan and Hou Youn. Their strategy is one of protracted war. Khmer Rouge, Cambodian Vietnamese and a few NLF and North Vietnamese cadres are attacking government outposts and taking towns and villages. More important, they are equipping and training the peasants to fight for themselves as part of the NUF. Even though North Vietnamese troops could easily have overrun the country and set up their own puppet government, the NUF, with North Vietnamese support, seems intent on organizing the countryside first, and only then seizing control of Phnom Penh and the government.

The NUF forces apply this same people's war strategy in their attacks. In mid-April 1970, small NLF forces, with an undetermined amount of support from pro-Sihanouk Cambodians, seized Angtassom, the scene of an earlier massacre of pro-Sihanouk people and a town embarrassingly close to the capital. Demonstrating both its ineffectiveness as a military force and its unerring ability to alienate the local population, the Cambodian Army surrounded the town in overwhelming numbers, called in air strikes, fired mortars and automatic weapons into the town and finally encircled it, leaving a convenient hole through which the guerrillas could escape. When the offensive finally came, the guerrillas had gone, leaving the town untouched and allowing the local inhabitants to flee. By contrast, the Cambodian troops, according to Allman, entered the town and, finding the shops in the market neatly shut and locked from the outside, proceeded to loot and burn them. By the time the Cambodian troops were finished, about 40 per cent of the town had been razed. While the government claimed that the NUF had attacked to replenish their supplies, at Angtassom, as at every other NUF halt in Cambodia, the communist troops seemed more interested in giving political lectures than in taking anything from the inhabitants. They left rice warehouses untouched and, according to one villager, even "turned down a chicken I offered them, saying they carried their own food with them."

By late June, the NUF had liberated more than half of Cambodia, and was carefully building its rural base. Fifteen of the nineteen Cambodian provinces had either military operations, people's uprisings, or an established revolutionary power. In Kratie province in the middle of May, for example, the NUF reported that it was sufficiently emplanted to hold elections for all levels of NUF government for the area. Michael Morrow, a journalist who was captured by the NUF, reported, according to the *San Francisco Chronicle* (June 27, 1970), that in the villages he traveled through on the way to his release, "there was no doubt that the guerrillas were in complete control and on good rapport with the people."

In its program, the NUF stresses one principal task: the unification of all classes, including the national bourgeoisie, against the invasion of the Americans and South Vietnamese and the government of Lon Nol. The program calls for modernization of the country, maintenance of a neutral foreign policy, and the guarantee of those rights generally associated with middle-class democracy—freedom of speech, the right to vote, religious freedom, sexual equality and the rights of ownership of land and property. The program makes no mention of socialism, and except for guaranteeing peasants the right of ownership of the land they cultivate, seems no more revolutionary than FDR's "Four Freedoms."

Yet in the course of fighting "the American imperialists," their Indochinese "satellites" and their Cambodian "flunkies," the NUF seems more likely to lead a full-scale social revolution than simply to reinstate Sihanouk as the middle-man in a fundamentally unbalanced social system. While the Prince still has great appeal among the tradition-minded peasantry, he has no independent organization; the Khmer Rouge are actually organizing the peasants and leading the military struggle. The entire NUF is cooperating closely with the communist-led revolutions in Laos and Vietnam.

Sihanouk said in an interview on July 3: "It is true that there are Vietnamese in Cambodia. But why should anyone be astonished that the

Indochinese unite? In Vietnam, the Americans erased the line of demarcation and they have turned the Vietnam war into an Indochinese war. Henceforth, Indochina must be considered as a single battlefield, and the Indochinese will remain united until final victory. But the Cambodian resistance exists. . . . [Cambodia] will be liberated by Cambodians and Phnom Penh will be taken by Cambodians."

And the NUF is receiving arms from China, despite Chinese wariness of further escalation of the Indochina war. "We will lend you money for the affairs of your country," Sihanouk quotes Mao. "But concerning arms: we are not in the habit of selling; we are not arms peddlers. We cannot sell you arms; we can only give them to you."

Cambodia's property owners and middle class, on the other hand, seem, hardly likely, or able, to restore the pre-coup political system. A number of the aristocrats, generals, and businessmen are linked so closely with Lon Nol that most of their countrymen clearly see them as traitors. Other aristocrats, still favorable to Sihanouk, are permanently losing their base of power to the Khmer Rouge. The Chinese businessmen are increasingly vulnerable and generally willing to form protective alliances with a revolutionary government. The Vietnamese shopkeepers have either been jailed or have fled. And the civil servants and office workers seem hardly strong enough to recreate Cambodia as a non-communist domino.

The road to Phnom Penh is still hard, blocked by Lon Nol, the Khmer Serai and the Khmer Krom, the CIA and the Pentagon, the Thais and the South Vietnamese. But when the NUF finally gets there, it will be not a coup but a social revolution.

chapter three

UNIVERSITIES AT WAR AND THE FIRES NEXT TIME

While the official hot wars are confined to Vietnam, Laos, and Cambodia, the conditions that created them—empire and poverty—are omnipresent. Moreover, many other countries are already in the early stages of insurgencies that could quickly escalate into major military confrontations with U.S. forces. The fact that these can develop beneath the surface and that many Americans are caught by surprise when open military intervention forces them to realize the extent of their government's "commitment" are direct consequences of the new style in empires. In contrast to the old imperialisms, whose initial emissaries arrived in gunboats and military armor, the modern American variant is more likely to extend its tentacles through the offices of foundation representatives, World Bank officials, and university professors.

The first American presence in Vietnam, in violation of the 1954 Geneva Accords, was a Michigan State University Team. Under the guise of a technical assistance contract, the MSU group contracted to do everything for Diem, from writing his constitution to training his police, thus paving the way for U.S. military domination. The MSU case was unusually dramatic but not especially unique.

Starting in the early '50s, nonmilitary American agencies of expansion and intervention—including the Rockefeller Foundation, the World Bank, and AID—worked together to reshape Thailand into a satellite of the "Free World" economy. In this program of what social scientists call nation building, AID commissioned the services of hundreds of American scholars to study every aspect of Thai life in order to facilitate the plans for capitalist economic development of the country.

In the process of development, insurgencies arose in opposition to the planners' attempts to integrate the minority peoples of Thailand into the new Thai political economy. These insurgencies, while not immediately threatening, became a laboratory for U.S. military and social scientists to test and further refine their techniques of counterinsurgency.

In Indonesia, the U.S. government backed postwar independence in a sophisticated plan to stem the tide of possible Communist revolution and to open Indonesia's markets and resources to U.S. economic interests. American strategists were careful to train a small but crucial segment of the Indonesian elite who would further this plan. As documented by DAVID RANSOM, in "The Berkeley Mafia and the Indonesia Massacre," the Ford Foundation philanthropically took on the entire operation, training Indonesian economists in American universities and creating a university in Indonesia as a base for the eventual takeover.

In 1965, a decade after the Ford Foundation and the American universities set to work, the pro-American segment of the Indonesian military seized power and set in motion a massacre of 500,000 to 1,000,000 of their countrymen. Immediately thereafter, those industries that President Sukarno had nationalized were returned to their original foreign owners, and Indonesia's valuable resources, particularly oil, were made available to Western investors.

While French journalist PHILLIPE GAVI's article, "Eruption in India," does not focus on the role of American intervention in creating the conditions of unrest, once again the ubiquitous Ford and Rockefeller foundations are significantly present, and this time they have brought their miracle grains with them and the so-called Green Revolution. The Green Revolution, according to David Rockefeller, "may ultimately have a cumulative effect in Asia, Africa, and Latin America such as the introduction of the steam engine had in the industrial revolution." The new miracle grains produced by the foundations were deliberately bred so that they require large use of fertilizers and pesticides and necessitate widespread mechanized farming to ensure their profitable production. One of the conditions that the U.S., through the World Bank, put on its aid during the famine of 1965, was that the Indian government maintain high food prices, as an incentive for growers; another condition was that the Indian government open the doors to U.S. investment in its fertilizer industry. "Call them 'strings,' call them 'conditions,' or whatever one likes," observed the *New York Times,* "India has little choice now but to agree to many of the terms." The "terms" have meant that the price of the new grain is so high that only relatively large commercial farmers have been able to receive the benefits of this revolution, and U.S. corporations, not the Indians, have been prospering from the increased need for fertilizer. Those who have no capital or credit are pushed off their land and are left with neither the means to produce their own food nor the money to pay the rising cost of the new "surplus." The inevitable outcome of such a trend is class and regional conflict. In *Foreign Affairs,* Cliff Wharton, Jr., reported that forty-three people died in a conflict between landlords and the landless peasants "who felt they were not receiving their proper share of the increased prosperity brought by the Green Revolution." Two Swedish journalists published pictures of "superfluous" Indian peasants burned in kerosene by a landlord.

In June 1970, after Gavi wrote his article, the *Far Eastern Economic Review* reported on the mounting violence in the countryside by the Naxalites, the first Maoist guerrilla force in India. The conflict between the peasants and the landlords (furthered by the Green Revolution's acceleration of the problems of unemployment and high food costs) have increased. Many student cadres have launched guerrilla attacks against anti-Chinese films, American study centers, and American propaganda. In the countryside, where 75 per cent of the Indian population lives, the Naxalite peasant organizations have been gaining strength, killing landlords or confiscating their farmlands.

The latest report (July 1970) of activity of this kind, though yet to be clarified, disclosed the arrest of 4,000 to 7,000 Indians, including two members of Parliament, who supposedly took part in a plan to take over 200,000,000 acres of land.

The magnitude of the conflicts in India is still unclear, as is the extent of U.S. intervention, which will inevitably grow as the Indian elite finds itself unable to repress the peasant revolution by itself, and as the U.S. perceives a growing threat to its national interests.

Thailand: The Next "Domino"?

Banning Garrett

In 1861, King Mongkut of Siam offered Abraham Lincoln elephants to aid the Union cause in the Civil War. The President politely refused the help, but that was not the end of military relations between the two countries. Thailand is no longer whimsically isolated from world realities; nor does it have a choice in the way it lines up on international issues. Over the past two decades, Thais have watched their country become a giant airstrip where American B-52s, fighter bombers and helicopter gunships roar off on missions of death for other Southeast Asian countries. They have seen their own troops become U.S. mercenaries, and their borders used as staging points for Special Forces and CIA personnel on missions of subversion into Laos and North Vietnam.

Thais have watched helplessly as their nation has become an American military base and neo-colony. U.S. Senator Gale McGee stated in a recent speech that "Southeast Asia is the last major resource area outside the control of any one of the major powers on the globe." And the mammoth Chase Manhattan Bank has been even more specific: "Thailand promises to be an excellent investment and sales area for Americans," its Economic Research Division writes, "if rebel insurgency can be contained."

The various minorities that make up Thailand have tried to resist the destruction of their culture and their forcible integration into a U.S.-controlled political economy. But the U.S. military advisors who train Thai troops to fight in South Vietnam, Cambodia and Laos have also trained them to fight rebels at home. Meanwhile hordes of AID and American university personnel comb the countryside, studying every aspect of Thai life and recommending and implementing programs of counter-insurgency.

Thailand has changed greatly in the century since its kings naively offered a U.S. President military aid. Since then America has decided to fight its wars abroad, not at home—wars that make sure countries like Thailand stay in the Free World bank account.

The Thai elite long prided itself on its ability to resist colonial domination. For a century and a half, the Thais had closed themselves to Western imperialism, and then tried to "modernize" Thailand through selective contact with the West. In the middle of the nineteenth century, the Thais established relations with the British, French, and other European powers, accepting technical advice as well as trade relations. Besides hiring European advisors, many members of the royal family studied in Europe and returned with Western ideas about the organization of the state and the economy. Under kings Mongkut (1851–1868) and Chulalongkorn (1868), the Thai elite built, from the basis of a quasi-feudal bureaucracy, a state administration similar to an inefficiently run colony, with the royalty and the Western-educated elite playing the role of colonial power. But the key element making possible Thailand's relative independence from Western domination was the British-French agreement to let Thailand remain as a buffer state between their respective colonial empires.

The Thais were responsible for only part of the modernization process. They provided leadership for building railroads and canals, and they "rationalized" the state apparatus. And the Thais tried to extend their rule to the outlying areas of the country, a process which is still continuing (with American help). But Chinese emigrants became the laboring and commercial classes for development. There had been a small community of Chinese traders in Thailand for centuries, but in the early part of the nineteenth century the Thais encouraged Chinese emigrants for coolie labor. By the late 1920s, 95 percent of Thailand's business was in foreign—Chinese or European—hands. The Chinese controlled most of the agricultural trade and small industry and merchandising, and the Europeans, primarily British, had investments in mining, teak, and other large-scale enterprises. For decades the Thai elite was content to take a share of the profits, through taxes, fees, and bribes, and allow the foreigners relatively free reign. The Thai economy became increasingly dependent upon foreign trade and investment, and thus tied into Western imperialism through the back door.

The growing dependence of Thailand upon foreign capitalists and the world market, combined with the conflict between an absolutist monarchy and a growing group of "professional," Western-educated bureaucrats, reached a crisis during the Depression. The world market prices of Thailand's exports fell, and the king responded by pruning the civil service while continuing his own extravagance. In 1932 a group of middle-level army officers and officials ended the rule of the royal family with a coup.

The coup group itself was hardly united. On the one hand, there were younger military men and the progressive civil servants, led by Pridi Phanomyong, and on the other hand there were conservative military men, led by Field Marshal Phibun Songkhram. Soon after the coup, Pridi, a brilliant young Paris-trained lawyer, proposed an elaborate plan for a national economy independent of foreign control and dominated by the state. But Pridi was forced into exile for his allegedly Bolshevik plan, and the civilian reformers lost out to the conservative military. Pridi was allowed to return in 1935 and was cleared of charges of being a communist, but Phibun became the dominant power and officially Prime Minister in 1938. Pridi had proposed national independence as essential for democracy and progress in Thailand. The conservative Phibun also pushed for independence from foreign, particularly Chinese, economic control, but in the name of Japanese-style Thai fascism. Phibun's pro-Japanese sentiments facilitated Thailand's transition to wartime status as a Japanese satellite.

The coups, counter-coups, and purges of Thai politics have always been merely struggles among the elite. The bulk of the Thai people have never been involved in official politics, and when Phibun acceded to Japanese domination, Pridi neither looked for nor found a popular base for his underground Free Thai Movement. Pridi and his followers worked with the American OSS, while Phibun became a Japanese puppet.

But Phibun, who had proven himself amenable to Japanese colonial interests, became the pro-American military dictator, while Pridi, who emerged from the underground as a popular leader among the Thai elite and was elected Prime Minister in 1946, was "coolly" received by the Americans. Apparently Pridi intended to pursue his plan for an independent, "top-down" socialist economy, and was organizing an alliance of anti-imperialist forces in Southeast Asia, which included the Viet Minh. The U.S., however, wanted the Thais to establish an Open Door for foreign investments and, after 1950, to commit themselves to an anti-communist alliance. So the U.S. set about cultivating a section of the elite amenable to its purposes, and that group was the military, under the leadership of the proven collaborator, Field Marshal Phibun.

By 1950, the Chinese Communists had liberated China, and the U.S. was fighting in Korea and backing British and French attempts to regain their former colonies of Malaya and Indochina. The U.S. considered Thailand's strategic position critical for establishing an American foothold on the Southeast Asian mainland, and by fall of 1950 U.S. military and economic aid began flowing to the Phibun regime.

The unpopular pro-American military regime set about smashing its opposition and consolidating power. In the early fifties, the Thai army and police began an anti-communist campaign which was used to attack Pridi (forcing him into exile in China) and his followers and to increase the

Phibun clique's control of the Chinese community. The attack on the Chinese began officially with the passage of the Un-Thai Activities Act in 1952, aimed supposedly at communist subversion. But the attack on the Chinese community as "communist" was absurd. Although the Communist Party of Thailand had been founded by a group of Thai Chinese in 1942, most of the Chinese were apolitical, and the sympathy of many of them for the successful communist revolution in China was merely a nationalist sentiment.

Since 1948 when he came to power with American approval, Phibun had been engaged in an extensive program to gain control of the economy for the military sector of the Thai elite. He tightened controls and restrictions on alien—meaning Chinese—businesses, and gave special privileges to Thai enterprises. The anti-communist attack on the Chinese culminated in forcing the Chinese to make protective alliances with army and police officials. The Chinese businessmen gave Thai officials positions on the boards of directors of Chinese corporations, and they created new Sino-Thai corporations with Chinese capital and Thai protection. These alliances increased the concentration of power in the Chinese community and gave the military regime a legal source of personal wealth and greater control over the economy.

Thai officials, however, had always had a parasitic relationship to the Chinese, and the Phibun ploy was merely a new twist to gain an economic base for his own political power. But another section of the elite had decided to forge a new kind of relationship with the Chinese capitalists. Some of the Thai elite and some Chinese businessmen had begun creating semi-private state corporations to which the Thai gave political security and some capital from government funds and the Chinese contributed their own capital and managerial skills. It might have been possible for such an alliance to slowly industrialize Thailand by relying on domestic rather than Western capital and the control and conditions attached. But for such a plan to be effective, the advocates from the Thai elite would have to have state power to plan the economy and to use government revenues to develop the "infrastructure" of the economy. This would have approximated the path taken by the Japanese elite, perhaps requiring a similarly repressive state to squeeze the maximum surplus from the peasantry in order to finance the investment in industry. This alliance with the Chinese businessmen would have required that the Thai officials subordinate their desire for personal gain through a many-faceted corruption to the overall long-range economic plan. In the long run, the Thai elite would have the increased benefits of an industrial economy, but they would have had to advance beyond the personal, parasitic relationships which they traditionally had with the Chinese businessmen.

Thailand's last hope for economic autonomy, however, was foreclosed by the U.S. Even if the pro-American Phibun regime had wanted to develop autonomously, Thailand's small measure of economic independence rested upon the government's ability to finance its infrastructure development from export surplus. But after the Korean War, the U.S. dumped large quantities of tin on the world market, forcing prices down. The price of rubber fell with the end of the wartime demand and the development of synthetics. And the price of rice fell, reducing the income on all three of Thailand's major exports. As that surplus dried up, the U.S. and its international financial arm, the World Bank, were conveniently prepared to offer the financial and technical assistance—subsidy—to underwrite the military regime, providing the Thais would cooperate by developing their economy along U.S.-prescribed lines. The U.S. enticed its client allies in the elite into accepting a multi-agency invasion of Thailand, which has meant U.S. intervention in nearly every aspect of Thai society and the final denouement of Thai independence.

The American relationship to Thailand which has developed in the last twenty years may be understood best as a new form of colonialism. After World War II, the U.S. government self-righteously proclaimed itself opposed to colonialism, and indeed the U.S. was generally in favor of liberation of the colonies from the European powers. The U.S. eagerly backed liberation movements which would make colonies free—in true Open Door fashion—for international capitalist investment. With the world's strongest postwar economy, the U.S. was sure to seize the lion's share.

But the U.S. soon found it necessary to intervene in Third World countries to ensure that their development would fit the resource and investment needs of the expanding U.S. economy. Since 1949, U.S. influence in Thailand has been underwritten by nearly $600 million in economic and $900 million in military aid. The U.S. has planned and aided the reordering of Thai society, from the military and administration to rice cultivation and education. (Thai officials get in the way of plans American administrators have for them. In a June 1967 memorandum for the U.S. Operations Mission (AID), Donald R. Mitchell proposes creation of a youth organization to occupy potential communist recruits. He comments that, "The biggest problem we face is the government officials to work with such an organization." His solution is for USOM to hire their own man and bypass the Thai governemnt. In other words, if it were not for the Thais, the U.S. could solve their problems.) U.S. government civilian and military personnel, heavily depending on American professors, have been probing, describing, and analyzing virtually every aspect of Thai life. US/AID uses the scholars' studies to program the development of Thailand for foreign investment.

By the late '50s, with the rise to power of Marshal Sarit Thanarit of the pro-American military clique, the U.S. was assured of an Open Door to Thailand. (Sarit's personal economic strength came from foreign companies. When he died, in 1963, he had amassed a personal fortune of nearly $140 million.)

Coincidental with Sarit's emergence as the Thai strong man, the World Bank, at the request of the Thai government, sent a mission to Thailand which drew up a plan for Thai public development. The mission report, published in 1959, suggested that the government liquidate most state-run enterprises and devote itself to creating the proper conditions for private enterprise by "special tax and other inducements," and by "institutional credit arrangements and provisions of such physical facilities as sites, buildings, power and water services, roads, housing, etc." A six-year plan, based on the Bank's survey, was adopted by the Sarit government in 1960. Since 1950, the World Bank has financed over $350 million in infrastructure development—for irrigation, railroads, port facilities, highways, education, and electric power. And in 1964 the World Bank, along with the Bank of America in Thailand, set up the International Finance Corporation of Thailand (IFCT), as an offshoot of the World Bank's IFC for financing private investment.

The U.S. government and the World Bank have been successfully preparing the way for U.S. investment. Since 1960, U.S. private investment in Thailand has grown from $25 million to over $200 million, and in 1968 the U.S. passed Japan as the largest investor in Thailand. By 1965 there were nearly 100 U.S. corporations in Thailand, from Walt Disney Productions and Coca-Cola to Esso-Standard Oil, Firestone, IT&T, and Chase-Manhattan Bank. American corporations have invested mainly in extraction of Thai raw materials—mostly tin—and in light manufacturing and tourist facilities. In a 1966 Thai-American treaty, the Thai regime officially granted the U.S. its hard-earned Open Door, as well as a "most favored nation" status for access to strategic resources. To make investment even more attractive for U.S. investors, AID grants investments guarantees for high-priority projects in Thailand, to protect against confiscation, expropriation, or damage due to war or revolution.

US/AID has worked with the Rockefeller Foundation and the World Bank to plan and implement programs for the new mechanized, capital-intensive agriculture. In 1967 AID proposed studies on peasant willingness to adopt new agricultural methods. "Will new crops and techniques increase surplus or peasant leisure?" AID asked—making it clear that it was the surplus it was interested in. Would the peasants consume the added income or have it for future investment in mechanization, like good Protestants? AID proposed marketing studies for chemical fertilizers, which should be particularly useful for U.S. exporters whose sales to Thailand increased 300 percent between 1966 and 1967.

AID has also worked closely with the Thai government and American business to rationalize problems with urban labor. The AID labor union project was originally funded in 1967, and labor unions were legalized in 1969 after an eleven-year ban. According to the AID proposal to Congress for funding fiscal year 1970, U.S. advisors are playing "a key role in preparing the necessary legislation." The Thai government legalized unions because foreign investors found that control of labor would be easier if they could deal with a representative who would have authority over the other workers. The U.S. Department of Commerce clearly spells out the advantages of the U.S.-developed unions to American investors: "While the labor situation in Thailand has tended to be stable, there have been wildcat strikes from time to time, usually as a result of poor communications between workers and management. Businessmen have reported that the lack of a legitimate employee organization has proven to be an obstacle in the settlement or prevention of such disputes."

AID also wants to thoroughly study its client government. Its program proposes studies of the effects of various government programs in rural Thailand and of "Thai government policies as they relate to private investment." From the extensive studies, it seems that AID must know much more about Thailand than the Thai elite and its bureaucracy.

As the American economy has expanded into Thailand, the Thai bureaucracy has expanded to outlying provinces to integrate previously isolated peoples into the Thai political economy. Peasant revolutionary movements are developing in at least three of these areas of Thailand, but the present insurgencies do not represent a major threat to the military regime in Bangkok. They are mounted mainly by minority peoples and are located at the geographical extremes from Bangkok. The government's attempt to integrate the northern hill tribesmen, the Malay and Chinese in the south, and the Lao-Thai in the northeast has brought rebellion. The U.S. has spent millions of dollars on counterinsurgency studies and projects to aid the Thai bureaucracy in "winning the hearts and minds of the people," but the Thai bureaucrats are more interested in collecting bribes than economic development and are more apt to use violence than persuasion.

Songha, Thailand. *(Photo by John Meckel, BBM.)*

Many of the peasants have organized resistance to this attempted domination and exploitation by the Thai elite and its U.S. backers. The Meo tribesmen began armed rebellion in 1967 in northern Thailand. The Thai government was trying to force the Meo out of the mountains, where they lived a semi-nomadic existence growing opium poppies as their only cash crop, and was trying to place them in "resettlement villages" where they could be controlled and taught to grow other marketable crops. The Meo resisted resettlement, and the government responded by napalming several villages, forcing even more people out of the mountains into resettlement villages as refugees.

Most of the young Meos are joining the guerrillas and escaping to live in the mountains when their tribes are forced into the resettlement camps. The Meo are treated with racist contempt by the Thai, who call them "savages." In fact, the Thai resettlement program is strikingly similar to the U.S. government policy toward the Indians in the nineteenth century, which forced surviving Indians onto reservations where they have been left to rot, physically, mentally, and culturally. Conditions in the Meo resettlement villages are similarly harsh. The people lack sufficient rice and water, and the corrupt local agents pocket the funds appropriated for the Meo in Bangkok. The results of this resettlement program are grimly described by reporter Arnold Abrams for the *Far Eastern Economic Review*:

> Physical hardship and psychological strain have taken a heavy toll on these people. They are gaunt and sickly; many are in a permanent state of semi-withdrawal stimulated by the shortage of opium to feed lifelong habits. Yet the decay of the Meo's spirit is even more distressing than the deterioration of their bodies. It is hard to associate the pitiful inhabitants of Ban Song San (a resettlement village) with the defiant rebels remaining in the mountains. They have lost all semblance of inner strength and independence; they seem to have withered while assuming the manner of the humbled.

However, the Meo insurgency involves only about a thousand armed guerrillas and is little threat to the Thai government. At least for the moment, the Thais have cancelled the resettlement program as counter-productive. But the Thais and Americans are continuing with the Accelerated Rural Development (ARD) program, which mainly consists of building a 125-mile road north of the provincial capital Chiang Mai into Meo territory for "movement of military vehicles, year-round transport of goods to and from Chiang Mai's markets, contact with Thai society."

In the south, Malay peasants have established some liberated areas near the Thai-Malaysia border. Eighty percent of the population of the four southernmost provinces are Malay Moslems who have been at best benignly neglected by the Thai government and at worst harassed like the Meo. The Thai government has suppressed Malay-language Moslem parochial schools and has generally neglected the development of public facilities. The government officials are almost all ethnic Thais, of course, and have similarly racist attitudes toward the Malay as they do toward the Meo.

As in the north, the southern guerrillas resist integration into Thai society. The guerrilla movement grew from the remnants of the Malayan Races Liberation Army, which fought the Japanese during World War II and the British in Malaya from 1948 to 1961. The British successfully suppressed the insurgency, reducing the guerrilla forces from about 10,000 to 500 men by the time the guerrillas moved to the Thai-Malaya border. Today the guerrillas have organized a thousand-man National Liberation Army, which apparently has been able to create an alliance with Thai Chinese in the area, and with a movement of ethnic Thais and Chinese further north. The NLA has an organization that collects taxes from the villagers besides carrying on propaganda work.

The insurgency is being met by combined Thai-Malaysian-U.S. government efforts. The Thai government has dispatched about 2,000 Border Patrol Police to the area. The border police, first organized by the CIA in 1957, supposedly has a dozen U.S. Special Forces advisers with it in the south. U.S. Information Service teams are distributing handbills and showing films to incredulous villagers, while local administrators and Mobile Development Units (MDUs) carry out emergency road construction, education, and community development programs. This operation is being aided by the counterinsurgency efforts of academic researchers from the Stanford Research Institute (SRI), on contract from the Pentagon's Advanced Research Projects Agency (ARPA). Reports have ranged from pinpointings of guerrilla camps and descriptions of "patterns of Communist Terrorist crop cultivation" to a "scenario for possible conflict in Southern Thailand." With Cornell and the University of Michigan, SRI has worked hard to perfect "infrared photographic surveillance" and other aerial reconnaissance techniques which have been used in counterinsurgency in the south to survey the base camps of the NLA. Once again, this increasing contact with the Thai government and their U.S. advisors may provoke even more insurgency.

The insurgency in the northeast, though also among a minority group, is more important. The northeast area, about one-third of the population and territory of Thailand, consists mainly of Lao-Thai, who are ethnically related to the Thai, but still considered second-class citizens. The northeast is the poorest region of the country, with the per capita income about half the national average. Although most of the people own their own land, it is poor and dry. Only about one-third of the villages have an adequate water supply, and education and other public services for the area have been neglected by Bangkok until recently. The northeast has long been considered exile for Bangkok bureaucrats, who were compensated only by the greater opportunities for corruption and petty authoritarianism.

The northeast insurgency began in 1965, shortly following the announcement in December 1964 of formation of the Thai Independence Movement (TIM). The TIM manifesto called on all patriotic Thai peoples to help drive out the U.S., overthrow the Thai government, and replace it with one composed of representatives of patriotic, democratic parties. Shortly after the announcement of the TIM, the Thai Patriotic Front (TPF) was organized by communist and nationalist forces as the political arm of the guerrilla struggle, like the National Front for Liberation of South Vietnam. Unlike the Indochinese liberation fronts, however, the TPF is completely oriented toward the Chinese, while the other fronts carefully play off the Russians and the Chinese to maintain their independence vis-à-vis both.

But the guerrillas apparently have not been very successful in organizing the northeast for revolutionary struggle. Guerrilla bands have been carrying out village propaganda—theatre as well as lectures—and they have received some support from the villagers. But they have apparently failed so far to create a strong peasant organization which is deeply embedded in the life of the villagers. This is partly a factor of the newness of the struggle, but there are also significant impediments to organization in the structure of Thai and Thai-Lao peasant society.

The Thai village is very different from the Vietnamese village. In Vietnam, as in Thailand, the elite and its administrative arm, the state bureaucracy, were suspended above the village rather than closely linked to it. But the Vietnamese village was in itself a tight-knit community, and this village solidarity and organization was easily mobilized by the Viet Minh, and now by the NLF, for the liberation struggle. On the other hand, there is little village solidarity among the Thai and Thai-Lao peasants. Other than the temple organization, there are no important organizations to bind the peasants together. Land is not held in common, as it is in Vietnam, and the peasants treat land as a commodity to be bought and sold at will, rather than an ancestral home as in many other peasant societies. Even the extended family is relatively loosely tied together, and young villagers quite freely move to other areas to settle. All these aspects of village life tend to atomize the peasantry, and make guerrilla organizing difficult.

But the Thai elite's attempts to "organize" their domination of the northeast has also proved difficult and AID has had to concentrate at least 75 percent of its funds for Thailand on the northeast counterinsurgency effort. Although AID continues its "development" projects, it no longer makes the distinction between counterinsurgency and development. The first sentence of the 1967 AID program for Thailand says that "the U.S. AID program in Thailand is concentrated upon a single objective: supporting the Royal Thai Government in its efforts to contain, control, and eliminate the Communist insurgency in rural areas." Indeed, AID manages to relate every U.S. study and project in Thailand to the problem of security. For example, they propose studies which would probe the following questions: "Is the prevailing pattern of village organization in the northeast adequate to cope with insurgency?" "What is the structure and function of the so-called wat (temple) committee in village life? Does this institution possess any relevance for promoting village security?" "Is there anything in the village pattern of economic organization that is relevant to the promotion of village security?" "What is the role of women in village life? Is it possible that, collectively and individually, they can make a significant contribution to the promotion of village security?"

Kathleen Gough Aberle once called anthropology the "child of imperialism." Nowhere is this more evident than in the AID studies on Thailand which also provide a vivid description of the way that the American university has joined the Southeast Asia war effort.

Many of these studies have been or will be performed by the AID-financed Academic Advisory Committee for Thailand (AACT), headed by UCLA professor David Wilson. Professor Wilson co-founded a faculty group opposed to "those faculty members and students who seek to impose their ideologies on the academic community by coercive or uncivilized means." Wilson's touching concern for "Academic neutrality," however, did not deter him from contributing one of the first counter-insurgency studies on northeastern Thailand. Written and researched for Rand in 1962 (although not published until 1964), the study—"Certain Effects of Culture and Social Organization on Internal Security in Thailand"—was done before armed insurgency developed in the northeast and elsewhere; but Wilson and Berkeley anthropologist Herbert Phillips nonetheless addressed themselves directly to the problem of "communist subversion."

The basic problem for rural security, Wilson and Phillips say, is the inadequacy of the communication between the government and the villagers. They delicately skirt the reasons for this, but rather discuss at length the problem of the link between the village and the government. The village headman, the official link, is usually ineffective: "When he meets the demands of the district office, he loses leadership and prestige in the eyes of the villagers; when he meets the expectations of his villagers, he loses his value to the district officer." But integration of the villagers is made even more difficult by competition with the communists, Wilson and Phillips say. The communists "are penetrating villages with agents and workers, who gather information and build organizations that mobilize the energies of the idle and disaffected." The professors propose that the government "must neutralize these efforts by using comparable techniques."

To do this, they recommend that the government recruit veterans, unemployed villagers and youth for a village defense corps which would also participate in public works programs. The scholars suggest that the government flatter the men with ceremonial rewards and distinctive uniforms. The village defense corps, however, should not receive military training "as such" because "a heavily militarized village defense corps, created to meet a communist threat that may never materialize, might very well constitute a hazard to the social order." The villagers might turn their guns on the government.

Though subsequent AID reports give the Thai government credit for the idea, the Village Security Force now being developed is suspiciously like that laid out by the California scholars. The "hazards" suggested by Wilson and Phillips, however, have also developed: many of the security force units have proved unreliable and a threat to Thai government control.

The Phillips and Wilson report is only one of hundreds done by American scholars for AID in Thailand. Organizations like AACT were specifically created by AID "to tap for AID the widest possible personnel resources" from American universities. Besides AID's statements that the single objective of its program is to counter insurgency, AACT's contract with AID requires that the professors supply AID with all research, done in universities and elsewhere, which "may relate to development and counterinsurgency activities in Thailand." AACT is supposed to coordinate its activities with the older regional organization, the Southeast Asia Development Advisory Group (SEADAG), which is also AID funded and is administered by the Asia Society in New York. The membership of SEADAG includes AID personnel, businessmen with interests abroad, professors from 34 major American universities, and 15 private foundations including Ford, Rockefeller, Asia Foundation and the Smithsonian Institute. SEADAG and AACT, together with these foundations, control (among other things) the scholarship funds that support budding Thai scholars and convince them to engage in studies at Thailand universities that will be useful to AID's program.

Private research groups have also gotten in on the action—and the Pentagon money—for counterinsurgency projects. The Research Analysis Corporation (RAC), one of the largest military think-tanks, has worked on problems the Thai Border Patrol Police face in the north, the ability of the Thai road network to provide logistic support for counterinsurgency operations, insurgent recruitment, and counterinsurgency organization in Thailand. The American Institutes for Research (AIR) have had a major project in Thailand dealing with "troop-community relations." Titled "The Impact of Economic, Social, and Political Action Programs in Thailand," and funded by ARPA at over a million dollars, the AIR proposal assured the Pentagon that it would "help the Defense Department and Thai government evaluate counterinsurgency programs, show both organizations how to do this for future programs, and indicate to the U.S. government how to apply similar counterinsurgency programs and evaluate them in other countries, including the United States."

AID has attempted to train Thais not only to eventually replace the development functions of colonial administrators, but also to take over the counterinsurgency programmed by American professors. Since 1950, AID has financed an education in the U.S. or elsewhere for an elite of more than 5,000 Thais. With the Thai government, it has set up "study centers" inside Thailand with ominous titles like the Hill Tribes Research Center in Chaing Mai.

Although the insurgencies that the SEADAG and AACT professors are hired to study are not presently threatening the American client regime in Thailand, the problems created in the future by capitalist development may not be so easily contained. In the central plains area, where a third of the population and most of the Thai peasants live, absentee landlordism and concentration of land holdings are growing—mostly as a result of the continually increasing capitalization of agriculture by the Bangkok rich. At present, nearly 70 percent of the land is in absentee ownership, in contrast to 20 percent a decade ago. Forced from their land, the peasants are becoming either rural or urban proletarians—threatening to become a vast industrial reserve army of the unemployed. Some Central Plains peasants have already organized armed resistance to the government and the economic pressures created by the reshaping of Thai society dominated by the needs of domestic and foreign capital. The AID professors are aware of the problems of unemployment and peasant discontent in rural areas, the growing slums, incredibly exploited wage labor (ten cents a day), and urban unemployment. Their understanding of these problems, however, does not mean they can solve them, for adequate solutions would threaten the military regime and Thai elite who are allowing the U.S. to turn Thailand into an economic colony and a military base.

U.S. military presence in Thailand, mainly related to the Indochina war, is aggravating the pressures created by "development." The U.S. has built eight major air bases in Thailand (of which only four are in full use) for bombing Laos and Vietnam. The major buildup of facilities began in 1964-1965 as the U.S. escalated the war, but the original landing strips for the bases at Ubon, Takhli, Udorn, and Korat were already completed by 1959-1960. (All of these bases are ostensibly Thai, not American; they each have the necessary Thai guards, Thai flag, and Thai base commander.) Several of the bases, particularly at Udorn and Nakhon Phanom, are used for flying supplies and personnel into Laos. And Nakhon Phanom is also used as a Special Forces base, both for training Thai counterinsurgency forces and for covert operations in Laos. By the late '60s, the U.S. had a total of about 50,000 military personnel in Laos. About 35,000 (of whom 6,000 have been withdrawn and another 10,000 are scheduled to be withdrawn) were Air Force personnel involved in the bombing of Indochina, 3,000 are still training Thais for counterinsurgency (so far, U.S. advisors do not engage in combat in Thailand), and the rest of the military personnel are working in construction and logistics in Thailand or in the covert CIA operations in Laos.

The American military presence accounts for the employment of at least 50,000 Thais, from laborers to translators to prostitutes, and contributes to a major share of the Thai national income. Towns around the U.S. bases (most of which are in the northeast and "aggravate" the insurgency) have become entertainment and service centers for U.S. soldiers, demonstrating more clearly than ever to the Thais their colonial status. But serving the Americans is much more profitable than comparable work for Thai employers. In fact, prostitutes and translators often make more than a

An American B-52 at Sattahirb, Thailand, with bombs under wings. *(Photo by Fred Goss.)*

provincial governor. And Bangkok too has become a hang-out for the colonial troops. Seventy thousand GIs each year travel to Bangkok from Vietnam for R & R (rest and recreation). They spend several hundred dollars each (the per capita income of the Thais is about $125) and further increase the class of people who serve the Americans.

Coupled with the overt U.S. presence in Thailand, the importation of American values and styles is creating a Thai nationalist resentment, even among the elite who owe their prosperity and continued rule to the U.S. In 1968, Kukrit Pramoj, a conservative monarchist, angrily attacked the Americans in his newspaper for exploiting the Thai people economically, for creating vast numbers of prostitutes, and for introducing Thai boys to homosexuality. He ended his article with the warning to the Americans that the Thais might "smash down your embassy" and burn the United States Information Service. "You American beasts," he concluded, "return to your holes."

Unfortunately, conservative members of an elite affronted at Western cultural imperialism do not make revolutions. When the choice has to be made, they will side with the U.S. against the masses of their own people. The anti-colonial future of Thailand lies in the hands of the Thai peasants.

The author wishes to thank David Ransom and Harry Cleaver of the Pacific Studies Center for use of their work on counterinsurgency research in Thailand. The author is also grateful to the Student Mobilization Committee to End the War in Vietnam, which came into possession of the liberated counterinsurgency documents and published a comprehensive report on counterinsurgency research in the Student Mobilizer *of April 2, 1970.*

The Berkeley Mafia and the Indonesia Massacre

David Ransom

Indonesia, which in the past fired the imagination of fortune-hunters and adventurers as the fabled East Indies, was long regarded as "the richest colonial prize in the world." Harking back to such times, Richard Nixon described Indonesia in 1967 as "the greatest prize in the Southeast Asian area." Not too many years earlier, however, the prize had been thought all but lost to the fiery nationalist, Peking-oriented Sukarno and the three million-strong Indonesia Communist Party waiting in the wings. Then in October 1965 an unsuccessful coup and a swift move by Indonesia's generals immobilized the leader and precipitated the largest massacre in modern history, in which from 500,000 to a million unarmed communists and their peasant sympathizers were killed. When the bloodletting was over, the immense nationalist spirit of a decade had vanished, and the Indies' vast natural treasures were opened by the new regime to U.S. oil companies and corporations.

To cut the ribbon on the Indonesian side was an extraordinary team of economic ministers known to insiders as "the Berkeley Mafia." Sporting PhDs from the University of California and acting as a closely-knit clique in the councils of power, these men shaped the post-nationalist policies of the new regime. Behind their rise to eminence and power lay a saga of international intellectual intrigue, of philanthropoids and university projects, of student Generals and political Deans, and a sophisticated imperial design beyond Cecil Rhodes's wildest dreams.

Part I—A Dean Is Born

Following Japan's defeat in World War II, wars of national liberation raged in China and Vietnam. Meanwhile, far away in Washington offices and New York living rooms, Indonesian independence was being sensibly arranged. By 1949 the Americans had persuaded the Dutch that if they took action before the Indonesian revolution went the way of China, they could learn to live with nationalism and like it. And sure enough, in that year the Indonesians accepted an independence agreement, drafted with the help of friendly American diplomats. It maintained the severely war-weakened Dutch economic presence, while swinging wide the Open Door to U.S. cultural and economic influences as well.

Among those who handled the diplomatic maneuvers in those years

Reprinted from *Ramparts,* October 1970.

were two young Indonesian aristocrats: Soedjatmoko,* called "Koko" by his American friends, and an economist and diplomat named Sumitro Djojohadikusumo. Both were members of the upper-class, nominally socialist PSI (Partai Sosialis Indonesia), one of the smaller and more Western-oriented of Indonesia's myriad political parties.

In New York the two were lionized by a group closely linked to the notorious Vietnam lobby which shortly thereafter launched Ngo Dinh Diem on his meteoric career in U.S.-Vietnamese politics. The group, which included Norman Thomas, was composed of members of the Committee for Independence of Vietnam and the India League. It occupied something of a vanguard position among socialist anti-communists. "We were concerned that the United States not be caught flatfooted in the post-war necessity to create non-communist governments in Asia," explains League member, Park Avenue attorney and legal counsel for Indonesia in the U.S., Robert Delson.

Delson squired Sumitro and "Koko" around town, introducing them to his friends in the Americans for Democratic Action (ADA) and to top anti-communist labor leaders. They also circulated in Establishment circles, particularly among members of the foundation-funded Council on Foreign Relations, the most influential elite policy-formulating group in the United States.

Distressed by Indonesia's peppery nationalist leader Sukarno and the strong left wing of the Independence forces, the Americans found that, as with Diem in Vietnam, the rather bland nationalism of "Koko" and Sumitro offered a most palatable alternative. In Council on Foreign Relations parlance, they were interested in "modernizing" Indonesia, not revolutionizing it. At the Ford-funded School of Advanced International Studies in Washington in early 1949, Sumitro explained that his kind of socialism included "free access" to Indonesian resources and "sufficient" incentives for foreign corporate investment.

When independence came later that year, Sumitro returned to Djakarta to become Minister of Trade and Industry in the coalition government and then, in two later cabinets, Minister of Finance. As Minister through the early '50s, Sumitro defended an economic "stability" that favored Dutch investments. Carefully eschewing radicalism, he appointed as advisor the German Hjalmar Schacht, economic architect of the Third Reich.

Sumitro was supported by the PSI and their numerically stronger "modernist" ally, the Masjumi Party, a vehicle of Indonesia's commercial and landowning *santri* Moslems. But he was clearly swimming against the tide. The Communist PKI, Sukarno's PNI, the Army, the orthodox Moslem NU—everybody, in fact, but the PSI and Masjumi—was riding the wave of post-war nationalism. In the 1955 national elections—Indonesia's first and last—the PSI polled a miniscule fifth place. It did worse in the local balloting of 1957, in which the Communist PKI emerged the strongest party.

*Many Indonesians have only one name.

Nevertheless, when Sukarno started nationalizing Dutch holdings in 1957, Sumitro joined Masjumi leaders and dissident Army commanders in the Outer Islands Rebellion, supported briefly by the CIA. It was spectacularly unsuccessful. From this failure in Sumatra and the Celebes, Sumitro fled to an exile career as government and business consultant in Singapore. The PSI and the Masjumi were banned.

America's Indonesian allies had colluded with an imperialist power to overthrow a popularly elected nationalist government, headed by a man regarded as the George Washington of his country—and they had lost. So ruinously were they discredited that nothing short of a miracle could ever restore them to power.

That miracle took a decade to perform, but now Sumitro has risen once again. He serves as Minister of Trade in a new Indonesian government. And he is no longer odd man out: today he is regarded as the number two man in Indonesia, and he and his comrades are firmly in control.

The "modernist" restoration was not imposed by American troops. The secular arm of the American imperium reached into Indonesian politics, often under the cloak of the CIA. But it was the hallowed private institutions of academia and philanthropy that worked the greatest wonders. For Sumitro had not simply been a minority politician and cabinet minister, but since 1951 Dean of the Faculty of Economics at the University in Djakarta. There he marshalled the young men with whom he planned to implement his program for Indonesia; there the Ford Foundation made common cause with him to do so.

Institution-Building

One of Sukarno's few lasting achievements was the creation of a university system (a rare instance in which foreign aid was put to good use).

—FORTUNE, June 1, 1968

Ford's interest in Indonesian education began in the early '50s, but it was the Rockefeller Foundation that had pioneered the area. Just before he left the Far East section of the State Department in 1952 to become the Rockefeller Foundation's president, Dean Rusk explained the purpose behind the program. "Communist aggression" required not only that Americans be trained for work in the Far East, but that "we must open our training facilities for increasing numbers of our friends from across the Pacific."

The head of the Ford Foundation, Paul Hoffman, who launched Ford's program in educational internationalism, was no stranger to the Indonesia situation. As head of the Marshall Plan in Europe, he had cut off Marshall Plan funds, which were vital to the Dutch counterinsurgency effort, and thus assisted the birth of the first pro-U.S. Indonesian government. The

Dutch themselves had practiced "indirect rule" in the Indies by simply adding their own administrators to the top of the existing aristocratic-administrative hierarchy (from which Sumitro's PSI was derived). As America supplanted the Dutch, Hoffman's Ford team laid the basis of a post-independence national bureaucracy trained to function under the new indirect rule of America—in Ford's words, to train a "modernizing elite."

"You can't have a modernizing country without a modernizing elite," explains the deputy vice president of Ford's international division, Frank Sutton. "That's one of the reasons we've given a lot of attention to university education." Sutton adds that there's no better place to find such an elite than among "those who stand somewhere in social structures where prestige, leadership, and vested interests matter, as they always do."

With the services it purchased from America's top universities, Ford managed to create a tough, sophisticated infrastructure that reached into every major power institution of Indonesian society. Students selected and molded by the Americans, trained in essential disciplines and skills, became in effect a paragovernment, representing the old PSI-Masjumi parties, but in reality far stronger than they.

Ford launched its effort to make Indonesia a "modernizing country" in 1954 with field projects out of MIT and Cornell. The scholars produced by these two projects—one in economics, the other in political development—have since effectively dominated the field of Indonesian studies in the United States. Compared to what they eventually produced in Indonesia, however, this was a fairly modest achievement. Working through the Center for International Studies (the CIA-sponsored brainchild of Max Millikan and Walt W. Rostow), Ford put together an MIT team to discover "the causes of economic stagnation in Indonesia." An interesting example of the effort was Guy Pauker's study of "political obstacles" to economic development, such as armed insurgency. Domination of natural and cultural resources by foreign institutions like Ford would be somewhat outside the theoretical framework of Pauker's Harvard training.

In the course of his field work, Pauker—an urbane and egocentric man—got to know the high-ranking officers of the Indonesian Army rather well. He found them "much more impressive" than the politicians. "I was the first who got interested in the role of the military in economic development," Pauker says. He also got to know most of the key civilians: "With the exception of a very small group," Pauker says, they were "almost totally oblivious" to what he called modern development. Not surprisingly, the "very small group" was composed of PSI aristocratic-intellectuals, particularly Sumitro and his students.

Sumitro, in fact, had participated in the MIT team's briefings in Cambridge. Some of Sumitro's students were also known by the MIT team, having attended a CIA-funded annual seminar run each summer at Harvard by Henry Kissinger, now President Nixon's top foreign policy strategist. One of them was Mohamed Sadli, son of a well-to-do *santri* trader, with whom Pauker became good friends. In Djakarta, Pauker had struck up friendships with members of the PSI clan and had formed a political study group among them, whose members included the head of Indonesia's National Planning Bureau, Ali Budiardjo, and his wife Miriam, "Koko's" sister.

Rumanian by birth, Pauker had helped found a group called "Friends of the United States" in Bucharest just after the Second World War. He then came to Harvard, where he got his degree. While many Indonesians have charged the professor with having CIA connections, Pauker denies that he was intimate with the CIA until 1958, after he joined the RAND Corporation. Since then, it is no secret that he briefs and is briefed by the CIA, the Pentagon and the State Department. Highly-placed Washington sources say he is "directly involved in decision-making."

In 1954 Ford grubstaked a Cornell Modern Indonesia Project with $224,000. With that money and subsequent Ford funds, program chairman George Kahin has built the social science wing of the Indonesian studies establishment in the United States. In Indonesia, Cornell's elite-oriented studies are what the universities use to teach post-Independence politics and history.

Among the several Indonesians brought to Cornell on Ford and Rockefeller grants, perhaps the most influential is sociologist-politician Selosoemardjan. Selosoemardjan is right-hand man to the Sultan of Jogjakarta, one of the strong-men of the present Indonesian regime.

Kahin's political science group worked closely with Sumitro's Faculty of Economics in Djakarta. "Most of the people at the university came from essentially bourgeois or bureaucratic families," recalls Kahin. "They knew precious little of their society." In a "victory" which speaks poignantly of the illusions of well-meaning liberals out of their depth, Kahin succeeded in prodding them to "get their feet dirty" for three months in a village. Many were to spend four years in the United States.

Together with Widjojo Nitisastro, Sumitro's leading protegé, Kahin set up an Institute to publish the village studies. It has never amounted to much, except that its American advisors helped Ford maintain its contact in the most difficult of the Sukarno days.

Kahin still thinks Cornell's affair with Ford in Indonesia "was a fairly happy marriage"—less for the funding than for the political cover it afforded. "AID funds are relatively easy to get," he explains. "But certainly in Indonesia, anybody working on political problems with [U.S.] government money during this period would have found their problem much more difficult."

Kahin, one of the leading academic Vietnam doves, has irritated the State Department on occasion, and many of his students are far more radical than he. Yet for most Indonesians, Kahin's work was really not that much different from Pauker's. One man went on to teach-ins, the other to RAND and the CIA. But the consequences of their nation-building efforts in Indonesia were much the same.

Berkeley East

MIT and Cornell made contacts, collected data, built up expertise. It was left to Berkeley actually to train most of the key Indonesians who would seize government power to put their pro-American lessons into practice. Dean Sumitro's Faculty of Economics provided a perfect academic boot camp for these political shock troops.

To oversee the project, Ford President Paul Hoffman tapped his old friend Michael Harris, a one-time CIO organizer who had headed Marshall Plan programs under him in France, Sweden and Germany. In the words of one Berkeley professor and close acquaintance, Harris was "a typical Lovestone kind of guy—the labor leader who makes a career out of anti-communist activities working with the government." Harris had been on a Marshall Plan survey in Indonesia in 1951, knew Sumitro, and before going out was extensively briefed by Sumitro's New York promoter, the Indonesian counsel Delson. Harris reached Djakarta in 1955 and set out to build Dean Sumitro a brand new Ford-funded graduate program in economics.

This time the professional touch and academic respectability were to be provided by Berkeley. The Berkeley team's first task was to replace the Dutch professors whom Sukarno was phasing out and to relieve Sumitro's Indonesian junior faculty so that Ford could send them back to Berkeley for advanced credentials. Already at Berkeley was Sadli, who shared a duplex with MIT's Pauker. Pauker had come to head the new Center for South and Southeast Asian Studies on his way to RAND and the CIA. Sumitro's protegé Widjojo led the first crew out to Berkeley.

While the Indonesian junior faculty learned American economics in Berkeley classrooms, the professors from Berkeley set to turning the Faculty in Djakarta into an American-style school of economics, statistics and business administration.

Sukarno objected. At an annual lecture to the Faculty, team member Bruce Glassburner recalls, Sukarno complained that "all those men can say to me is 'Schumpeter and Keynes.' When I was young I read Marx." Sukarno might grumble and complain, but if he wanted any education at all he would have to take what he got. "When Sukarno threatened to put an end to Western economics," says John Howard, long-time director of Ford's International Training and Research Program, "Ford threatened to cut off all programs, and that changed Sukarno's direction."

The Berkeley staff also joined Sumitro's protegés in the effort to prevent the Faculty's being brought more in line with Sukarno's "socialism" and Indonesian national policy. "We got a lot of pressure through 1958–1959 for 'retooling' the curriculum," Glassburner recalls. "We did some dummying up, you know—we put 'socialism' into as many course titles as we could—but really tried to preserve the academic integrity of the place." A very academic integrity, indeed.

The project, which continued for six years at a cost of $2.5 million, had a clear, if not always stated, purpose. John Howard explains the purpose quite simply: "Ford felt it was training the guys who would be leading the country when Sukarno got out."

There was little chance, of course, that Sumitro's miniscule PSI would outdistance Sukarno at the polls. But "Sumitro felt the PSI group could have influence far out of proportion to their voting strength by putting men in key positions in government," recalls the first project chairman, a feisty Irish business prof named Len Doyle.

When Sumitro went into exile, his university carried on. His students visited him surreptitiously on their way to and from the U.S. Powerful Americans like Harry Goldberg, a lieutenant of labor boss and CIA-coordinator Jay Lovestone, kept in close contact and saw that Sumitro's messages got through to his Indonesian friends. No dean was appointed to replace him; he was the "chairman in absentia."

All of the unacademic intrigue caused hardly a ripple of disquiet among the scrupulous professors. A notable exception was the essentially conservative business professor, Doyle.

"I feel that much of the trouble that I had probably stemmed from the fact that I was not as convinced of Sumitro's position as the Ford Foundation representative was, and, in retrospect, probably the CIA," recalls Doyle.

Harris tried to get Doyle to hire "two or three Americans who were close to Sumitro." One was Sumitro's friend from the MIT team, William Hollinger. Doyle refused. "It was clear that Sumitro was going to continue to run the Faculty from Singapore." But it was a game Doyle didn't want to play. "I felt," Doyle explains, that the University should not be involved in what essentially was becoming a rebellion against the government—whatever sympathy you might have with the rebel cause and the rebel objectives."

Back home, Doyle's lonely defense of academic integrity against the political pressures exerted through Ford was not appreciated. Sent there for two years, Berkeley recalled him after one. "He tried to run things," University officials say politely. "We had no choice but to ship him home." In fact, Harris had him bounced. "In my judgment," Harris recalls, "there was a real problem between Doyle and the Faculty."

Ralph Anspach, a Berkeley team member now teaching at San Francisco State, got so fed up with what he saw in Djakarta that he will no longer work in applied economics. "I had the feeling that in the last analysis I was supposed to be a part of this American policy of empire," he says, "bringing in American science, and attitudes, and culture . . . winning over countries—doing this with an awful lot of cocktails and high pay. I just got out of the whole thing."

Doyle and Anspach were the exceptions. Most of the academic professionals found the project—as Ford meant it to be—the beginning of a career. "This was a tremendous break for me," explains Glassburner. "Those three years over there gave me an opportunity to become a certain kind of economist. I had a category—I became a development economist—and I got to know Indonesia. This made a tremendous difference in my career."

Berkeley phased its people out of Djakarta in 1961–62. The running battle between the Ford representative and the Berkeley chairman as to who would run the project had some part in hastening its end. More important, the professors were no longer necessary; in fact, they were probably an increasing political liability. Sumitro's first string had returned with their degrees and resumed control of the school.

The Berkeley team had done its job, "kept the thing alive," Glassburner recalls proudly. "We plugged a hole . . . and with the Ford Foundation's money we trained them 40 or so economists." What did the University get out of it? "Well, some overhead money, you know." And the satisfaction of a job well done.

Part II—School for Soldiers

The marvel is that the modernists have had so much of a chance to steer events. They got in because this military regime, unlike some others in the world, chose to make an alliance with the intellectual and academic community.

—FORTUNE, June 1, 1968

In 1959, Pauker set out the lessons of the PSI's electoral isolation and Sumitro's abortive Outer Islands Rebellion in a widely-read paper entitled "Southeast Asia as a Trouble Area in the Next Decade." Parties like the PSI were "unfit for vigorous competition with communism, he wrote. "Communism is bound to win in Southeast Asia . . . unless effective countervailing power is found." The "best equipped" countervailing forces, he wrote, were "members of the national officer corps as individuals and the national armies as organizational structures."

From his exile in Singapore, Sumitro concurred, arguing that his PSI and Masjumi parties, which the Army had attacked, were really the Army's "natural allies." Without them, the Army would find itself politically isolated, he said. But to consummate their alliance "the Sukarno regime must be toppled first." Until then, Sumitro warned, the generals should keep "a close and continuous watch" on the growing and powerful Communist peasant organizations. Meanwhile, Sumitro's Ford-scholar protegés in Djakarta began the necessary steps toward a rapprochement.

Fortunately for Ford and its image, the Army had a school: SESKOAD (Army Staff and Command School). Situated 70 miles southeast of Djakarta in cosmopolitan Bandung, SESKOAD was the Indonesian Army nerve center. There, generals decided organizational and political matters; there, senior officers on regular rotation were "upgraded" with manuals and methods picked up at the U.S. command school back in Fort Leavenworth, Kansas.

When the Berkeley team phased itself out in 1962, Sadli, Widjojo and others from the Faculty began regular trips to Bandung to teach at SESKOAD. Ford's Frank Miller—who rcplaced Harris in Djakarta and who, like Harris, had worked under Ford President Hoffman in Germany—says that they taught "economic aspects of defense."

Pauker tells a different story. Since the mid-'50s, he had come to know the Army General Staff rather well, first on the MIT team, then on trips for RAND. One good friend was Colonel Suwarto (not to be confused with General Suharto), the deputy commander of SESKOAD and a 1959 Fort Leavenworth graduate. In 1962, Pauker brought him to RAND.

Besides learning "all sorts of things about international affairs" while at RAND, Suwarto also saw how RAND "organizes the academic resources of the country as consultants," Pauker says. According to Pauker, Suwarto had "a new idea" when he returned to Bandung. "The four or five top economists became 'cleared' social scientists lecturing and studying the future political problems of Indonesia in SESKOAD."

In effect, this group became the Army's high-level civilian advisors. They were joined at SESKOAD by other PSI and Masjumi alumni of the university programs—Miriam Budiardjo from Pauker's MIT study group, and Selosoemardjan from Kahin's program at Cornell, as well as senior faculty from the nearby Bandung Institute of Technology, where the University of Kentucky had been "institution-building" for AID since 1957.

The economists were quickly caught up in the generals' anti-communist conspiracy. Lieutenant General Achmad Yani, Army commander-in-chief, had drawn around him a "brain trust" of generals. It was an "open secret," says Pauker, that Yani and his brain trust were discussing "contingency plans" which were to "prevent chaos should Sukarno die suddenly." The contribution of Suwarto's mini-RAND, according to Colonel Willis G. Ethel, U.S. defense attaché in Djakarta at the time, was that the professors "would run a course in this contingency planning." Col. Ethel was a close confidant of Commander-in-Chief Yani and others of the Army high command. He even introduced them to golf.

Of course, it wasn't "chaos" the Army planners were worried about, but the PKI. "They weren't about to let the Communists take over the country," Col. Ethel says. Moreover, any but the most dense officer or advisor knew that since there was immense popular support for Sukarno and the PKI, a lot of blood would flow when the showdown came.

Other institutions joined the Ford economists in preparing the military. High-ranking Indonesian officers had begun U.S. training programs in the mid-'50s. By 1965 some 4000 officers had been taught big-scale army command at Fort Leavenworth and counterinsurgency at Fort Bragg. Beginning in 1962, hundreds of visiting officers at Harvard and Syracuse were provided with the skills for maintaining a huge economic, as well as military, establishment, with training in everything from business administration and personnel management to air photography and shipping. AID's "Public Safety Program" in the Philippines and Malaya trained and equipped the Mobile Brigades of the Indonesian military's fourth arm, the police.

While the Army developed expertise and perspective (courtesy of the generous American aid program), it also increased its political and economic influence. Under the martial law declared by Sukarno at the time of the Outer Islands Rebellion, the Army had become the predominant power in Indonesia. Regional commanders took over provincial governments—depriving the Communist PKI of its plurality victories in the 1957 local elections. Fearful of a PKI sweep in the planned 1959 national elections, the generals prevailed on Sukarno to cancel them for six years. Then they moved quickly into the upper reaches of Sukarno's new "guided democracy," increasing the number of ministries under their control right up to the time of the coup. Puzzled by the Army's reluctance to take complete power, journalists called it a "creeping coup d'état." General Nasution termed it the "Middle Way."

The Army also moved into the economy, first taking "supervisory control," then key directorships of the Dutch properties that the PKI unionists had seized "for the people" during the confrontation over West Irian in late 1957. As a result, the generals controlled plantations, small industry, state-owned oil and tin, and the state-run export-import companies, which by 1965 monopolized government purchasing and had branched out into sugar milling, shipping and distribution.

Those high-ranking officers not born into the Indonesian aristocracy quickly married in, and in the countryside they firmed up alliances—often through family ties—with the *santri* Moslem landowners who were the backbone of the Masjumi Party. "The Army and the civil police," wrote Robert Shaplen of the New York Times, "virtually controlled the whole state apparatus." American University's Willard Hanna called it "a new form of government—military-private enterprise."

The economists' "economic aspects of defense" thus became a wide-ranging subject. To make it even broader, the professors undertook preparing post-Sukarno economic policy at SESKOAD, too.

Deprived of their victory at the polls and unwilling to break with Sukarno, the Communist PKI tried to make a poor best of this "guided democracy," participating with the Army in coalition cabinets. Pauker has described the PKI strategy as "attempting to keep the parliamentary road open," while seeking to come to power by "acclamation." That meant building up PKI prestige as "the only solid, purposeful, disciplined, well-organized, capable political force in the country," to which Indonesians would turn "when all other possible solutions have failed."

By 1963, three million Indonesians, most of them in heavily populated Java, were members of the PKI, and an estimated 17 million were members of its associated organizations in 1963—making it the world's largest Communist Party outside Russia and China. At Independence the party had numbered only 8000.

In December 1963, PKI Chairman D. N. Aidit gave official sanction to "unilateral action" which had been undertaken by the peasants to put into effect a land reform and crop-sharing law already on the books. Though landlords' holdings were not large, less than half of the Indonesian farmers owned the land they worked, and of these, the majority had less than an acre. As the peasants' "unilateral action" gathered momentum, Sukarno, seeing his coalition endangered, tried to check its force by establishing land reform courts which included peasant representatives. But in the countryside, police continued to clash with peasants and made mass arrests. In some areas, *santri* youth groups began murderous attacks on peasants.

Since the Army held state power in most areas, the peasants' "unilateral action" was directed against its authority. Pauker calls it "class struggle in the countryside" and suggests that the PKI had put itself "on a collision course with the Army." But unlike Mao's Communists in pre-revolutionary China, the PKI had no Red Army. Having chosen the parliamentary road, the PKI was stuck with it. In early 1965, PKI leaders demanded that the Sukarno government (in which they were cabinet ministers) create a people's militia—five million armed workers, ten million armed peasants. But Sukarno's power was hollow. The Army had become a state within a state. It was they—and not Sukarno or the PKI—who held the guns.

The test of strength came in September 1965. On the night of the 30th, troops under the command of dissident lower-level Army officers, in alliance with officers of the small Indonesian Air Force, assassinated General Yani and five members of his SESKOAD "brain trust." Led by Lt. Colonel Untung, the rebels seized the Djakarta radio station and next morning broadcast that their September 30th Movement was directed against the "Council of Generals," which they declared was CIA-sponsored and had itself planned a coup d'état for Armed Forces Day, four days later.

Untung's preventive coup quickly collapsed. Though he did not denounce it, Sukarno, hoping to restore the pre-coup balance of forces, gave it no support; on the other hand, the PKI had prepared no street demonstrations, no strikes, no coordinated uprisings in the countryside. For their part, the dissidents missed assassinating General Nasution and apparently left General Suharto off their list; Suharto rallied the elite paracommandos and units of the West Java division, the Siliwangi, against Untung's colonels. Untung's troops, unsure of themselves, their mission and their loyalties, made no stand as Suharto drove them from their strongpoints. It was all over in a day.

The Army high command quickly blamed the Communists for the coup, a line the Western press has followed ever since. Yet the utter lack of activity in the streets and the countryside makes PKI involvement unlikely, and many Indonesia specialists believe, with Dutch scholar W. F. Wertheim, that "the Untung coup was what its leader . . . claimed it to be—an internal army affair reflecting serious tensions between officers of the Central Java Diponegoro Division, and the Supreme Command of the Army in Djakarta . . ."

Leftists, on the other hand, assumed after the ensuing massacres and

Sukarno's overthrow that the CIA had a heavy hand in the affair. Indeed, embassy officials had long wined and dined the student *apparatchiks* who rose to lead the demonstrations that brought Sukarno down. And old Indonesia hands casually mention the CIA's connections with the Army, especially with Intelligence Chief Achmed Sukendro, who retrained his agents after 1958 with U.S. help and then studied at the University of Pittsburgh in the early '60s. But Sukendro and most other members of the Indonesian high command were equally close to the embassy's military attachés, who seem to have made Washington's chief contacts with the Army both before and after the attempted coup. And considering the make-up and history of the generals and their "modernist" allies and advisors, it is clear that at this point neither the CIA nor the Pentagon needed to play any more than a subordinate role.

Student Power

The professors may have helped lay out the Army's "contingency" plans, but no one was going to ask them to take to the streets and make the generals' "revolution." Fortunately, they could leave that to their students. Lacking a mass organization, the Army depended on the students to give authenticity and "popular" leadership in the events that followed. It was the students who demanded—and got—Sukarno's head; and it was the students—as propagandists—who carried the cry of *jihad* (religious war) to the villages.

In late October, Brigadier General Sjarif Thajeb—the Harvard-trained Minister of Higher Education—brought student leaders together in his living room to create the Indonesian Student Action Command (KAMI). Many of the KAMI leaders were the older student *apparatchiks* who had been courted by the U.S. embassy. Some had traveled to the U.S. as American Field Service exchange students, or on year-long jaunts in a "Foreign Student Leadership Project" sponsored by the U.S. National Student Association in its CIA-fed salad years.

Only months before the coup, U.S. Ambassador Marshall Green had arrived in Djakarta, bringing with him the reputation of having masterminded the student overthrow of Syngman Rhee in Korea and sparking rumors that his purpose in Djakarta was to do the same there. Manuals on student organizing in both Korean and English were supplied by the embassy to KAMI's top leadership soon after the coup.

But KAMI's most militant leadership came from Bandung, where the University of Kentucky had mounted a ten-year "institution-building" program at the Bandung Institute of Technology, sending nearly 500 of their students to the U.S. for training. Students in all of Indonesia's elite universities had been given paramilitary training by the Army in a program for a time advised by an ROTC colonel on leave from Berkeley. Their training was "in anticipation of a Communist attempt to seize the government," writes Harsja Bachtiar, an Indonesian sociologist (alumnus of Cornell and Harvard).

In Bandung, headquarters of the aristocratic Siliwangi division, student paramilitary training was beefed up in the months preceding the coup, and *santri* student leaders were boasting to their Kentucky friends that they were developing organizational contacts with extremist Moslem youth groups in the villages. It was these groups that spearheaded the massacres of PKI followers and peasants.

At the funeral of General Nasution's daughter, mistakenly slain in the Untung coup, Navy chief Eddy Martadinata told *santri* student leaders to "sweep." The message was "that they could go out and clean up the Communists without any hindrance from the military," wrote Christian Science Monitor Asian correspondent John Hughes. "With relish they called out their followers, stuck their knives and pistols in their waistbands, swung their clubs over their shoulders, and embarked on the assignment for which they had long been hoping." For starters, they burnt the PKI headquarters. Thousands of PKI and Sukarno supporters were arrested and imprisoned in Djakarta; cabinet members and parliamentarians were permanently "suspended"; and a purge of the ministries was begun.

On October 17, Col. Sarwo Edhy took his elite paratroops (known as the "red berets") into the PKI's Central Java stronghold in the Bojolali-Klaten-Solo triangle. His assignment, Hughes says, was "the extermination, by whatever means might be necessary, of the core of the Communist Party there." He found he had too few troops. "We decided to encourage the anti-communist civilians to help with the job," he told Monitor correspondent Hughes. "In Solo we gathered together the youth, the nationalist groups, the religious [Moslem] organizations. We gave them two or three days training, then sent them out to kill Communists."

The Bandung engineering students, who had learned from the Kentucky team how to build and operate radio transmitters, were tapped by Col. Edhy's elite corps to set up a multitude of small broadcasting units throughout strongly-PKI East and Central Java, some of which exhorted local fanatics to rise up against the Communists in *jihad.* Providing necessary spare parts for these radios was one of the ways the U.S. embassy found of helping the generals' anti-communist pogrom that followed.

Time magazine described the slaughter in Java in mid-December 1965: "Communists, Red sympathizers and their families are being massacred by the thousands. Backlands army units are reported to have executed thousands of Communists after interrogation in remote jails. . . . Armed with wide-blade knives called *parangs,* Moslem bands crept at night into the homes of Communists, killing entire families and burying the bodies in shallow graves. . . . The murder campaign became so brazen in parts of rural East Java, that Moslem bands placed the heads of victims on poles and paraded them through villages. The killings have been on such a scale that the disposal of the corpses has created a serious sanitation problem in

East Java and Northern Sumatra, where the humid air bears the reek of decaying flesh. Travelers from these areas tell of small rivers and streams that have been literally clogged with bodies; river transportation has at places been seriously impeded."

Graduate students from Bandung and Djakarta were dragooned by the Army to research the number dead. Their report, never made public, but leaked by correspondent Frank Palmos—something of an insider—estimated a million victims. "In the PKI 'triangle stronghold' of Bojolali, Klaten, and Solo," Palmos said they reported, "nearly one third of the population is dead or missing." Most observers think their estimate high, positing a death toll of 3–500,000.

The KAMI students' most important task was bringing life in Djakarta to a standstill with anti-Communist, anti-Sukarno demonstrations whenever necessary. By January, with Col. Edhy back in Djakarta addressing KAMI rallies, his elite corps providing KAMI with trucks, loudspeakers and protection, KAMI demonstrators could tie up the city at will.

"The ideas that Communism was public enemy number one, that Communist China was no longer a close friend but a menace to the security of the state, and that there was corruption and inefficiency in the upper levels of the national government were introduced on the streets of Djakarta," says Bachtiar, whose scholarly output includes recording these activities.

The old PSI and Masjumi leaders nurtured by Ford and its professors were home at last. They gave the students advice and money, while the PSI-oriented professors maintained "close advisory relationships" with the students, later forming their own Indonesian Scholars Action Command (KASI). One of the economists, Emil Salim, recently returned with a Berkeley PhD, was counted among the KAMI leadership. Salim's father had purged the Communist wing of the major pre-war nationalist organization, and then served in the pre-Independence Masjumi cabinets.

In January the economists made Djakarta headlines with a week-long Economic and Financial Seminar at the Faculty. "Principally . . . a demonstration of solidarity among the members of KAMI, the anti-Communist intellectuals, and the leadership of the Army," Bachtiar says, the seminar heard papers from Gen. Nasution, Adam Malik and others who "presented themselves as a counter-elite challenging the competence and legitimacy of the elite led by President Sukarno."

It was Djakarta's post-coup introduction to Ford's economic policies.

In March Suharto stripped Sukarno of formal power and had himself named Acting President, tapping old political warhorse Adam Malik and the Sultan of Jogjakarta to join him in a ruling triumvirate. The generals whom the economists had known best as SESKOAD—Yani and his brain trust—had all been killed. But with the help of Kahin's protegé, Selosoemardjan, they first caught the Sultan's and then Suharto's ear, persuading them that the Americans would demand a strong attack on inflation and a swift return to a "market economy." On April 12, the Sultan issued a major policy statement outlining the economic program of the new regime —in effect announcing Indonesia's return to the imperialist fold. It was written by Widjojo and Sadli.

In working out the subsequent details of the Sultan's program, the economists got aid from the expected source. When Widjojo got stuck in drawing up a stabilization plan, AID brought in Harvard economist Dave Cole, fresh from writing South Korea's banking regulations, to provide him with a draft. Sadli, too, required some post-doctoral tutoring. According to an American official, Sadli "really didn't know how to write an investment law. He had to have a lot of help from the embassy." It was a team effort. "We were all working together at the time—the 'economists,' the American economists, AID," remembers Calvin Cowles, the first AID man on the scene.

By early September the economists had their plans drafted and the generals convinced of their usefulness. After a series of crash seminars at SESKOAD, Suharto named the Faculty's five top men (the "Berkeley Mafia") his Team of Experts for Economic and Financial Affairs, an idea Ford man Frank Miller claims as his own.

Armed with Sadli's January 10, 1967, investment law, the economists could put on their old school ties and play host to the lords of the great American corporations. In August the Stanford Research Institute—a spin-off of the university-military-industrial complex—brought 170 "senior executives" to Djakarta for a three-day parley and look-see. "The Indonesians have cut out the cancer that was destroying their economy," an SRI executive later reported approvingly. Then, urging that big business invest heavily in Suharto's future, he warned that "military solutions are infinitely more costly."

In November, Malik, Sadli, Salim, Selosoemardjan and the Sultan met in Geneva with a select list of American and European businessmen flown in by Time-Life. Surrounded by his economic advisors, the Sultan ticked off the selling-points of the New Indonesia—"political stability . . . abundance of cheap labor . . . vast potential market . . . treasurehouse of resources." The universities, he added, have produced a "large number of trained individuals who will be happy to serve in new economic enterprises."

David Rockefeller, chairman of the Chase Manhattan Bank, thanked Time-Life for the chance to get acquainted with "Indonesia's top economic team." He was impressed, he said, by their "high quality of education."

Part III—Harvard: Bringing It All Back Home

We couldn't have drawn up a more ideal scenario than what happened. All of those people simply moved into the government and took over the management of economic affairs, and then they asked us to continue working with them.

—Gus Papanek, Chief of the Harvard Development Advisory Service

To some extent, we are witnessing the return of the pragmatic outlook which was characteristic of the PSI-Masjumi coalition of the early Fifties when Sumitro . . . dominated the scene," observed a well-placed insider in 1966. That same year, Sumitro slipped quietly into Djakarta, opened a business consultancy and prepared himself for high office. The prospect was not long in coming. Having received its bona fides from the lords of international finance, the Indonesian generals' regime was ready to name its "Development Cabinet." In June 1968 Suharto organized an impromptu reunion for the class of Ford, known in Djakarta as the "Berkeley Mafia." As Minister of Trade and Commerce he appointed Dean Sumitro (PhD, Rotterdam); as Chairman of the National Planning Board he appointed Widjojo (PhD, Berkeley, 1961); as Vice Chairman, Emil Salim (PhD, Berkeley, 1964); as Secretary General of Marketing and Trade Research, Subroto (Harvard, 1964); as Minister of Finance, Ali Wardhana (PhD, Berkeley, 1962); as Chairman of the Technical Team of Foreign Investment, Mohamed Sadli (MS, MIT, 1956); as Secretary General of Industry, Barli Halim (MBA, Berkeley, 1959). "Koko" Soedjatmoko, who had been functioning as Malik's advisor, became ambassador in Washington.

"We consider that we were training ourselves for this," Sadli told a reporter from Fortune—"a historic opportunity to fix the course of events." To make the most of the opportunity, Ford provided the Indonesians with a post-graduation present—a development team from Harvard.

Since 1954, Harvard's Development Advisory Service (DAS), the Ford-funded elite corps of international modernizers, had brought Ford influence to the national planning agencies of Pakistan, Greece, Argentina, Liberia, Colombia, Malaysia and Ghana, Officially the Harvard-DAS Indonesia project began July 1, 1968, but DAS head Gus Papanek had people in the field well before that, joining with AID's Cal Cowles in bringing back the old Indonesia hands of the '50s and '60s. Dave Cole returned to work with Widjojo on the Ford/Harvard payroll. Leon Mears, the agricultural economist who had learned Indonesian rice-marketing in the Berkeley project, came for AID and stayed on for Harvard. Sumitro's old buddy from MIT, Bill Hollinger, transferred from the DAS-Liberia project and now shares Sumitro's office in the Ministry of Trade.

The Harvard people are "advisors," explains DAS Deputy Director Lester Gordon—"foreign advisors who don't have to deal with all the paperwork and have time to come up with new ideas." They work "as employees of the government would," he says, "but in such a way that it doesn't get out that the foreigners are doing it." Indiscretions got them bounced from Pakistan. "We stay in the background."

They stayed in the background for the five-year plan. In the winter of 1967–68, a good harvest and a critical infusion of U.S. "Food for Peace" rice had kept prices down, cooling the political situation for a time. Hollinger, the DAS's first full-time man on the scene, arrived in March and helped the economists lay out the plan's strategy. As the other DAS technocrats arrived, they went to work on its planks. "Did we cause it, did the

Ford Foundation cause it, did the Indonesians cause it?" asks AID's Cal Cowles rhetorically. "I don't know."

The plans went into force without fanfare in January 1969. With its key elements being foreign investments and agricultural self-sufficiency, it is a late-20th century American "development" plan that sounds suspiciously like the mid-19th century Dutch colonial strategy. Then, Indonesian labor —often *corvée*—substituted for Dutch capital in building the roads and digging the irrigation ditches necessary to create a plantation economy for Dutch capitalists, while a "modern" agricultural technology increased the output of Javanese paddies to keep pace with the expanding population. The plan brought an industrial renaissance to the Netherlands, but only an expanding misery to Indonesia.

As in the Dutch strategy, the Ford scholars' five-year plan introduces a "modern" agricultural technology—the so-called "green revolution" of high-yield hybrid rice—to keep pace with Indonesian rural population growth and to avoid "explosive" change in Indonesian social—i.e., class—relationships.

Probably it will do neither, though AID is currently supporting a project at Berkeley's Center for South and Southeast Asian Studies to give it the old college try. Negotiated with Harsja Bachtiar, the Harvard-trained sociologist now heading the Faculty's Ford-funded research institute, the project is to train Indonesian sociologists to "modernize" relations between the peasantry and the Army's state power.

The agricultural plan is being implemented by the central government's agricultural extension service, whose top men were trained by a University of Kentucky program at the Bogor Agricultural Institute. In effect, the agricultural agents have been given a monopoly in the sale of seed and the buying of rice, which puts them in a natural alliance with the local military commanders—who often control the rice transport business—and the local *santri* landlords whose higher returns are being used to quickly expand their holdings. The peasants find themselves on the short end of the stick, but if they raise a ruckus they are sabotaging a national program and must be PKI agents, and the soldiers are called in.

The Indonesian ruling class, observes Dutch scholar Wertheim, is now "openly waging [its] own brand of class struggle." It is a struggle the Harvard technocrats must "modernize." Economically the issue is Indonesia's widespread unemployment; politically it is Suharto's need to legitimize his power through elections. "The government . . . will have to do better than just avoiding chaos if Suharto is going to be popularly elected," Papanek reported in October 1968: "A really widespread public works program, financed by increased imports of PL480 ["Food for Peace"] commodities sold at lower prices, could provide quick economic and political benefits in the countryside."

Harvard is pushing its Indonesian New Deal with a "rural development" program that will further strengthen the hand of the local Army commanders. Supplying funds meant for labor-intensive public works, the program is supposed to increase local autonomy by working through local authorities. The money will merely line military pockets. DAS Director Papanek admits that the program is "civilian only in a very broad sense, because many of the local administrators are military people." And the military has two very large, and rather cheap, labor forces which are already at work in "rural development."

One is the 300,000-man Army itself. The other is composed of the 120,000 political prisoners still being held after the Army's 1965–66 anti-Communist sweeps. Some observers estimate there are twice as many prisoners, most of whom the Army admits were not PKI members, though they fear they may have *become* Communists in the concentration camps.

Despite the abundance of "Food for Peace" rice for other purposes, there is none for the prisoners, for whom the government's daily food expenditure is slightly more than a penny. At least two journalists have reported on Sumatran prisoners quartered in the middle of a Goodyear rubber plantation where they had worked before the massacres as members of a PKI union. Now, the correspondents report, they daily work its trees for the substandard wages paid to their guards.

In Java, the Army uses the prisoners in public works. Australian professor Herbert Feith was shown around one Javanese town in 1968 where prisoners had built the prosecutor's house, the high school, the mosque, and (in process) the Catholic church. "It is not really hard to get work out of them if you push them," he was told.

Just as they are afraid and unwilling to free the prisoners, so the generals are afraid to demobilize the troops. "You can't add to the unemployment," explained an Indonesia desk man at the State Department, "especially with people who know how to shoot a gun." Consequently, the troops are being worked more and more into the infrastructure labor force—to which the Pentagon is providing roadbuilding equipment and advisors.

But it is the foreign investment plank of the five-year plan that is the pay-off of Ford's 20-year-long strategy in Indonesia and the pot of gold that the Ford modernizers—both American and Indonesian—are paid to protect. The 19th century colonial Dutch strategy built an agricultural export economy. But the Americans are interested primarily in resources, mainly mineral.

Freeport Sulphur will mine copper on West Irian. International Nickel has got the Celebes' nickel. Alcoa is negotiating for most of Indonesia's bauxite. Weyerhaeuser, International Paper, Boise Cascade and Japanese, Korean and Filipino lumber companies will cut down the huge tropical forests of Sumatra, West Irian and Kalimantan (Borneo). A U.S.-European consortium of mining giants, headed by U.S. Steel, will mine West Irian's nickel. Two others, U.S.-British and U.S.-Australian, will mine tin. A fourth, U.S.-New Zealander, is contemplating Indonesian caoline. The Japanese will take home the archipelago's shrimp and tuna and dive for her pearls.

Another unmined resource is Indonesia's 120 million inhabitants—half of the people in Southeast Asia. "Indonesia today," boasts a California electronics manufacturer now operating his assembly lines in Djakarta, "has the world's largest untapped pool of capable assembly labor at a modest cost." The cost is ten cents a day.

But the real prize is oil. During one week in 1969, 23 companies, 19 of them American, bid for the right to explore and bring to market the oil beneath the Java Sea and Indonesia's other coastal waters. In one 21,000-square-mile concession off Java's northeast coast, Natomas and Atlantic-Richfield are already bringing in oil. Other companies with contracts signed have watched their stocks soar in speculative orgies rivaling those following the Alaskan North Slope discoveries.

Ford, like an over-attentive mother, is sponsoring a new Berkeley project at the U.S. law school in "developing human resources for the handling of negotiations with foreign investors in Indonesia."

Meanwhile in Indonesia, the "chaos" that Ford and its modernizers are forever preventing is one more gathering force. Late last year, troops from West Java's crack Siliwangi division rounded up 5000 surprised and sullen villagers in an odd military exercise that speaks more of Suharto's fears than of Indonesia's political "stability." Billed as a test in "area management," officers told reporters that it was an exercise in preventing a "potential fifth column" in the once heavily-PKI area from linking up with an imaginary invader. But the Army got no cheers as it passed through, an Australian reporter wrote. "To an innocent eye from another planet it would have seemed that the Siliwangi division was an army of occupation."

There is no more talk about land reform or arming the people in Indonesia now. But the silence is eloquent. In the Javanese villages where the PKI was strong before the pogrom, now landlords and officers fear going out after dark. Those who do so are sometimes found in the morning with their throats cut. The generals mutter about "night PKI."

David Ransom, a member of the Pacific Studies Center, is currently at work on a book on Indonesia. His views do not necessarily represent those of the Center.

Eruption in India

Phillipe Gavi

Calcutta: capital of turbulent West Bengal. Lenin appears under a burning sun shining through the palm trees. Impudent slogans, clenched fists, suspicious looks. A student asks me how to make a Molotov cocktail. The round smiling face of Mao looks on. These are the Naxalites from the little town of Naxalbari in West Bengal where a peasant insurrection broke out in the spring of 1967. Today there are 5000 Naxalites to commemorate the anniversary of the uprising. All firmly believe in peasant guerrilla war. The most militant have already gone out into the villages. It is the beginning of armed struggle. The sea of red flags is refreshing in starving, wretched India. Perhaps red is the color of hope as more than 200,000 gaunt bodies stretched out along the sidewalks pave the Calcutta nights.

Calcutta: city of four million dying people, although it accounts for 20 per cent of all of India's industries, according to one expert. It is impossible for India to feed her 525 million inhabitants; what will she do with the 170 million additional mouths expected in the next ten years in spite of the family planning institute which is supposed to solve all problems?

In the official census taken in March 1961 there were ten million people unemployed (in fact, there are at least 30 million). Seventy-six per cent of the population is illiterate, a third of the peasants have no land, the caste system is still powerful. Government corruption exists at every level. Only foreign "charity"—almost $600 million annually—makes the budget deficit good.

From 1961–62 to 1965–66, the years of the Third Plan, the national revenue was only increased by 12 per cent. The same goes for the population. The Indian people run, but they don't ever get anywhere. The director of the Unit Trust of India said to me in Bombay: "The ground is moving backwards under us." An elegant man of 50 who is equally at home in Paris, London, or the New York Hilton, he is the president of the first Indian company that has variable investments.

The volcano certainly had to erupt one day or another.

On December 18, 1968, in a small town on the border between Bihar and West Bengal, a rich farmer wakes up to find a disagreeable surprise: 500 peasants are surrounding his house. His house is destroyed and his reserves of wheat, rice and fertilizer are seized. Several shots are fired into the air and the mob flees.

In Bihar one month later a farmer is killed; his harvest is looted by about 40 people shouting Maoist slogans. In the State of Kerala, more than 2000 kilometers away, police stations are attacked. Everywhere, in

Reprinted from *Ramparts*, April, 1970.

the states of Andra Pradesh, Uttar Pradesh, Bihar, West Bengal and Kerala, the disturbances take on alarming proportions. Revolutionary peasant committees are formed. Wealthy landowners and *jotedars* (small farmers) are attacked, sometimes massacred, by crowds of infuriated peasants. Estates are occupied by force. In the cities: strikes and demonstrations, *gheraos* (workers surrounding the places—or the managers—where they work), street-fighting. In mid-July of 1969, bombs explode in the American Consulate in Calcutta. The repression is correspondingly intensified: men are killed on both sides. Entire villages in revolt are burned; the women raped, the peasants massacred. Striking workers give in to bullets or the *lathi,* the bamboo cane which the Indian police use as clubs.

On July 31, 3000 cops, infuriated by the death of one of their men, march in the streets of Calcutta carrying their friend's body on their shoulders. Three hundred people break into the West Bengal Parliament, destroying furniture and microphones and attempting to molest certain Members of Parliament. They demand that Deputy Chief Minister Jyoti Basi, who is supposed to be the head of the police in the State, explain why he always sides with the demonstrators and criticizes the police who enforce the law with force. Keeping law and order is the duty of the police. It is true that the Minister of the Interior belongs to the Indian Marxist Communist Party (CPI-M). How did it happen?

The Congress Party, which has ruled India since independence, is losing strength. General elections were held in India in February 1967, the fourth general elections since the Proclamation of the Constitution in 1950. The Congress Party underwent a decisive defeat, losing 81 Members of Parliament in the Lok Sabha (Indian Parliament) where it had only 280 seats left out of 520. Its defeat was helpful to everybody—the right (Swatantra, Jan Sangh) and the left (Praja Socialist Party, Samyukta Socialist Party,

(Photo by Jeanne Thwaites, BBM.)

the Communist Party of India [pro-Soviet], the independent Indian Marxist CP).

The Congress Party also lost power in the States of Punjab, Bihar, Orissa, Madras (which voted on the right), West Bengal, and Kerala (which voted on the left). It pays heavily for having failed in the projects it had set up and for the economic and social chaos into which the country had fallen.

As Chandra Sekhar, who is considered to be one of the powerful members of the Congress Party, explained to me: "The Congress Party is not a political party: it's a front that has no coercive power. This is both its strength and its weakness. It is popular because it was the lever for independence, not because of what it's doing right now. Revolutions are always more progressive than when they're being put into effect. The new generation doesn't worry about the past. It wants something concrete. This is how the Congress Party has begun to lose its popularity."

Mr. Chandra Sekhar, a sworn enemy of totalitarian Communism "based on violence," lives in New Delhi. New Delhi is green and pink like a bag of bitter candy. Huge and bureaucratic, its avenues are lined with trees and its Parliament is navel-colored. On the other side is Old Delhi, the ancient city of the Moghuls. That's the Delhi that President Nixon didn't visit. On that side is death. Neon signs lose some of their brightness in the dusty, shady heat. Purple spots of slow agony that overflow the human leprosy, the huge mob is nothing but an explosion of starved corpuscles. Violet night bathes the Fort and the Grand Mosque. Time no longer exists. Time is mutilated, like the stumps which the lepers hold out to foreign visitors. Flies are everywhere, oppressive. Car horns and noisy engines—the human race is swarming. The half-naked *sadhus* look syphilitic. In these wretched alleys you feel like crying out "Enough!" But the city keeps on voting for the Congress Party. The same for the Maharashtra area and Bombay, where thousands of prostitutes who aren't even 12 years old beg for customers for ten rupees behind the bars of a cage whose door doesn't even have to be closed any longer.

And yet the cry of protest has been uttered. Two states, Kerala and West Bengal, gave way. In each, a government on the left directed by the Communists was elected in 1967. Two states out of 17 isn't much, but their population put together is equal to the combined population of France and Belgium. Kerala has 20 million inhabitants in 39,000 kilometers, and West Bengal has 40 million inhabitants in 87,167 kilometers. The two states have in common the highest population density and the highest rate of literacy in India, factors which contributed to the victory in both states of a United Front that includes all leftist or supposed leftist factions, and is led by the Indian Marxist Communist Party.

Two men dominated the electoral campaign: Mr. EMS Namboodiripad, Chief Minister of Kerala, author of many theoretical books and one of the founders of the CPI-M, and Mr. Jyoti Basu, Deputy Chief Minister of West Bengal. Both have defended the line "Administration with agitation." But how far can they go with agitation? Outside of education, the Constitution grants no more power to the state governments than is granted to a French municipality. If the authorities of a state take measures which are thought to be against the Constitution, or if they do not take measures which are provided for by the Constitution, the central government and its representative, the state governor, with the approval of the President of the country, can dismiss the state government and organize new elections. That is what they call President's Rule—the President has the final say.

In 1959, President's Rule was applied to the state of Kerala after two years of a strong-man government directed by EMS Namboodiripad. In November 1967 the central power attempted this operation again in West Bengal. It was in vain, for in the February 1969 elections the people showed their discontent with the government's abuse of power and voted heavily for the left-wing United Front after months of rioting. In the legislative assembly of Calcutta, the Congress Party won only 55 seats, compared with 127 in 1967. The United Front of West Bengal and the left coalition in Kerala are therefore similar: they are both caught between Scylla and Charybdis. Either they follow the popular sentiment for radical change, risking President's Rule being held over their heads again, or they follow a more moderate road, keeping the power—but the people will lose all caution. The latter risk has obviously been chosen.*

"We don't have any hope of doing much, and we say this honestly to the masses. We are practically impotent so long as we don't have the central power. In this sense, we don't believe in parliamentary means. But one shouldn't refuse the parliamentary weapon right off. We can be in power and help strikes perfectly well. The only thing is that one has to let the people know that there are limits."

Eight A.M. The little man with the debonair appearance looks almost like an accused man in his modest office of Tribandrum where he consults the day's files. EMS Namboodiripad, familiarly called EMS, is the target of many people's rage. The industrialists treat him like a "red," the Naxalites like a "turncoat." For others, like the American Consul of Bombay, the "Chief Minister of Kerala is a remarkable man, perhaps the most remarkable man in India, but he can't do anything." In fact, Kerala is perishing because of a lack of industrialization, which is especially strange since it is this state which, thanks to its spice, tea, and copra, supplies 25 per cent of the foreign currency of the central government. Kerala is reduced to drawing part of its resources from money orders sent to families by Kerala men living in other states of India or abroad. Yet how can a Communist government which is favorable "a priori" to the workers and not to capital attract the industrialists and get them to invest in an area which is threatened by social upheaval?

*The United Front in Kerala broke down in October 1969, and the CPI-M left the government, which is now led by a chief minister of the still more revisionist CPI. [*Editor's note.*]

Two directors of the First National City Bank confided to me in the very exclusive English-type Bengal Club of Calcutta that "it's out of the question for the industrialists to invest in Kerala or in West Bengal." At the bar sit "ladies and gentlemen"—mostly European, mixed with a couple of Indian magnates to whom the club has only recently been opened; with monocles and mustaches they look so "British" that they become caricatures. This whole universe has subsisted, and in fact done well, during the CP's take-over. And this sovereign elite society has no intention of risking anything at all—especially since in spite of the United Front's efforts to extinguish the fire, social "agitation" continues to spread. Strikes and *gheraos* are now daily events. Sometimes the police intervene, killing demonstrators. The government disclaims unjustified brutality. To sum it up, things are in an impossible state.

The CPI-M has actually produced its own Trojan Horse. In 1967 the United Front encouraged the movements for peasant demands. These demands took on special meaning in the Naxalbari area, which is a sub-district of Siliguri at the foot of the Himalayan chain of Darjeeling, in West Bengal. Gradually, thanks to CPI-M organizers like Mr. Kanu Sanyal, revolutionary peasant committees began appearing. The estates of large landowners were taken over; their farms were burned. Despite the appeals for calm by the Central Committee and by the government of the United Front, the movement turned into insurrection. The United Front became resigned to the fact that police forces sent to the spot brutally repressed the rebellion which, being poorly organized and without arms, was crushed in

(Photo by Jeanne Thwaites, BBM.)

a couple of months, costing many lives. The limit was reached because of the Party's attitude: a group of the most militant members broke off, forming a revolutionary committee.

Little by little, the Naxalite movement—the name they have adopted in homage to Naxalbari—took on larger proportions. On May 1, 1969, while tens of thousands of pro-Naxalite demonstrators rushed to the march organized by the CPI-M, Kanu Sanyal, recently let out of prison, announced the constitution of a third Communist party, the Indian Marxist-Leninist-Maoist Communist Party (CPI[M-L]), calling for Chinese-type armed struggle in which groups of men surround the cities. Besides the CPI (M-L), other groups of Naxalites, such as the Nagi Reddy group in the Srikakulam district, led an armed struggle.

"Our country has no hope; we lose before we begin," I was told by the director of an insurance company. A Communist in his youth, he thinks of himself as an "average Indian." "We can't get angry: not even when people were dying in the streets like flies during the famines in Calcutta."

Around us, behind the barbed wire fence, lies Calcutta, the monstrous city. From a study made by the Calcutta Chamber of Commerce in December 1968, it was learned that the city has one hospital bed per 333,000 inhabitants. Three million people are unemployed in West Bengal. The water is 45 per cent virus-infested; 200,000 people sleep on the sidewalks while 50 per cent of the industrial capacity of the country is concentrated in this state. Hell must be like Calcutta. Calcutta is paved with thin brown flesh. Lizards. Mutilated bodies. The blind. Rickshaws pursue me, ringing their bells. Poverty-stricken civil servants are squeezed together in old busses. Intellectuals are out of work: there are 80,000 engineers without jobs in India. Students don't have the right books. Peasants from Bihar who have neither land nor work come to fail and perhaps to die under the commercial arcades of Jawaharlal Nehru Road. Workers with salaries of 150 to 200 rupees live in sewers. Solemn old buildings of the colonial period are falling apart. The country is falling apart. The country is going downhill although the birth rate, according to documents of the International Monetary Fund, is down by 0.7 per cent since 1947.

The fact that nothing has changed since the victory of the United Front is not normal. How absurd it was to nationalize the banks—which has nothing to do with socializing the country. How absurd the campaign of Mr. Giri for President—using axes, the symbol of the United Front, and alarm clocks, the symbol of the Congress Party, to decorate a city in which a man can walk down the road completely naked without being noticed at all. And yet the clenched fists, the cries of protest, the riots, the farmers who are attacked, the estates which are taken over, the red flags which are beginning to show through the long gray Indian night, certainly show that hope is not as dead as my insurance director would like to think. On the contrary, hope is appearing a little everywhere. Sometimes it bursts out. Little by little power is being set up in the streets.

Neither Mr. Desai (formerly Deputy Prime Minister and Finance Minister, and one of the powerful members of the "Syndicate"—those in the Congress Party who represent big business) nor Mr. Namboodiripad takes the Naxalite movement lightly, because they know very well that it corresponds to an unbelievable feeling of frustration. One of them proposes repression and economic development; the other rightly shows how economic development in the present system is not possible, but puts off insurrection "till tomorrow." The "average Indian" still believes in a passive India, even though people are getting angry everywhere. Often the anger doesn't take political form. Sometimes it takes the form of criminal action or acts of spontaneous violence, like the riots in February 1969 which stopped the city of Bombay for five days. This pressure explains the safety valves which are opening up: On August 16, 1969, Mr. Giri, the "left" candidate, supported by the left wing and center of Congress and notably by Prime Minister Mrs. Gandhi, beat Mr. Sanjiva Reddy, the candidate of the Official Congress and of the right. In a way, Congress votes against the Congress. The "left," Socialists, Communists, Congress supporters, claim the victory. But whose victory is it?

While traditional political parties are still fighting it out among themselves to gain a couple of seats and to protect some of their interests, a large movement is being born without their knowledge. In its political form it is affecting only two states, and only several pockets within those states. But the movement is growing, gnawing at borders and social barriers. Undoubtedly India still doesn't have her new Yenan. But India does not and will never again conform to the classic model of non-violence.

Phillipe Gavi is a French journalist and a contributor to Jean-Paul Sartre's Magazine, Le Nouvel Observateur. *Translated by Judy Oringer.*

---

chapter four

THE POWERS RESPONSIBLE

"Why, then," the critic of the war is asked, *"are* we fighting in Vietnam?" For many pondering this question for the first time, the answer seemed to be that the war in Vietnam was the result of some awful mistake, a terrible misunderstanding of events by incompetent leaders.

But pointing out this "mistake" did not seem to rectify it: even My Lais could be acknowledged and the war escalated throughout Indochina. Furthermore, the war seemed to be connected to racism and poverty at home and the American role of global policeman abroad—it seemed to be symptomatic of a larger pattern, not an aberration. Student leftists who put their intellects to examining the *why* of the war began to understand that the system of American expansion was an updated version of the old-style European imperialism.

As CARL OGLESBY, former president of Students for a Democratic Society, explains in "The Vietnam Case," anti-communism is a cloak behind which the United States has relentlessly moved to extend its domination. The basic question in Vietnam, Oglesby argues, is foreign versus local control. The U.S. is using its political and military power to prevent the development of Vietnam by the Vietnamese and the organization of the Asian political economy by the Asians. As a strong, independent China has emerged which threatens to cause a drastic reorientation of forces in Asia, the U.S. has had to intensify and militarize the struggle for Indochina in order to counter the Chinese challenge to its hegemony. Though a militarized, politicized, and costly enterprise, the Vietnam war is not the result of bureaucratic or military intransigence or adventurism, but rather an instance of economic imperialism. Unlike some liberal critics who trace the war's origins to Cold War anti-communism and power-seeking bureaucracies, Oglesby, and DAVID HOROWITZ in "Corporations and the Cold War," argue that these government agencies *serve* rather than create U.S. foreign policy aims. And those aims are the interests and needs of U.S. big business, which are justified by anti-communist idealogy.

As Horowitz shows, there need not be one-to-one agreement on every issue between government and corporate leaders in order to establish the fact of corporate dominance of U.S. foreign policy. The interests and needs of the economy—particularly the dominant forces within that economy, the large corporations—set the parameters for foreign policy decisions. Corporate needs and "political realism" dictate the direction and limits of political decision-making.

One consequence of capitalist corporate expansion has been to make the rich richer and the poor poorer—both within the so-called underdeveloped countries and between the developed and underdeveloped countries. In fact, such U.S. expansion has thwarted, and indeed even "underdeveloped," the economies of the Third World countries. In response, social revolutionary movements have developed against the domestic elites serving U.S. interests, elites which have become increasingly dependent on the U.S. for their survival. If Vietnam is the bloodiest case of U.S. intervention, others, such as the Dominican Republic and Guatemala, have been no less blatant.

In the struggle for elementary social justice, the people of Third World countries find that imperialism and domestic capitalism/feudalism are the causes of their impoverishment and powerlessness, and are the primary impediments to social change. In this context accusations (as in the Dominican Republic invasion) that reformist movements are "communist" becomes a self-fulfilling prophecy; as the U.S. and the domestic elites mobilize their forces to prevent social change, the reformers begin to see their enemy not as particular injustices or unjust rulers, but as an entire system which needs to be changed at the root and transformed into another system. National independence for these countries can only be assured by social revolution.

Thus, as Oglesby points out, some of the myths of anti-communism have reality: there is an international system—imperialism—that creates similar conditions in Third World countries, which in turn give rise to revolutionary movements that see themselves struggling against the same enemy and therefore are an international movement—the International Communist Conspiracy. These revolutions are "communistic," if by that we mean that they will forcibly dismantle rich elites and probably develop noncapitalist economies. These movements have tried to coordinate themselves, though not by any dramatically conspiratorial means. And the revolutions do aim at America itself, or rather at the American elite and its expanding global economy. From this basis the Cold Warriors have developed the ideology of anti-communism which can justify genocide in the course of maintaining and expanding their empire.

The Vietnam Case

Carl Oglesby

The commercial supremacy of the Republic means that this nation is to be the sovereign factor in the peace of the world. For the struggles of the future are to be conflicts of trade—struggles for markets—commercial wars for existence. And the golden rule of peace is impregnability of position and invincibility of preparedness.

—SENATOR ALBERT J. BEVERIDGE, 1898

If Cold War anticommunism is most basically an ideological mask for Free World imperialism, then one should be able to show somehow that the issue of the Vietnam war is not Western freedom versus Eastern slavery but foreign versus local control of Vietnam—to show, that is, that the war is being fought to determine how and by whom the Vietnamese political economy is going to be developed. And since the United States has committed itself so unreservedly to Vietnam's Free World salvation, this line of analysis is also obliged to show that Vietnam is somehow crucial for the security and growth of the American commercial state.

It is precisely on this point that the imperialism theory confronts a simple, serious objection: Are American commercial interests in that very poor, very backward part of the world so substantial as to justify so dangerous and unlimited a war? The war is now costing Americans upward of $20 billion a year. How many years will it take for a "saved" Vietnam to start paying dividends on that kind of military investment? The accountant will observe that saving Vietnam is costing us a great deal more than any resulting "colonial" advantage will ever be worth. This entirely commonsensical observation, on its face quite persuasive, directs us to dismiss the imperialist theory (at least for *this* war) and return to a more purely "political," noncommercial explanation.

But probe the case more curiously. We shall find that America's Vietnam policy does not merely illustrate American imperialism, it is a paradigm instance of it; and that in its fusion of imperial motive and anticommunist ideology, the war is not only exemplary, it is also climactic.

There are four important points, argued below in ascending order of importance.

First, a direct American commercial interest in Vietnam exists. For the most part it is potential. That makes it no less real.

In its issue of January 1, 1966, *Newsweek* ran an essay called "Saigon: A Boomtown for U.S. Businessmen." A similar piece by Edmund K. Faltermayer appeared in the March 1966 issue of *Fortune* under the title "The Surprising Assets of South Viet-Nam's Economy." There is the possibility that both pieces may have been a bit contrived or calculated. Perhaps they were brought forth to bolster the business community's enthusiasm for a war which creates a few domestic nuisances (e.g., inflation, labor scarcities in key-skill areas, higher taxes, tighter credit). But whatever the motive, these pieces—and Faltermayer's especially—must have convinced many that South Vietnam is a plum quite delectable enough to be saved. "A South Viet-Nam preserved from Communism," Faltermayer wrote, "has the potential to become one of the richest nations in Southeast Asia." He notes that the country could become an exporter of sugar and cotton, both of which it now imports; that it exported a record 83,000 tons of rubber in 1961, and could easily surpass that record under normal conditions; that the Mekong Delta, the "rice bowl" which now produces about four million tons of rice annually, could produce 12 to 15 million tons. It is not by magic that the rice, the rubber, the sugar, the cotton—and the promising industrial crops, jute, ramie, and kenaf—will come leaping from the ground into the holds of cargo ships. That will require capital, whether the socialist or the capitalist kind.

The capitalist pioneers are already staking their claims. Chase Manhattan and the Bank of America have opened branch offices in Saigon. The New York firm of Parsons & Whittemore holds 18 percent interest in a $5-million American-managed paper mill at Bien Hoa. Foremost Dairies of California has controlling interest in a new condensed-milk plant and half-interest in a new textile mill. Another textile mill has been partly financed by the Johnson International Corporation. The American Trading Co. and Brownell Lane Engineering Co. are selling and servicing heavy equipment—bulldozers, tractors, trucks, and railroad locomotives—and averaging 20 to 30 percent returns on their investments.[1]

The giant is RMK-BRJ, a construction combine formed by Raymond International, Morrison-Knudsen, Brown & Root, and J. A. Jones Construction. RMK-BR is the major contractor for the enormous military construction program in airbases, ports, and roads (economic "infrastructure"), and its contracts may eventually reach $700 million. As of March 1966, it was already the biggest private employer in the country, with 15,000 workers on its payroll and plans for an increase up to 75,000.

"Never before," said *Newsweek,* "have U.S. businessmen followed their [*sic!*] troops to war on such a scale." Faltermayer is careful not to exaggerate the size of the present stake. He emphasizes that our total direct investment in Vietnam is at the moment no more than $6 million. But the niggardliness of that amount is itself a clear enticement: There is a new wide-open frontier's-worth of opportunity in Vietnam. The situation, he says,

> could change radically in the next few years. Esso and Caltex . . . are studying proposals to build a $16-million oil refinery, the country's first. Shell Oil and the South Vietnamese Government would participate in the venture, and the refinery might be included in the proposed Cam Ranh Bay industrial complex.

(It is surprising, however, that Faltermayer represents this "venture" as something new. The same $16-million refinery plans were already "under study" as early as April 1962, according to Indochina scholar Bernard B. Fall, who adds to the story a touching note: "There is strong evidence that the American Government 'urgently invited' the oil companies to proceed with the contract in order to show American confidence in the future of Viet-Nam."[2])

An important aspect of the commercial picture is, of course, the donation of American dollars to finance the Vietnamese import of American goods. We have already quoted *Forbes* (which calls itself a "capitalist tool") on the Agency for International Development: It "is the principal agency through which the U.S. Government finances business abroad. . . . AID distributes about $2 billion a year. Of this, 85 percent is spent in the U.S. for American products and raw materials." In 1966, AID allocations to Vietnam were about a sixth of the $2 billion total. In 1967, this goes to a fourth: $550 million. If 85 percent of that is spent on American exports, South Vietnam will rank among our ten top buyers.

All new frontiers need their Paul Bunyans. Faltermayer offers a strong candidate in a New York entrepreneur named Herbert Fuller, head of an investor group which since 1958 has been promoting a $10-million sugar mill for the coastal city of Tuy Hoa:

> When the troops arrive to clear the area, as they sooner or later must, this American capitalist will literally be one step behind them. "I am in it for the money," Fuller says. "We could get back our investment in two years." Like all entrepreneurs, Fuller once again is pushing ahead with his plans because he assumes the U.S. is now committed to saving Viet-Nam.

But so what? Why is it so wrong for our businessmen to be right behind "their" troops? There is nothing strange about the pursuit of profit and opportunity; and that the businessmen should at once occupy, settle in, and begin to develop the ground just cleared by our troops does not mean that it is for them that the troops are there. Does it?

We encounter a problem of vision. It is hard to see these particular businessmen as being in any way crucial to the Vietnam drama. Their appearance in it seems incidental—important perhaps, but not especially sig-

(Photo by Joseph W. Carey, BBM.)

nificant. The war would be the same with or without them. It is being fought for freedom or to hold back the Communists. Is is not being fought for this Herbert Fuller, "American capitalist."

No doubt. If Fuller decided the Tuy Hoa project was a bad bet and went back to New York, another coastal city, no one thinks the Marines would forgo the conquest of Tuy Hoa. But what do we suppose "freedom" means? And what is the real purpose of keeping the Communists back? Our functional definition of a free country is clear from our behavior. The definition says that a country is free when Americans like Fuller are free to do business in it if they have the skill and the drive to do so. It is free when there are native counterparts of Fuller. It is free when there is free enterprise. When there is *no* free enterprise, the country is Communist. It cannot be doubted that Vietnam's importance lies far more basically in its geographic and *historical* position than in its inherent commercial potentials, whether immediate or long-term. But, as we shall see, that is only because Vietnam is imagined to be the key to larger areas—areas whose commercial accessibility *is* important to us, and which will or will not themselves be "free," depending on the possibility of our doing business in them. Thus, when Faltermayer talks of "saving Vietnam," he is at one and the same time talking about saving both it and the region for Fuller, free enterprise, and Western-style freedom—for the last two are considered to define each other, and the first is an instance of their realization. "After the war," says Arthur Tunnell, of Investors Overseas Services' Saigon office, "there is going to be a big future for American business here."[3] Analyze to the surface the vision which that statement makes concrete, and one will approach an exhaustive ideological description of the Vietnam war.

Second, the militarized economy demands a militarized politics; a militarized politics demands a militarized economy. Vietnam, as conflict colony, helps turn this wheel.

Consider that since 1946 the federal government has laid out about 60 percent of its budget for support of the military-industrial complex, a 20-year total of better than $850 billion. This is a *political* fact.

In 1959, when Khrushchev came to Camp David and the Cold War seemed up for reappraisal, the stock market took its sharpest downturn in nearly four years. This was called "peace jitters." In 1960, when Eisenhower came back from Paris via that broken U-2 (a Lockheed novelty), *The New York Times*' financial page headlined: "Summit Failure a Market Tonic."[4]

During the summer of 1965, as is very well known, certain informed people were again fretful about the national economy. Having cantilevered themselves out into the future on act of faith after vote of confidence, the lenders and the borrowers and their analysts began to make uneasy murmurs. News of an important inner-sanctum debate about the national metabolism drifted out in bits and pieces. The Administration seemed to favor confidence. But then the Federal Reserve Board's chairman, William McChesney Martin, Jr., began to say aloud in public places that he was not convinced things were as right as they ought to be. He even confessed that the economy was putting him in mind of 1929. No one knew quite how to react to this crack in the expert consensus. Was it deep? Was there any real danger? There was a ripple of discreet uncertainty.

In this subdued Perils-of-Pauline atmosphere, there all of a sudden appeared an unexpected hero whom no one was really surprised to see. The hero was the war: It would not get smaller, much less come to a quick end, and it became common knowledge that its direct costs would go to at least $21 billion a year. However nervous it might remain, the bull market had won its reprieve.

Those who argue that the Vietnam war *must* have been forced upon us since it is so uneconomical do not grasp the economics of state capitalism. The economic effects of the war are anything but unambiguous. The war generates very real fiscal management problems and disturbing anomalies in the pattern of foreign exchange. But over all, the war is good for the economy because the economy is addicted to federal subsidy in general and to military subsidy in particular. It appears that we *have* to spend, because what a high-employment economy produces has to be vended. Whether it goes into the sweet life or the limbo of government silos, the product has to go some place and it has to be paid for. Consider, then, a key economic fact about the defense product: *It is not produced at the expense of recognized domestic necessities.* It is not as if Americans are standing in queues to purchase automobiles, which, for the sake of tanks, are going unbuilt. The opposite comes closer to being the case: If it were not for the tanks, the planes, the submarines, the missiles—where would the economy be? Which is very much like asking: If it were not for the heroin, where would the junkies be? Obviously: in hospitals undergoing very painful therapy. Perhaps even of a revolutionary nature.

One does not claim that the Vietnam war was escalated only to cheer up an overblown, dour economy with that "external" and "expanded" market which it could not otherwise procure. But what if the Vietnam war ended and China said, Have it your way? What if the Cold War faded and faded until one day someone noticed that it had disappeared? What would become of this gargantuan Lockheed with its $500 million in research and development contracts alone? What would become of the intensively specialized scientists, engineers, technicians, administrators, and line workers it employs? Or of the tens of thousands of shopkeepers, middlemen, lenders, and suppliers their salaries keep in business? Where are the concrete plans, the great Congressional debates, the enabling legislation on the management of defense-to-civilian industrial conversion? Who is hammering out the answers?

We have a scatterfire from assorted blue-ribbon commissions of scientists, economists, and businessmen whom everyone very well knows to be nonserious. They are a step wiser than Sisyphus, for they only circle their rock, staring at it soberly, poking at it now and then. What else? Are they foolish, these men of science, economics, and business? But it really seems not to matter. Not so deep down inside at all, quite on the surface of intuition, we are all privy to the main secret of state, which is that we are in no real danger of being abandoned by this "threat" that keeps the corporate state in its fighting trim.

Look at Europe, where there is no claim that the "threat" is increasing. The reverse is true: more trade with East Europe and the U.S.S.R., moves on both sides of the Curtain (of which de Gaulle's in the West and Ceausecu's in the East are only the most dramatic) to bring Europe toward accord and integration. Yet in this atmosphere of calm and confidence, after several years of the preaching and the apparent practice of coexistence, what is America's policy on European militarization? Over the past fifteen years we have given or sold to other countries some $35 billion worth of military equipment. Since mid-1961, military export sales have run to more than $9 billion, and the profit to American defense suppliers totals about $1 billion—nicely concentrated in the hands of three big and highly influential firms, General Dynamics, Lockheed, and McDonnell. Overseas military sales for 1965 were about $2 billion and, let the cold War thaw as it pleases, they will run on at that high rate into the foreseeable future.[5] Why does this happen, if the threat is diminishing? It happens because our military sales abroad represent one of our major handles on our chronic balance-of-payments deficit. These sales are actively promoted by the Pentagon, which seems to care little more about the buyers' need and ability to pay for guns than any ordinary used-car salesman: The goodness of the guns is a good enough need, and if the price seems high, never mind, another part of our government will put up an easy-term loan. The number-one salesman—the Pentagon calls him a "negotiator"—is Henry J. Kuss, Jr., Deputy Assistant Secretary of Defense for International Logistics Negotiations. In May 1965, in recognition of his section's "intensive sales effort," Kuss was awarded the Meritorious Civilian Service Medal.[6]

Here is a prime instance: Germany earns about $675 million a year from the American troops who are stationed there. To offset these U.S. payments, Germany "has been encouraged" to purchase $1.3 billion worth of American military goods over the 1966–67 period. Very convenient, that Germany's military equipment "needs" so closely match our expenses. But Germany seems reluctant to buy what we insist she cannot do without. Foreign military sales in the first quarter of 1966 were the lowest since 1964, and the big reason was Germany's tardiness in making the agreed-upon purchases. That tardiness might have something to do with Germany's recession and budget problems. But that is small concern of ours. We have to move these goods.

It is argued that these weapons stabilize the world and make peace, as if the financial benefit which accrues to us from their sale were only a happy incidental. But the most elementary survey of what is now happening in European politics will make it clear that armaments—on both sides—are increasingly irrelevant to peace and stability, and that if they have any effect at all on the larger pattern of European reintegration, it is a negative and obstructing one. Outside Europe, realities counter the arms-for-stability thesis even more ominously. Former Ambassador to India John Kenneth Galbraith testified before the Foreign Relations Committee on April 25, 1966, that "the arms we supplied . . . caused the war between India and Pakistan. . . . If we had not supplied arms, Pakistan would not have sought a military solution [to the Kashmir dispute]."[7]

As bad as it was—and may yet be again—the India-Pakistan encounter will be nothing compared to what may at any moment erupt in the Near and Middle East. Neither the Arabian war with Israel nor Nasser's vendetta with Saudi Arabia has anything at all to do with the Cold War; no one thinks the Russians are about to come howling down the Caspian or across the Kopet Mountains, and once upon a time it was American policy (as Rusk put it as recently as January 1966) "not to stimulate and promote the arms race in the Near East and not to encourage it by our direct participation."[8] Little more than two months after that statement, the State Department announced an agreement to sell Jordan (which already had American tanks) "a limited number" of advanced fighter-bomber aircraft, reportedly Lockheed F-104s. Senator Eugene McCarthy commented: "It is not clear how Jordan, which has an annual per capita GNP of $233 and which has been dependent on U.S. military grants and economic aid, will pay for these planes, which cost $2,000,000 apiece. *The availability of U.S. credit for arms purchases is undoubtedly an important factor.*"[9] [Emphasis added.]

Selling arms to both Israel and the Arab world at the same time is an embarrassing business, so we do it behind the barn as much as we can—but do it nevertheless because we suppose we have to. One interesting sequence begins with our demand that Britain purchase American fighter planes. Having complied, Britain now has need of sales to "offset" *her* imbalance. Britain is therefore allowed to bid on American munitions contracts. But should she win such bids, *that would result in a market loss for American munitions-makers.* So the Pentagon arranges to find British bids not quite up to standard. American sellers are content. But Britain still has her deficit. Enter Saudi Arabia, convinced that she will be unsafe so long as she does not have a big fleet of fighters. She would like to have American ones, the best. But against the background of American policy on Israel, this is a "need" which it would be politically ticklish for us to service—at least openly. So we persuade Saudi Arabia that ours are not the only aircraft in the world worth flying and she will be just as happy with a British mark. Britain thereupon sells Saudi Arabia what she wants—$400 million worth of supersonic fighters. And we, having lost no market which we might gracefully have entered, *count this British aircraft sale to Saudi Arabia as the quid-pro-quo balancer of our original aircraft sales to Britain.*[10]

So it goes. Apparently we are not really proud of this sort of thing, but what can we do? There stand the bright weapons in a row. Behind them stand their engineers. Behind the engineers, the executives, who serve on presidential committees and travel often to the capital. Behind the executives, the booming system for which they work, for which they speak, in which they have their being. The system must boom, the executives must have their being, the military engineers must design, the riveters must rivet, and the shining bright weapons must therefore be *marketed.* And that marketing is easier if there is a certain uneasiness in the world, a little tension and anxiety. Who could market aspirin if there were no headaches? Yet what is more antiheadache than aspirin? Preventive aspirin, these sleek fighter aircraft. But the world should not forget what a headache is. So to go with that conceptual beauty called "preventive war," we have preventive *threats,* just bit enough to put an edge on things and keep the system from coming unstuck.

Harvard economist Sumner Slichter explained the system very movingly in a 1949 address to a group of bankers. The Cold War, he said, "increases the demand for goods, helps sustain a high level of employment, accelerates technological progress and thus helps the country to raise its standard of living. . . . So we may thank the Russians for helping make capitalism in the United States work better than ever."[11]

Sad to say, we have had to watch Russia's glory fade, her power to inspire our capitalism decline. Besides, when we have put 7000 long-range nuclear rockets in West Europe alone,[12] we have perhaps begun to saturate a good market. But we are in luck, for new Russians keep entering the Cold War market. Today we have China—and therefore Vietnam. And in the wings, tomorrow's starlets—Guatemala? the Philippines? Iran?—are even now trying on their black-pajama *campesino* costumes and rehearsing their most splenetic Marxist curses. And the Third World is crawling with CIA and Special Forces talent scouts.

Third, the strategic heart of the matter.

Increasingly from the turn of the century, American policy has been preoccupied with the problem of pacifying the global commercial environment. As early as the mid-1890s we had already become the world's leading manufacturer and therefore internationalist in spite of ourselves. It had become critical to us that our foreign markets should not be disturbed. How were the required stability and freedom of access to be won? A distinctly minority opinion was that they could not be: The old nations were too bent on conquering one another. America should therefore be neutral and trade with all who would trade on proper terms. (This is one of the so-called isolationist positions. It is not isolationist, it is neutralist. Neutralism *might* be isolationist, but it need not be and usually is not. Neutralist Switzerland, for example, is anything but isolationist. For an example closer home, there is the prewar period of the New Deal, during which time we were internationalist, politically partisan, and economically neutralist all at once: our trade with Germany, Italy, and Japan remained basically solid in the years 1933–40.[13])

But what came to be the dominant belief was that the problems of advanced-power aggression and backward-state revolution *had* to be solved, *could* be solved, and *would* be solved through some combination of the advanced powers. The world needed a concert of industrial giants whose collective strength, will, and prestige would restrain aggressions and suppress revolutions. The question for statesmanship was which powers should make up the club. The question for diplomacy was how to get them into it.

Before World War I, the general belief was that the proper combination would consist of the United States, Britain, and France. After that war, Wilson explicitly revised this outlook, holding that Germany and Japan would now have to be integrated into the Atlantic concert. In this way, revolutionary Russia could be isolated and the Big Powers acting coordinately could protect the security of the world's increasingly integrated political economy. So in the 1920s the United States underwrote the reconstruction of Germany's prewar industrial structure, and in 1922 (the Nine-Power treaty) brought Japan by the ears into a modern open-doorist agreement on hapless China. When trouble began to brew in the 1930s, Chamberlain struggled with all the considerable anxiety at his command to establish Four-Power hegemony in Europe (i.e., Britain, France, Germany, and Italy). The New Deal, not much more instructed by Japan's invasion of Manchuria than was Britain by Germany's Rhineland remilitarization, maneuvered with carrots and sticks through most of that period to secure a China accommodation with Japan.

We were steadily trying, that is, with a really remarkable constancy, to establish that political integration of the Big Powers which finally *was* established—at least temporarily—as one of the chief results of World War II. De Gaulle's France portends change today, and perhaps (it is debatable) Gaullism represents genuinely different ideas about how European power should be arranged and what its fundamental goals should be. But at least well into the mid-sixties, the postwar world was dominated by explicit or implicit alliances that linked the United States, Britain, France, Germany, and Japan into one another's economies, all our partners sharing our belief in a democratic-liberal political philosophy, and all of them more or less willing to accept and support our views on the Communist threat.

This system has two separate but integrated domains, the Atlantic and the Pacific. As Germany is the pivotal state of the Atlantic domain, Japan is the pivot of the Pacific. It is the situation of this Japan which we shall now examine more closely.

The first point is that Japan is a traditionally vigorous trader, one which has long been important to the commerce of the United States. From 1929 through 1940, our total volume of trade with Japan was surpassed only by our trade with Canada and Britain. The much-lusted-after China trade was not even half as heavy (over that period, about $3.5 billion total volume with Japan as opposed to about $1.5 billion with China). Our view of Japan's distinction is reflected in the fact that besides the quite special cases of Vietnam, Korea, and Formosa, no country outside Europe has received as much assistance from the United States (some $4 billion over the 1945–63 period). Her comeback in the postwar period was rapid and strong. Her 1965 volume of trade was close to $17 billion (more than double her 1960 volume), placing her ahead of Italy among the world's business-doers behind the United States, West Germany, England, France, and Canada. By 1961, she had taken over second place among our trade partners, with only Canada ahead. In 1965 she sold us $2.5 billion and bought from us $2.4 billion, achieving for the first time a favorable balance of trade both with the United States and the world ($8.5 billion exports vs. $8.3 billion imports).[14]

The second point is that a healthy, westward-looking Japan is just as crucial to the containing of China as containing China is to the health and Western-orientation of Japan. To understand the essentials of this dynamic, we have to unpack the meaning of this concept "containment."

It can, of course, mean several things. For a pathetically brief period, Czechoslovakia's Beneš "contained" Hitler by answering the German troop concentration at his border with a military mobilization of his own. Thus, there is a type of containment that is distinctively military. The United States "contained" the growth of domestic communism by a program of systematic legislative, judicial, and propaganda harassment. Containment, then, can be political and legalistic. We could go through a set of such differing situations and define for each a differing form of containment. The common characteristic would be that in each case a perception of an active threat elicits a countermeasure that is specifically pitched to the threat's nature, and that does not commit itself to the direct and final liquidation of the threat.

What is the nature of the Chinese Communist threat? As should be perfectly clear, the threat is not basically military. No real threat ever is. China's power to aggress against her neighbors is not to be doubted. But two other things are also not to be doubted. One is that she would be all but defenseless against the kind of strategic nuclear attack which a clear act of aggression would surely provoke. The other is that she has never attacked for spoils, nor without provocation. (The Korean "invasion" came only after repeated U.S. bombings of Manchuria, the Tibetan "invasion" only after a clear mutiny of the theocracy, the Indian "invasion" as a result of a very plain border dispute in which she had by no means the worst of the argument.)

The threat is political. And as with any political threat, the guts of it are economic. It has long been a statesmanly wisdom in the West that any China which could organize herself would be a China indeed. Only recall Napoleon's words about the slumbering giant who will awaken to shake the world, Lenin's observation that "for world communisim the road to Paris lies through Peking and Calcutta." She has the people, the resources, the energy, and the ingenuity to be—what? Given equity in what time can purchase, what time will inevitably bring, China could become the peer of America, Europe, and the U.S.S.R. What she lacked for centuries was order, a sense of national unity, and positive control over her inherent resources. The people—industrious—and the land—rich—have been there all along, waiting for some iron-minded Johnny Appleseed.

China's rate of growth in the first ten years following Chiang's flight to Formosa was anywhere from 15 to 30 percent, depending on which of several experts one believes. Apart from the problem of insufficient data, none seems to be really sure how to measure the performance of an immature planned economy. But there is general agreement that growth was strong, even allowing for the very abysmal state of the initial conditions. Assessments of the Great Leap experience vary even more widely, some scholars arguing a "catastrophe" interpretation, others claiming that the failure, now mostly recouped, was chiefly agricultural and the basic industrial growth remained healthy. To dare to say anything conclusive about China's economy one would have to base it on a lengthy analysis, and a major reason for its lengthiness would be the need to explain why nothing exactly conclusive could be said. But we need not be so technical here. What is important is that no one denies that for the first time in centuries there *is* such a thing as a Chinese nation, that it *has* an economy, and that this economy has established contact with the intrinsic potential of the land and the people. That potential, plagued as it is with natural and political difficulties, is as great as it needs to be. Reflect then, as our statesmen surely must, on the China of a hundred or even fifty years from now. Imagine a world in which creative action—economic, political, cultural—is no longer so densely and disproportionately concentrated in the North Atlantic global core—a world, that is, in which an independent and dynamic Asia *exists.*

Our response to the mammoth fact of Chinese revolution—something which has nothing at all to do with communism, but rather with the independent organization of China and her acquisition of modern fire—has not been exactly pragmatic. First we chose to believe that it was not happening. We exhausted ourselves in mirthful tales of the new China's blunders, sorrows, and epidemic pain, and poised ourselves for the next news dispatch, for it would tell us of the end of this extravagant mistake. The news was different. Then we adopted the view that its own inner evil would in time surely destroy this most total of totalitarianisms. Merely to give its self-destruction a little nudge, a little momentum, we set up an embargo. And it did not die. But then surely the Chinese people would rise against the "yellow peril" internalized, demanding capitalism and Chiang Kai-shek. Merely to give them pluck, we ostentatiously armed their real and true hero, that leashed whirling dervish of Formosa. And the people did not rise up. Strange ways of the Orient! Our recriminations meanwhile were endless. Clearly, this was all the work of Joe Stalin and certain State Department infidels. Reputations were garroted. China was still there, however, coming on like a freight train.

And there sits Japan in the very beam of the Manchurian industrial headlamp, *quite powerless to move.* (A roughly comparable situation would be one in which England found herself politically misallied against a Europe united to the Urals, a battering ram.) What are Japan's options? Isolationism vis-à-vis China was never even thinkable. Whether coerced by future political apprehensions or lured by present commercial opportunities, Japan is already China's foremost trade partner,* surpassing even the Soviet Union (with which, adroitly enough, Japan's businessmen are also arranging increased commerce). It is not as if Japan could pretend that China is just not there. It would be strange economics, politics, and history if she tried to. The only questions that are at all open are how much, when, and on what terms. Most specifically: Will Japan contrive to maintain her present pro-American political bias? Will she submit to world history's commonest law that the Higher Economics determines the Lower Politics and so cast in with Peking? Or will she try instead the Greek way of golden-meansmanship and make of herself a bridge between the two supergiants, well knowing (as one Japanese has remarked) that bridges get walked on?

It will be clear what the United States expects Japan to do. But how much pressure do we ask that nation to bear in our name whose principal cities we atomized? Japan understands that she bombed Pearl Harbor with

*Japan's sales to China, $245 million in 1935, are rising annually at a rate matched only by her purchases from China. Exports (and imports) in her China trade from 1960 through 1965 are as follows (in millions of U.S. dollars): 2.7 (20.7); 16.0 (30.9); 38.5 (46.0); 62.4 (74.6); 152.8 (157.8); 245.3 (224.7).[15]

no very great moral finesse. Japan understands that her new economy was built by us. But there is something especially memorable about that bomb, callous about our nuclear appearances at her ports of call, humiliating about the 1960 Mutual Security Treaty for which the Kishi government had to pay with its life, infuriating about our overt colonization of Okinawa and the Ryukyu chain, frightening about our Vietnam war, which three quarters of her people oppose: the elements of Japanese anti-Americanism subsist. Japan, the keystone of our Asian containment perimeter, may do what she can to remain our long-haul affiliate. She will not do what she cannot do. If America has certain expectations, it is up to America to make their possibility concrete.

We now ask: Does Vietnam bear materially on this drama? The key facts would seem to be the following: (1) Two of China's principal import needs are rubber and rice, improved access to which will in some measure accelerate her rate of development and thus her over-all power. (2) The two principal export commodities of a normalized South Vietnam will be rubber and rice. (3) Japan's unemployment figure is an irreducible one percent. Increased industrialization will draw more workers from the farm to the factory. Urbanization of labor will reduce yield of unmechanized farms at the same time that the resultant higher purchasing power will raise demand. (4) Japan is traditionally a food importer, and she is becoming a greater one, her food imports being on the rise both proportionately and absolutely. Of 1962's total $5.6 billion imports, $700 million (12 percent) went for food; of 1963's $6.7 billion total, $1 billion (16 percent) went for food; of 1964's $7.9 billion total, $1.3 billion (17 percent) went for food.[16] (5) Japanese are the world's foremost shipbuilders and among its strongest steelmakers and textilers. They need markets. China needs ships, steel, and textiles. A developing Vietnam will want steel certainly and probably ships, but may be inclined to protect her textile industry.

Let us join a final fact with a professional observation. The fact is reported by the Indochina scholar Bernard B. Fall:

> DRVN [North Vietnamese] trade with Japan, after a period of coolness when Japan decided to pay war reparations to South Viet-Nam only, has reached important proportions that might well provoke concern in the United States. Trade rose from about $10 million in 1959 to more than $40 million in 1961–62 and involves such items as chemicals, machinery of all kinds, and four seagoing 5,000-ton cargo ships and one of 2,000 tons; for these, North Viet-Nam pays in raw materials, notably coal.[17]

The observation was made by President Eisenhower at his press conference of April 7, 1954, almost exactly one month before the French collapse at Dien Bien Phu and the opening of the Geneva Conference on Indochina. The stenographic reports reads:

> In its economic aspects, the President added, [loss of Indochina] would take away that region that Japan must have as a trading area, or it would force Japan to turn toward China and Manchuria, or toward the Communist areas in order to live. The possible consequences of the loss [of Japan] to the free world are just incalculable, Mr. Eisenhower said.[18]

All the foregoing would appear to support the following propositions:

1. Japan's economic strength is the crucial element in America's policy of containing China and maintaining the peace in Asia. Japan is the bastion.

2. Behind only Canada among our trade partners, Japan is of major commercial importance to us. In fact, a primary direct purpose of containing China is the safeguarding of our commercial interest in Japan. Japan is thus both the bastion of the containment-expansion struggle and the prize of victory.

3. South Vietnam is an important prospective trade area for both Japanese sellers and Chinese buyers.

4. But China is also an important Japanese trade partner and cannot fail to become increasingly magnetic. The authoritative *Finance* (June 1966) said: "Some trade experts in Washington expect the Communist Bloc to supersede the U.S. as Japan's biggest trading partner during the next decade." (West Germany's sale of a steel plant to China further disarms the ideological argument against mainland trade and can only sharpen the commercial appetite of the Japanese businessman.)

5. If Japan and China develop economic interdependency—and as things now stand only shattering disturbances can even postpone that—then the brute mathematics of the relationship will doom Japan to juniority (much as Britain would be junior to an economically integrated European continent). If Japan has no long-term alternative to massive China trade, she will be left without an alternative to a progressively more pro-Chinese orientation. The bastion and the prize, one and the same, hear the same clock ticking.

6. Japan's only remote chance (it *is* remote) for a long-term alternative to the developing market of China lies with the more slowly developing and less organizable markets of the South Pacific, South Asia, and Southeast Asia. In the first, America's position is traditionally privileged, especially in the crucial Philippines (where economic nationalism is growing) and in Australia (where direct U.S. investments, at about $1.5 billion, are greater than in all other countries but Canada, Britain, Venezuela, and Germany). In the second, India proves all but inert under the most exasperated Western proddings. In the third, South Vietnam's position is central owing to her coasts, harbors, resources wealth, and the fact that the war has *made* it central. South Vietnam's now buried treasures mean that her markets, once developed, will exert a great pull on Japan the Trader *regardless of who develops them.*

We can simplify this.

What the West faces in the Pacific is the formation of a regional economic system (*a*) whose potential and power are inherent in the Pacific situation itself, (*b*) which must include Japan, and (*c*) which would quite naturally be dominated by China. This is the "threat." America feels it most keenly because among the Western powers she now enjoys the dominant economic position there in the Pacific, because her postwar Asian investment in blood and treasure is steep, and because she is by any measure the most international of the international states. Our purpose, then, is to frustrate the drawing together of this geoeconomic system by imposing political and military barricades between its elements and by holding out the alternative of other economic configurations. Thus, the struggle to hold South Vietnam. Thus, the United States-promoted Northeast Asia Treaty Organization (NEATO), which died a-borning. And thus, for more recent and more sensible approaches, the Asian Bank and the new, tentatively titled Asian and Pacific Cooperation Council (so it can be called ASPAC—"an attractive name with a masculine sound," said Thailand's Foreign Minister Thanat Khoman[19]). *New York Times* reporter Robert Trumbull, reporting the manly ASPAC's birth at Seoul in June 1966, quoted the chief of one delegation as saying that "although the organization initially will be purely for economic cooperation [e.g., a regional bank to handle development of rice and other commodities, and an international technician pool], it cannot avoid strengthening the policies of these non-Communist and anti-Communist countries."[20] The nine members are South Korea, Thailand, Malaysia, the Philippines, Australia, New Zealand, Nationalist China, South Vietnam, and Japan.

We lead from this into a final deduction:

The aim of the North Atlantic political economy is to frustrate the independent organization of the Pacific political economy.

Such has been Europe's traditional policy in Africa. Such has been the United States' traditional policy in Latin America. Such has been the traditional Asian policy of the Atlantic powers together. Nor does it very much matter that such a policy may or may not have been made explicit and consciously acted upon. An eloquent two and a half centuries of Western mucking about in Asia tell the story quite clearly enough. Everywhere in the poor world, in fact, the inveterate habit of the Western powers has been to absorb and integrate what they could command and to scatter and harass what they could not.

The most elemental meaning of the hit-and-miss, chaotic, and in many respects chronically malformed poor-world revolution is that to the traditional alternatives of subservient integration and harassment there shall now be added a third course: a South American South America, an African Africa, an Asian Asia—the very straightforward argument of it being that there can be no equable integration of the several global spheres (that's where peace is) until there is an approximate economic and political equity among them. Whether we happen to like it or not, and however we conceal the roots of our antagonism to it with panegyrics on democracy and equally irrelevent diatribes against Communism, this is the testament of revolution and this is what we are struggling to resist with our isolation of China, quarantining of Cuba, and pacifying in Vietnam.

The *fourth* point—for its powers of commentary on our culture, it seems to me, much the most important—is coiled up in a not very puzzling puzzle.

Saving Vietnam at the price of deploying some 600 Special Forces guerrilla experts, or even 16,000 Marine "advisers," whatever one thinks of the political motive, seems at least to be a proportionate act, cost-conditional and controllable. But half a million men? Who will apparently have to become a million? And a hundred billion dollars? Moreover, this "military solution" has long since proved to be no solution at all. Everyone can see that the air raids on North Vietnam, officially described as the best way to stop infiltration, have led only to stepped-up infiltration. In the south, the B-52s kill more monkeys, tigers, and civilians than Vietcong. The napalm destroys more villages than fighting forces. Sophisticated reports on our ground war argue most persuasively (if sometimes unintentionally) that it is fought without relevant pattern and without significant effect, our mechanized forces being unable to engage in any sustained and decisive way the guerrillas, whose mobility is not of the machine but of the culture itself.* And besides being militarily ineffectual, this destruction exacts a steadily higher toll in that political good will in which Johnson's America is in such miserably short supply. It means decades, if not centuries, of recrudescent anti-Americanism in Vietnam, the rest of Indochina, all of Asia; even West Europe begins to gag. One might suppose that a rational imperialist could invent other, more sensible ways to shore up the quivering dominoes of the Pacific—indeed, that he could see problems there that make Vietnam's "salvation" seem a small item. Without a wholly new order of concentrated Western will and wisdom, India will be communist within two decades. Every day, South Korea slips further behind North Korea in economic development and political independence. The political economy of the Philippines is stagnant and the Huks are again on the rise. Thailand's northeast remains as vulnerable as ever to those "outside agita-

*See, for example, Special Forces veteran Donald Duncan's "I Quit!" in the February 1966 *Ramparts*, reprinted in this book. Or a piece from the hand of a protagonist of the war, S. L. A. Marshall's "The Death of a Platoon" in the September 1966 *Harper's*, an essay of disaster whose between-the-lines message is distinct and harrowing. Or one of the few really powerful psychological studies of the ground war, John Sack's "M, An Account of One Company of American Soldiers in Fort Dix, New Jersey, Who Trained for War and Who Found It in South Viet-Nam Fifty Days Later" in the October 1966 *Esquire*. Or Marshall Sahlins' close-in study of Special Forces operations, "The Destruction of Conscience in Viet-Nam," *Dissent*, Jan.–Feb. 1966.

tors" whose main crime is pointing out the emperor's nakedness. Above all, there is what Stillman and Pfaff have strikingly called "the furious material energy and the eerie political passivity of contemporary Japan,"[21] an energy which we have seen to be in fact freighted with political meanings of the most momentous sort.

In sum: The military solution to the problem of Vietnam is not working; the attempt to achieve such a solution worsens and may begin to cripple our political position in Asia; and the really important and defensible eastern salients of the Western world—India, Thailand, the Philippines, Korea, Japan—drift every day a bit closer to that distinctively Oriental future which our policy-makers can hardly fail to see.

The government's computers have been no guard against a loss of control which may very well be unparalleled. Why does this happen?

This happens because the ideology that demanded and vindicated this "necessary" act of war continues to demand and vindicate the act even after it has overreached its necessity and become, on its own terms, *irrational.* What Western power opposes is the anti-imperialist social revolution of the poor. But in a time in which Western liberals have oversold themselves on their own slick humanism-*cum*-realpolitics, that position is not easy to sloganize. We have ourselves lately cursed imperialism—the more primitive imperialism of others; have ourselves once glorified revolution—our own. Perhaps because of this, America's leaders seem to have doubted that their subjects had the stomach for a repressive counterrevo-

Wrecked helicopter. *(Photo by Joseph W. Carey, BBM.)*

lutionary and imperialist war. Such a war, since it had to be fought, would have to be sweetened with a different name. Imperialism is thus rechristened as anticommunism, and our foe is instantly transformed from a human being into a pawn, a dupe, or an outright hard-core agent of that International Communist Conspiracy whose ultimate objective (so we are guaranteed) is the conquest of America.

This theory of the International Communist Conspiracy is not the hysterical old maid that many leftists seem to think it is. It has had an intimate affair with reality and it has some history on its mind when it speaks. There *is* a revolution which *is* international—one only has to count the perturbations and look at a map to see as much. In some less than technical sense, this revolution *is* "communistic," if by that we mean that it will probably not produce capitalist economies, that it will probably create autarchic and controlled economies, authoritarian central governments, programs of forced-march wealth accumulation, and the forcible dismantling of rich elites. And if not by any means melodramatically conspiratorial, the several national liberation movements, in their early stages especially, *do* make an effort to coordinate themselves; they do so, pathetically unadept, because they consider their enemy to be internationally coordinated himself—a view which is entirely correct. And to the extent to which this revolution aims at terminating the masterdom of the rich, an aim which automatically implicates America, the revolution *does* aim itself at America—it aims itself, rather, at an America which most Americans have forgotten about: Rockefeller, Engelhard, U.S.A. There is just no use being deluded about that. But what is added on for pure political effect is that ugly edge of clandestinity, pointless and merciless ambition, that cloud of diabolism which has nothing to do with the sustaining force of the revolution itself. And what is *subtracted* from the reality—much more important—is the *source* of the ferment, the *cause* of the anger, the supreme question of the *justice* of rebellion. What this theory gives us is a portrait whose outlines are not unreal, but whose colors have been changed from human blacks and browns and yellows into devil's red, and whose background has been entirely erased. Thus, the theory wildly disorganizes and mismanages the very real history that allows it to survive. And if it lies within the power of an idea to pervert a nation's generosity and curse its children, then the widespread American acceptance of this view of revolution may forecast a bitter future for us all.

It is through the ideology of Cold War anticommunism (a cynic might abbreviate it to CWAC and call it "cwackery") that the masters of American power have rationalized and quite successfully dissembled their opposition to the Third World's diffuse and uneven movement for independence. This ideology is the root-and-branch descendant of that ideology by which the fathers of these same masters once sought to break the American labor movement. It has the sort of truth in it now, and the same sort of lies, that it had in the long bitter period between the Civil War and World

War II. After years of perfection, and applied now to a remote world familiar to Americans only as the well-controlled mass media see fit to make it so, one has to say of this ideology that it is more effective now than ever. It entirely rearranges the moral terms of the encounter between the rich and the poor, and in one stroke deprives the revolutionary of the very right to name and explain himself. He stands already named—a criminal; already explained—an enemy. He is *not* the revolutionary which he pretends to be. The *real* social revolutionaries, it seems, are ourselves. This other one is a fraud, whether willfully so or not; and, whether or not *he* knows it, *we* happen to know that he is an imposter, an intruder on the scene of social change whose real hope, real demand—is the destruction of our country. Whatever he may think, we know that he will never be satisfied with Moscow or Peking, Havana or Algiers, Caracas or Saigon. He is out to get *us*—Kansas City, Birmingham, Washington, D.C. So it follows that the inner, central, driving theme of the drama being acted out in Vietnam's jungles is nothing less than the question of our own national survival. This is the theory by which the war has been explained to us.

If it is a good theory, then it is good *absolutely*. If it is correct to say that our national well-being requires the defeat of the NLF, then the NLF will have to be defeated. The explanation will remain correct regardless of how hard it might be to carry out its implicit commands. Preserving the well-being of the nation is an overriding and transcendent objective. It is not possible to imagine that such an objective can be qualified or repealed *even for one moment* by any other objective. It is an imperative. The awesome consequence of this is that *any struggle that is rationalized in its name is one from which we cannot withdraw.*

Everyone knows that some people in this country, some of them strong, consistently demand that we use all needed force to bring this war to a "speedy and favorable conclusion." If their view of history is not backward, then their moral system is; but to characterize them as ultraconservatives, to try to erase their argument by calling them names like warmongers, is to miss entirely the good, clear point which they make. The main thing wrong with this "ultraconservative warhawk" may in fact have nothing at all to do with conservatism or bellicosity, but rather with his unreserved acceptance of a theory which liberal American administrations have been drumming into his head for at least a quarter of a century—namely, the theory that there is an International Communist Conspiracy that threatens to capture the world, including *us*; the bleakest tyranny that history ever saw; and that aims to achieve all this through the piecemeal conquest of increasingly less marginal states.

Let it be remembered that the government speaks to its people with a measure of authority. People do not expect it to lie, distort, or deceive. People trust it. When this self-same trustworthy government informs the people that the war takes place because agents of the world-hungry tyranny came to a happy land from outside and proceeded to agitate, propagandize, subvert, terrorize, and spread chaos, hatred, and ammunition, then the people have every right to demand, Why not go after such a threat *at its source?* When our trusted government explains to us that the Red takeover of Vietnam (Laos, Cuba, Hispaniola, the Congo) is merely secondary, nothing but a conquistadorial way station on the road to this Xanadu of ours, then the people have every right to demand, *Why not act now?* Looked at *in itself,* as a problem of national survival, it does not seem to me that this has anything very much to do with conservatism. There is a murder going on out there in the street: A man with a knife is killing Kitty Genovese; after he finishes her off, he aims to invade the apartment house itself and kill one by one the empty-headed, empty-hearted cowards who gape at the atrocity from their windows. So *of course* the right thing to do is to leap now to her defense. First, because she is an innocent victim and not to defend her is dishonorable. Second, because her murder will not appease but only whet the killer's appetite, and we have before us an official American fact that unless someone stops him he will soon be putting his fangs into us. What is "conservative" about wanting to fight in that situation? What kind of whimpering lunatic thinks it is "warmongering" to intervene under such circumstances? The bravest case to be made against these reactionaries of ours is that they are so overeager to believe what the liberals have been feeding them. On terms of that belief, what nonsense it is to talk about a "limited" war with "limited" objectives.

"We are at total war right now," say the right-wingers—only making more succinct what Truman told them, what Eisenhower and Kennedy allowed them to believe, what Johnson's homilies have convinced them of all over again.

An ideology which originates in a distortion of history acquires an intrinsic power to sustain and add to historical distortions. It achieves an independent authority in the explanation of events and therefore in the forcing of national policy. We go to Vietnam to maintain a segment of the Western, North Atlantic community's sphere of influence—an objective which on its own terms is practical, concrete, definite, and perhaps not at all without limits; one which is subject to a cost accounting and for which there may be an excessive price to pay. But because they have rationalized this venture in terms of the ideology of anticommunism, our leaders are obliged to insist that we are in Vietnam to protect our vital organs of national increase—an objective that is not practical and cost-conditional but absolute and sacred. To ask what is the value of holding Vietnam becomes, in the grip of this ideology, as pointless as asking the value of the king in a game of chess. The war escapes the political relativity to become transcendent and sublime.

This is an affliction of the people. We might assume (although Johnson, Rusk, and Rostow make us shaky about it) that the political technicians of the State and Defense Departments only purvey, but themselves do not use, the quasi-religious doctrine of the Great Conspiracy. That will not help those whom they have made true-believer addicts to it. A big minority of Americans is one day going to be *betrayed.* The ideological bridgework between the fact and the fancy is coming unstuck today as perhaps never before for America. And when it crumbles, a great many good, strong people are going to find themselves marooned in the unreal. Their anger will shake the nation. To them, the conduct of the war already seems an act of madness if not perfidy. Here we are in a death duel with a most relentless foe, and look at us pulling our punches! The two basic criticisms of the war, which correlate with the leftist and the rightist dissents, aim at resolving the tension that exists between the war's most common political and military descriptions. The rightist accepts the political description and therefore wants the war to be more fiercely waged. The leftist repudiates that political description and therefore wants the war to be broken off. Both aim at a more rational position. Both have a much more solid line of argument than the center, which is only confused and trapped by its own dissembling gobbledygook. In a way, this warhawk is even more humane than the slow-death advocates, for he may at least lay claim to the stark compassion of Macbeth: "If it were done when 'tis done, then 'twere well it were done quickly." If we must destroy Vietnam, then let us have the mercy to do it with dispatch and put those poor people, broken-legged horses, out of their misery.

And the very sad fact is that when the time comes to pay the piper, it will not be to these "moderates" of ours that the deepest, most spirit-tearing agony will come. The example of the French experience in Algeria is all too instructive.

France fought to maintain her colonial control of Algeria for many of the same reasons that mobilize America in Vietnam today. Like America, France rationalized the colonial war in terms of transcendent national imperatives. When it became clear to the leaders of France that disengagement was required, important elements in the French army were outraged. The Secret Army Organization (OAS) was formed to resist what its members felt was the betrayal of the nation. The OAS aimed at nothing less than a *coup d'état,* and its existence created for France the most punishing internal torment. How did this happen in France, the heartland of European humanism? Western liberals have a theory about that which restores their confidence: The OAS happened because there were fascists in the French army who wanted it to happen. The OAS was only the last gasp of the old Nazi collaborationists. There is nothing like that in America.

But look again—not at America to find fascists, but beyond the fascist label itself, which has merely substituted a curse where an explanation is required.

On the first of August 1962, Captain Estoup, a lawyer of the First Foreign Legion Paratroop Regiment, arguing before a high French military tribunal, summed up his defense of one of the OAS conspirators: "How can it happen," he asked, "that a brilliant young St.-Cyr cadet, one of the outstanding young men . . . at the military academy . . . today stands accused (of treason) before a military court . . .?"[22]

Let us fix our eye on the American counterpart of this "brilliant young cadet" before we go on. Let us imagine a good blond and upright young man, square-shouldered with a heart full of bravery, a West Point graduate from some very American place like Colorado Springs or Trenton or Seattle—in E. E. Cummings' phrase, "a yearning nation's blue-eyed pride." We must imagine the ballgames he has played, the cotton candy and the sweet spring nights and the sweetheart he has left behind him; the strong old clapboard houses, the gracious elms, the broad green lawns of the quiet streets from which he came. All that. He is not monocled or mustached. There is no *Mein Kampf* hidden in his footlocker. His voice is well modulated, his demeanor perhaps a bit retiring. He is proud but not arrogant about his Green Beret. He is not happy to be in Vietnam. He would prefer to be home. There is, however, a job to be done. Such is the villain of the peace: the traitor.

Estoup proceeds to explain that it was to the members of the elite forces —men like our young St.-Cyr cadet from Wyoming—that the most odious and dangerous of assignments fell. It was the cadet's duty to procure vital information about the enemy—"by all means available." That is, he was instructed to use torture. "I do not know," says Estoup,

> what sort of mental turmoil someone who gives an order like this must go through; but I do know the sense of shock and revulsion suffered by those who have to carry it out. All the fine ideas and the illusions of the young St.-Cyr cadet crumble. . . . But you will say, "Then why did not the young St.-Cyr cadet refuse to carry out the order?" Because the ultimate end had been so described to him that it appeared to justify the means. It had been proved to him that the outcome of the battle depended on the information he obtained, that the victory of France was at stake. . . . If the means are justified only by the end, there is no justification at all unless the end is achieved. If it is not, nothing is left but a senseless pattern of dirty indelible stains. . . . It is my testimony that for the most part the true motive for [the actions of the conspirators] was a secret, silent, inward, gnawing determination not to have committed crimes that achieved no object. In the final analysis, these are the actions of the damned souls making their last desperate effort to wreak vengeance on the devil who has lured them into hell. The people of France, in whose name justice is now being done, should know that it was in their name and for their sake that the accused were pushed, by those in authority, over the edge of this pit of destruction.[23]

No one knows better than the torturer himself what torture means. No one understands bombing better than the bomber, guns than the gunner, death than he who kills. You need not inform this Wyoming lad that his hands are bloody. He is the expert about that. But the blood will wash away, will it not? The dirty indelible stains will one day be removed? The cleansing water is victory. The sacrifice is redeemed by the rebirth for which it prepares the conquered land. But if the water is not brought, that deferred innocence in whose name the present guilt is borne vanishes from the future. And what becomes of this strange savage blood? It fuses permanently with the skin of the hands that shed it.

We ought to be able to understand a very simple thing: From now on in America it shall be with such hands that children are soothed, office memoranda signed, cocktails stirred, friends greeted, poems written, love made, the Host laid on the tongue and wreaths on graves, the nose pinched in meditation. In the forthcoming gestures of these hands—this is really very simple—we shall behold an aspect of Vietnam's revenge.

Notes

[1]*Newsweek,* January 1, 1966.

[2]Bernard B. Fall, *The Two Viet-Nams,* Praeger Publishers, Inc., New York, rev. eds., 1964, 1966, p. 304.

[3]*Fortune,* March 1966.

[4]Fred J. Cook, *The Warfare State,* The Macmillan Company (Collier book), New York, 1964, p. 181.

[5]Eugene J. McCarthy, "The U.S.: Supplier of Weapons to the World," *Saturday Review,* July 9, 1966.

[6]*Ibid.*

[7]*Ibid.*

[8]*Ibid.*

[9]*Ibid.*

[10]*U.S. News & World Report,* July 11, 1966.

[11]New York *Herald Tribune,* October 26, 1949; *quoted in* Cook, p. 183.

[12]*New York Times,* September 18, 1966.

[13]*Almanac,* p. 470. U.S. export (and import) figures for 1933 and 1937–40 are as follows (in millions of U.S. dollars): Germany: 140 (78); 126 (93); 107 (65); 47 (52); and 0.2 (5). Italy: 61 (39); 77 (48); 58 (41); 59 (40); and 51 (23). Japan: 143 (128); 288 (204); 240 (27); 232 (161); and 227 (158).

[14]Alex Campbell, "Japan Plays the Field," *New Republic,* March 5, 1966.

[15]International Monetary Fund, *Direction of World Trade* (monthly). For an expert analysis of such trade figures, see Alexander Eckstein, *Communist China's Economic Growth and Foreign Trade,* McGraw-Hill Book Company, New York, 1966, pp. 200-212.

[16]*Direction of World Trade.*

[17]Fall, p. 194.

[18]William Appleman Wiliams, *The Shaping of American Diplomacy,* Rand McNally & Co., Chicago, 1956, p. 1119.

[19]*New York Times,* June 16, 1966.

[20]*Ibid.*

[21]Edmund Stillman and William Pfaff, *The Politics of Hysteria,* Harper & Row (Colophon book), New York, 1964, p. 40.

[22]Pierre Vidal-Naquet, *Torture: Cancer of a Democracy,* Penguin Books, Baltimore, Md., 1963, p. 194.

[23]*Ibid.*

Carl Oglesby, long a member of the New Left, is a past president of the Students for a Democratic Society.

Corporations and the Cold War

David Horowitz

Who makes U.S. foreign policy? The question is by no means academic, for the historical record shows that over the last fifty years and more, U.S. policy has consistently run in channels which are antagonistic to the most cherished ideals of the American Republic, issuing finally in the conflicts which we associate with the Cold War. Those ideals—enshrined in the Declaration of Independence—are democratic in character, and recognize above all the right of nations to self-determination, the freedom to carve out their own paths of historical development. Included in this freedom is the equally sacred privilege of any oppressed people to overthrow by force the institutions of their oppressors and to secure for themselves, after the example of the American revolutionaries, the rights to "life, liberty, and the pursuit of happiness."

Yet the record shows that as the United States has assumed the role of a great and then dominant world power, it has more and more consistently opposed the major social revolutions of our time. Moreover, in violation of the principle of self-determination, it has intervened militarily, diplomatically, and economically to crush or to cause grave setbacks to these revolutions, whether in Russia or Mexico, China or Cuba, Greece or Vietnam.

Nowhere has this pattern of policy been more evident, certainly, than in the American intervention in Vietnam. In 1945, the Democratic Republic of Vietnam was proclaimed in a document modeled on the American Declaration of Independence and at first was recognized by the former colonial power, France. Yet when that power sought to reassert control of its former colonial territory, establishing a puppet regime in Saigon for this purpose, it found support in U.S. policy. Not only did Washington back France's illegitimate war of conquest with economic and military aid, but when the French failed, Washington itself took over the struggle to defeat the Vietnamese Republic through the quisling government in Saigon. Indeed, more than twenty years after the proclamation of Vietnam's Declaration of Independence, the Vietnamese peasants are still being assaulted by the U.S. armed forces in what has undoubtedly become the most savage and ruthless intervention on historical record.

Nor was this counterrevolutionary expedition exceptional as U.S. Cold War policy, despite the unprecedented ferocity and outright depravity of its execution. As already noted, it formed rather a consistent pattern with other U.S. interventions in Santo Domingo, Cuba, Guatemala, the Congo, the Middle East, China, Greece, and elsewhere during the Cold War years,

Reprinted from David Horowitz, ed., *Corporations and the Cold War* (New York: Monthly Review Press, 1969).

(Photo by Arthur S. Boyle.)

and in Russia, Mexico, Cuba, China, and other countries earlier in the century. Indeed, counterrevolutionary intervention, which is at the heart of the Cold War and its conflicts, has been a characteristic of U.S. foreign policy ever since the United States embarked on a course of overseas economic expansion following the closing of the geographical frontier more than seventy years ago.

How is this counterrevolutionary policy, which runs directly counter to the high ideals of the American Republic, to be explained? How is it to be explained that the largest "defense" program of any nation in history (and of the United States in particular, which, prior to the postwar decades, never in peacetime maintained a conscription army) is organized around the unprecedented, "un-American," and patently interventionary concept of *counter-insurgency?*

These paradoxes can only be explained if it can be shown that there is a group wielding predominant power in the American policy; one whose interests run counter to what have been America's most basic ideals, and which can impose its own interpretation of the American tradition onto the framework of policy-making in the state. If it can be shown that there is a *class* among the plurality of competing interest groups which enjoys a predominance of power and can establish its own outlook as a prevailing ideology, and if it can be shown that these interests are expansionist, antirevolutionary, and tending to be militarist by nature, then an explanation of the paradoxical character of American policy will have been found and, beyond that, the sources of the Cold War conflicts and their permanence.

Such a "ruling class" can, in fact, be readily shown to exist. Its locus of power and interest is the giant corporations and financial institutions which dominate the American economy, and, moreover, the economy of the entire Western world. "In terms of power," writes one authority on the corporations (himself a corporation executive and former U.S. policy-maker), "without regard to asset positions, not only do 500 corporations control two-thirds of the non-farm economy, but within each of that 500 a still smaller group has the ultimate decision-making power. This is, I think, the highest concentration of economic power in recorded history." In addition, "since the United States carries on not quite half of the manufacturing production of the entire world today, these 500 groupings—each with its own little dominating pyramid within it—represent a concentration of power over economies which makes the medieval feudal system look like a Sunday school party."[1]

As this observer points out, many of these corporations have budgets, and some of them have payrolls which, with their customers, affect a greater number of people than most of the hundred-odd sovereign countries of the world. Indeed, the fifty largest corporations employ almost three times as many people as the five largest U.S. states, while their combined sales are over five times greater than the taxes the states collect. As one American political scientist summarized it:

> Our ideology permits us to rest happy in the thought that the Anti-Trust Division of the Justice Department could, if it so desired, "break up" General Dynamics or International Business Machines into congeries of separate companies. The fact of power, however, is that this has not, cannot, and will not be done because government is weaker than the corporate institutions purportedly subordinate to it. This is the politics of capitalism. It is not at all expressive of a conspiracy but rather a harmony of political forms and economic interests on a plane determined by the on-going needs of corporate institutions.[2]

It is, in the last analysis, the dependence of men individually and collectively on the corporately organized and controlled economy that provides the basis of the corporate domination of U.S. policy, especially U.S. foreign policy. The basic fulcrum of this corporate power is the investment decision, which is effectively made by a minute group of men relative to the economy as a whole. This decision includes how much the corporations spend, what they produce, where the products are to be manufactured, and who is to participate in the processes of production.

> A single corporation can draw up an investment program calling for the expenditure of several billions of dollars on new plants and products. A decision such as this may well determine the quality of life for a substantial segment of society: Men and materials will move across continents; old communities will decay and new ones will

> prosper; tastes and habits will alter; new skills will be demanded, and the education of a nation will adjust itself accordingly; even government will fall into line, providing public services that corporate developments make necessary.[3]

But this is not the whole extent of the power of the corporate investment decision. In the national economy, the small oligarchy of corporate and financial rulers, who are responsible to no one,[4] determine through the investment outlays the level of output and employment for the economy as a whole. As Keynes observed, the national prosperity is excessively dependent on the confidence of the business community. This confidence can be irreparably injured by a government which pursues a course of policy inimical to business interests. In other words, basic to the political success at the polls for any government, as to the success of its specific programs, will be the way the government's policies affect the system of incentives on which the economy runs—a system of incentives which is also the basis of the privileges of the social upper classes.

This does not mean of course that the business community as such must prefer a particular candidate or party for that candidate or party to be victorious. It means, much more fundamentally, that, short of committing political suicide, no party or government can step outside the framework of the corporate system and its politics, and embark on a course which consistently threatens the power and privileges of the giant corporations. Either a government must seize the commanding heights of the economy at once, i.e., initiate a course of social revolution, or run things more or less in the normal way, that is, according to the priorities and channels determined by the system of incentive payments to the corporate controllers of the means of production. This is an unspoken but well understood fact conditioning politics in capitalist countries, which explains among other things why the pattern of resource allocation—the priority of guns over butter, of highway construction over schools and hospitals—is so similar in all of them. It also explains why, despite the congressional and parliamentary enactment of progressive tax laws in all these countries, the spirit of the law has everywhere been thwarted, and nowhere has the significant redistribution of income promised by these democratically ratified statutes taken place.

The sheer economic pressure which the corporations can exert over the policies of democratically elected governments is lucidly manifest in the experience of the Wilson Labor government in England. For, while owing its office to labor votes and labor money, this government was forced by "the economic situation," i.e., by domestic and international capital, to pursue precisely the policies which it had condemned as *anti*-labor while in opposition.

Of course, under normal conditions, and particularly in the United States, where no labor party exists, the corporations have less subtle means at their disposal for ensuring policies conducive to their continued vigor and growth. For

> all the political activities and functions which may be said to constitute the essential characteristics of the [democratic] system—indoctrinating and propagandizing the voting public, organizing and maintaining political parties, running electoral campaigns—can be carried out only by means of money, lots of money. And since . . . the big corporations are the source of big money, they are also the main sources of political power.[5]

The means by which the upper classes maintain their privileged position and vested interests in countries where universal suffrage prevails vary with the differing traditions, social institutions, and class structures of the countries involved. They vary also with their historical roles. Thus, in the twentieth century, as the United States has replaced Britain as the guardian power and policeman of the international system of property and privilege, the corporate ruling class, with its equally expanding overseas interests, has less and less been able to entrust policy to indirectly controlled representatives and has more and more had to enter directly the seats of government itself.

In the postwar period, the strategic agencies of foreign policy—the State Department, the CIA, the Pentagon, and the Treasury, as well as the key ambassadorial posts—have all been dominated by representatives and rulers of America's principal corporate-financial empires. In addition, all the special committees and task forces on foreign policy guidelines have been presided over by the men of this business elite, so that on all important levels of foreign policy-making, "business serves as the fount of critical assumptions or goals and strategically placed personnel."[6]

While the corporate-based upper class in general occupies a prodigious number of positions in the highest reaches of the "democratic" state, it need not strive to occupy all the top places to impose its own interpretation of the national interest on American policy. For precisely because the prevailing ideology of U.S. politics in general, and of the federal government in particular, is corporate ideology, reflecting the corporate outlook and interests, and because, therefore, the framework of articulated policy choices lies well within the horizon of this outlook, political outsiders may be tolerated and even highly effective in serving the corporate system and its programs.

There are two principal ways (in addition to those already discussed) by which corporate ideology comes to prevail in the larger political realm. In the first place, it does so through the corporate (and upper class) control of the means of communication and the means of production of ideas and ideology (the mass media, the foundations,[7] universities, etc.). However, even this control, which is vast but not ubiquitous in ensuring the general predominance of the ideas of the dominant class, is not left to work at random. Thus, in Professor Domhoff's investigation of the American ruling class, he found that "in most instances" non-upper class political leaders "were selected, trained, and employed in [special] institutions which function to the benefit of members of the upper class and which are controlled by members of the upper class." Such leaders, Professor Domhoff concluded, "are selected for advancement in terms of the interests of members of the upper class."

The second basic way in which corporate ideology comes to prevail, particularly at the foreign policy level, is by the very fact that the dominant reality of society is corporate, and therefore political "realism" dictates for any statesman or politician that he work in its framework and accept its assumptions. If the horizon of political choice is limited to an area in which the corporate interest is not directly challenged, because it would be both imprudent and impractical (utopian) to do so, if the framework of private property in the means of production is accepted as not realistically subject to change, then the "national" interest, which is the concept under which politicians and statesmen tend to operate (particularly in foreign policy), necessarily coincides with the interests of the corporations, the repositories of the nation's wealth, the organizers of its productive power, and hence the guardians of the material basis of its strength. In a class-divided society under normal (i.e., non-revolutionary) conditions, the national interest vis-à-vis external interests inevitably is interpreted as the interest of the dominant or ruling class. Thus, in a corporate capitalist society, the corporate outlook as a matter of course becomes the dominant outlook of the state in foreign affairs.

This is not to say that there is never a conflict over foreign policy between the corporations as such and the state. Just as inevitably there are differences between the corporate interests themselves, within a general framework of interests, so there are differences between the corporate community outside the state and the corporate representatives and their agents in the state, resulting from the difference in vantage and the wider and narrower interests that each group must take into account.* But here, too, the horizon of choice, the framework of decisive interests, is defined by the necessity of preserving and strengthening the status quo order of corporate capitalism and consequently the interests of the social classes most benefited by it.

What then is the nature of corporate ideology as it dominates U.S. foreign policy, and what is its role in the development of the Cold War? As a result of the pioneering work of Professor William Appleman Williams and his students,[8] these questions can be answered precisely and succinctly. The chief function of corporate ideology is, of course, to make an ex-

*We are dealing here with the United States. In countries where a labor party assumes government office, the relationship is more complex, but for the reasons outlined above the policy results are basically the same.

plicit identification of the national tradition and interest—the American Way of Life—with its own particular interest. This identification is accomplished by means of an economic determinism which takes as its cardinal principle the proposition that political freedom is inseparably bound up with corporate property, that a "free enterprise" economy is the indispensable foundation of a free policy (where "free enterprise" is defined so as to coincide with the status quo order of corporate capitalism, not with an outdated system of independent farmers and traders).

Starting from this root premise, the ideology, as articulated by American policy-makers since the nineteenth century, maintains that an expanding "frontier" of ever new and accessible markets is absolutely essential for capitalist America's domestic prosperity,[9] and hence that the extension of the American system and its institutions abroad is a primary necessity for the preservation of the American, democratic, free-enterprise order at home. Originally formulated as an "Open Door" foreign policy to prevent the closing of the external frontier by European colonialism, and to ensure American access to and eventual domination of global markets, this policy has become in the postwar period a policy of preserving and extending American hegemony and the free enterprise system throughout the external frontier, or, as it is now called, the "free world." From Woodrow Wilson's First World War cry that the world must be made safe for democracy, it was but a logical historical step to Secretary of State Byrnes's remark at the close of the Second World War that the world must be made safe for the United States. This is the core of America's messianic crusade: that the world must be made over in the American image (read: subjected to the American corporate system) if the American Way of Life (read: the corporate economy) is to survive at home.

If expansion (and militarism) had held the key not only to American prosperity,[10] but to American security as well, the postwar period would undoubtedly have realized Secretary of State Byrnes's ambitious goal. In the last stages of the war and the first of the peace, the United States successfully penetrated the old European empires (mainly those of France, Great Britain, and the Netherlands), assumed control of Japan and its former dependencies, and extended its own power, globally, to an unprecedented degree. By 1949, the United States had liens on some 400 military bases, while the expansion of direct overseas investments was taking place at a phenomenal rate. Thus, while between 1929 and 1946 U.S. foreign investments had actually declined from $7.9 to $7.2 billion, between 1946 and 1967 they increased an incredible eight-fold to more than $60 billion. It is this global stake in the wealth and resources of the external frontier that forms the basis of the U.S. commitment to the worldwide status quo (though it may not always provide the whole explanation for particular commitments and/or engagements). It is this commitment to the internal status quo in other countries (the State Department actually runs a course for foreign service officers and ambassadors called "Overseas Internal Defense") that renders Washington's expansionist program not the key to security but the very source of Cold War conflict, with its permanent menace to mankind's survival.

For the expansion of corporate overseas investment has to an overwhelming degree not produced beneficial results, and the status quo, of which the corporations inevitably constitute a dominating part, is almost everywhere a status quo of mass human misery and incalculable suffering. In the words of one observer of the corporate scene:

> No one acquainted with the behavior of Western corporations on their pilgrimages for profit during the last fifty years can really be surprised that the . . . explosions now taking place [in the underdeveloped world] are doing so in an anti-American, anti-capitalist, anti-Western context. For many years these continents have been happy hunting grounds for corporate adventurers, who have taken out great resources and great profits and left behind great poverty, great expectations and great resentment. Gunnar Myrdal points out that capitalist intervention in underdeveloped countries thus far has almost uniformly had the result of making the rich richer and the poor poorer. . . ."[11]

This has indeed been the undeniable historical consequence of capitalist corporate expansion, although this is not what one is led to believe by the orthodox theorists and academic model builders who function so frequently as the sophisticated apologists of the American empire and the policy of counterrevolutionary intervention necessary to maintain it.

In the writings of such theorists, the expansion of America's monopolistic giants and their control of the markets and resources of the poverty-stricken regions is presented as entailing the *net* export of capital to these capital-starved areas, the transfer of industrial technologies and skills, and the flow of wealth generally from the rich world to the poor. From this point of view, revolutions in the underdeveloped world which challenge the presence and domination of foreign corporations and their states are either misguided or sinister in intent, and contrary to the real needs and interests of the countries involved. Indeed, for those who maintain this view, revolutions are regarded as alien-inspired efforts aimed at subverting and seizing control of the countries in question during the period of great difficulty and instability prior to the so-called take-off into self-sustaining growth. This is the argument advanced by W. W. Rostow, former director of the State Department's Policy Planning Staff and the chief rationalizer of America's expansionist counterrevolutionary crusade.

In fact, this view rests neither on historical experience, which shows the presence of foreign capital and power to have had a profoundly adverse effect on the development potential of the penetrated regions, nor on a sound empirical basis. Far from resulting in a transfer of wealth from richer to poorer regions, the penetration of the underdeveloped world by the imperialist and neo-imperialist systems of the developed states has had the opposite effect. As a result of direct U.S. overseas investments between 1950 and 1965, for example, there was a *net* capital flow of $16 billion *to the United States,* and this was just a part of the negative transfer. Similarly, when looked at in their political and economic settings, the much heralded benefits of the advanced technologies transplanted into these areas, but remaining under the control of international corporations, also tend to be circumscribed and even adverse in their effects. Indeed, regarded in terms of its impact on total societies, rather than on particular economic sectors, the operation of opening the backward and weak areas to the competitive penetration of the advanced and powerful capitalist states has been nothing short of a catastrophe. For as Paul Baran showed in his pioneering work, *The Political Economy of Growth,* it is precisely the penetration of the underdeveloped world by advanced capitalism that has in the past obstructed its development and continues in the present to prevent it. Conversely, it has been primarily their ability to escape from the net of foreign investment and domination that has made a chosen few of these countries, like Japan, an exception to the rule. Professor Gunder Frank and others have continued the work that Baran initiated, showing how foreign capitalist investment produces the pattern of underdevelopment (or "growth without development," as it is sometimes called) which is the permanent nightmare of these regions.

The view expounded by these writers, which is based on a thoroughgoing and concrete historical and social analysis, makes fully intelligible the fact of anti-imperialist revolution in the underdeveloped world and its inevitable conflict with the Western powers. Only this view can show revolution as the real full-blooded historical phenomenon that it is, rather than the implausibly contrived product of foreign-generated conspiratorial intrigue.* It also explains why communist and socialist revolutions have been so intimately and integrally bound up in the contemporary era with struggles for national liberation and self-determination. For the gateway to national political independence and economic development in the penetrated and dependent regions leads inevitably through the *class* revolution—i.e., the expropriation of the corporations' foreign and domestic agents who dominate the politics and economies of these countries, siphon off the national wealth, and prevent its utilization for overall national industrial development.

However, while the recent history of the Cold War can be seen to fall easily into this structural pattern of corporate expansion and national resistance, of social revolutionary upsurge and counterrevolutionary intervention, the international conflicts of the entire postwar period present a

*Perhaps the acme of absurdity in promoting the conspiracy theory was reached when President Johnson justified the intervention of 30,000 Marines in the Dominican Republic by the presence of 53 alleged Communists supposed to be behind the Dominican Revolution.

somewhat more complicated problem for analysis. For in the early postwar years, the conflict between Russia and the United States over the peace settlement in Europe dominated relations between all states to an exceptional degree. Moreover, while this conflict was certainly related to the Open Door expansion of the corporate system[12] and the rising nationalist and anti-capitalist revolutions in the underdeveloped world (from southeastern Europe to Asia), its domination by great-power politics, and by the abrupt power shifts resulting from the war, gave to it a different appearance and a character somewhat different from the conflicts of the later period.

This exception notwithstanding, the fanatical anti-Communism which took root in this period, and which has been such a central and consistent feature of America's messianic Cold War crusade, fulfills a clearly discernible and indispensible function in corporate ideology and the success of the corporate program. For as a system which is by nature expansionist (from the sheer pressure of the world market and the competitive struggle to control it) and which generates nationalist resistance and revolt that must be countered and contained, the American corporate empire is beset by a real and basically insoluble problem: How can it justify the counterrevolutionary intervention necessary to extend and to preserve itself in an American ideology of democratic pluralism and revolution self-determination? The corporate answer to this dilemma, arrived at early in American history, and in which anti-Communism now plays the central role, is to present the intervention as a program of "containment" against a third threatening imperial force or party. Thus just as the U. S. thrust into the markets of China at the turn of the century was carried out under the cover of containing European colonialism, so the takeovers in Cuba and the Philippines were presented as efforts to save those countries from the clutches of imperial Spain. The pre-Communist origins of what has become a crucial ideological gambit in U.S. foreign relations are symbolized in the fact that when Bolshevism first triumphed in Russia, and there was no external Communist power on which to blame the revolution, Lenin and Trotsky were presented as *German* agents, and U.S. counterrevolutionary intervention as an attempt to contain German imperialist expansion.[13] When the second major Communist revolution was occurring in China, it could of course be presented by the State Department as a takeover by Russia, despite the substantial evidence available to document the rift between Stalin and Mao, about which the State Department was well aware. From then on, any Communist revolution, no matter how nationalist in character or content, became in State Department White Papers the illegitimate offspring of "Communist imperialism" centered in some conveniently located Communist capital.

Historically, of course, there has never been a legitimate resistance or revolt from the point of view of the ruling power. American revolutionaries themselves were portrayed by their opponents as agents of the French. So it is as but part of this old historical pattern that U.S. counterrevolutionary intervention in defense of the social status quo in Vietnam should be officially justified by portraying the Vietnamese guerrillas in the south as mere agents of their brothers in the north, and then by insinuating that the north is a puppet of Moscow or Peking. In this way, Washington, like all previous ruling powers, seeks to present its own role as that of the would-be protector of its intended victim, and in this case also as defending self-determination and therefore acting in accord with America's traditional ideals.

The increasingly violent contradiction between the American policies of expansion and counterrevolutionary intervention and American ideals has its roots in a past that long pre-dates the Cold War, although it is undoubtedly the Cold War ascendance of U.S. power that has made the contradiction so acute. This contradiction between American program and American creed reflects an equally important conflict between the structures of American social and political life, and the American democratic framework. For in a profound sense, foreign policy is but an extension of domestic policy: the inequality of privilege and power in American society mirrors (and serves) an even more insidious global inequality. Similarly, the gathering revolt against the corporate system at home is but one of the outward ripples of the post-1917 global revolutionary upsurge against the imperialist world system that America in part inherited and in part has taken over from the old European colonial powers. It should be clear from this that neither world history nor American policy, neither the Cold War nor the U.S. role in it, can be understood without a previous understanding of the class character of American society and the nature of the corporate system that underpins and structures it.

Notes

[1]A. A. Berle, Jr., "Economic Power and the Free Society," in Andrew Hacker, ed., *The Corporation Take-Over* (New York: Doubleday, 1965), p. 97. This is a collection of papers originally prepared for the Center for the Study of Democratic Institutions, Santa Barbara.

[2]Hacker, *The Corporation Take-Over*, Introduction, pp. 10–11.

[3]Hacker, *The Corporation Take-Over*, p. 9.

[4]Berle, in Hacker, p. 91. Cf. C. Wright Mills, *The Power Elite* (New York: Oxford University Press, 1956), p. 126n: "As political organizations [the corporations] are of course totalitarian and dictatorial, although externally, they display much public relations and liberal rhetoric of defense."

[5]Paul Baran and Paul M. Sweezy, *Monopoly Capital* (New York: Monthly Review Press, 1966), p. 155.

[6]Gabriel Kolko, *The Roots of American Foreign Policy* (Boston: The Beacon Press, 1969), p. 26.

[7]See Horowitz, "Charity Begins at Home," *Ramparts*, April 1969; "The Billion Dollar Brains," *Ramparts*, May 1969; and "The Sinews of Empire," *Ramparts*, October 1969.

[8]William Appleman Williams, *The Tragedy of American Diplomacy* (New York: Delta Books, 1962); Walter LaFeber, *The New Empire, An Interpretation of American Expansion 1860-1898* (Ithaca: Cornell University Press, 1963); Lloyd C. Gardner,

Economic Aspects of New Deal Diplomacy (Madison: University of Wisconsin Press, 1964). On the immediate Cold War origins, see also Gar Alperovitz (another Williams student), *Atomic Diplomacy: Hiroshima and Potsdam* (New York: Simon & Schuster, 1965).

[9]See the essays by Professors Lloyd C. Gardner, "The New Deal, New Frontiers, and the Cold War: A Re-examination of American Expansion, 1933-1945," pp. 105-141; David W. Eakins, "Business Planners and America's Postwar Expansion," pp. 143-171; and William Appleman Williams, "The Large Corporation and American Foreign Policy," pp. 71-104 in David Horowitz, ed., *Corporations and the Cold War* (New York: Monthly Review Press, 1970).

[10]On the ultimate connection between corporate capitalist prosperity and militarism, see Rosa Luxemburg, *The Accumulation of Capital* (New York: Monthly Review Press, 1968); Joan Robinson, "Marx, Marshall and Keynes," in *Collected Economic Papers II* (New York: Oxford University Press, 1960); and Baran and Sweezy, *Monopoly Capital.* Cf. also the essays by Professor Phillips and C. Nathanson in the present volume.

[11]W. H. Ferry, "Irresponsibilities in Metrocorporate America," in Hacker, *The Corporation Take-Over.*

[12]See the essay by Professor Gardner.

[13]Cf. William Appleman Williams, "American Intervention in the Russian Revolution, 1917–1920," in *Containment and Revolution.*

chapter five

THE WAR COMES HOME

Without setting a foot on American soil the Vietnamese have brought the war home to the United States. Their resistance to U.S. domination, their will to fight, and their refusal to die silently have begun to shake America at its very roots.

For different groups of Americans, outrage against the war came at different times. For some it came in August 1964, when the U.S. began bombing the North, supposedly in retaliation for a dubious attack on an American ship in the Bay of Tonkin. For many it came because of the Administration's hypocritical moves toward a "bombing halt," "peace negotiations," and "withdrawal," while at the same time it increased the intensity and destruction of the war in the South. Still others held their faith until the invasion of Cambodia. But all along, more and more Americans began to ask, "What in the name of humanity are we doing in Vietnam?" And with the end of innocence, some Americans began to organize active resistance.

Young American protestors began with the disarmingly simple assumption that America needed only to realize her immorality and hypocrisy to correct it. The protestors of the '60s had been taught that in the U.S. there was equality and freedom for all, and that the Cold War was a crusade to bring these rights to other nations. Once, so they thought, they exposed America's Cold War crusade as a cloak for an expansionism that resulted in the *denial* of freedom rather than its preservation, the struggle would be virtually won—popular pressure would put an end to the war. With this hope, hundreds of thousands petitioned Washington, marched, campaigned, voted, even burned draft cards. Still the war escalated, and as it did so, many protestors came increasingly to the conclusion that to end the violence they would have to take on the System itself. Since voting, protest, and resistance could not change the system, they would have to overturn it altogether. And for this the Vietnamese became not merely victims deserving sympathy but revolutionary models inspiring emulation.

In November 1965 CARL OGLESBY, a leading intellectual figure in the early movement, outlined the New Left analysis of the war and U.S. foreign policy in a famous speech, "Trapped in a System," delivered to 25,000 peace marchers in Washington, D.C. Blaming "those who mouthed my liberal values and broke my American heart" for his seemingly anti-American protest, Oglesby attacked head-on the hypocrisy of American liberalism.

American economic interests, Oglesby believes, are the real motivations behind U.S. intervention against movements for social and economic justice, but since the United States itself was founded by revolution, its leaders must make their counterrevolutionary interventions appear to be progressive rather than reactionary. The ideology of anti-communism provides the necessary guise. Looking at the American empire as a part of the American economic and political structure, Oglesby maintains that we cannot expect its leaders—who are not "moral monsters" but in fact liberal politicians—to simply abandon the empire on request. These leaders are merely instruments of it and their choices are limited by its demands. Americans working to dismantle the system, Oglesby says, are dealing with a "colossus that does not want to be changed. It will not change itself. It will not cooperate with those who want to change it." The movement cannot rely on political leaders and their piecemeal bureaucratic changes. Rather, Oglesby advises, the left must work toward a mass democratic movement which, "in the name of simple human decency and democracy," calls for a radical change of the American system whose very imperialist structure necessitates wars against human freedom.

In his 1967 speech "Declaration of Independence from the War in Vietnam," MARTIN LUTHER KING, JR., martyred black leader of the civil rights movement, places himself very close to the white radical movement which Oglesby spoke for earlier. According to King, American society needs a "radical revolution of values," for as long as profits and property rights are more important than people and human rights the "giant triplets of racism, materialism, and militarism" cannot be altered. For King it was cruelly ironic that black people and poor people were fighting in Vietnam to defend liberties they do not have at home. With John F. Kennedy's warning in mind—that "those who make peaceful revolution impossible will make violent revolution inevitable"—King believed that he could not criticize the violence of the oppressed "without first speaking to the greatest purveyor of violence in the world, the U.S. government." If King did not entirely understand the nature of Third World communist movements, he nevertheless urged that the United States, instead of resisting the world revolutions against old systems of exploitation and oppression, should support the new systems of justice and equality fighting to be born and rededicate itself to the struggle for a new world.

The civil rights movement had been based on the same assumptions as the early anti-war protests—that pointing out the evils and demanding their correction would compel a response from the system. Thus, from the late '50s to the mid-'60s, blacks simply petitioned nonviolently for the equal place that America long had promised them. But as the anti-war protestors realized that imperialism was inherent to American capitalism, so many blacks came to realize that racism was part of the imperial pattern of American history, and so there grew the black revolutionary movement.

In "The Black Man's Stake in Vietnam," ELDRIDGE CLEAVER, Minister of Information for the Black Panther Party, stresses that blacks in America are colonized and terrorized just as Third World peoples are dominated abroad. Cleaver maintains that if white America is successful in repressing the liberation movements of non-whites abroad, it will then turn even more viciously on blacks struggling for freedom at home. But, he believes, the organization and unity of American blacks—into a black Trojan Horse within America—will bring their own liberation as well as that of the Third World.

Three years ago Cleaver said that "Black Americans are considered to be the world's biggest fools to go to another country to fight for something they don't have for themselves." When he wrote this, the black soldiers in Vietnam, although comprising 22 percent of the fatalities, generally supported the war, were anxious to prove themselves to white America, and were critical of black leaders who opposed the war. Yet in the end, sending black people to fight against the Vietnamese has only heightened their awareness of their oppression at home and increased their determination to organize and struggle for their freedom. According to the series of *New York Times* articles by WALLACE TERRY II, black soldiers now are bitter and enraged with fighting and dying in a war they consider to be the white man's folly. Angered at racism in the army and in the United States rather than at "communism" and the "enemy" in Vietnam, they feel that their fight is in America, against their repression there. Or, as the Panthers chant at their rallies, "The Revolution has come; time to pick up the gun."

TOM HAYDEN has followed the course of the movement, from being a civil rights activist in Mississippi, to helping establish Students for a Democratic Society, to working in the black ghetto in Newark, to being a defendant in the Chicago Conspiracy trial. In "All for Vietnam," a selection from the last chapter of his new book, Hayden argues that members of the left have failed to realize that the Vietnam war is the major "international showdown of our time" and have failed to envision the role they must play in resolving the crises that the war has created at home.

Since the 1968 Democratic Convention in Chicago, he feels, the left has lacked a coherent strategy. On one hand, the Weathermen have bravely committed their lives to physically attacking imperialism, but, doubtful of achieving popular support, they have failed to embrace the struggles of oppressed groups in the U.S., thereby alienating themselves from a potential base among the people. On the other hand, radical groups such as the Yippies and Women's Liberation have concentrated only on their particular oppression and failed to focus on the overriding issue of the war and imperialism.

Hayden calls for an Emergency Consciousness about the danger of further escalation of the war. The left must once again place Vietnam in the forefront. Although Vietnam should always be linked to racism and repression at home, he believes, "the practice of organizing *only* around one's particular oppression must be seen as self-indulgence in the face of what threatens Vietnam." The task, he says, is "an all-out siege against the war machine."

Only the power of a democratic upsurge can cripple the war machine, prevent the destruction of Vietnam, and begin to radically change American society. Liberal arguments about the impossibility of working outside the system have deceived young people about their own power. For Hayden, "that power does not reside in their electoral potential but only in their potential to disrupt the vital institutions containing them—the universities—and to threaten the stability of the country's future."

Trapped in a System

Carl Oglesby

Seven months ago at the April [1965] March on Washington, Paul Potter, then President of Students for a Democratic Society, stood in approximately this spot in Washington and said that we must name the system that creates and sustains the war in Vietnam—name it, describe it, analyze it, understand it, and change it.

Today I will try to name it—to suggest an analysis which, to be quite frank, may disturb some of you—and to suggest what changing it may require of us.

We are here again to protest again a growing war. Since it is a very bad war, we acquire the habit of thinking that it must be caused by very bad men. But we only conceal reality, I think, by denouncing on such grounds the menacing coalition of industrial and military power, or the brutality of the blitzkrieg we are waging against Vietnam, or the ominous signs around us that heresy may soon no longer be permitted. We must simply observe, and quite plainly say, that this coalition, this blitzkrieg, and this demand for acquiescence are creatures, all of them, of a government that since 1932 has considered itself to be fundamentally *liberal.*

The original commitment in Vietnam was made by President Truman, a mainstream liberal. It was seconded by President Eisenhower, a moderate liberal. It was intensified by the late President Kennedy, a flaming liberal.

Reprinted from a pamphlet published by Students for a Democratic Society.

Think of the men who now engineer that war—those who study the maps, give the commands, push the buttons, and tally the dead: Bundy, McNamara, Rusk, Lodge, Goldberg, the President himself.

They are not moral monsters.

They are all honorable men.

They are all liberals.

But so, I'm sure, are many of us who are here today in protest. To understand the war, then, it seems necessary to take a closer look at this American liberalism. Maybe we are in for some surprises. Maybe we have here two quite different liberalisms: one authentically humanist; the other not so human at all.

Not long ago, I considered myself a liberal. And if someone had asked me what I meant by that, I'd perhaps have quoted Thomas Jefferson or Thomas Paine, who first made plain our nation's unprovisional commitment to human rights. But what do you think would happen if these two heroes could sit down now for a chat with President Johnson and McGeorge Bundy?

They would surely talk of the Vietnam war. Our dead revolutionaries would soon wonder why their country was fighting against what appeared to be a revolution. The living liberals would hotly deny that it is one: there are troops coming in from outside, the rebels get arms from other countries, most of the people are not on their side, and they practice terror against their own. Therefore, *not* a revolution.

What would our dead revolutionaries answer? They might say: "What fools and bandits, sirs, you make then of us. Outside help? Do you remember Lafayette? Or the 3,000 British freighters the French navy sunk for our side? Or the arms and men we got from France and Spain? And what's this about terror? Did you never hear what we did to our own loyalists? Or about the thousands of rich American Tories who fled for their lives to Canada? And as for popular support, do you not know that we had less than one-third of our people with us? That, in fact, the colony of New York recruited more troops for the British than for the revolution? Should we give it all back?"

Revolutions do not take place in velvet boxes. They never have. It is only the poets who make them lovely. What the National Liberation Front is fighting in Vietnam is a complex and vicious war. This war is also a revolution, as honest a revolution as you can find anywhere in history. And this is a fact which all our intricate official denials will never change.

But it doesn't make any difference to our leaders anyway. Their aim in Vietnam is really much simpler than this implies. It is to safeguard what they take to be American interests around the world against revolution or revolutionary change, which they always call Communism—as if that were that. In the case of Vietnam, this interest is, first, the principle that revolution shall not be tolerated anywhere, and second, that South Vietnam shall never sell its rice to China—or even to North Vietnam.

There is simply no such thing now, for us, as a just revolution—never mind that for two-thirds of the world's people the 20th Century might as well be the Stone Age; never mind the melting poverty and hopelessness that are the basic facts of life for most modern men; and never mind that for these millions there is now an increasingly perceptible relationship between their sorrow and our contentment.

Can we understand why the Negroes of Watts rebelled? Then why do we need a devil theory to explain the rebellion of the South Vietnamese? Can we understand the oppression in Mississippi, or the anguish that our Northern ghettoes make epidemic? Then why can't we see that our proper human struggle is not with Communism or revolutionaries, but with the social desperation that drives good men to violence, both here and abroad?

To be sure, we have been most generous with our aid, and in Western Europe, a mature industrial society, that aid worked. But there are always political and financial strings. And we have never shown ourselves capable of allowing others to make those traumatic institutional changes that are often the prerequisites of progress in colonial societies. For all our official feeling for the millions who are enslaved to what we so self-righteously call the yoke of Communist tyranny, we make no real effort at all to crack through the much more vicious right-wing tyrannies that our businessmen traffic with and our nation profits from every day. And for all our cries about the international Red conspiracy to take over the world, we take only pride in the fact of our 6,000 military bases on foreign soil.

We gave Rhodesia a grave look just now—but we keep on buying her chromium, which is cheap because black slave labor mines it.

We deplore the racism of Verwoerd's fascist South Africa—but our banks make big loans to that country and our private technology makes it a nuclear power.

We are saddened and puzzled by random back-page stories of revolt in this or that Latin American state—but are convinced by a few pretty photos in the Sunday supplement that things are getting better, that the world is coming our way, that change from disorder can be orderly, that our benevolence will pacify the distressed, that our might will intimidate the angry.

Optimists, may I suggest that these are quite unlikely fantasies. They are fantasies because we have lost that mysterious social desire for human equity that from time to time has given us genuine moral drive. We have become a nation of young, bright-eyed, hard-hearted, slim-waisted, bullet-headed make-out artists. A nation—may I say it?—of beardless liberals.

You say I am being hard? Only think.

This country, with its thirty-some years of liberalism, can send 200,000 young men to Vietnam to kill and die in the most dubious of wars, but it cannot get 100 voter registrars to go into Mississippi.

What do you make of it?

The financial burden of the war obliges us to cut millions from an al-

(Photo by David Goldstein.)

ready pathetic War on Poverty budget. But in almost the same breath, Congress appropriates $140 million for the Lockheed and Boeing companies to compete with each other on the supersonic transport project—that Disneyland creation that will cost us all about $2 billion before it's done.

What do you make of it?

Many of us have been earnestly resisting for some years now the idea of putting atomic weapons into West German hands, an action that would perpetuate the division of Europe and thus the Cold War. Now just this week we find out that, with the meagerest of security systems, West Germany has had nuclear weapons in her hands for the past six years.

What do you make of it?

Some will make of it that I overdraw the matter. Many will ask: What about the other side? To be sure, there is the bitter ugliness of Czechoslovakia, Poland, those infamous Russian tanks in the streets of Budapest. But my anger only rises to hear some say that sorrow cancels sorrow, or that *this* one's shame deposits in *that* one's account the right to shamefulness.

And others will make of it that I sound mighty anti-American. To these, I say: Don't blame *me* for *that!* Blame those who mouthed my liberal values and broke my American heart.

Just who might they be, by the way? Let's take a brief factual inventory of the latter-day Cold War.

In 1953 our Central Intelligence Agency managed to overthrow Mossadegh in Iran, the complaint being his neutralism in the Cold War and his plans to nationalize the country's oil resources to improve his people's lives. Most evil aims, most evil man. In his place we put in General Zahedi, a World War II Nazi collaborator. New arrangements on Iran's oil gave 25-year leases on 40 percent of it to three U.S. firms, one of which was Gulf Oil. The CIA's leader for this coup was Kermit Roosevelt. In 1960 Kermit Roosevelt became a vice president of Gulf Oil.

In 1954, the democratically elected Arbenz of Guatemala wanted to nationalize a portion of United Fruit Company's plantations in his country, land he needed badly for a modest program of agrarian reform. His government was overthrown in a CIA-supported right-wing coup. The following year, Gen. Walter Bedell Smith, director of the CIA when the Guatemala venture was being planned, joined the board of directors of the United Fruit Company.

Comes 1960 and Castro cries we are about to invade Cuba. The Administration sneers "poppycock," and we Americans believe it. Comes 1961 and the invasion. Comes with it the awful realization that the United States Government had lied.

Comes 1962 and the missile crisis, and our Administration stands prepared to fight global atomic war on the curious principle that another state does not have the right to its own foreign policy.

Comes 1963 and British Guiana, where Cheddi Jagan wants independence from England and a labor law modeled on the Wagner Act. And Jay Lovestone, the AFL-CIO foreign policy chief, acting, as always, quite independently of labor's rank and file, arranges with our Government to finance an eleven-week dock strike that brings Jagan down, ensuring that the state will remain *British* Guiana, and that any workingman who wants a wage better than 50¢ a day is a dupe of Communism.

Comes 1964. Two weeks after Under Secretary Thomas Mann announces that we have abandoned the *Alianza's* principle of no aid to tyrants, Brazil's Goulart is overthrown by the vicious right-winger, Ademar Barros, supported by a show of American gunboats at Rio de Janeiro.

Within 24 hours, the new head of state, Mazzilli, receives a congratulatory wire from our President.

Comes 1965. The Dominican Republic. Rebellion in the streets. We scurry to the spot with 20,000 neutral Marines and our neutral peacemakers—like Ellsworth Bunker, Jr., Ambassador to the Organization of American States. Most of us know that our neutral Marines fought openly on the side of the junta, a fact that the Administration still denies. But how many also know that what was at stake was our new Caribbean Sugar Bowl? That this same neutral peace-making Bunker is a board member and stock owner of the National Sugar Refining Company, a firm his father founded in the good old days, and one which has a major interest in maintaining the status quo in the Dominican Republic? Or that the President's close personal friend and advisor, our new Supreme Court Justice Abe Fortas, has sat for the past 19 years on the board of the Sucrest Company, which imports black-strap molasses from the Dominican Republic? Or that the rhetorician of corporate liberalism and the late President Kennedy's close friend Adolf Berle, was chairman of that same board? Or that our roving ambassador Averell Harriman's brother Roland is on the board of National Sugar? Or that our former ambassador to the Dominican Republic, Joseph Farland, is a board member of the South Puerto Rico Sugar Co., which owns 275,000 acres of rich land in the Dominican Republic and is the largest employer on the island—at about one dollar a day?

Neutralists! God save the hungry people of the world from such neutralists!

We do not say these men are evil. We say, rather, that good men can be divided from their compassion by the institutional system that inherits us all. Generation in and out, we are put to use. People become instruments. Generals do not hear the screams of the bombed; sugar executives do not see the misery of the cane cutters—for to do so is to be that much *less* the general, that much *less* the executive.

The foregoing facts of recent history describe one main aspect of the estate of Western liberalism. Where is our American humanism here? What went wrong?

Let's stare our situation coldly in the face. All of us are born to the colossus of history, our American corporate system—in many ways, an awesome organism. There is one fact that describes it: With about 5 percent of the world's people, we consume about half the world's goods. We take a richness that is in good part not our own, and we put it in our pockets, our garages, our split-levels, our bellies, and our futures.

On the *face* of it, it is a crime that so few should have so much at the expense of so many. Where is the moral imagination so abused as to call this just? Perhaps many of us feel a bit uneasy in our sleep. We are not, after all, a cruel people. And perhaps we don't really need this superdominance that deforms others. But what can we do? The investments are made. The financial ties are established. The plants abroad are built. Our system *exists*. One is swept up into it. How intolerable—to be born moral, but addicted to a stolen and maybe surplus luxury. Our goodness threatens to become counterfeit before our eyes—unless we change. But change threatens us with uncertainty—at least.

Our problem, then, is to justify this system and give its theft another name—to make kind and moral what is neither, to perform some alchemy with language that will make this injustice seem to be a most magnanimous gift.

A hard problem. But the Western democracies, in the heyday of their colonial expansionism, produced a hero worthy of the task.

Its name was free enterprise, and its partner was an *illiberal liberalism* that said to the poor and the dispossessed: What we acquire of your resources we repay in civilization. The white man's burden. But this was too poetic. So a much more hard-headed theory was produced. This theory said that colonial status is in fact a *boon* to the colonized. We give them technology and bring them into modern times.

But this deceived no one but ourselves. We were delighted with this new theory. The poor saw in it merely an admission that their claims were irrefutable. They stood up to us, without gratitude. We were shocked—but also confused, for the poor seemed again to be right. How long is it going to be the case, we wondered, that the poor will be right and the rich will be wrong?

Liberalism faced a crisis. In the face of the collapse of the European empires, how could it continue to hold together our twin need for richness and righteousness? How can we continue to sack the ports of Asia and still dream of Jesus?

The challenge was met with a most ingenious solution: the ideology of anti-Communism. This was the bind: we cannot call revolution bad, because we started that way ourselves, and because it is all too easy to see why the dispossessed should rebel. So we will call revolution *Communism*. And we will reserve for ourselves the right to say what Communism means. We take note of revolution's enormities, wrenching them where necessary from their historical context and often exaggerating them, and say: Behold, Communism is a bloodbath. We take note of those reactionaries who stole the revolution, and say: Behold, Communism is a betrayal of the people. We take note of the revolution's need to consolidate itself, and say: Behold, Communism is a tyranny.

It has been all these things, and it will be these things again, and we will never be at a loss for those tales of atrocity that comfort us so in our self-righteousness. Nuns will be raped and bureaucrats will be disembowelled. Indeed, revolution is a fury. For it is a letting loose of outrages pent up sometimes over centuries. But the more brutal and longer-lasting the suppression of this energy, all the more ferocious will be its explosive release.

Far from helping Americans deal with this truth, the anti-Communist ideology merely tries to disguise it so that things may stay the way they are. Thus, it depicts our presence in other lands not as a coercion, but a protection. It allows us even to say that the napalm in Vietnam is only another aspect of our humanitarian love—like those exorcisms in the Middle Ages that so often killed the patient. So we say to the Vietnamese peasant, the Cuban intellectual, the Peruvian worker: "You are better dead than Red. If it hurts or if you don't understand why—sorry about that."

This is the action of *corporate liberalism.* It performs for the corporate state a function quite like what the Church once performed for the feudal state. It seeks to justify its burdens and protect it from change. As the Church exaggerated this office in the Inquisition, so with liberalism in the [Joseph] McCarthy time—which, if it was a reactionary phenomenon, was still made possible by our anti-Communist corporate liberalism.

Let me then speak directly to humanist liberals. If my facts are wrong, I will soon be corrected. But if they are right, then you may face a crisis of conscience. Corporatism or humanism: which? For it has come to that. Will you let your dreams be used? Will you be a grudging apologist for the corporate state? Or will you help try to change it—not in the name of this or that blueprint or "ism," but in the name of simple human decency and democracy and the vision that wise and brave men saw in the time of our own Revolution?

And if your commitment to human value is unconditional, then disabuse yourselves of the notion that statements will bring change, if only the right statements can be written, or that interviews with the mighty will bring change if only the mighty can be reached, or that marches will bring change if only we can make them massive enough, or that policy proposals will bring change if only we can make them responsible enough.

We are dealing now with a colossus that does not want to be changed. It will not change itself. It will not cooperate with those who want to change it. Those allies of ours in the Government—are they really our allies? If they *are,* then they don't need advice, they need *constituencies;* they don't need study groups, they need a *movement.* And if they are *not,* then all the more reason for building that movement with a most relentless conviction.

There are people in this country today who are trying to build that movement, who aim at nothing less than a humanist reformation. And the humanist liberals must understand that it is this movement with which their own best hopes are most in tune. We radicals know the same history that you liberals know, and we can understand your occasional cynicism, exasperation, and even distrust. But we ask you to put these aside and help us risk a leap. Help us find enough time for the enormous work that needs doing here. Help us build. Help us shake the future in the name of plain human hope.

Declaration of Independence from the War in Vietnam

Martin Luther King, Jr.

Over the past two years, as I have moved to break the betrayal of my own silences and to speak from the burnings of my own heart, as I have called for radical departures from the destruction of Vietnam, many persons have questioned me about the wisdom of my path. At the heart of their concerns this query has often loomed large and loud: Why are *you* speaking about the war, Dr. King? Why are *you* joining the voices of dissent? Peace and civil rights don't mix, they say. Aren't you hurting the cause of your people, they ask. And when I hear them, though I often understand the source of their concern, I am nevertheless greatly saddened, for such questions mean that the inquirers have not really known me, my commitment or my calling. Indeed, their questions suggest that they do not know the world in which they live.

In the light of such tragic misunderstanding, I deem it of signal importance to try to state clearly why I believe that the path from Dexter Avenue Baptist Church—the church in Montgomery, Alabama, where I began my pastorage—leads clearly to this sanctuary tonight.

I come to this platform to make a passionate plea to my beloved nation. This speech is not addressed to Hanoi or to the National Liberation Front. It is not addressed to China or to Russia.

Nor is it an attempt to overlook the ambiguity of the total situation and the need for a collective solution to the tragedy of Vietnam. Neither is it an attempt to make North Vietnam or the National Liberation Front paragons of virtue, nor to overlook the role they can play in a successful resolution of the problem. While they both may have justifiable reasons to be suspicious of the good faith of the United States, life and history give eloquent testimony to the fact that conflicts are never resolved without trustful give and take on both sides.

Tonight, however, I wish not to speak with Hanoi and the NLF, but rather to my fellow Americans who, with me, bear the greatest responsibility in ending a conflict that has exacted a heavy price on both continents.

Since I am a preacher by trade, I suppose it is not surprising that I have seven major reasons for bringing Vietnam into the field of my moral vision. There is at the outset a very obvious and almost facile connection between the war in Vietnam and the struggle I, and others, have been waging in America. A few years ago there was a shining moment in that struggle. It seemed as if there was a real promise of hope for the poor—both black and white—through the Poverty Program. Then came the build-up in Vietnam, and I watched the program broken and eviscerated as if it were some idle political plaything of a society gone mad on war, and I knew that America would never invest the necessary funds or energies in rehabilitation of its poor so long as Vietnam continued to draw men and skills and money like some demonic, destructive suction tube. So I was increasingly compelled to see the war as an enemy of the poor and to attack it as such.

Perhaps the more tragic recognition of reality took place when it became clear to me that the war was doing far more than devastating the hopes of the poor at home. It was sending their sons and their brothers and their husbands to fight and to die in extraordinarily high proportions relative to the rest of the population. We were taking the young black men who had been crippled by our society and sending them 8000 miles away to guarantee liberties in Southeast Asia which they had not found in Southwest

Martin Luther King, University of California, Berkeley, May 1967. *(Photo by Gerhard E. Gscheidle, Photophile, S.F.)*

Georgia and East Harlem. So we have been repeatedly faced with the cruel irony of watching Negro and white boys on TV screens as they kill and die together for a nation that has been unable to seat them together in the same schools. So we watch them in brutal solidarity burning the huts of a poor village, but we realize that they would never live on the same block in Detroit. I could not be silent in the face of such cruel manipulation of the poor.

My third reason grows out of my experience in the ghettos of the North over the last three years—especially the last three summers. As I have walked among the desperate, rejected and angry young men, I have told them that Molotov cocktails and rifles would not solve their problems. I have tried to offer them my deepest compassion while maintaining my conviction that social change comes most meaningfully through non-violent action. But, they asked, what about Vietnam? They asked if our own nation wasn't using massive doses of violence to solve its problems, to bring about the changes it wanted. Their questions hit home, and I knew that I could never again raise my voice against the violence of the oppressed in the ghettos without having first spoken clearly to the greatest purveyor of violence in the world today—my own government.

For those who ask the question, "Aren't you a Civil Rights leader?" and thereby mean to exclude me from the movement for peace, I have this further answer. In 1957 when a group of us formed the Southern Christian Leadership Conference, we chose as our motto: "To save the soul of America." We were convinced that we could not limit our vision to certain rights for black people, but instead affirmed the conviction that America would never be free or saved from itself unless the descendants of its slaves were loosed from the shackles they still wear.

Now, it should be incandescently clear that no one who has any concern for the integrity and life of America today can ignore the present war. If America's soul becomes totally poisoned, part of the autopsy must read "Vietnam." It can never be saved so long as it destroys the deepest hopes of men the world over.

As if the weight of such a commitment to the life and health of America were not enough, another burden of responsibility was placed upon me in 1964; and I cannot forget that the Nobel Prize for Peace was also a commission—a commission to work harder than I had ever worked before for the "brotherhood of man." This is a calling that takes me beyond national allegiances, but even if it were not present I would yet have to live with the meaning of my commitment to the ministry of Jesus Christ. To me the relationship of this ministry to the making of peace is so obvious that I sometimes marvel at those who ask me why I am speaking against the war. Could it be that they do not know that the good news was meant for all men—for communist and capitalist, for their children and ours, for black and white, for revolutionary and conservative? Have they forgotten that my ministry is in obedience to the One who loved His enemies so fully that He died for them? What then can I say to the Viet Cong or to Castro or to Mao as a faithful minister of this One? Can I threaten them with death, or must I not share with them my life?

And as I ponder the madness of Vietnam, my mind goes constantly to the people of that peninsula. I speak now not of the soldiers of each side, not of the junta in Saigon, but simply of the people who have been living under the curse of war for almost three continuous decades. I think of them, too, because it is clear to me that there will be no meaningful solution there until some attempt is made to know them and their broken cries.

They must see Americans as strange liberators. The Vietnamese proclaimed their own independence in 1945 after a combined French and Japanese occupation and before the communist revolution in China. Even though they quoted the American Declaration of Independence in their own document of freedom, we refused to recognize them. Instead, we decided to support France in its re-conquest of her former colony.

Our government felt then that the Vietnamese people were not "ready" for independence, and we again fell victim to the deadly Western arrogance that has poisoned the international atmosphere for so long. With that tragic decision, we rejected a revolutionary government seeking self-determination, and a government that had been established not by China (for whom the Vietnamese have no great love) but by clearly indigenous forces that included some communists. For the peasants, this new government meant real land reform, one of the most important needs in their lives.

For nine years following 1945 we denied the people of Vietnam the right of independence. For nine years we vigorously supported the French in their abortive effort to re-colonize Vietnam.

Before the end of the war we were meeting 80 per cent of the French war costs. Even before the French were defeated at Dien Bien Phu, they began to despair of their reckless action, but we did not. We encouraged them with our huge financial and military supplies to continue the war even after they had lost the will to do so.

After the French were defeated it looked as if independence and land reform would come again through the Geneva agreements. But instead there came the United States, determined that Ho should not unify the temporarily divided nation, and the peasants watched again as we supported one of the most vicious modern dictators—our chosen man, Premier Diem. The peasants watched and cringed as Diem ruthlessly routed out all opposition, supported their extortionist landlords and refused even to discuss reunification with the North. The peasants watched as all this was presided over by U.S. influence and then by increasing numbers of U.S. troops who came to help quell the insurgency that Diem's methods had aroused. When Diem was overthrown they may have been happy, but the long line of military dictatorships seemed to offer no real change—especially in terms of their need for land and peace.

The only change came from America as we increased our troop commitments in support of governments which were singularly corrupt, inept and without popular support. All the while, the people read our leaflets and received regular promises of peace and democracy—and land reform. Now they languish under our bombs and consider us—not their fellow Vietnamese—the real enemy. They move sadly and apathetically as we herd them off the land of their fathers into concentration camps where minimal social needs are rarely met. They know they must move or be destroyed by our bombs. So they go.

They watch as we poison their water, as we kill a million acres of their crops. They must weep as the bulldozers destroy their precious trees. They wander into the hospitals, with at least 20 casualties from American firepower for each Viet Cong-inflicted injury. So far we may have killed a million of them—mostly children.

What do the peasants think as we ally ourselves with the landlords and as we refuse to put any action into our many words concerning land reform? What do they think as we test out our latest weapons on them, just as the Germans tested out new medicine and new tortures in the concentration camps of Europe?* Where are the roots of the independent Vietnam we claim to be building?

Now there is little left to build on—save bitterness. Soon the only solid physical foundations remaining will be found at our military bases and in the concrete of the concentration camps we call "fortified hamlets." The peasants may well wonder if we plan to build our new Vietnam on such grounds as these. Could we blame them for such thoughts? We must speak for them and raise the questions they cannot raise. These too are our brothers.

Perhaps the more difficult but no less necessary task is to speak for those who have been designated as our enemies. What of the NLF—that strangely anonymous group we call VC or communists? What must they think of us in America when they realize that we permitted the repression and cruelty of Diem which helped to bring them into being as a resistance group in the South? How can they believe in our integrity when now we speak of "aggression from the North" as if there were nothing more essential to the war? How can they trust us when now we charge *them* with violence after the murderous reign of Diem, and charge *them* with violence while we pour new weapons of death into their land?

How do they judge us when our officials know that their membership is

*The press and some critics have quoted this sentence out of context. I had no intention of equating the U.S. and Nazi Germany. Indeed, recognition of American democratic traditions and the absence of them in Nazi Germany, makes it all the more disturbing if even some elements of similarity of conduct appear.

less than 25 per cent communist and yet insist on giving them the blanket name? What must they be thinking when they know that we are aware of their control of major sections of Vietnam and yet we appear ready to allow national elections in which this highly organized political parallel government will have no part? They ask how we can speak of free elections when the Saigon press is censored and controlled by the military junta. And they are surely right to wonder what kind of new government we plan to help form without them—the only party in real touch with the peasants. They question our political goals and they deny the reality of a peace settlement from which they will be excluded. Their questions are frighteningly relevant.

Here is the true meaning and value of compassion and non-violence—when it helps us to see the enemy's point of view, to hear his questions, to know his assessment of ourselves. For from his view we may indeed see the basic weaknesses of our own condition, and if we are mature, we may learn and grow and profit from the wisdom of the brothers who are called the opposition.

So, too, with Hanoi. In the North, where our bombs now pummel the land, and our mines endanger the waterways, we are met by a deep but understandable mistrust. In Hanoi are the men who led the nation to independence against the Japanese and the French, the men who sought membership in the French commonwealth and were betrayed by the weakness of Paris and the willfulness of the colonial armies. It was they who led a second struggle against French domination at tremendous costs, and then were persuaded at Geneva to give up, as a temporary measure, the land they controlled between the 13th and 17th parallels. After 1954 they watched us conspire with Diem to prevent elections which would have surely brought Ho Chi Minh to power over a united Vietnam, and they realized they had been betrayed again.

When we ask why they do not leap to negotiate, these things must be remembered. Also, it must be clear that the leaders of Hanoi considered the presence of American troops in support of the Diem regime to have been the initial military breach of the Geneva Agreements concerning foreign troops, and they remind us that they did not begin to send in any large number of supplies or men until American forces had moved into the tens of thousands.

Hanoi remembers how our leaders refused to tell us the truth about the earlier North Vietnamese overtures for peace, how the President claimed that none existed when they had clearly been made. Ho Chi Minh has watched as America has spoken of peace and built up its forces, and now he has surely heard the increasing international rumors of American plans for an invasion of the North. Perhaps only his sense of humor and irony can save him when he hears the most powerful nation of the world speaking of aggression as it drops thousands of bombs on a poor, weak nation more than 8000 miles from its shores.

At this point, I should make it clear that while I have tried here to give a voice to the voiceless of Vietnam and to understand the arguments of those who are called enemy, I am as deeply concerned about our own troops there as anything else. For it occurs to me that what we are submitting them to in Vietnam is not simply the brutalizing process that goes on in any war where armies face each other and seek to destroy. We are adding cynicism to the process of death, for our troops must know after a short period there that none of the things we claim to be fighting for are really involved. Before long they must know that their government has sent them into a struggle among Vietnamese, and the more sophisticated surely realize that we are on the side of the wealthy and the secure while we create a hell for the poor.

Somehow this madness must cease. I speak as a child of God and brother to the suffering poor of Vietnam and the poor of America who are paying the double price of smashed hopes at home and death and corruption in Vietnam. I speak as a citizen of the world, for the world as it stands aghast at the path we have taken. I speak as an American to the leaders of my own nation. The great initiative in this war is ours. The initiative to stop must be ours.

This is the message of the great Buddhist leaders of Vietnam. Recently, one of them wrote these words: "Each day the war goes on the hatred increases in the hearts of the Vietnamese and in the hearts of those of humanitarian instinct. The Americans are forcing even their friends into becoming their enemies. It is curious that the Americans, who calculate so carefully on the possibilities of military victory, do not realize that in the process they are incurring deep psychological and political defeat. The image of America will never again be the image of revolution, freedom and democracy, but the image of violence and militarism."

If we continue, there will be no doubt in my mind and in the mind of the world that we have no honorable intentions in Vietnam. It will become clear that our minimal expectation is to occupy it as an American colony, and men will not refrain from thinking that our maximum hope is to goad China into a war so that we may bomb her nuclear installations.

The world now demands a maturity of America that we may not be able to achieve. It demands that we admit that we have been wrong from the beginning of our adventure in Vietnam, that we have been detrimental to the life of her people.

In order to atone for our sins and errors in Vietnam, we should take the initiative in bringing the war to a halt. I would like to suggest five concrete things that our government should do immediately to begin the long and difficult process of extricating ourselves from this nightmare:

1. End all bombing in North and South Vietnam.
2. Declare a unilateral cease-fire in the hope that such action will create the atmosphere for negotiation.

3. Take immediate steps to prevent other battlegrounds in Southeast Asia by curtailing our military build-up in Thailand and our interference in Laos.
4. Realistically accept the fact that the National Liberation Front has substantial support in South Vietnam and must thereby play a role in any meaningful negotiations and in any future Vietnam government.
5. Set a date on which we will remove all foreign troops from Vietnam in accordance with the 1954 Geneva Agreement.

Part of our ongoing commitment might well express itself in an offer to grant asylum to any Vietnamese who fears for his life under a new regime which included the NLF. Then we must make what reparations we can for the damage we have done. We must provide the medical aid that is badly needed, in this country if necessary.

Meanwhile, we in the churches and synagogues have a continuing task while we urge our government to disengage itself from a disgraceful commitment. We must be prepared to match actions with words by seeking out every creative means of protest possible.

As we counsel young men concerning military service we must clarify for them our nation's role in Vietnam and challenge them with the alternative of conscientious objection. I am pleased to say that this is the path now being chosen by more than 70 students at my own Alma Mater, Morehouse College, and I recommend it to all who find the American course in Vietnam a dishonorable and unjust one. Moreover, I would encourage all ministers of draft age to give up their ministerial exemptions and seek status as conscientious objectors. Every man of humane convictions must decide on the protest that best suits his convictions, but we must *all* protest.

There is something seductively tempting about stopping there and sending us all off on what in some circles has become a popular crusade against the war in Vietnam. I say we must enter that struggle, but I wish to go on now to say something even more disturbing. The war in Vietnam is but a symptom of a far deeper malady within the American spirit, and if we ignore this sobering reality we will find ourselves organizing clergy- and laymen-concerned committees for the next generation. We will be marching and attending rallies without end unless there is a significant and profound change in American life and policy.

In 1957 a sensitive American official overseas said that it seemed to him that our nation was on the wrong side of a world revolution. During the past ten years we have seen emerge a pattern of suppression which now has justified the presence of U.S. military "advisors" in Venezuela. The need to maintain social stability for our investments accounts for the counterrevolutionary action of American forces in Guatemala. It tells why American helicopters are being used against guerrillas in Colombia and why American napalm and green beret forces have already been active against rebels in Peru. With such activity in mind, the words of John F. Kennedy come back to haunt us. Five years ago he said, "Those who make peaceful revolution impossible will make violent revolution inevitable."

Increasingly, by choice or by accident, this is the role our nation has taken—by refusing to give up the privileges and the pleasures that come from the immense profits of overseas investment.

I am convinced that if we are to get on the right side of the world revolution, we as a nation must undergo a radical revolution of values. When machines and computers, profit and property rights are considered more important than people, the giant triplets of racism, materialism, and militarism are incapable of being conquered.

A true revolution of values will soon cause us to question the fairness and justice of many of our past and present policies. True compassion is more than flinging a coin to a beggar; it is not haphazard and superficial. It comes to see that an edifice which produces beggars needs re-structuring. A true revolution of values will soon look uneasily on the glaring contrast of poverty and wealth. With righteous indignation, it will look across the seas and see individual capitalists of the West investing huge sums of money in Asia, Africa and South America, only to take the profits out with no concern for the social betterment of the countries, and say: "This is not just." It will look at our alliance with the landed gentry of Latin America and say: "This is not just." The Western arrogance of feeling that it has everything to teach others and nothing to learn from them is not just. A true revolution of values will lay hands on the world order and say of war: "This way of settling differences is not just." This business of burning human beings with napalm, of filling our nation's homes with orphans and widows, of injecting poisonous drugs of hate into the veins of peoples normally humane, of sending men home from dark and bloody battlefields physically handicapped and psychologically deranged, cannot be reconciled with wisdom, justice, and love. A nation that continues year after year to spend more money on military defense than on programs of social uplift is approaching spiritual death.

America, the richest and most powerful nation in the world, can well lead the way in this revolution of values. There is nothing, except a tragic death wish, to prevent us from re-ordering our priorities, so that the pursuit of peace will take precedence over the pursuit of war. There is nothing to keep us from molding a recalcitrant status quo until we have fashioned it into a brotherhood.

This kind of positive revolution of values is our best defense against communism. War is not the answer. Communism will never be defeated by the use of atomic bombs or nuclear weapons. Let us not join those who shout war and through their misguided passions urge the United States to relinquish its participation in the United Nations. These are days which demand wise restraint and calm reasonableness. We must not call everyone a communist or an appeaser who advocates the seating of Red China in the United Nations and who recognizes that hate and hysteria are not the final answers to the problems of these turbulent days. We must not engage in a negative anti-communism, but rather in a positive thrust for democracy, realizing that our greatest defense against communism is to take offensive action in behalf of justice. We must with positive action seek to remove those conditions of poverty, insecurity and injustice which are the fertile soil in which the seed of communism grows and develops.

These are revolutionary times. All over the globe men are revolting against old systems of exploitation and oppression, and out of the wombs of a frail world, new systems of justice and equality are being born. The shirtless and barefoot people of the land are rising up as never before. "The people who sat in darkness have seen a great light." We in the West must support these revolutions. It is a sad fact that, because of comfort, complacency, a morbid fear of communism, and our proneness to adjust to injustice, the Western nations that initiated so much of the revolutionary spirit of the modern world have now become the arch anti-revolutionaries. This has driven many to feel that only Marxism has the revolutionary spirit. Therefore, communism is a judgment against our failure to make democracy real and follow through on the revolutions that we initiated. Our only hope today lies in our ability to recapture the revolutionary spirit and go out into a sometimes hostile world declaring eternal hostility to poverty, racism, and militarism.

We must move past indecision to action. We must find new ways to speak for peace in Vietnam and justice throughout the developing world—a world that borders on our doors. If we do not act we shall surely be dragged down the long, dark and shameful corridors of time reserved for those who possess power without compassion, might without morality, and strength without sight.

Now let us begin. Now let us re-dedicate ourselves to the long and bitter—but beautiful—struggle for a new world. This is the calling of the sons of God, and our brothers wait eagerly for our response. Shall we say the odds are too great? Shall we tell them the struggle is too hard? Will our message be that the forces of American life militate against their arrival as full men, and we send our deepest regrets? Or will there be another message, of longing, of hope, of solidarity with their yearnings, of commitment to their cause, whatever the cost? The choice is ours, and though we might prefer it otherwise we *must* choose in this crucial moment of human history.

The above address was given by Dr. Martin Luther King, Jr., at the Riverside Church, New York City, April 4, 1967, sponsored by Clergy and Laymen Concerned about Vietnam. It has been slightly condensed.

The Black Man's Stake in Vietnam

Eldridge Cleaver

The most critical tests facing Johnson are the war in Vietnam and the Negro revolution at home. The fact that the brains in the Pentagon see fit to send 16 per cent black troops to Vietnam is one indication that there is a structural relationship between these two arenas of conflict. And the initial outrageous refusal of the Georgia Legislature to seat representative-elect Julian Bond, because he denounced the aggressive U.S. role in Vietnam, shows, too, the very intimate relationship between the way human beings are being treated in Vietnam and the treatment they are receiving here in the United States.

We live today in a system that is in the last stages of the protracted process of breaking up on a worldwide basis. The rulers of this system have their hands full. Injustice is being challenged at every turn and on every level. The rulers perceive the greatest threat to be the national liberation movements around the world, particularly in Asia, Africa, and Latin America. In order for them to wage wars of suppression against these national liberation movements abroad, they must have peace and stability and unanimity of purpose at home. But at home there is a Trojan Horse, a Black Trojan Horse that has become aware of itself and is now struggling to get on its feet. It, too, demands liberation.

What is the purpose of the attention that the rulers are now focusing on the Trojan Horse? Is it out of a newfound love for the horse, or is it because the rulers need the horse to be quiet, to be still, and not cause the rulers, already with their backs pressed to the wall, any trouble or embarrassment while they force the war in Vietnam? Indeed, the rulers have need of the horse's power on the fields of battle. What the black man in America must keep constantly in mind is that the doctrine of white supremacy, which is a part of the ideology of the world system the power structure is trying to preserve, lets the black man in for the greatest portion of the suffering and hate which white supremacy has dished out to the non-white people of the world for hundreds of years. The white-supremacy-oriented white man feels less compunction about massacring "niggers" than he does about massacring any other race of people on earth. This historically indisputable fact, taken with the present persistent efforts of the United States to woo the Soviet Union into an alliance agains China, spells *DANGER* to all the peoples of the world who have been victims of white supremacy. If this sweethearting proves successful, if the United States is finally able to make a match with Russia, or if the U.S. can continue to frighten the Soviet Union into reneging on its commitments to international socialist solidarity (about which the Soviets are always trumpeting, while still allowing the imperialist aggressors to daily bomb the Democratic Republic of North Vietnam), and if the U.S. is able to unleash its anxious fury and armed might against the rising non-white giant of China, which is the real target of U.S. policy in Vietnam and the Object-Evil of U.S. strategy the world over—if the U.S. is successful in these areas, then it will be the black man's turn again to face the lyncher and burner of the world: and face him alone.

Black Americans are too easily deceived by a few smiles and friendly gestures, by the passing of a few liberal-sounding laws which are left on the books to rot unenforced, and by the mushy speechmaking of a President who is a past master of talking out of the thousand sides of his mouth. Such poetry does not *guarantee* the safe future of the black people in America. The black people must have a guarantee, they must be *certain,* they must be sure beyond all doubt that the reign of terror is ended and not just suspended, and that the future of their people is secure. And the only way they can ensure this is to gain organizational unity and communication with their brothers and allies around the world, on an international basis. They must have this power. There is no other way. Anything else is a sellout of the future of their people. The world of today was fashioned yesterday. What is involved here, what is being decided right now, is the shape of power in the world tomorrow.

Eldridge Cleaver and Bobby Seale speaking to Black Panther rally, Oakland, Calif., January 1968. *(Photo by Gerhard E. Gscheidle, Photophile, S.F.)*

The American racial problem can no longer be spoken of or solved in isolation. The relationship between the genocide in Vietnam and the smiles of the white man toward black Americans is a direct relationship. Once the white man solves his problem in the East he will then turn his fury again on the black people of America, his longtime punching bag. The black people have been tricked again and again, sold out at every turn by *mis*-leaders. After the Civil War, America went through a period similar to the one we are now in. The Negro problem received a full hearing. Everybody knew that the black man had been denied justice. No one doubted that it was time for changes and that the black man should be made a first-class citizen. But Reconstruction ended. Blacks who had been elevated to high positions were brusquely kicked out into the streets and herded along with the masses of blacks into the ghettos and black belts. The lyncher and the burner received virtual license to murder blacks at will. White Americans found a new level on which to cool the blacks out. And with the help of such tools as Booker T. Washington, the doctrine of segregation was clamped firmly onto the backs of the blacks. It has taken a hundred years to struggle up from that level of cool-out to the miserable position that black Americans now find themselves in. Time is passing. The historical opportunity which world events now present to black Americans is running out with every tick of the clock.

This is the last act of the show. We are living in a time when the people of the world are making their final bid for full and complete freedom. Never before in history has this condition prevailed. Always before there have been more or less articulate and aware pockets of people, portions of classes, etc., but today's is an era of mass awareness, when the smallest man on the street is in rebellion against the system which has denied him life and which he has come to understand robs him of his dignity and self-respect. Yet he is being told that it will take time to get programs started, to pass legislation, to educate white people into accepting the idea that black people want and deserve freedom. But it is physically impossible to move as fast as the black man would like to move. Black men are deadly serious when they say *FREEDOM NOW*. Even if the white man wanted to eradicate all traces of evil overnight, he would not be able to do it because the economic and political system will not permit it. All talk about going too fast is treasonous to the black man's future.

What the white man must be brought to understand is that the black man in America today is fully aware of his position, and he does not intend to be tricked again into another hundred-year forfeit of freedom. Not for a single moment or for any price will the black men now rising up in America settle for anything less than their full proportionate share and participation in the sovereignty of America. The black man has already come to a realization that to be free it is necessary for him to throw his life —everything—on the line, because the oppressors refuse to understand that it is now impossible for them to come up with another trick to squelch

(Photo by Gerhard E. Gscheidle, Photophile, S.F.)

the black revolution. The black man can't afford to take a chance. He can't afford to put things off. He must stop the whole show *NOW* and get his business straight, because if he does not do it now, if he fails to grasp securely the reins of this historic opportunity, there may be no tomorrow for him.

The black man's interest lies in seeing a free and independent Vietnam, a strong Vietnam which is not the puppet of international white supremacy. If the nations of Asia, Latin America, and Africa are strong and free, the black man in America will be safe and secure and free to live in dignity and self-respect. It is a cold fact that while the nations of Africa, Asia, and Latin America were shackled in colonial bondage, the black American was held tightly in the vise of oppression and not permitted to utter a sound of protest of any effect. But when these nations started bidding for their freedom, it was then that black Americans were able to seize the chance; it was then that the white man yielded what little he did—out of sheer necessity. The only lasting salvation for the black American is to do all he can to see to it that the African, Asian, and Latin American nations are free and independent.

In this regard, black Americans have a big role to play. They are a Black Trojan Horse within white America and they number in excess of 23,000,000 strong. That is a lot of strength. But it is a lot of weakness if it is disorganized and at odds with itself. Right now it is deplorably disorganized, and the overriding need is for unity and organization. Unity is on all black lips. Today we stand on the verge of sweeping change in this wretched landscape of a thousand little fragmented and ineffectual groups and organizations unable to work together for the common cause. *The need for one organization that will give one voice to the black man's common interest* is felt in every bone and fiber of black America.

Yesterday, after firmly repudiating racism and breaking his ties with the Black Muslim organization, the late Malcolm X launched a campaign to transform the American black man's struggle from the narrow plea for "civil rights" to the universal demand for human rights, with the ultimate aim of bringing the United States government to task before the United Nations. This, and the idea of the Organization of Afro-American Unity, was Malcolm's dying legacy to his people. It did not fall on barren ground. Already, black American leaders have met with the ambassadors of black Africa at a luncheon at UN headquarters. The meaning of this momentous event is lost on no one. The fact that it was the issue of Julian Bond, his denunciation of U.S. aggression in Vietnam, and the action of racist elements in the Georgia legislature which brought the leaders of black Africa and black America together is prophetic of an even clearer recognition by black men that their interests are also threatened by the U.S. war of suppression in Vietnam. This dovetailing of causes and issues is destined to bring to fruition the other dream which Malcolm's assassination prevented him from realizing—the Organization of Afro-American Unity, or perhaps a similar organization under a different name. Black Americans now realize that they must organize for the power to change the foreign and domestic policies of the U.S. government. They must let their voice be heard on these issues. They must let the world know where they stand.

It is no accident that the U.S. government is sending all those black troops to Vietnam. Some people think that America's point in sending 16 per cent black troops to Vietnam is to kill off the cream of black youth. But it has another important result. By turning her black troops into butchers of the Vietnamese people, America is spreading hate against the black race throughout Asia. Even black Africans find it hard not to hate black Americans for being so stupid as to allow themselves to be used to slaughter another people who are fighting to be free. Black Americans are considered to be the world's biggest fools to go to another country to fight for something they don't have for themselves.

It bothers white racists that people around the world love black Americans but find it impossible to give a similar warm affection to white Americans. The white racist knows that he is the Ugly American and he wants the black American to be Ugly, too, in the eyes of the world: misery loves company! When the people around the world cry "Yankee, Go Home!" they mean the white man, not the black man who is a recently freed slave. The white man is deliberately trying to make the people of the world turn against black Americans, because he knows that the day is coming when black Americans will need the help and support of their brothers, friends, and natural allies around the world. If through stupidity or by following hand-picked leaders who are the servile agents of the power structure, black Americans allow this strategy to succeed against them, then when the time comes and they need this help and support from around the world, it will not be there. All of the international love, respect, and goodwill that black Americans now have around the world will have dried up. They themselves will have buried it in the mud of the rice paddies of Vietnam.

Eldridge Cleaver, Minister of Information for the Black Panther Party, is the author of Soul on Ice.

The Angry Blacks in the Army

Wallace Terry II

Angry Blacks in the Vietnam War

Cambridge, Mass.

Racial harmony between black and white American troops in Vietnam has disintegrated to the most dangerous level of the war.

The result has been numerous racial incidents—even killings—and clear signs that black militancy and attitudes of separatism and black power thrive in Southeast Asia.

The first scientific survey to be made public of black and white troops in war discloses attitudes that are not only frightening but which could add significantly to the racial problem in the United States.

For example:

• Black soldiers are fed up with fighting and dying in a war they consider to be white man's folly.

• Their anger is not directed toward Communism in Vietnam, but toward racism in America.

• They feel that they have no business fighting in southeast Asia—that their fight is in the United States, against repression and racism.

• A frightening number—schooled in the violent art of guerrilla warfare—say they would join riots and take up arms, if necessary, to get the rights and opportunities they have been deprived of at home.

• The spirit of black militancy has enveloped the GI on the battleground as much as it has the student on the college campus and many black soldiers say they will join the ranks of radical groups like the Black Panthers or Students for a Democratic Society when they return home.

This is in direct contrast to the black American fighting man of 1967 and 1968 who was anxious to prove himself in the most integrated war in U.S. history—and did so by accounting for up to 22 per cent of U.S. combat fatalities while back home newspapers, magazines, and television networks were heralding the spirit of brotherhood between blacks and whites in the foxholes.

Moreover, the black soldier of 1967 would roundly criticize Martin Luther King, Jr., and Cassius Clay for publicly objecting to the war. But today, King, Clay, and other outspoken critics of the war such as Eldridge Cleaver and Julian Bond stand highest in the black soldier's esteem.

"The immediate cause of racial problems in Vietnam is black people themselves," said Navy Lieutenant Owen Heggs, a black attorney from

Washington, D.C. "White people haven't changed. The same people in the military today were in the military in 1930, 1940, and so on. What has changed is the black population. As the military represents in microcosm the society we live in, black people in the lower ranks represent the young black movement in our country.

"Today there is a different breed of young blacks, not satisfied being in the Marine Corps with their hair cut short. Either they say, 'Hell no, we won't go,' or 'Yeah, I got to go and I'm here, but I'm not going to take any pushing around.' "

In six months I personally interviewed 833 black and white men of all ranks and branches of service along the Vietnam landscape, asking each to answer 109 questions. The results of that survey, many of which are included here, were recently computed with the assistance of members of the Harvard and Boston university faculties.

Following is an example of some of the findings of Wallace Terry's survey of the racial attitudes of servicemen in Vietnam. They are based on interviews with 833 servicemen, enlisted and officers, black and white.

Should America continue to fight in Vietnam?

	Black Enlisted	*White Enlisted*	*Black Officers*	*White Officers*
Yes. Because communism will spread if we do not stop it here	32.1%	54.1%	41.7%	49.4%
Yes. To help South Vietnam build a democracy	13.5	21.0	14.3	30.6
No. This is a civil war in which America has no business	25.8	11.6	21.7	7.1
No. This is an Asian problem which should be settled by Asians	17.6	7.2	15.4	8.2
Don't know	11.0	6.1	6.9	4.7

Should black people fight in Vietnam?

	Black Enlisted	*Black Officers*	*Black Combat Troops*	*Black Support Troops*
No. They have problems back home	63.8%	25.1%	67.1%	68.3%
Yes. The same as white people	21.9	62.3	17.8	16.3
Yes. As many as can should so that we can prove ourselves	7.7	8.0	8.9	8.7
Not sure	6.6	4.6	6.2	6.7

A large majority of the black enlisted men agreed that black people shout not fight in Vietnam because they have problems of discrimination to deal with at home—a striking contrast with the typical attitude of the black soldiers I talked with in 1967.

Of 392 black enlisted men surveyed, 63.8 per cent believe that their fight is in the U.S.

"I think the black man in Vietnam is definitely fighting two enemies," Ken Bantum, a black Air Force sergeant from Philadelphia told me. "And he should only be at home fighting one." One-fourth of the black officers and senior non-commissioned officers agreed.

More than half of the enlisted men objected to taking part in the war because they believe it is a race war pitting whites against nonwhites or because they flatly don't want to fight against people of dark skin. Less than half agreed that they were fighting a common Communist enemy with their white buddies in arms—the prevailing attitude among blacks three years ago.

"America is just fighting this war so that the white man can put boo-coo money in his pocket," Private Bruce Jessup of Washington, D.C., said in Pleiku. "He just lets you die so he can send his little war materials over there. To hell with this war. We should say, come on in, Ho Chi Minh, this is yours." Jessup drove a gas truck for the 815th Army Engineer Battalion.

"I can't see dying in Vietnam to make someone else money," said Marine Corporal James E. Baker, Jr., of Chicago. "The way whites treat the natives of this country I know they don't give a damn about their freedom."

Less than a third of the blacks and whites agreed that the best way to pursue the war was by new attacks on North Vietnam and invasions into Laos and Cambodia, while much larger groups argued for a reduction in the battle tempo and a U.S. pullout as soon as the South Vietnamese could shoulder the full burden.

As for why America is involved, most blacks and a significant minority of whites rejected the notion that the war is stemming the spread of Communism. More than 40 per cent of the blacks and nearly 20 per cent of the whites believe that America should not be fighting in what is essentially a civil war or Asian problem.

"Give it (Vietnam) to them," said Claude E. Bowen, a black Marine from Los Angeles. "If the cracker wants to stay here and fight, let him. If they kick his ass, too damned bad. It's about time somebody did."

Black GIs—Bringing the War Home

What is frightening many black officers and a few knowledgeable white ones is not so much the course of the war as the potential of the young black to bring the lessons of violence he has learned in the war against the Viet Cong to America with him.

"It's a new breed of black over here," said Army Captain Robert Robbins, a black officer from Wilmington, N.C., serving in the 9th Division.

"He has graduated from peaceful demonstrations up to the riots. He comes here to put his life on the line for some cause he probably doesn't believe in. When he goes home, he'll think the only way he can get what he wants is to take it."

Lieutenant Colonel Frank Petersen of Washington, D.C., a black Marine pilot who led a squadron of Phantoms at Chu Lai, agreed. "You have some very angry blacks who are here who are going to go back and are going to be more angry once they return. There is a hell of a chance that many of the blacks who are being discharged, if they encounter the right set of conditions, will become urban guerrillas."

Indeed, only 37.8 per cent of the black enlisted men surveyed agreed that weapons have no place in the struggle for their rights in the U.S. Nearly 50 per cent said that they would use weapons, while 13 per cent said they would consider arming themselves if forced to.

"Half the brothers over here can build their own weapons," observed Washington. "They are going back ready for anything."

"I ain't coming back playing, 'Oh, say can you see,' " said Marine Sergeant Paul Thomas of Chesapeake, Va., in Da Nang. "I'm whistlin' 'Sweet Georgia Brown,' and I got the band."

"When you come back to the States and the [white] man's going to say, 'Sorry, son, but I'm going to give you some of these rights, but you ain't ready for the rest of them yet,' after I put my life on the line. Uh-uh," said Sergeant Randolph Doby, a black Marine from Milwaukee stationed in Da Nang. "The man who says that, I'm going to try to kill him. If I can't kill him, he's going to wish he were dead."

Only one black enlisted man in three believed that the use of weapons

(Photo by Robert C. Scheu, Photon West.)

would damage the black move for independence of choice and full opportunity, and a significantly high percentage promised to carry home the lessons they learned in self-defense and black unity to radical groups like the Black Panthers.

"The Black Panthers is what we need as an equalizer," said seaman James Cannon of Gary, Ind. "The beast [white man] got his Ku Klux Klan. The Black Panthers gives the beast something to fear like we feared from the Ku Klux Klan all our lives."

Seaman Milton Banion of Maywood, Ill., another sailor at Da Nang, said, "The Honkies made the Panthers violent like they are. I'd join 'em, and I'd help 'em kill all these Honkies, because do unto him before he do unto you."

Albert Jackson of Chicago, a black Marine stationed at Chu Lai, promised, "If at all possible, I plan to move as quickly as possible with a group that is ready to move. The Panthers are definitely the readiest group in the world, because they move so awesomely."

The vast majority of the blacks believe that America is in for more race violence than has marred the Nation in the last decade, and most of these believe that they would join renewed rioting.

"There's going to be more violence back in the world because we're goin' back," said Claude Bowen. "Hell, yes, I'd riot. If they're kicking crackers' asses, I'm going to get in and kick a few myself. I'm just doing what my grandfather wanted to do and couldn't."

Said another black Marine: "My ancestors said, please. Yeah, they said, please. Did they get any mercy? Why should we turn around and say, please, may I have this? Hell, no. I say start an armed revolution."

"I always back a riot," said a black sailor. "Riots is good. It makes people wonder what's going on, and they come in and check it out."

Only 14 per cent of the black enlisted men said they would follow without reservation orders to put down rebellious blacks at home and more than 45 per cent said they would refuse the order.

"I'd put 'em right down," said Jessup sarcastically. "And put myself right down in the heart of the riot, and riot right with them, Army clothes and all. As a matter of fact, I'd get out there and put down the police."

The white student movement against the war drew surprising support from black troops. Most black students have ignored the war issue, pressing instead for separate curriculums and housing while protesting police assaults on blacks. But 60.2 per cent of the black enlisted men and 49.7 per cent of the black officers agreed that the right to make the war protest should be protected: 14 per cent of the enlisted and 12 per cent of the officers said they supported the campus stand.

A strong majority of white GIs took exception to the protest, including 46.9 per cent who would either draft or jail the student dissenters.

I'd like to kick them in the ass," said James Pole, a white private from Waycross, Ga.

"They should be made to see how we live and die over here," argued James Bennett, a white soldier from San Lorenzo, Calif., "then perhaps they would appreciate college more."

Following is an example of some of the findings of Wallace Terry's survey of the racial attitudes of servicemen in Vietnam.

RACE VIOLENCE IN AMERICA

	Black Enlisted	*Black Officers*
Race violence will increase in America	82.9%	78.3%
Race violence will decrease	4.8	4.0
Race violence will remain about the same as it has been in recent years	7.7	10.3
Don't know	4.6	7.4

Do you plan to join a militant black group like the Black Panthers when you return home?

	Black Enlisted	*Black Officers*	*Black Combat Troops*	*Black Support Troops*
Yes	30.6%	6.3%	36.3%	26.9%
No	52.3	79.4	45.9	58.7
Maybe	17.1	14.3	17.8	14.4

Would you join a ghetto riot or revolt in order to gain black demands?

	Black Enlisted	*Black Officers*	*Black Combat Troops*	*Black Support Troops*
Yes	44.6%	15.4%	45.2%	48.1%
No	40.6	76.0	39.0	37.5
Maybe	14.8	18.6	15.8	14.4

Would you use weapons to secure your rights back home?

	Black Enlisted	*Black Officers*	*Black Combat Troops*	*Black Support Troops*
Yes	49.2%	31.4%	43.8%	55.8%
No. Weapons have no place in the black revolution	37.8	54.3	42.5	35.6
Maybe	13.0	14.3	13.7	8.7

Blacks are more tolerant; the right to protest means more to them. "I'd either join the Black Panthers or SDS (Students for a Democratic Society), preferably SDS," said Jessup, "because SDS is down on the whole thing, down on this war, down on society, the Establishment. The society and the Establishment are messed up. They need changin', man, so that people can live, live equally. Get all this racist stuff on out of here."

"Hell, yes, I'd riot," said Corporal Toby Hoffler, a black Marine from Brooklyn. "The white man had his goddamn Boston Tea Party, so why can't we have our riots, and the white students their marches? Is there any difference? Check it. Is there any difference?"

Despite the military's contention that life for blacks is better in service than out, fewer than three black GIs in 10 believe they get along better with whites in Vietnam than they did back home. And nearly 65 per cent of them expect the racial strife there to grow.

The Angry Reaction of Black GIs

In the past three years, mistrust and hostility between black and white American troops in Vietnam have increased to a dangerous extent. There have been beatings, killings, racial slurs from both sides, and cross-burnings.

In one incident, more than 200 black inmates of the Long Binn stockade donned white kerchiefs and African-style robes made from Army blankets and went on a rampage that left one white inmate dead, scores injured, and the stockade in shambles. Military officials blamed overcrowding and racial tensions.

In another incident, a black guard was shot to death when a black sailor went on a wild shooting spree at a camp near Da Nang. That episode followed rioting along China Beach by black Marines and sailors with M-16 rifles.

Other incidents:

- A black Marine sergeant with a reputation for being tough on black militants and a white major narrowly escaped death when a black Marine exploded a grenade under the orderly room of the Fifth Communication Battalion at Da Nang.
- When white officers at Chu Lai refused to give rides to black Marines they were severely beaten. Later name-calling whites triggered a riot at the enlisted men's club; two whites were so badly injured that they were evacuated home. Clubs at Qui Nhon and a dozen other places have been wrecked by racial melees.
- On the walls of bars and latrines throughout the country, whites infuriate blacks by scrawling such phrases as "niggers eat s--t" and "I'd prefer a gook to a nigger."
- At Tan Son Nhut Air Base near Saigon, a white soldier was shot by a black GI he had been stalking with shouts of "I'm going to kill you, nigger."
- When Martin Luther King, Jr., was murdered, whites burned crosses at Cam Ranh Bay and flew confederate flags over bases at Da Nang. After appearing on the cover of *Time* magazine in the story of "The Negro in Vietnam," Army Airborne Sergeant Clide Brown found a cross burning outside his tent.

"The military establishment is hailed as being one of the most democratic institutions in America," observed Lieutenant Colonel Frank Petersen, a black Marine pilot. "This implies that everything is as it should be. There are no separate and dual standards. Once the young black arrives in the military, however, he finds that this is not the case. The military is simply an extension of American society. Furthermore, in any war zone, once you've committed your life to a 'true cause' and find that you are still subjected to different standards, it tends to infuriate you to the extreme. That is what's happening out here."

The black soldier is no longer silent over the discrimination he experienced a decade ago. "When I came into the Army in 1956 everything was quiet," said Major Wardell C. Smith of Des Moines, Iowa, a black who was Inspector General for the Third Brigade of the 82nd Airborne Division.

"No one was raising any hell about the prejudice and discrimination going on. The Negro soldier didn't know which way to go as far as speaking out against it. Every time he tried to, he got kicked in the head. Now they can speak and somebody will listen. And some feel that since they are going to face death, it doesn't matter what happens."

Following is an example of some of the findings of Wallace Terry's survey on the racial attitudes of servicemen in Vietnam.

What kind of military would you prefer to serve in?

	Black Enlisted	*White Enlisted*	*Black Officers*	*White Officers*	*Black Combat Troops*	*Black Support Troops*
Integrated	35.5%	88.7%	68.9%	83.3%	33.9%	38.6%

How do you feel about whites?

	Black Enlisted	*Black Officers*	*Black Combat Troops*	*Black Support Troops*
I hate them	20.2%	7.4%	19.9%	23.1%
I don't care for them, but I try to get along with them	35.5	39.4	34.9	31.7
Their color makes no difference to me. I get along with them	32.4	49.1	37.7	29.8
Despite differences with some, I like many whites	.3			1.
Don't know	11.7	4.	7.5	14.4

After racial slurs, confederate flags, and the intimidation that comes with wearing Afro-style haircuts and using black power signs and trappings, blacks most complain about their failure to get coveted rear area assignments, medals, and promotions on an equal basis with whites.

Among all black enlisted men surveyed, nearly half believe that blacks are assigned more dangerous duty than whites.

But the black soldier's bitterness deepens when his natural gravitation toward other blacks, his use of black power signs and banners, and his wearing of Afro-styled haircuts is repressed.

These frustrations were illustrated in a remarkable, though confidential, report made by a Marine Division Commander in the First Corps battle zone.

His insight into the "very deep layer of bitterness" among his black troops demonstrated an understanding of racial tensions at that high level. The two-star general summarized the grievances that he found in this set of questions:

- Why is the natural gravitation of blacks to each other viewed as bad and subsequently labeled as black power plotting?
- If restrictions are placed on banners, why is not the same restriction placed on the display of confederate flags as is placed on the display of black power banners?
- Why are black soldiers ostracized by superior noncommissioned officers and labeled as troublemakers within the units?
- Why is there a feeling among enlisted blacks that their superiors are not concerned with their problems?
- Why are whites who freely associate with black soldiers ostracized by superior noncommissioned officers and also labeled as troublemakers?
- Why are blacks threatened with transfer to the northernmost region of the division's area of operation—the most dangerous place—at the slightest provocation?

Most black GIs and many black officers use the clenched fist sign as a form of greeting or recognition of one black by another. But a third of the white enlisted men and more than 40 per cent of the white officers condemn its use.

Six black enlisted men in ten, and half as many officers, now wear Afro-style haircuts, though most whites object to them.

Black pride and culture, as on the college campus, have spilled over into other areas:

- At remote fire support bases along the Cambodian border, scores of blacks have banded together to present their complaints against racial epithets and slow promotions.
- Aboard the boats that sweep the Mekong Delta and on the roads that connect bases, black sailors and soldiers raise black power salutes in common recognition and often fly black flags.
- One company commander leading his First Cavalry Division troops into the field was startled to find his black soldiers wearing black berets and shirts instead of the regulation helmets and fatigues.
- In the First Marine Division, Lance Corporal Gene Johnson of Norfolk, Va., joined the Ju Ju's, a 200-member black protective (against white prejudice and intimidation) group "because the white man won't mess over us if we stick together. By acting in unity we can make our protest

much stronger." Lance Corporal Roddie Latimer of Washington, D.C., joined the Mau Mau's, a sister group of similar size and philosophy begun by blacks in the same division. "Whites think we're starting some sort of black power movement," said Latimer, "or plotting some kind of riot. But if you're not tight with the brothers (blacks) in the 'Nam, you can't get over. We want them (whites) to know that we are definitely together. Mess with one of us, and you mess with all of us."

• And in Da Nang, black Marines have designed a flag for black soldiers in Vietnam. A red background symbolizes blood shed by blacks in the war and in racial conflicts in America. A black foreground represents the face of black culture. At the center are crossed spears and a shield, meaning "violence if necessary," surrounded by a wreath, symbolizing "peace if possible." The flag bears a legend in Swahili, meaning "my fear is for you."

The heroes of the black soldiers today are drawn among the most militant black spokesmen. Eldridge Cleaver receives the approval of most, followed by Malcolm X and Cassius Clay. Edward Brooke, the only black U.S. Senator, draws the approval of less than half; black sailors refer to him as an "Oreo"—a cookie, black on the outside, white on the inside. Another moderate, Roy Wilkins, the NAACP leader, highly popular with black soldiers of 1967, is roundly criticized today for condemning the black studies movement. "I dig the militant blacks," said Jessup.

"Nonviolence didn't do anything but get Martin Luther King killed."

Wallace Terry II spent more than two years in Vietnam as a correspondent for Time *magazine. During that time he interviewed 833 black and white servicemen on their racial attitudes as part of a private survey. Each was asked 109 questions on a questionnaire. Terry's conclusions are based on 2500 scientifically comprised tables derived from the servicemen's replies by the Harvard Computer Center.*

All for Vietnam

Tom Hayden

The Cambodian invasion, the killings at Kent State, and Nixon's Cold War rhetoric all caused a sudden panic among millions of Americans who yearned to believe in "Vietnamization" and other promises of peace in Southeast Asia. The national reaction was great enough to send Nixon before the TV cameras, and ultimately to the Washington Monument, to cool the threat of disruption in his own capital. Nixon's promise to withdraw from Cambodia did have a temporary cooling effect, but it also blew away many lingering illusions about peace in Asia. The government had served notice to all but the most blind that its intention was to win the war through escalation—even with nuclear weapons, if necessary.

Why did anyone ever doubt it?

The U.S. government already had demonstrated its willingness to attempt subtle genocide in Vietnam under the pretense of waging a "war of attrition." The military ruthlessly bombed the social structure—schools, hospitals; used chemicals to poison the dams of Vietnam, the rivers, and farmlands; drove the rural population in the South into concentration camps; and spoke of "destroying cities to save them," "fighting against the Vietnamese birth rate," and "threatening their existence as a nation." The toll of suffering in Vietnam long ago surpassed that which would have resulted from a Hiroshima-type attack. Genocide by any other name is still genocide. Regardless of the intent of particular officials during the last 21 years of American intervention, the dynamic is unmistakable: relentless American military action has attempted to crush the Vietnamese revolution by any means necessary, by any escalation required.

The Pattern of Liberal Protest

But there is a very human desire to recover from shock, to return to normalcy, to disbelieve that nightmare can become reality. All these feelings operate among Americans who want peace, and it is precisely these feelings that Nixon has sought to manipulate. Feelings such as these quite likely moved people involved in national protests against the Cambodian invasion to feel satisfaction with Nixon's agreement to "withdraw" in two months.

If the New Haven weekend offered a glimpse of the Apocalypse, the calm protest in Washington, D.C., just one week later returned most people to the conventional world of anti-war protest.

Reprinted from *Ramparts,* September 1970.

It was not the Nixon Administration which implemented this pacifying strategy but, paradoxically, the liberal establishment that Nixon and Agnew despise. Much of the effort to keep young people from believing that the nightmare had come was made by liberal politicians and college administrators.

On Yale's signal, college administrators adopted a sudden new tolerance, even cooperation, towards dissent on the campuses. Just as Yale was "reconstituted" for a weekend to accommodate the Panther protests, so did schools everywhere allow students and faculty to work against the war. On the political front, a score of senators came forward with anti-war amendments and proposals for channeling student energies into fall electoral campaigns.

The underlying motive of the administrators and politicians in all this was certainly not withdrawal of troops from Vietnam or radical transformation of the war-oriented university. Their immediate concern was peace in the schools and peace between the generations.

A perfect embodiment of this concern could be found in the figure of Cyrus Vance, a Yale trustee who was intimately involved in keeping his alma mater from being destroyed during the May Day protests. Vance, of course, previously represented the U.S. government in the Paris peace talks. Like Yale President Brewster and Yale trustee John Lindsay, Vance by now preferred a retreat in Vietnam to save America's interests elsewhere, particularly at home.

These men knew quite well the level of discontent on the campuses. They knew that the school year's two peaceful and legitimate Moratoriums had only widened the generation gap. They knew that the Chicago Conspiracy Trial had added greatly to the despair the young felt toward established institutions. Above all they knew that since the beginning of the year the level of revolutionary violence in America had taken a quantum jump forward. Demonstrators in large numbers were breaking windows and trashing buildings. Young guerrillas were burning and bombing hundreds of institutions, such as ROTC and draft boards. They knew, finally, that Yale would be levelled in any confrontation during May Day weekend, setting off perhaps hundreds of violent rebellions on less guarded campuses. In their calculation it was time for a new policy: to allow for peaceful dissent within their institutions even at the risk of ruffling Establishment feathers and exciting Spiro T. Agnew.

This is not to say that all the protest energy generated by the spontaneous national student strike was wasted or co-opted. Overnight, thousands of new activists were made; Nixon was forced to limit the timetable of his invasion; and shock over the blood spilled at Kent State, Augusta, Jackson, and Cambodia probably increased the conviction of millions of Americans that the war was wrong.

Now that the strike is over, however, we can see its limits clearly. No colleges were really "reconstituted"; no fundamental pressures were built against the war machine; most of the activity dissipated into summer vaca-

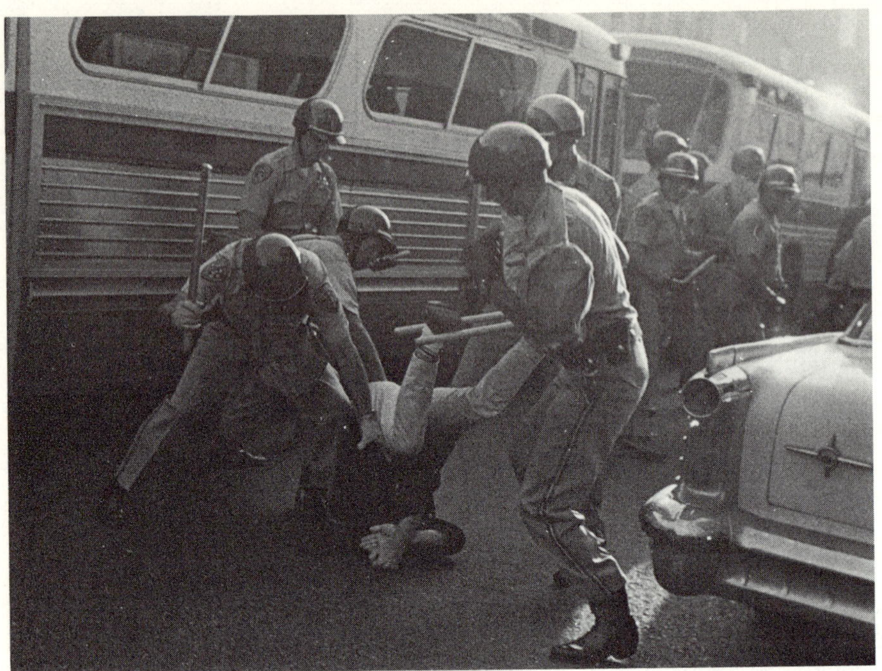

Confrontation at Armed Forces Induction Center, Oakland, Calif., 1968. *(Photo by Gerhard E. Gscheidle, Photophile, S.F.)*

tion; most college administrations were able finally to preserve their buildings from violence. In contrast to this strike, there was a bloodbath in Cambodia; 40,000 South Vietnamese troops remain there; and the U.S. is planning to bomb Cambodia as mercilessly as it does Laos.

The sense of *déja vu* this syndrome creates is overpowering. We went through a precisely analogous experience in 1967-68 leading up to the Chicago confrontation. Then members of the "lunatic fringe" of the American left were not guerrilla-bombers; they were burning draft cards, obstructing Dow recruiters, and storming Pentagon walls. Then, too, the Establishment's crisis-managers (McGeorge Bundy comes to mind) were urging a cutback in Vietnam to prevent a breakdown at home. Then as now the message to young America was: don't believe the radicals, work within the system, create a constructive alternative to nihilism—and remember, you'll be crushed if you try to rebel. Then also the young people went to the Silent Majority, worked in the very guts of the electoral system, became Clean for Gene. Then came the bloody finish in Chicago. Senator McCarthy went off to cover the World Series for *Life* magazine. The moderates won their demands—negotiations with the other side, an end to the bombing of North Vietnam—only to realize they were meaningless. The government had ended the anti-war movement under the pretext of ending the war.

It is amazing that within a year optimism could bloom again among the same liberal forces that were shattered in Chicago. A group of former

McCarthy and Kennedy workers (and politicians even including Averell Harriman) formed a movement curiously called The Moratorium. Everyone hailed it as a respectable alternative to the kind of politics The Chicago Conspiracy represented (we had to fight their bureaucracy even to appear on stage in the Chicago Moratorium in October 1969). Indeed, a million people were mobilized around rather humble slogans like "Give peace a chance." The response to this upstanding, respectable protest? Nixon declared he would be unaffected by their numbers, and Agnew branded the organizers "effete snobs."

Evidentally the Agnew criticism contained some truth, since the Moratorium organizers swiftly gave up their plans for an escalating, month-by-month boycott and work stoppage, and closed the Moratorium to return to the more familiar environment of electoral politics. The Cambodian invasion came three weeks later.

The pattern of liberal failure is by now obvious. From the McCarthy campaign to the Moratorium to the present campus "reconstitution" movement, we have seen a moderate, Democratic Party-oriented program tried and frustrated again and again. The problem in this political strategy seems to be an over-reliance on politicians and an under-reliance on popular pressure. This is not the way liberal strategists would argue their cause, of course. They would say that the war can only be ended by respectable efforts within the mainstream of politics, and that disruptive protest only alienates the public and strengthens the hawks. But they cannot be blind to the fact that if they have any leverage at all, it is precisely because they are a safe alternative to radicalism. For a better explanation of their politics we would have to conclude that they want to end the war but also save the system. They do not themselves follow the natural path of radicalization which many of their followers do. They remain instead a loyal opposition working within the electoral arena for changes—changes, not in the system, but in its priorities.

The tragedy is that many young people who accept the liberal theory of change are simply not aware of their own power. It is not that they want above all to stay within the system, but only that they are conditioned to believe that working outside the system is impossible. They are still blind to the source of their tremendous power, the power to make Nixon rush to the Washington Monument. That power does not reside in their electoral potential but only in their potential to disrupt the vital institutions containing them—the universities—and to threaten the stability of the country's future. It was this threat which caused Brewster to "open" Yale and Nixon to pledge "withdrawal" from Cambodia. There is a constant tendency among students and young people in general to disbelieve the reality of their own power, to continue believing that power is with their parents or the politicians. But they should instead consider the formula the Vietnamese have for American politics: *if we are strong, even a Goldwater will withdraw; if we are weak, even a McCarthy will attack.*

Radicalism and Its Impasse

The radicals have always been more correct about Vietnam than have the architects of liberal protest. The former goals of the radicals, once condemned by liberals as utopian, now are quite acceptable—for example, the demand for immediate withdrawal instead of negotiations. The radical strategy of relying on people in the streets instead of in the ballot box has also been productive, at least up through 1968, when the radical strategy reached a peak of success which has been followed by a prolonged impasse.

In 1968 we administered the first clear setback to America's strategy of escalation. It was the year of military defeat (the Tet offensive) and of political catastrophe, with Westmoreland, McNamara, and Johnson bowing out unceremoniously. Those who came to Chicago to protest were prophets without honor holding to two convictions: that despite Johnson's retirement, despite the Paris talks, the U.S. aggression would continue; and that the anti-war movement should remain independent in the streets instead of placing itself at the disposal of "peace candidates." The Chicago confrontation was the peak in a year of demonstrations showing that any political leadership committed to staying in Vietnam would face domestic chaos and, ultimately, electoral defeat.

But at the same time we learned that in the face of chaos, "law and order" would be implemented long before withdrawal from Vietnam. Moreover, from Johnson's abdication we realized that America's stake in Vietnam took precedence over the personal fortunes of whoever happened to be President. The costs we were imposing on the American Establishment were real but at least for a while acceptable.

And with that discovery, radicalism came to an impasse.

Up to that point, and even today, most peace activists and radicals believe that Vietnam is a flaw—a terrible flaw—in the working of the American Empire, which could be repaired by a loud enough outcry of disagreement. Who would have believed that a supreme egomaniac like Lyndon Johnson would make winning the war more important than winning re-election? Who would have thought that with half the Senate and most of the press and public believing the war a "mistake," it would nevertheless continue to expand?

There has been a widespread failure to recognize in Vietnam the most serious international showdown of our time.

Radical intellectual theories about Vietnam, for example, have assumed that U.S. involvement is irrational—not in the sense liberals assert when they blame faulty Presidential advisers for our Vietnam commitment, but "irrational" in the sense that Vietnam is not in the "true interests" of corporate capitalism. In the radical view, America is ruled by a flexible corporate elite with many interests throughout the world. In this empire, Vietnam is a rather unimportant economic and political area (compared to India, Indonesia, Japan, or Brazil). Since the corporate elite is concerned with the smooth over-all maintenance of empire, and not with the occasional loss of a small domino (the radical reasoning goes), our powerful gentry will cut their losses in Vietnam and dig in better elsewhere. In this view, the U.S. can withdraw to Thailand and India-Indonesia, keeping a forward base against China while consolidating its grip on richer possessions.

This world-view provided most of the operating assumptions of the major anti-war groups in the late Sixties—the Mobilization and the SDS—even though the two organizations were constantly at odds over strategy.

The Mobe did just what its name implied: it mobilized people to demand withdrawal from Vietnam. In most cases, its demonstrations were large, legal, and peaceful, designed to allow a variety of people to surface their opposition to Vietnam. Between mass mobilizations there were numerous attempts to do educational work among new constituencies, but local branches of the Mobe existed primarily to pull out people to rallies. The presence of ever larger numbers in the streets was effective in several ways: first, it helped individuals feel they were not alone in opposing the war; second, it gave politicians and influential figures confidence that they could oppose the war without being crucified, which in turn legitimized dissent among larger numbers of people; and third, it gave encouragement to the Vietnamese revolutionaries while demoralizing the American military and the puppets they supported.

But eventually the underlying assumption—that decision-makers would end the war if enough widespread pressure was created—was proven inadequate by the government's repeated escalation. While its structure remains, the Mobe direction has blurred and support has waned since 1968.

The SDS radicals actually created the first national mobilization in the spring of 1965, but then very quickly shunned a leadership role in the anti-war protests because they did not believe in the "pressure" strategy. Their radicalism, however, often led in perverse and sectarian directions. They assumed the anti-war mobilizations would be deceptively "successful" because the American Establishment, sensing a bad investment in Vietnam, would use the anti-war sentiment as a popular basis for pulling out. The peace movement would be co-opted in the process, used by a new set of politicians (Robert Kennedy) for their rise to power. The real issue, for SDS, was not Vietnam but the imperialist system which would continue beyond the withdrawal, a system which would strangle and threaten Vietnam (as the American blockade does Cuba) and other nations, until overthrown. In SDS language, there had to be an anti-imperialist movement able to muster resistance "seven wars from now."

In various local actions, SDS chapters made important anti-war contributions by their confrontations with recruiters and official spokesmen. But in the two major national confrontations against the war—at the Pentagon and Chicago—SDS stayed aloof and hostile until the sheer heat of the conflict persuaded them to participate.

The SDS outlook was clearer than the liberal and humanitarian politics of most of the movement, but it was a terribly elitist view. Instead of regarding Vietnam as the crisis which would tear America apart and create conditions for domestic radicalism, a crisis which SDS would be deeply involved in resolving, they saw it more as an important issue for liberals.

There were other strands of radicalism—the life-style, or cultural, rebellion—which were even further removed from the issue of the war. Taking Vietnam only as a symptom of what was wrong with the country, many chose to fight primarily against their own oppression as longhairs. They opted totally out of the anti-war movement into what would become the Woodstock Nation. To the early Merry Pranksters as well as to the later Yippies, the anti-war activists were "straight" or "too political" or "on a death trip," not in touch with their own oppression and therefore building no alternative to America. And so there developed a genuine alternative culture, but its outlook, until quite recently, has been that of revolution-for-the-hell-of-it, revolution-for-ourselves, "Dope, Rock 'n' Roll, and Fucking in the Street," etc. Whatever impulse there has been in this culture against the war has had no outlet (except during Chicago) or has been channeled into a diffuse rage against America.

The women's liberation movement, too, has been through a long alienation from the issues of Vietnam and the Third World. Rebelling against male-dominated structures in the anti-war movement, and focusing primarily on their particular oppression, they have assumed that the problem of Vietnam would be solved by others.

Even during our Chicago trial, though it was aimed at the anti-war movement, we could not generate a new level of interest in Vietnam. In our speeches we emphasized the government's attack on anti-war militants. We observed the Moratorium in court. We sent Bill Kunstler to Paris to obtain news of American prisoners held in North Vietnam. We supported the idea of a release of U.S. prisoners in exchange for Bobby Seale and Huey Newton. . . . Yet Yippie theatrics and Judge Hoffman's personal quirks dominated popular consciousness of the trial. The same people whose nerves were deadened to the massive atrocity of Vietnam could be aroused by the relatively minor oppressiveness of our Chicago courtroom.

Paradoxically, the Vietnamese knew best that the trial was about the future of the anti-war struggle. Throughout Vietnam, people were concerned about our fate and, when we were jailed after the trial, our immediate release was demanded at the Paris peace talks.

Given the vacuum of militant anti-war leadership, it was predictable that a group like Weatherman would re-assert a revolutionary interest in Third World struggles. And the vacuum may also explain the extreme one-sidedness with which they would assert their politics.

Against the view that emphasized the stability and flexibility of imperialism, the Weathermen began with the view that the Vietnamese and other Third World peoples are winning; that imperialism was in its death throes. They advanced a fifth-column strategy, although cloaked in a hippie lifestyle and invoking Dylan and the Stones as well as Regis Debray and Lin Piao.

Their view: "The pump don't work 'cause the vandals stole the handle." The exclusive task of white radicals, in their view, is irregular warfare behind enemy lines inside American imperialism's fragile structure. Irregular, rather than conventional, guerrilla warfare, because the Weathermen are doubtful of ever achieving broad popular support inside the United States. They are essentially agents, John Browns, for the Third World revolution, with the goal of materially weakening imperialism by overextending its resources.

The immense contribution of the Weathermen has been in the assertion of internationalism and in their commitment to give their lives, rather than lip service, in solidarity with Third World people. But the problem in their vandalism or fifth-column strategy is that it fails to embrace the legitimacy of other struggles against oppression: women's liberation, the cultural revolution, and so forth. Thus the Weathermen create a basic rupture between themselves and their natural base for revolution. The intertwined problem is that the Weathermen are underground by choice and necessity, thus cutting themselves off from any open leadership role in mass struggles against the war. They do not carry out the basic Vietnamese teaching that legal demonstrations, even activity by the liberal wing of the Establishment, can be more important on certain occasions than guerrilla attack.

So the liberal anti-war movement is trapped in electoral politics, the radical strategy is at an impasse, other revolutionaries have abandoned Vietnam for the issue of their own oppression, and a few people have gone underground. Clearly, we have come to the crossroads: either the Vietnamese people will win, or they will be maimed horribly in a larger war. Either we will stop this war, or we will live under an intolerable barbarism. *Our task: an all-out siege against the war machine. Our watchword: All for Vietnam.*

What Is to Be Done

First and foremost, we need an Emergency Consciousness about the real danger of further escalation. The only way the Vietnamese, the Cambodians, and the Laotians can secure their national rights is if the U.S. government is prevented from enlarging the war to include China and the use of advanced chemical or nuclear weapons. We cannot rely on liberal politicians to initiate this alert. At most we can include them in a united front, but the strongest Emergency must be sounded by students on campuses like the University of California, where the bombs are being processed, by the scientists who know what is going on, by the local anti-war groups outside military institutions, and by all groups who are supposedly defending the Vietnamese Revolution. By forcing the government to answer in advance whether it is planning an ultimate genocidal blow, we can develop an international alarm which will make such an escalation far more difficult. We will also be laying the foundation for renewed militancy at home, since no tactics are too extreme in the face of this threat.

Second, Vietnam has become once more a leading priority for all groups struggling to change the country. It cannot be assigned to an anti-war movement that is no more than a bureaucratic skeleton which goes into motion several times annually. The practice of organizing *only* around one's particular oppression must be seen as self-indulgence in the face of what threatens Vietnam. It is also illogical because there are no Vietnamese inside this country, and therefore we have to speak for them.

Third, the Vietnam war should be linked always with the issues of racism and repression at home. There still are many who prefer to keep the issue of Vietnam "separate" for the purpose of drawing the greatest popular support. This political line is self-defeating for at least two reasons: it depresses and holds back the swiftly growing consciousness of hundreds of thousands of people who long ago were awakened to the war issue; and it neglects the obvious repression of the anti-war radicals and blacks who are being crushed precisely because they are causing difficulties for imperialism. If the Administration can gun down and silence Panthers, one might ask, why would that Administration have to worry about an unarmed and less disciplined peace movement?

Fourth, it is time for the core of the anti-war movement to intensify the struggle with the goal of "cutting the supply lines" that feed the war machine. It is all well and good to make "reaching larger numbers of people" the goal of organizing, but there comes a moment when time is running out, when there can be no more waiting for the Silent Majority or the Working Class to be taking the stand we have to take. It is time to ask what has become of the hundreds of thousands who have been mobilized in the past for orthodox demonstrations, but who are never called upon to do more than repeat those performances. Is our "lack of numbers" and "isolation" the problem, or is it the cynicism and defeatism of those who have given up stopping the war machine?

The image of "cutting the supply lines" is meant to deflect focus away from politicians and towards the precious institutions that must run smoothly if this war is to go forward. Now is the time to cripple this machinery of war by extending the "siege of the Pentagon" from one end of the country to another. The revolt of black GIs—and many whites as well —is a prime example of the way to do it. Delegitimizing and shutting down ROTC, which supplies the junior officers, is another example. Preventing nuclear and chemical warfare research is another. We need to be assailing corporations doing Vietnam business, striking at the authority of every important individual and agency involved in Vietnam, exposing and identifying the Vietnam lobby as a group of war criminals, isolating, weakening, and stopping their murderous program.

This siege strategy embraces both the "mobilization" and "guerrilla" tactics. The immediate problem is not whether the tactics are too moderate or too militant. The problem is to recommit the energies of every sincere person for a last stand on Vietnam. The problem is to make people see that Vietnam is not a permanent part of the American Way of Life; it is a war with a dynamic leading to a showdown.

The only way to brush off our cynicism is to realize that we are not alone and isolated inside the United States. We should follow the war not as a "tragedy" but as a struggle in which the side of humanity is making a stand so heroic that it should shatter the hardest cynicism.

One of the best ways to gain strength for the struggle is to explore and measure the contribution of the Vietnamese people to ourselves and the rest of the world. Developing this sense of internationalism means going beyond the conceptions of Vietnam offered by dove professors in the teaching. Their view, accepted widely in the anti-war movement, is that Vietnam is a case of "civil war" in which the U.S. should not have intervened. The notion of "civil war" suggests that there are several Vietnamese sides with different ethnic, religious, and political backgrounds, all quarreling among themselves. The implication is that Vietnam always has had internal problems which should not be important to the U.S. government. There is no basis for solidarity with Vietnam in this view, only a basis for paternalistic regret.

This kind of thinking hides from people a history which is both informative and stirring. What has happened in Vietnam is no more a "civil war" than the American Revolution was a "civil war." The fact that some

(Photo by David Goldstein.)

Vietnamese have identified first with the French and now with the Americans is no more significant than the fact that some American colonists were linked to the British.

The real history of Vietnam is a history of successful revolution which the Western powers have been trying to erase for 25 years. The important fact about Ho Chi Minh's 1945 Proclamation of Independence is not that he quoted the American Declaration (which the doves constantly use to show how cooperation would have been possible with him) but that he declared the independence of his county. The basic conflict since that time has not been among the Vietnamese. The Diem government and the Thieu-Ky government were established by the U.S. and would fall without the U.S.: they have no significant roots among the Vietnamese people. The basic conflict is between the Vietnamese Nation and American Imperialism.

This Vietnamese Nation is a threat not only to American generals but to American professors and liberals, because of the revolutionary example it is establishing. The Vietnamese defy the military assumption that weapons can preserve America's power, and in their defiance revive a romantic revolutionary spirit that is supposed to be out of style.

In Vietnam the word "individualism" does not exist. The Vietnamese word that comes closest to individualism is "cannibalism." Their culture and their oppression have helped them approach the communist ideal of suffering, sharing, and struggling together. In order to survive they have had to become brothers and sisters in everything *before* achieving the technology and abundance that is supposed to make such a socialist lifestyle possible.

Their age-old fight against foreign aggression makes struggle seem to be in their blood. Their existence, like that of Cuba and Korea, demonstrates not only that socialist and national liberation struggles can be joined; it demonstrates that the Modern Imperial Colossus can be fought and beaten by a small country with primitive technology.

The Vietnamese people have fired the modern "shots heard round the world." They are defeating the United States in war, destroying the myth of American superiority.

In this triumph they have raised the spirit of millions of Third World people.

They have provided the triggering issue for the new student movements in Western Europe.

They have inspired black and brown people, and young white people, inside the United States itself.

More than any other people, they have come to represent the conscience of humanity. When Ho Chi Minh died he was the most revered statesman in the world.

And they have done all this alone. The initiative has been theirs. They began fighting and dying long before there was a peace movement in

America. They fought despite the fact that their communist allies were impossibly divided.

If it seems embarrassing or fuzzy-headed to mention these truths in America, it is only because our country is an emotional wasteland too decadent to believe in being born again.

But if these truths continue to inspire greater numbers of Americans, the Vietnamese people will have to be thanked for a final gift: opening our eyes to our own history as a genocidal nation, and starting us on the road to our own revolution.

This article is an abridged chapter from Tom Hayden's The Trial, *published Fall 1970 by Holt, Rinehart and Winston, Inc. The rest of the book appeared in* Ramparts, *September 1970.*

Bibliography

Vietnam, Laos, Cambodia, and the War

Historical Background: French Colonialism, War Between France and the Vietminh

Buttinger, J. *Vietnam: A Dragon Embattled.* 2 vols. New York: Praeger, 1967.

———. *Vietnam: A Political History.* New York: Praeger, 1968. A condensation of *Vietnam: A Dragon Embattled.*

Devillers, Philippe, and Jean Lacouture. *End of a War: Indochina Nineteen Fifty-Four.* New York: Praeger, 1969. Written by a team of French historians and journalists, this book gives an excellent account of the Geneva Conference of 1954. It also deals with the French Indochina War and the period 1954–55, when France's involvement in Indochina was transferred to the United States.

Lacouture, Jean. *Ho Chi Minh.* New York: Random House, 1968.

Vietnam and the War

American Friends Service Committee. *Peace in Vietnam: A New Approach in Southeast Asia.* New York: Hill & Wang, 1966. A short book illustrating the major issues in Vietnam. Includes extensive appendices plus bibliography.

Berrigan, D. *Night Flight to Hanoi.* New York: Macmillan, 1968. Highly personal and poetic account by war-resisting priest.

Burchett, Wilfred. *Vietnam North: Inside Story of the Guerrilla War.* New York: International Publishers Co., 1965. Account by Australian reporter of long visit with the NLF.

Chaliand, G. *Peasants of North Vietnam.* Baltimore, Md.: Penguin Books, 1969. By a French scholar, this book presents long interviews with North Vietnamese peasants. Highly recommended.

Chomsky, Noam. *American Power and the New Mandarins.* New York: Pantheon Books, 1969. Articles on the relationship of scholars to the war in Vietnam and to the cold war.

Fall, Bernard B., and M. G. Raskin, eds. *The Viet-Nam Reader.* New York: Vintage Books, 1965. Articles and documents representing all points of view.

Gerassi, John. *North Vietnam: A Documentary.* New York: Bobbs-Merrill, 1968.

Giap, Vo Nguyen. *People's War, People's Army.* New York: Bantam Books, 1968. Vietminh general says Vietminh won against the French because they were fighting a people's war.

Kahin, George, and John Lewis. *The United States in Vietnam,* rev. ed. New York: Dial, 1969. History of U.S. involvement. Highly recommended. 1969 revision is up to date through early 1969. Includes discussion of Chinese attitudes and U.S. involvement in the manipulation of Saigon politics.

Kolko, Gabriel. *The Roots of American Foreign Policy: An Analysis of Power and Purpose.* Boston: Beacon Press, 1969. Written by a sociologist, this book stresses economic aspects of policy formation.

Luce, Donald S., and John Sommer. *Viet Nam: Unheard Voices.* Ithaca, N.Y.: Cornell University Press, 1969. Two Americans with over ten years' experience in Vietnam with International Voluntary Service give the South Vietnamese peasants' view of the war—they want the war to end.

Lynd, Staughton, and Thomas Hayden. *The Other Side.* New York: Signet Books, 1969. Account of a trip to Hanoi.

McCarthy, Mary. *Vietnam.* New York: Harcourt, Brace and World, 1967. Well-known author's account of her trip to South Vietnam. Includes critique of war policy and suggested solution.

Schell, J. *The Military Half.* New York: Vintage Books, 1968. The destruction of Quang Ngai province (where My Lai is) from the air. First appeared as an article in *New Yorker.*

———. *The Village of Ben Suc.* New York: Vintage Books, 1967. U.S. operation in a single village in South Vietnam. First appeared as an article in *New Yorker.*

Schurmann, Franz, and others. *Politics of Escalation in Vietnam.* New York: Fawcett, 1966. Documents how under President Johnson every publicized "peace feeler" was accompanied by escalation of the war.

Zinn, Howard. *Vietnam: The Logic of Withdrawal.* Boston: Beacon Press, 1967. Highly recommended book on why we should get out of Vietnam and how. Gives perspective on the war. Arguments apply equally to Cambodia. One chapter is titled "Munich, Dominoes, and Containment."

Laos

Burchett, Wilfred. *Mekong Upstream.* 1957.

———. *The Second Indochina War, June 1970.* New York: New World Paperbacks, 1970. Written after the U.S. invasion of Cambodia.

Far East Economic Review. Highly recommended for current reporting.

Le Monde. English weekly edition has included excellent articles by Jacques Decornoy and Claude Pomonti.

McCoy, Al, and Nina Adams, eds. *Laos: War and Revolution.* New York: Harper & Row, 1970. An excellent collection of articles on the background and impact of the American war in Laos.

Toye, Hugh. *Laos: Buffer State or Battleground.* New York: Oxford University Press, 1968. Outstanding book on Laos. Written by former British intelligence officer in Laos.

Cambodia

Lacouture, Jean. *The Demi-Gods.* 1970. A quarter of the book is devoted to a discussion of Sihanouk as a charismatic leader.

Unger, Jonathan, Laurence Moss, and Jonathan Grant. *Cambodia: The Widening War in Indochina.* New York: Simon & Schuster (in press).

Southeast Asia and Indochina

Chomsky, Noam. *At War with Asia.* New York: Pantheon Books, 1970. A collection of Chomsky's perceptive essays on America in Indochina. Includes a report of the author's trip to Laos and North Vietnam in March 1970.

Committee of Concerned Asian Scholars. *The Indochina Story.* New York: Bantam, 1970. An excellent attempt to answer who, how, and why the U.S. is fighting in Indochina.

Scott, Peter Dale, *The War Conspiracy* (tentative). Indianapolis, Ind.: Bobbs-Merrill (in press). A study revealing how American escalations created an ever larger war, with emphasis on relevant U.S. economic, military, and intelligence institutions.

Selden, Mark, and Edward Friedman, eds. *America's Asia.* New York: Pantheon, 1970. Essays by the new generation of Asia scholars. Highly recommended.

Weisberg, Barry, ed. *Ecocide in Indochina.* San Francisco: Canfield Press, 1970. Documents the full complexity of U.S. destruction of individuals, societies, and landscapes of Indochina. The book deals with issues such as defoliation, craterization, refugees, anti-personnel weapons, and air power.

Asian Official Documents

Publications by Peking, North Vietnam, National Liberation Front of South Vietnam, and Pathet Lao are available from China Books and Periodicals, 2929 24th Street, San Francisco, California 94110. A catalogue available on request. Some of these publications can also be found in university libraries and in other specialized bookstores. Particularly recommended: *Vietnamese Studies,* a quarterly published in Hanoi treating problems and topics in North Vietnam and NLF areas.

America and the War

American Expansionism, 1860–1970

Alperovitz, Gar. *Atomic Diplomacy: Hiroshima and Potsdam.* New York: Simon and Schuster, 1965.

———. *Cold War Essays.* New York: Doubleday, 1968.

Barnet, Richard J. *Intervention and Revolution: America's Confrontation with Insurgent Movements Around the World.* Cleveland, Ohio: World Publishing Co., 1968.

Beard, Charles. *American Foreign Policy in the Making, 1932–1940.* New Haven, Conn.: Yale University Press, 1946.

———. *President Roosevelt and the Coming of the War,* 1941. New Haven, Conn.: Yale University Press, 1948.

Bernstein, Barton, ed. *Politics and Policies of the Truman Administration.* Chicago: Quadrangle Books, 1970.

Fleming, D. F. *The Cold War and Its Origins, 1917–1960.* 2 vols. New York: Doubleday, 1961.

Gardner, Lloyd. *Architects of Illusion.* Chicago: Quadrangle Books, 1969.

———. *A Different Frontier: Readings in the Foundation of American Economic Expansion, 1870–1905.* Chicago: Quadrangle Books, 1966.

———. *Economic Aspects of New Deal Diplomacy.* Madison, Wis.: University of Wisconsin Press, 1964.

Horowitz, David, ed. *Containment and Revolution.* Boston: Beacon Press, 1967.

———, ed. *Corporations and the Cold War.* New York: Monthly Review Press, 1969.

———. *The Free World Colossus: A Critique of American Foreign Policy in the Cold War.* New York: Hill and Wang, 1965.

———. *Empire and Revolution: A Radical Interpretation of Contemporary History.* New York: Random House, 1969.

Kolko, Gabriel. *The Politics of War, 1943–1945.* New York: Random House, 1969.

La Feber, Walter. *The New Empire: An Interpretation of American Expansion. 1860–1898.* Ithaca, N.Y.: Cornell Press, 1963.

McCormick, Thomas. *China Market: America's Quest for Informal Empire, 1893–1901.* Chicago: Quadrangle Books, 1967.

Oglesby, Carl, and Richard Shaull. *Containment and Change: Two Dissenting Views of American Foreign Policy.* London: Macmillan, 1969.

Parrini, Carl. *Heir to Empire: U.S. Economic Diplomacy, 1916–1923.* Pittsburgh, Pa.: University of Pittsburgh Press, 1969.

Williams, William Appleman. *The Tragedy of American Diplomacy.* New York: Dell Publishing Co., 1962.

———. *The Roots of the Modern American Empire: A Study of the Growth and Shaping of Social Consciousness in a Marketplace Society.* New York: Random House, 1969.

American Policymakers

Domhoff, G. William. *The Higher Circles: the Governing Class in America.* New York: Random House, 1970.

———. *Who Rules America?* Englewood Cliffs, N.J.: Prentice-Hall, 1967.

——— and H. Ballard. *C. Wright Mills and the Power Elite.* Boston: Beacon Press, 1968.

Gillam, R., ed. *Power in Postwar America.* (In press.)

Kolko, Gabriel. *Wealth and Power in America: An Analysis of Social Classes and Income Distribution.* New York: Praeger, 1962.

Mills, C. Wright. *The Power Elite.* New York: Oxford University Press, 1956.

Capitalism and Imperialism

Baran, Paul. *The Political Economy of Growth.* New York: Monthly Review Press, 1957.

——— and Paul Sweezy. *Monopoly Capital: An Essay on the American Economic and Social Order.* New York: Monthly Review Press, 1966.

Hacker, Andrew, ed. *The Corporation Take-Over.* New York: Doubleday, 1965.

Jalee, Pierre. *The Third World in World Economy.* New York: Monthly Review Press, 1969.

———. *The Pillage of the Third World.* New York: Monthly Review Press, 1968.

Magdoff, Harry. *The Age of Imperialism: The Economics of U.S. Foreign Policy.* New York: Monthly Review Press, 1969.

The War Comes Home

Cleaver, Eldridge. *Soul on Ice.* New York: Delta Books, 1968.

Cohn-Bendit, Daniel and Gabriel. *Obsolete Communism: The Left-Wing Alternative.* New York: McGraw-Hill, 1969.

Douglas, William O. *Points of Rebellion.* New York: Random House, 1970.

Hayden, Tom. *The Trial.* New York: Holt, Rhinehart & Winston, 1970.

Hoffman, Abbie. *Revolution for the Hell of It.* New York: Dial, 1968.

Jacobs, Paul, and Saul Landau. *The New Radicals: A Report with Documents.* New York: Vintage Books, 1966.

Jaffe, Harold, and John Tytell, eds. *The American Experience: A Radical Reader.* New York: Harper & Row, 1970.

Keniston, Kenneth. *Young Radicals: Notes on Committed Youth.* New York: Harcourt, Brace and World, 1968.

Lasch, Christopher. *New Radicalism in America.* New York: Vintage Books, 1966.

Marcuse, Herbert. *An Essay on Liberation.* Boston: Beacon Press, 1969.
Roszak, Theodore. *The Making of a Counter Culture.* New York: Doubleday, 1969.
Seale, Bobby. *Sieze the Time: The Story of the Black Panther Party and Huey P. Newton.* New York: Random House, 1968.
Teodori, Massimo. *The New Left: A Documentary History.* New York: The Bobbs-Merrill Co., 1969.

Appendix A

Chronologies of Events*

U.S. Involvement in Vietnam

Key to Frequent Abbreviations:

ARVN—Army of the Republic of Vietnam
NLF—National Liberation Front
NVA—North Vietnamese Army
VC—Vietcong

1940 (Sept.) Japan enters French Indochina. Has full economic and military use of the country nominally ruled by a Vichy-French administration.

1941 (May) Vietnam Independence League (the Vietminh) founded. This communist-led united front organization includes many non-communist nationalists.

1945 (July) At Potsdam, the U.S. persuades the Allies to agree to a post-war occupation of Indochina by British forces south of the 16th parallel, and by Chinese forces in the North.

American Office of Strategic Services (OSS), forerunner of the CIA, actively supports Ho Chi Minh and the Vietminh in their struggle against Japanese imperialism.

(Sept.) Ho Chi Minh declares the independence of the Democratic Republic of Vietnam in Hanoi.

British arrive in Saigon to disarm the Japanese, re-establishing the French in Saigon and later rearming the Japanese against the Vietminh.

1946 (Dec.) Attempts at negotiations between France and the Vietminh fail. The Vietminh want independence; the French want their colony. War breaks out, to last almost 8 years.

1949 The Communist Party comes to power in China.

The French begin to groom Bao Dai, a member of Vietnamese royal family, to head a French-controlled "State of Vietnam" in opposition to Ho Chi Minh.

1950 In response to communist control of China and the beginning of the Korean War, U.S. decides that the French war in Indochina should be supported for anti-communist reasons. By 1953, the U.S. will be supplying 80% of the costs of the French war effort.

*Chronologies courtesy Concerned Asian Scholars at Stanford.

Time magazine cover story on May 29, 1950, explains, "It is Bao Dai's mission, and the U.S.–French hope, to rally his countrymen to the anti-communist camp of the West. In this undertaking he needs time. 'Nothing can be done overnight,' he says."

1953 (Sept.) Special U.S. grant of $385 million to implement the Navarre Plan, designed to build French and Vietnamese troops up to a level permitting the destruction of the Vietminh forces by the end of 1955.

1954 (April) Vietminh siege of French forces at Dien Bien Phu. Admiral Radford (Chairman of Joint Chiefs of Staff), Secretary of State John Foster Dulles, and Vice-President Nixon favor American armed intervention. Use of air strikes around Dien Bien Phu or troop commitment considered. High government officials reported to favor use of tactical nuclear weapons to "save" French position at Dien Bien Phu. Eisenhower will not commit U.S. forces to Indochina without congressional and Allied support, neither of which is forthcoming. (For fullest discussion, see Melvin Gurtov, *The First Vietnam Crisis,* Columbia University Press, 1967.)

(July) Geneva Accords signed: cease-fire arrangements signed only by France and the Democratic Republic of Vietnam (Vietminh). (For text of accords, see Kahin and Lewis, *The United States in Vietnam,* rev. ed., Dial, 1969.) The Accords provided for:

1. a provisional military demarcation line at the 17th parallel to permit the regrouping of forces, the French to the south and Vietminh to the north. Each of the parties would administer its respective zone pending general elections for all of Vietnam, to be held in July, 1956.

2. a ban on the introduction of new military personnel, materiel, or bases and the adherence of either party to any military alliance with an outside power.

3. the military demarcation line to be provisional and not in any way to be interpreted as constituting a political or territorial boundary. U.S. does not join in signing the Geneva Accords, but makes a unilateral declaration pledging to refrain from disturbing the Accords by force and endorsing fair, free elections for all of Vietnam under UN supervision. A private communique to the French government, however, makes it clear that the U.S. does not intend to honor its public commitment: it will only abide by an armistice in Vietnam if it does not ". . . contain political provisions which would risk loss of the retained area [Southern Vietnam] to communist control," and does not impose on Laos, Cambodia, and southern Vietnam ". . . restrictions impairing their right to maintain adequate forces for internal security, to import arms and to employ foreign advisors." (From Anthony Eden, *Full Circle,* Houghton Mifflin, 1960, pp. 132–133.)

(Sept.) Establishment of Southeast Asia Treaty Organization (SEATO), a collective defense pact sponsored by the U.S. The State of Vietnam, headed by Bao Dai, does not sign the treaty. No provision in the treaty commits the signatories to provide troops or other support to any government in southern Vietnam. An additional protocol, however, designates the southern zone of Vietnam as falling under SEATO protection. This unilateral protocol is designed to circumvent the provision of the Geneva Accords that the south could *not* adhere to a military alliance.

(Nov.) U.S. puts decisive support behind Ngo Ninh Diem by refusing to train or give aid to Vietnamese armed forces not committed to the U.S. candidate (See Kahin and Lewis, p. 68.)

1955 (July) Hanoi proposes establishment of normal relations between the northern and southern zones to prepare for the elections scheduled by the Geneva Accords. Diem consolidates control, establishing a state of "South Vietnam." Supported by the U.S., he refuses to cooperate in carrying out Geneva Accords for elections. The key to South Vietnamese and U.S. reluctance to hold the elections is found in a statement in Eisenhower's memoirs: if there were free elections, ". . . possibly 80% of the population would have voted for the Communist Ho Chi Minh."

1956 In violation of Geneva Accords, Diem initiates a policy of imprisoning all people who had been involved in war against the French. Large concentration camps are set up; police actions are taken against religious sects and mountain peoples. This is the origin of the so-called "Vietcong" which means "Vietnamese Communists," for Diem knew he could obtain U.S. support by calling all his opponents "Communists," whether communist or not.

In violation of Geneva Accords, U.S. continues to supply military materiel and advisors to the South Vietnamese government.

1958 First appearance of southern resisters to Diem's dictatorship, many of whom were non-communist, calling themselves "The National Liberation Front of South Vietnam."

1959 Diem steps up repression by promulgating the death sentences for anyone engaged in anti-government activities. The number of political prisoners rises from 40,000 in 1958 to nearly 160,000 in 1961.

1960 (April) Former government officials and professionals in Saigon (the Caravellists) publicly protest Diem's policies; all are imprisoned.

(Nov.) Abortive palace revolt by Diem's paratroop battalion.

(Dec.) U.S. acknowledges presence of 773 U.S. personnel in Vietnam.

The National Liberation Front (NLF) formally established in response to southern political factors and not as a result of infiltration from the north. Little other than verbal support from the Democratic Republic of Vietnam (North Vietnam) for the NLF at this time. (For detail and documentation, see Kahin and Lewis, Chapter V, 'The Origins of the Civil War.')

1961 (Sept.) Sir Robert Thompson, British counter-insurgency expert, arrives in South Vietnam. Influential in developing a strategic hamlet program consisting of moving peasants into fortified villages. Program alienates people and only adds to NLF strength.

(Oct.) Diem declares a state of emergency as a result of growing insurgent strength.

1962 Great U.S. optimism about success of strategic hamlet program. Secretary of Defense McNamara makes his first visit to Vietnam. Says, "Every quantitative measurement we have shows we're winning this war." U.S. troop strength in Vietnam: 10,000.

1963 (May) Growing Buddhist and student opposition to Diem regime. Self-immolation of Buddhist monk gets world-wide publicity. Strong U.S.

and world public opinion against Catholic Diem government's treatment of Buddhists. Certain U.S. agencies reported to withdraw support from Diem, making way for his overthrow. U.S. troop strength: 14,000.

(Oct.) Military coup ends Diem regime. Diem and his brother Nhu, head of secret police, assassinated. Beginning of rule by military oligarchy, starting with General Minh.

Secretary of Defense McNamara and General Maxwell Taylor report that ". . . by the end of this year, the U.S. program for training Vietnamese should have progressed to the point where 1,000 U.S. military personnel assigned to South Vietnam can be withdrawn." (From White House statement on Vietnam, *Department of State Bulletin.*)

(Nov.) Kennedy assassinated; Johnson becomes President.

1964 (Jan.) General Khanh overthrows the Minh junta. Minh had come under criticism from the U.S. and some of his own generals for failing to stem the tide of neutralist feeling in favor of negotiations with the NLF. Growing Americanization of the war.

(July) Khanh calls for attack on North Vietnam. Nguyen Cao Ky, Commander of the Vietnamese Air Force, says he is prepared to bomb North Vietnam at any time.

(Aug.) President Johnson persuades Congress to pass Tonkin Gulf Resolution authorizing President to take all necessary action to protect U.S. Armed Forces, as a result of alleged North Vietnamese attack on U.S. vessels in international waters.

(Dec.) Saigon army virtually defeated militarily, as a result of NLF campaign to annihilate Saigon's strategic reserves. This makes necessary a key decision by President Johnson: accept negotiations with NLF for coalition government and a neutral South Vietnam, or greatly increase U.S. involvement.

1965 (Jan.) Renewed outbreak of pro-neutralist, anti-junta, and anti-American sentiments in Saigon, led by same Buddhists and students who had caused the downfall of Diem's dictatorship.

(Feb.) U.S. begins to bomb North Vietnam, using pretext of a guerrilla raid on Pleiku which took eight American lives. No more than twelve hours pass from Pleiku incident to bombing on Feb. 7. Yet Arthur Krock in *New York Times* on Feb. 10 reveals that Washington had informed several other governments about the planned escalation prior to Feb. 7 attack on Pleiku.

State Department releases white paper claiming a "Communist government has set out deliberately to conquer a sovereign people in a neighboring state."

(March) Marked escalation of the bombing, including nonmilitary targets (bridges) and daily raids. Nonaligned nations appeal for negotiations without preconditions.

(June) Government of South Vietnam fails again. Replaced by a military junta dominated by Ky and Thieu.

U.S. takes more active, independent role in an intensified war. Troops increased to total of 53,500. Johnson first publicly authorizes U.S. troops to perform search and destroy operations. (Troops formerly limited to "patrolling.")

(July) McNamara visits South Vietnam and reports that the situation has deteriorated since his last visit five months before.

(Dec.) U.S. combat troops number 160,000.

1966 (Jan.) Senate Foreign Relations Committee openly challenges legality of U.S. military involvement in Vietnamese war and demands an explanation of administrative policy.

(Feb.) Broad anti-junta coalition of Buddhists and students demonstrates against Ky regime. U.S. fears return of civilian government to power in Saigon, which would negotiate settlement with NLF.

(May) "Buddhist Struggle Movement" in Central Vietnam crushed by Ky, resulting in the death and imprisonment of thousands. The besieged coalition, led by General Thi, includes Buddhist monks, students, peasants, and South Vietnamese army forces desiring peace. Intense resentment in Central Vietnam engendered by the fact that the U.S. supplied helicopter transport for Ky's troops to crush this non-Communist regional uprising.

(July) U.S. combat troop level jumps to 267,000 men. Intensification of bombing of the North, where B-52 strategic bombers are used for the first time, close to urban, populated areas.

(Oct.) Manila Conference between Johnson and Ky. Communique stresses that U.S. will withdraw its troops from Vietnam six months after Communists (including Southern NLF) withdraw their forces to the North.

1967 (Aug.) McNamara testifies before Senate Armed Services Committee on ineffectiveness of the bombing of the North. The ". . . quantity of externally supplied material, other than food, required to support the VC/NVA forces in South Vietnam at their current level of combat activity is very, very small. The reported figure is fifteen tons per day, but even if the quantity were five times that amount, it could be transported by only a few trucks."

(Sept.) Thieu wins Presidential elections. Prominent advocates of peace and negotiations not allowed to run. Despite election irregularities and the overwhelming influence of the military, a lawyer named Truong Dinh Dzu, who only declared himself for peace *after* he was accepted as a candidate, comes in a strong second. After election, Dzu jailed on trumped-up charges. National Assembly refuses to ratify the election results until after pressured by the secret police. (See Kahin and Lewis.)

(Oct.) General Westmoreland shifts strategy from "pacification" (search and destroy missions in villages) to "free-fire zone" tactics—saturation bombing in VC and civilian areas to preclude the use of the land for food or shelter. This generates huge number of "refugees from communism."

1968 (Feb.) Vietcong Tet offensive: attacks on 36 of 44 provincial capitals. U.S. Air Force bombs cities. 5,000 civilian casualties in Hué as result of bombing.

President Johnson calls for major review of policy. Westmoreland requests 206,000 more troops, an increase of 40% over the existing U.S. military strength of 535,000 men. This request refused.

(March) Johnson announces he will not run for a second term. Ends bombing north of the 19th parallel in North Vietnam. (Until total bombing halt in October, bombing between 17th and 19th parallels is more intensive than previous bombing of all North Vietnam.) U.S. sends 13,500 additional troops to Vietnam.

(May) Preliminary peace talks finally begin in Paris, although resolution of the conflict through political means is still less important to the U.S. command than achievement of military victory.

(Oct.) Johnson accepts NLF participation at Peace Talks on condition that Hanoi agrees to presence of Saigon delegation. Johnson assures TV audience that "attendance by representatives of NLF in no way involves recognition of NLF in any form."

(April) Thieu maintains no political settlement is possible unless all North Vietnamese forces are withdrawn to the north (before departure of U.S.) and all NLF members renounce communism.

1969 (May) NLF calls for unconditional withdrawal of U.S. and Allied troops, and for determination by Vietnamese parties (not foreign parties) of a cease-fire and of a provisional coalition government.

President Nixon states his administration does not oppose a coalition government, although U.S. must demonstrate that ". . . confrontation with the U.S. is costly and unrewarding." Initiation of "Vietnamization" strategy and withdrawal of U.S. troops.

(Dec.) Saigon government arrests fifteen student leaders at Saigon University, and closes two newspapers on charges of pro-neutralism and anti-security. Evidence of torturing political opponents in jail.

1970 (April) U.S.–ARVN joint invasion of Cambodia.

(May) U.S. conducts large bombing raid on North Vietnam (120 planes), first large-scale attack since November, 1968, and first bombing north of 19th parallel since March, 1968.

U.S. Involvement in Laos

Key to Frequent Abbreviations:

ARVN—Army of the Republic of Vietnam
DRV—Democratic Republic of Vietnam (North Vietnam)
FAC—Forward Air Control
JUSMAG THAI—Joint United States Military Advisory Group in Thailand
MAAG—Military Assistance Advisory Group
NVA—North Vietnamese Army
PEO—Programs Evaluation Office
PL—Pathet Lao
RLG—Royal Laotian Government
RO/AID—Requirements Office of U.S. Aid
SEATO—Southeast Asia Treaty Organization

1949 Mutual Defense Assistance Act. Leads to a five-sided agreement among France, the United States, and the countries of Indochina (1950) governing the furnishing of military assistance.

1950 (August 13) Formation of the Pathet Lao.

1951 (March 11) Joint meeting of Khmer Issarak (Thai movement), Pathet

Lao, and Vietminh; allows the Vietminh to use Laos as a staging ground to fight the French.

1954 (Spring) Dien Bien Phu.

(May–June) Geneva Conference. Phong Saly and Sam Neua provinces given to PL as regroupment areas. By 1954, PL had liberated two-thirds of Laotian provinces.

United States begins backing right-wing elements, displeased with Souvanna Phouma's efforts at neutralism and integration of PL into Laotian government, 1954–1957.

1955 Southeast Asian Treaty Organization (SEATO) organized on the initiative of the United States Government.

First U.S. Agency for International Development (AID) office set up in Laos.

1957 Royal Laotian Government agrees on integration of the PL into national life. Souphanouvong and Phoumi Vongvichit (PL leaders) enter coalition government.

1958 (May) Elections held. Left wing wins thirteen out of twenty additional seats provided. Neo Lao Hak Sat (political party of the PL organized to participate in the coalition government) organized.

(Aug.) American-backed right-wing coup led by Phoumi Nosavan ousts Souvanna Phouma. New right-wing government under Phoumi Sanaikone.

Programs Evaluations Office, first CIA front in Laos, set up: leads to organization of the Military Assistance Advisory Group.

1959 Military integration of PL into the RLG Army sabotaged by right-wing maneuver. Final battalion of PL forces escapes to North Vietnam. Souphanouvong and colleagues placed under arrest.

1960 (Jan.) CIA backs Phoumi Nosavan coup ousting Phoumi Sanaikone. Kon Abhay government dominated by Phoumi Nosavan.

(April) Rigged elections seen as legitimizing the coup.

(August 9) Kong Le takes over Vientiane in a successful coup. Declares policy of neutrality. Puts Souvanna Phouma back in power.

CIA continues to aid Phoumi.

1961 PEO officially transformed into Military Assistance Advisory Group (MAAG).

(March) President Kennedy sends 500 marines with helicopters into Udorn Thailand (major B-52 base for raids over Northern Laos and North Vietnam).

1962 Phoumi still attempting a coup despite established ceasefire.

(July 23) Geneva Accords: withdrawal of all foreign troops from Laos; respect of sovereignty, neutrality, and integrity of Laos. Article VI allows for the possibility of RLG requesting military aid in cases of self-defense. Signed by People's Republic of China, the U.S.S.R., the United States, the United Kingdom, the Democratic Republic of North Vietnam, Laos, and Cambodia.

Three-way coalition formed within Laos between Souvanna Phouma, Souphanouvong, and Boun Oum. In violation of Accords, U.S. maintains Special Forces organizing General Vang Pao's "Secret Army."

The United States creates office of Deputy Chief of Joint United States

Military Advisory Group in Thailand (JUSMAG THAI) specifically to handle military assistance in Laos, since presence of U.S. military interests in Laos is prohibited by the Accords.

U.S. sets up the Requirements Office of U.S. AID (RO/AID) to coordinate communications between the deputy chief of JUSMAG THAI and the Laotian military forces.

RLG asks U.S. to provide supplies, repair parts for U.S.-furnished equipment, training assistance, and ammunition.

(November 6) The U.S. agrees to aid requests.

U.S.S.R. in agreement with the Accords, cuts off aid to the neutralists, undermining independent position of Kong Le's forces. The neutralists split; Kong Le first turns to the U.S., then goes into exile in 1966.

Beginning of Chinese roadbuilding in northern Laos.

1963 Assassination of important neutralist and PL political figures. More fighting breaks out between RLG army and PL.

(April) Following RLG atacks against the PL on the Plain of Jars, U.S. responds favorably to further aid requests by the RLG.

U.S. special forces, still in eastern Laos since late 1950's, training minority tribes, especially with Vang Pao.

Chinese road from Meng La in Yunnan to Phong Saly province completed.

1964 (February) U.S. obtains Royal Thai Government agreement to allow United States Air Force Special Air War Units to train Lao pilots in Thailand.

(April 19) Chief of Phoumi's secret police takes control of Vientiane. Final disintegration of neutralist position.

Souvanna Phouma accepts beginning of U.S. air reconnaissance flights.

(May 19) First U.S. bombing flight over southern Laos.

(May 21) U.S. bombing extended to the Plain of Jars.

(June 16) Agreement reached with Souvanna Phouma to keep information on U.S. flights secret. Firing on ground targets by U.S. escort planes not to be acknowledged.

Royal Thai Government allows use of Thai bases for U.S. photo reconnaissance flights over Laos.

Phou Pha Thi constructed. Includes radar and electronic control of bombings over North Vietnam, rescue helicopter base, and base for small Meo guerrilla harassment raids into North Vietnam.

1965 Reported existence of 250,000 to 430,000 refugees as a result of American escalation, particularly in northern Laos.

Attempted coup by right-wing faction led by Siho.

1966 American Forward Air Control (FAC) begins flying target and spotting missions for Laotian bombing.

Attempted coup by right-wing faction led by General Ma.

1967 Luang Prabang used as a temporary staging base for FAC (a stated violation of the 1962 Accords).

1968 FAC first permanently assigned to Luang Prabang.

(March 11) PL troops overrun secret U.S. radar base at Phou Pha Thi.

(March 31) Limited U.S. bombing halt over DRV.

(April) *Le Monde* correspondent reports all but two villages in Sam Nuea province destroyed; remaining villagers living in hill caves.

(September) 3,000 sorties per month over northern Laos.

(October) 4,000 sorties per month over northern Laos.

(November) 12,000 sorties per month over northern Laos. After November elections, bombing escalated. Sam Thong base (U.S.) near Long Cheng, major base for Vang Pao's "Secret Army," overrun by PL and NVA troops.

1969 (April 9) Xieng Khoung bombed and destroyed by U.S. planes as it is overrun by Pathet Lao.

(June 26) Muong Long bombed by B-52's.

(September 7) Plain of Jars bombed by B-52's after North Vietnamese and Pathet Lao had withdrawn. 20,000 peasants forcibly evacuated prior to bombing.

(December 16) Church-Cooper Amendment passed by U.S. Senate to bar U.S. ground troops from Laos. *New York Times* notes presence of Special Forces units in Laos and Vang Pao's 30,000 man "Secret Army" supported by Pentagon and CIA. Mansfield and Fulbright reveal U.S. bombing has increased.

1970 (January 24) U.S. Senate reveals U.S. Aid to RLG for fiscal year 1970 approximately $190 million.

(February 22) PL and North Vietnamese troops overrun the Plain of Jars.

(March 12) U.S. A-1 fighter shot down over Laos, apparently flying air support for RLG forces fighting PL and North Vietnamese rather than bombing Ho Chi Minh trail.

(March 14) Fulbright reports he has confirmation that CIA is using AID as a screen for its operations in Laos.

(March 21) Two Thai battalions flown by U.S. planes to Long Cheng to help defend it against North Vietnamese and PL attacks.

(March 23) USAF spotter plane shot down over Plain of Jars.

(March 17–24) 80,000 to 100,000 refugees driven from Plain of Jars.

(March 25) Marine helicopters downed over Laos.

(April 1) Town of Attopeu (American base) captured by PL and North Vietnamese.

(May 7) Kennedy's Senate Sub-Committee on refugees reports that, of 700,000 refugees in Laos (total population: 2½–3 million), *most* were fleeing U.S. bombing.

(May 18) South Vietnamese Foreign Minister announces ARVN invasion of Southern Laos ". . . has been under way for some time." American advisors and air support confirmed.

(May 19) Laird admits U.S. ground troops involved in brief incursions in Southern Laos. "In his Senate testimony, Laird stressed that the 'protective reaction' missions—short incursions into Laos to prevent enemy troops from launching attacks on American or South Vietnamese forces—are permissible under an amendment to the Current Defense Appropriations Act *which prohibits U.S. Ground troops in Laos or Thailand.*" (From *San Francisco Chronicle,* May 19, 1970.)

U.S. Involvement in Cambodia

Key to Frequent Abbreviations

ARVN—Army of the Republic of Vietnam
COSVN—Vietcong Headquarters for Operations in South Vietnam
KR—Khmer Rouge
NLF—National Liberation Front
NV—North Vietnamese
NVA—North Vietnamese Army
SEATO—Southeast Asia Treaty Organization
VC—Vietcong

1884 King Norodom forced to abandon independence and place his country under control of France in order to avoid division of Cambodia between Thailand and Vietnam.

1941 Sihanouk declared King at age 18. Japanese occupy Cambodia.

1945–1950: Post-War Settlement—A French-Controlled Cambodia

1945 Authority over Cambodia returned to France.

Collaborationist Premier Son Ngoc Thanh wins national referendum in independence move. Thanh arrested; supporters flee to Thailand and form dissident nationalist movement (Khmer Issarak).

1946 Cambodia becomes "autonomous state within French Union." Sihanouk reinstated with French retaining veto power and control of army, police, finances, and judiciary. An anti-French line would win elections, but King Sihanouk favors gradual achievement of negotiated independence.

1949 French sign treaty transferring de jure independence to Kingdom of Cambodia, providing Cambodia with control over its own army and police except in time of war; but French officially stipulate a continuing state of war.

1950 U.S. establishes diplomatic relations. Nationalist activity increases as total independence proves hollow reality. "Liberation government" named by Vietminh for Cambodia. Cambodia sends troops to fight (with French) against the Vietminh in Vietnam.

Sihanouk takes stronger nationalist stance in face of increased Vietminh activity in Cambodia.

1951–1956: Cambodia Becomes Independent—Sihanouk Announces Neutral Foreign Policy

1952 Increasing anti-government activity from both communists and non-communists. Sihanouk takes emergency powers.

1953 Sihanouk's "royal crusade for independence" seeks U.S. aid to pressure French. U.S. refuses. Continued French presence causes many non-communist elements to join insurgents. Sihanouk enters voluntary exile and declares intent to lead "holy war for independence."

(Oct.–Dec.) French finally agree to independence in effort to prevent two-front war in Indochina. Sihanouk begins efforts to oust Vietminh forces; U.S. offers aid.

1954 Geneva Conference agreement provides for evacuation of Vietminh from Cambodia. Under Sept. 1954 SEATO treaty (ratified by U.S. Senate Feb. 1955), Cambodia is designated a protected state. U.S. promises further aid. French withdraw from Indochina.

(Dec.) Sihanouk announces Cambodia will remain unaligned and will conduct a neutral foreign policy.

1955 Sihanouk abdicates throne and forms the Sangkum Party to compete in national elections. His party wins overwhelming victory. Bandung Conference establishes understanding between Sihanouk and Communist China for peaceful co-existence and no foreign bases in Cambodia. Sihanouk renounces SEATO protection.

1956 Thailand and South Vietnam impose economic blockade of Cambodia in retaliation for Sihanouk signature of aid agreement with China. U.S. suspends aid. Subsequent negotiations result in lifting of blockade. Cambodia resists U.S. pressure to join SEATO. American and Soviet aid accepted.

1957–1960: Foreign Elements Work Against Sihanouk

1958 South Vietnamese army units invade Cambodian border areas. Cambodia appeals to U.S. to restrain Saigon; U.S. refuses. Cambodia proposes diplomatic relations with China. U.S. considers cutting off aid as anti-Sihanouk move. Khmer Serei (Free Cambodia) movement organized reportedly with CIA, Thia, and Vietnamese aid. Thais begin anti-Combodian campaign; Cambodia suspends diplomatic relations with Thailand.

1959 Bangkok Plot exposed. Plot called for anti-Sihanouk invasion from Thailand by foreign-supported Khmer Serei forces and creation of new opposition political party. U.S., Thailand, and South Vietnam are implicated in plot. Eisenhower denies U.S. involvement, Thailand and South Vietnam cease provocative actions, and diplomatic relations with Thailand are restored.

1960 National referendum gives near-unanimous support to Sihanouk policies. (Non-communist opposition elements compromised by implication in Bangkok Plot.) Sihanouk made Chief of State for life.

Sihanouk calls for international conference on Laos.

Kennedy assumes U.S. Presidency.

1961–1966: Sihanouk Strives for Neutral Cambodia

1961 At Geneva Conference on Laos, Sihanouk proposes that neutralization of Laos be extended to Cambodia. Saigon persecution of Cambodian minority in Vietnam results in refugees fleeing to Cambodia. Thais accuse Cambodia of giving sanctuary to communist elements which seek to subvert rest of Southeast Asia; Cambodia breaks diplomatic relations with Thailand.

1962 Sihanouk calls for new conference in Geneva, this time to extend "international protection" to Cambodia; U.S. is noncommittal. Sihanouk offers to accept international control in return for recognition of existing borders. South Vietnamese oppose, continue border violations.

1963 Cambodian protest at continued Saigon repression of Vietnamese Buddhists and discrimination against Cambodian minority in Vietnam;

diplomatic relations are broken. Anti-Sihanouk activity by Khmer Serei resumes at new intensity; includes virulent propaganda from CIA-furnished transmitters in agreements. Pentagon reacts by calling for intervention in Cambodia. Liu Shao Ch'i, President of People's Republic of China, visits Cambodia. Sihanouk seeks Chinese support in controlling North Vietnamese and NLF forces in Cambodian border areas.

1964 Continuing border violations from South Vietnam (including at least one attack [in mid-March] by South Vietnamese unit with American adviser). U.S.S.R. and France ask U.S. support for declaration of Cambodian neutrality. U.S. refuses unless Cambodia first resolves its difference with its neighbors.

U.S. aid totals $403.7 million for the period 1956–1964. Soviet aid totals $57.7 million for the same period.

(April) Cambodia recalls its diplomatic mission from Washington. U.S. delegate in UN denies Cambodian charges concerning continuing U.S. involvement in border violations and states that U.S. is convinced "Vietnam has no aggressive designs toward Cambodia."

(Autumn) North Vietnam infiltrates first large force of regular troops through Cambodia into Mekong Delta. U.S. requests negotiations with Cambodia.

(Dec.) U.S. and Cambodia open talks in Cambodia; disagree over question of border determinations. Cambodia wants recognition of boundaries before international conference takes place. Talks broken off.

1965 (April) Rusk indicates U.S. would participate in international conference on Cambodian neutrality.

(May–Oct.) Cambodia severs diplomatic relations with U.S. Border violations continue; U.S. planes attack two Cambodian border villages in May and napalm a third in October.

(Nov.) Sihanouk states conditions for renewed U.S. relations: recognition of Cambodian territorial integrity, cessation of military incursion, and indemnity for losses to life and property.

1966 (Jan.) U.S. fourteen-point peace plan for Southeast Asia includes possibility of neutralization. Armed border incursions continue. Rusk announces continued U.S. support for Cambodian neutrality, adds that Hanoi and Vietcong have abused it. UN mediation of Thai-Cambodian border conflict fails; border attacks continue. Conservative general, Lon Nol, Minister of National Defense, is transferred by Sihanouk to position of Prime Minister. Sihanouk's neutralist policies come under increasing attack from this time on by Lon Nol and other right-wing elements. Right-wing elements seek more military and economic aid from the U.S. (primarily to increase the flow of funds and material into hands of Cambodian generals) and encourage a much more anti-communist posture in Cambodian foreign policy.

1967–1968: Leftist as Well as Rightist Elements Pressure Sihanouk

1967 (April–May) Sihanouk sends army against communist rebels and continues his military action to counter Khmer Serei attacks still being mounted from South Vietnam and Thailand. Sihanouk given full powers by National Assembly. Lon Nol dropped as Prime Minister after leftist pressures. Sihanouk refuses U.S. request for talks on use of Cambodia by North Vietnamese troops.

(June) Cambodia establishes diplomatic relations with North Vietnam; offers to renew relations with Thailand if borders are recognized.

(July-Aug.) U.S.-sponsored Khmer Serei attacks continue into Cambodia and penetrate up to twelve miles.

(Sept.–Oct.) Cultural Revolution begins to influence the Chinese minority in Cambodia. Sihanouk accuses China of imperialism and internal interference in Cambodia and threatens to seek aid from U.S.

(Nov.) Reconciliation between Cambodia and Peking.

(Nov.–Dec.) U.S. continues refusal to recognize existing borders; it considers this a matter for negotiations between Cambodia and its neighbors. U.S. upholds border incursions by U.S. army in "hot pursuit."

1968 (Jan.) Bowles' mission to Cambodia inconclusive in matter of re-establishing diplomatic relations. U.S.S.R. condemns violation of Cambodian territorial integrity but opposes strengthening of International Control Commission. Sihanouk accuses communist elements of fomenting civil war in northwestern Cambodia.

(March–July) Sihanouk charges that communists support rebel activity in northeastern Cambodia. Sihanouk complains to U.S. on continuing U.S. and South Vietnamese border violations in south.

(Sept.) U.S. charges that use of northeast Cambodia and Svayrieng provinces for bases of Vietcong and North Vietnamese forces has tripled.

(Nov.–Dec.) Cambodia charges that U.S. air attacks killed 300 Cambodians in border villages. Four captured American flyers released.

1969–1970: Sihanouk Rapprochement with U.S.—Military Coup Ousts Sihanouk

1969 Economic situation worsening, with budget deficit of $20 million and devaluation of the Riel.

(April) Cambodia offers to re-establish diplomatic relations with U.S. in exchange for recognition of her territorial integrity. U.S. states that it "recognizes and respects sovereignty, independence, neutrality, and territorial integrity" of Cambodia. U.S. planes bomb border regions.

(May) Two U.S. helicopters downed in Cambodia; NLF mission in Cambodia raised to Embassy status.

(Aug.) American Embassy reopened in Phnom Penh. Sihanouk says new cabinet formed under General Lon Nol will re-examine issue of U.S. aid.

(Aug.) Sihanouk alleges 40,000 communist troops in Cambodia.

(Oct.) Sihanouk protests U.S. bombing of border provinces.

(Dec.) Denationalization of banking and import/export. In late December, Cambodia admitted to International Monetary Fund and World Bank, and given U.S. aid.

1970 (Jan.) U.S. pays compensation for Cambodian losses resulting from continuing border clashes.

(Mar. 8) Cambodian army organizes anti-VC demonstrations in Svayrieng.

(Mar. 11) 10,000 students, soldiers, and monks ordered to demonstrate at Independence monument in Phnom Penh, then marched to VC and NV embassies. Forty-five civilian-dress soldiers sack embassies. National Assembly approves the demonstration.

(Mar. 12) Cabinet cables Sihanouk in Paris of radical change in foreign and military policy. Army expands from 25,000 to 30,000.

(Mar. 13) Lon Nol expresses "sincere regrets" for embassy demonstrations. Orders VC/NV to remove troops by Sunday, March 15.

(Mar. 16) 10,000 students demonstrate at National Assembly against VC/NV troops and move onto embassies in Phnom Penh. Government begins talks with VC/NV to remove troops. Pro-Sihanouk police launch abortive coup by attempting to arrest Lon Nol. Failing, leaders forced to resign.

(Mar. 17) Phnom Penh airport closed; government offices and radio station surrounded. Cambodian army and South Vietnamese army fight together against VC on border. Sihanouk meets Brezhnev, who offers support.

(Mar. 18) Sihanouk removed by National Assembly and Council of Kingdom. Lon Nol appointed Premier and Defense Minister. Sirik Matak made First Deputy Premier. U.S. reacts with surprise; hopes war situation in South Vietnam will improve with new friendly regime. Sihanouk telegrams home, indicating U.S.S.R. refuses to restrain VC/NV. Sihanouk leaves for Peking.

(Mar. 19) Sihanouk arrives in Peking without ceremony. National Assembly declares state of emergency, suspends constitutional liberties, and closes port of Sihanoukville to the Democratic Republic of Vietnam (North Vietnam). Lon Nol notes no change in strict neutrality.

(Mar. 20) Sihanouk argues National Assembly and Council of Kingdom cannot legally depose him as head of state, blames CIA for coup, and calls for referendum in Cambodia under auspices of the International Control Commission. Continued South Vietnamese Air Force aid to Cambodian army, 2 miles inside Cambodia.

(Mar. 23) Lon Nol hopes for "strict neutrality" through withdrawal of VC/NV troops. Airport reopens. Sihanouk plans "Army of Liberation" in Peking.

(Mar. 24) U.S. noncommittal on Cambodian request for aid.

(Mar. 25) Soviets warn against change in Cambodia's neutral status. Saigon jets execute fourth air raid in Cambodia.

(Mar. 26) U.S. fighters attack NV/VC gun opposition in Cambodia in fifth U.S. exercise of "inherent right of self-defense." Three Khmer Rouge leaders issue statement of support for Sihanouk.

(Mar. 27) Pro-Sihanouk demonstration in provinces; curfew imposed in Phnom Penh. First large-scale South Vietnamese army sweep into Cambodia. U.S. gunships fire into Cambodia from South Vietnamese border.

(Mar. 28) U.S. forces first allowed to cross border. Ziegler declares: "This does not represent widening of the war." White House announces American troops may cross Cambodian border in response to enemy threats.

(Mar. 29) Government fires on pro-Sihanouk supporters marching on the capital. Dozens killed, hundreds wounded. NVA (North Vietnamese Army), VC, and Khmer Rouge troops move against government forces. Vietnamese residents in Cambodia flee to South Vietnam as result of persecution in eastern provinces.

(Mar. 30) Lon Nol says in no case would Cambodia request help from foreign troops.

(Apr. 1) Cambodian government spokesman says Cambodia would never request U.S. aid or troop intervention. France calls for general conference on Indochina.

(Apr. 2) Cambodia frees 480 political prisoners. Cambodian government denies right of U.S. or South Vietnamese troops to pursue enemy into Cambodia.

(Apr. 3) *New York Times* reports that authoritative Nixon administration sources say Vietcong headquarters for operations in South Vietnam (COSVN) was moved in late March from Cambodia to South Vietnam.

(Apr. 5) NVA/VC/KR (Khmer Rouge) forces move deeper into Cambodia.

(Apr. 9) 100 Vietnamese and Chinese massacred in Prasavat. Cambodian troops withdraw from Parrot's Beak. U.S. advisors allowed to make protocol visits to Cambodia.

(Apr. 14) Lon Nol requests military aid.

(Apr. 15) Nixon replies that there are no immediate plans to reply to Lon Nol's appeal for arms. Joint ARVN/Cambodian Army attacks on VC/KR/NVA troops. All diplomatic missions in Phnom Penh receive official request for arms and equipment for use against communist forces.

(Apr. 16) U.S. discloses official Cambodian request for aid. Senator Mansfield pleads for U.S. to go no further. Cambodian government says it is unable to protect rights of Vietnamese minorities in Cambodia. An estimated 1,000 bodies of Vietnamese float down Mekong.

(Apr. 17) Of seventeen provinces in Cambodia, three totally controlled by NLF/KR/NVA and five more in question. U.S.S.R. delegate to UN indicates a Geneva Conference could find a solution and relax tensions in Indochina.

(Apr. 18) Vietnamese residents arrested along whole border region. Cambodian soldiers shoot 100 Vietnamese civilians, including thirty children in grade school.

(Apr. 20) NLF/KR capture Saang, twenty miles from Phnom Penh, without a fight, and distribute weapons to Vietnamese civilians.

Nixon announces withdrawal of 150,000 U.S. troops from South Vietnam over the next year.

(Apr. 21) Nixon indicates Cambodia has urgently appealed for U.S. arms and military assistance and active intervention in Cambodia.

(Apr. 22) Lon Nol requests return of U.S.-trained and -equipped Cambodian troops in South Vietnam to Cambodia. Le Duan (Secretary/General of the North Vietnamese Communist Party) says people of North Vietnam, Laos, and Cambodia would unify efforts against U.S. imperialists who intend to widen war in Indochina.

Nixon announces first airlift of captured arms to Cambodia. U.S. calls situation in Cambodia a "foreign invasion of a neutral country."

(Apr. 23) Cambodia denies massacres and begins repatriation of Vietnamese.

(Apr. 24) Cambodian foreign ministry protests U.S. incursions into Cambodia. Cambodian government denounces VC/NVA attacks in border areas as violations of Cambodian neutrality, and contrary to Geneva Accords. *New York Times* describes Nixon as convinced that a U.S. attack on Cambodia would kill any chance of a negotiated settlement for Indochina. Sihanouk meets with Chou En-lai (Premier of People's Republic of China), Pham Van Dong (Premier of Democratic Republic of Vietnam), Souphanouvong (leader of the Pathet Lao), Nguyen Huu Tho (President of the National Liberation Front, commonly known as Vietcong), and representatives of the Khmer Rouge at a summit conference of the Indochinese Peoples in Southern China.

(Apr. 26) Hanoi reports a United National Front Committee established in East Cambodia. Sihanouk may go to liberated areas.

(Apr. 27) Senate Foreign Relations Committee opposes arms to Cambodia in a bipartisan stand. Rogers testifies before Committee, announces second weapons lift to Cambodia; promises to consult Senate before any major move in Cambodia. Pentagon proposes U.S. landing in Sihanoukville. Nixon rejects the idea.

(Apr. 28) Peking hails establishment of Eastern Cambodian National Front. Sihanouk tried in absentia for treason by military tribunal in Phnom Penh.

(Apr. 29) ARVN announces assault of 15,000 ARVN troops into Cambodia with U.S. advisors.

(Apr. 30) Nixon announces U.S.-ARVN invasion. 8,000 U.S. troops enter Fishhook and Parrot's Beak regions to attack ". . . the headquarters for the entire communist military operation in South Vietnam." U.S.S.R. calls the U.S. invasion of Cambodia ". . . direct aggression against a member of the United Nations." B-52 saturation bombing precedes the invasion. Cambodian government notified of speech and invasion 45 minutes after speech.

(May 1) Nixon labels campus activists "bums."

ARVN commanders call Allied invasion of Cambodia "Operation Total Victory."

(May 2) Resumption of air strike over North Vietnam.

(May 3) U.S. forces in Cambodia meet "little resistance." Monsoon rains begin. 120 U.S. planes bomb North Vietnam. Four shot down.

(May 4) Agnew claims Cambodian operation consistent with Administration's goal of "complete withdrawal and separation" from Vietnam conflict.

Supply cache found in Fishhook area, few enemy troops, and no headquarters. U.S. bombing sixty miles inside Fishhook. 2000-man Green-Beret-trained mercenary unit sent to Phnom Penh.

Four students killed at Kent State University.

NLF shells 56 U.S. targets within Vietnam, the largest attacks of the year. NLF/KR forces capture strategic river crossing east of Phnom Penh.

(May 5) Sihanouk creates exile government in Peking, which is immediately recognized by Communist China.

Third U.S.-South Vietnamese foray begins, this time at the northeastern corner of Cambodia.

(May 6) Laird tells press conference that Cambodia's changed political situation ". . . led to the invasion of sanctuaries in Cambodia." Saigon regime closes all schools because of demonstrations. U.S. launches three new thrusts into Cambodia. More Cambodian mercenaries flown to Phnom Penh. Communist troops continue to advance on capital.

Nixon tells Congressional leaders that U.S. forces will be in Cambodia no longer than eight weeks. Sets 21.7-mile limit on penetration of Cambodian territory.

Sixty U.S. Army soldiers refuse to join their unit in invading Cambodia.

(May 7) Thieu announces ARVN has no time limit for withdrawal from Cambodia. Snoul captured and destroyed by U.S. Workers from Snoul join Khmer Rouge. First official shipment of U.S. weapons to Lon Nol.

(May 8) Nixon's news conference claims troops will be out of Cambodia by mid-June. 410 colleges and universities on strike.

Three major Khmer Rouge leaders named as key ministers in Sihanouk's government in exile, the "National United Front of Kampuchea." Saigon announces plan for sending South Vietnamese gunboat flotilla up Mekong to rescue Vietnamese refugees in Phnom Penh.

(May 9) 75,000-150,000 Americans protest in Washington.

(May 10) Flotilla (U.S.-ARVN, including thirty U.S. ships) begins Mekong invasion. U.S. advisors accompany 1300 Viet Marines. White House terms Cambodian drive a success, as destruction of enemy bases will prevent widened enemy activity; admits COSVN (headquarters for South Vietnamese communist operation) was not found.

(May 11) U.S. advisors continue with Vietnamese ships past the 21.7-mile limit. U.S. field commanders say Nixon time limit is too short to allow thorough search of the sanctuaries.

(May 12) South Vietnamese flotilla reaches Phnom Penh to evacuate Vietnamese. Cambodians held in "assembly camps." Combat to secure Mekong River banks. Laird vows all American ground combat troops will be out of Vietnam by July 1, 1971; Americans will protect only their own bases.

(May 13) Sihanouk announces in Peking that three members of his new cabinet are now in Cambodia leading resistance forces there—all three are members of Khmer Rouge.

First U.S. forces leave Cambodia.

Thieu urges four-nation cooperation (South Vietnam, Laos, Cambodia, Thailand) to battle communists.

South Vietnam plans extensive military operations in eastern and central Cambodia after U.S. leaves.

Allied boats begin blockade of Cambodian coastline from Kompong Sam to South Vietnam border.

(May 14) Rogers pledges no U.S. troops of air support for Lon Nol; suggests Cambodia elicit help through third countries (e.g., South Vietnam, Thailand).

(May 15) Laird, Kissinger, and Under Secretary of State Richardson tell G.O.P. caucus that administration prefers no restriction on Presidential powers.

Appendix B

Programs of the Liberation Fronts

The Ten Points of the South Vietnam National Front for Liberation

The South Vietnam National Front for Liberation sets forth the principles and main content of an overall solution to the South Vietnam problem to help restore peace in Vietnam as follows:

1. To respect the Vietnamese people's fundamental national rights, i.e., independence, sovereignty, unity and territorial integrity as recognized by the 1954 Geneva Agreements on Vietnam.

2. The U.S. Government must withdraw from South Vietnam all U.S. troops, military personnel, arms and war materiel, and all troops, military personnel, arms and war materiel of the other foreign countries of the U.S. camp without posing any condition whatsoever; liquidate all U.S. military bases in South Vietnam; renounce all encroachments on the sovereignty, territory and security of South Vietnam and the Democratic Republic of Vietnam.

3. The Vietnamese people's right to fight for the defense of their Fatherland is the sacred, inalienable right to self-defense of all peoples. The question of the Vietnamese armed forces in South Vietnam shall be resolved by the Vietnamese parties among themselves.

4. The people of South Vietnam settle themselves their own affairs without foreign interference. They decide themselves the political regime of South Vietnam through free and democratic general elections. Through free and democratic general elections, a Constituent Assembly will be set up, a Constitution worked out, and a coalition Government of South Vietnam installed, reflecting national concord and the broad union of all social strata.

5. During the period intervening between the restoration of peace and the holding of general elections, neither party shall impose its political regime on the people of South Vietnam.

The political forces representing the various social strata and political tendencies in South Vietnam that stand for peace, independence, and neutrality, including those persons who, for political reasons, have to live abroad, will enter into talks to set up a provisional coalition government based on the principles of equality, democracy, and mutual respect with a view to achieving a peaceful, independent, democratic, and neutral South Vietnam.

The provisional coalition government is to have the following tasks:

(a) To implement the agreements to be concluded on the withdrawal of the troops of the U.S. and other foreign countries of the American camp, etc.

(b) To achieve national concord and a broad union of all social strata, political forces, nationalities, religious communities, and all persons, no matter what their political beliefs and their past may be, provided they stand for peace, independence, and neutrality.

(c) To achieve broad democratic freedoms—freedom of speech, freedom of the press, freedom of assembly, freedom of belief, freedom to form political parties and organizations, freedom to demonstrate, etc.; to set free those persons jailed on political grounds; to prohibit all acts of terror, reprisal, and discrimination against people having collaborated with either side, and who are now in the country or abroad, as provided for in the 1954 Geneva Agreements on Vietnam.

(d) To heal the war wounds, to restore and develop the economy, to restore normal life of the people, and to improve the living conditions of the laboring people.

(e) To hold free and democratic general elections in the whole of South Vietnam with a view to achieving the South Vietnam people's right to self-determination, in accordance with the content of point mentioned above.

6. South Vietnam will carry out a foreign policy of peace and neutrality:

To carry out a policy of good neighborly relations with the Kingdom of Cambodia on the basis of respect for her independence, sovereignty, neutrality, and territorial integrity within her present borders.

To carry out a policy of good neighborly relations with the Kingdom of Laos on the basis of respect for the 1962 Geneva Agreements on Laos.

To establish diplomatic, economic, and cultural relations with all countries, irrespective of political and social regime (including the U.S.), in accordance with the five principles of peaceful co-existence: mutual respect for independence, sovereignty and territorial integrity, non-aggression, non-interference in the internal affairs, equality and mutual benefit; and peaceful co-existence.

To accept economic and technical aid with no political conditions attached from any country.

7. The re-unification of Vietnam will be achieved step by step, by peaceful means, through discussions and agreement between the two zones, without foreign interference.

Pending the peaceful re-unification of Vietnam, the two zones shall reestablish normal relations in all fields on the basis of mutual respect.

The military demarcation line between the two zones at the 17th parallel, as provided for by the 1954 Geneva Agreements, is only of a provisional character and does not constitute in any way a political or territorial boundary. The two zones shall reach agreement on the statute of the Demilitarized Zone, and work out modalities for movements across the provisional military demarcation line.

8. As provided for in the 1954 Geneva Agreements on Vietnam, pending the peaceful re-unification of Vietnam, the two zones, North and South of Vietnam, undertake to refrain from joining any military alliance with foreign countries, not to allow any foreign country to maintain military bases, troops, and military personnel on their respective soil, and not to recognize the protection of any country or military alliance or bloc.

9. To resolve the aftermath of the war:

(a) The parties will negotiate the release of the army men captured in the war.

(b) The U.S. Government must bear full responsibility for the losses and devastations it has caused to the Vietnamese people in both zones.

10. The parties shall reach agreement on an international supervision of the

withdrawal from South Vietnam of the troops, military personnel, arms, and war materiel of the U.S. and other foreign countries of the American camp.

The principles and content of the overall solution expounded above form an integrated whole. On the basis of these principles and content, the parties shall reach understanding to the effect of concluding agreements on the above-mentioned questions with a view toward ending the war in South Vietnam, and toward contributing to the restoration of peace in Vietnam.

Excerpts from the Political Program of National United Front of Kampuchea (Cambodia)

The Cambodian people are unanimously determined to liberate the country from the dictatorship of Lon Nol-Sirik Matak, valets of the American imperialists, and from all other forms of American imperialist domination.

The Cambodian society, which will be established in the liberated zone and then in the whole country, will be rid of all defects impeding its rapid and full bloom: elimination of depraving customs, corruption, all sorts of illicit trading, smuggling and means of inhuman exploitation of the people. The N.U.F.K. declares that "power is, and will always be, in the hands of the progressive, industrious, and genuine working people who will ensure our motherland a bright future on the basis of social justice, equality and fraternity among all the Khmers." (Solemn Declaration of Samdech, Head of State, on March 23, 1970.) The people are the source of all power.

The democratization of Cambodian society is being carried out in the liberated zone as of March 23, 1970, and will be carried out in the whole country later in the following ways:

Guarantee to all Cambodians, except traitors known to the country, the freedom of vote, the freedom of standing for election, the freedom of speech, the press, opinion, association, demonstration, residence, travel at home and abroad, etc. . . . Safeguard the inviolability of the person, property, wealth, and privacy of correspondence.

Guarantee effective equality to both sexes, strive to wipe out backward traditions discriminating against women. Encourage by all means the cultural and professional development of women to enable them fully to participate in the common struggle. Give primary importance to training and educating women cadres at all levels in the national life. Abolish polygamy.

Buddhism is and will remain the state religion. But the N.U.F.K. recognizes and guarantees the freedom of all other religions and beliefs: Islamism, Brahmanism, the belief of the Khmers-Louer, Catholicism, Protestantism and Caodaism, etc. . . . Places of worship protected.

Look after with greatest solicitude the needs of our disabled servicemen and the families of our fighters who gave their lives for the country, and reserve privileged treatment for them.

Ensure the protection of the legitimate rights and interests of foreign nationals who respect our laws and customs, the independence and sovereignty of Cambodia.

See to it that the legitimate rights and interests of the minority nationalities and Cambodian nationals living abroad are respected.

The N.U.F.K. is devoted to building up and developing an independent national economy by relying principally on the resources and productive forces of Cambodia.

This economic policy finds concrete expression in:

—Freeing the national economy from persons who engage in profiteering, smuggling, blackmarketeering, and inhuman exploitation of the people.

—Protecting and guaranteeing the rights of ownership of land and property in accordance with the laws of the state.

—Confiscating the land and property of traitors who are active accomplices in the pay of the American imperialists and who have committed crimes against the people. The land and property seized will be distributed among the needy peasants.

—Guaranteeing to the peasants the right of ownership of the land they cultivate. Establishing a fair system on land rent and rates of interest on loans.

—Helping the peasants resolve the agrarian problem through a fair solution of unreasonable debts.

—Helping the peasants increase production and labor productivity. Protecting and developing cooperation and the good customs of mutual aid in the countryside.

—Ensuring conditions of safe and rational management and ensuring the marketing and economical transportation of products.

—Encouraging the formation of trade unions. Guaranteeing security of employment and reasonable remuneration to the laboring classes. Improving working conditions. Ensuring a system of social insurance.

—Developing the industrialization of the country and carrying out a rational industrial policy so that production will meet the principal needs of the people to the maximum. Studying adequate measures for the elimination of faults in the administration of state or joint enterprises.

—Encouraging the national bourgeoisie to run well and set up enterprises beneficial to the people in conformity with the laws concerning wage-earners. Ensuring rational and uninterrupted sale of manufactured goods.

—Helping the handicraftsmen raise labor productivity and diversify their products and ensuring the sale of their products under the best conditions.

—Developing communication lines and means of transportation.

—Safeguarding the interests of school and university students, intellectuals, and functionaries; providing employment for "those without occupation" and the unemployed in accordance with their ability and helping them develop further their ability to serve the motherland.

—Maintaining the nationalization of the banks and foreign trade.

—With regard to foreign trade, encouraging and developing export, limiting imports to equipment and products necessary to the national economy.

—Protecting national products from foreign competition. Safeguarding the purchasing power of the *riel* and paying attention to improving the public finance.

Alongside the democratization and the realization of the above-mentioned economic policies, the N.U.F.K. pays attention to the training of persons capable of correctly applying these objectives. The policy of the N.U.F.K. concerning education and culture is based on the following points:

—Develop the good traditions of the Angkor civilization handed down to us till now. Build a national culture on the basis of patriotism and love for work well done, and love for art. Protect historical relics and monuments.

—Khmerize gradually the curricula for the different stages of education, including higher education.

—Adopt the national language as the sole official language in the public services.

—Adapt the educational programs and methods to the needs of the country.

—Encourage and assist scientific research and experimentation, and encourage the efforts of those who wish to deepen their studies.

—Promote the research in our national history which is often distorted by foreign authors, and include our national history in the educational program.

—Ensure continuous education through established school terms or practical training.
—Develop pre-school education: nurseries, kindergartens, and pre-school classes.
—Ensure free education and provide scholarships for the needy children and youth.
—Ensure and support an extensive political, civic and cultural education among the people and the youth. Help every citizen realize his duties to himself, to society, and to the people. Instill actively the ideas of public interest and love for service to the community and of making himself useful to the people. This political, civic and cultural education should be carried out at all levels—in the ministries, in public services and administrations, in factories, shops and co-operatives, in the capital and in provinces, districts, and villages and in families. Develop the ideas of morality, honor, national dignity, patriotism, mutual aid, usefulness of collective labor, the sense and nobleness of rendering sacrifices for the people's cause, the spirit of working conscientiously and practicing economy, and the respect for public property.

The Ten-Point Program of the Thai Communist Party*

"To meet the present situation in our country, the Communist Party of Thailand hereby proclaims to our compatriots its present policy as follows:

1. Resolutely carry out people's war, drive U.S. imperialism out of Thailand, and overthrow the fascist dictatorial and traitorous government of the Thanom clique which brings ruin to the people and to the country. Establish a people's government which consists of representatives of the working class, peasants, petty bourgeoisie and national bourgeoisie and of the patriotic and democratic personages and which genuinely carries out an independent and democratic policy.
2. Abolish all laws, notices, orders, and regulations detrimental to the people and the country. The people have the rights of freedom of speech, writing, publication, holding meetings, organizing associations, holding demonstrations, of security of employment, maintaining religious belief, and preserving their customs and habits and livelihood which are not harmful to the people and the country.
3. Confiscate all property and land of the U.S. imperialists, the Thanom clique, counter-revolutionaries and tyrannical landlords, and distribute them for the benefit of the people and the nation. Resolutely punish counter-revolutionaries and reactionaries who have done evil deeds to the people according to the seriousness of their crimes; the opportunity to turn over a new leaf will be given to those who have done evil deeds and admitted them, and are willing to repent.
4. Abolish all traitorous and unjust agreements and treaties, unite with all the countries which support the Thai people's revolution; together with the world's revolutionary people, oppose imperialism, modern revisionism, and all reaction; support the just struggle of the oppressed peoples and nations the world over, promote friendly relations with various countries on the basis of equality, mutual respect for sovereignty, and territorial integrity.
5. The various nationalities shall enjoy the right of autonomy within the big family of Thailand; they shall enjoy equal rights, respect each other, support and help each other; religions, languages, cultures as well as customs and habits

*Reprinted from *Peking Review,* January 17, 1969, pp. 19–20.

which are not harmful to the people shall be respected: oppose national oppression and racial discrimination; economy, culture, education, and public health shall be developed generally in the areas of all the nationalities.

6. Abolish the feudal system of exploitation step by step; reduce rents and interest, abolish all unjust debts; the agrarian revolution shall be carried out according to the conditions of various places, so that peasants shall be given land to earn a livelihood. Develop irrigation, improve production, raise the standard of living, and bring the role of the peasants into full play in the revolutionary movement.

7. Promote and develop state industrial and commercial enterprises; protect private industrial and commercial enterprises which are not detrimental to the national economy; assist handicraft and small commercial enterprises which are still beneficial to the people.

8. Ensure the worker's employment, wages, and security; workers doing the same kind of work and with the same productivity shall get the same wages without distinction of sex, age, and nationality; bring the role of the working class into full play in the revolutionary movement.

9. Women shall enjoy equal rights with men in the political, economic, cultural, educational and vocational fields; bring the role of women into full play in the revolutionary movement and production; promise full welfare work among women and children; ensure education and work to the youth; foster in the youth love of the motherland, democracy, the people and labor; to actively participate in revolution, and to have the spirit of sacrifice for the collective.

10. Weed out the reactionary and corrosive U.S. imperialist and feudal culture which poisons the spirit of the people; promote and develop revolutionary culture; examine critically the cultural heritage of the nationalities of Thailand and of other countries; promote and develop education which is patriotic, democratic, scientific, and of mass character; promote and develop public health, especially in the entire countryside.

[The present policy of our Party] represents the urgent demand of the people of the whole country and the common objectives of their current struggle. On the basis of this present policy, our Party is ready to cooperate with all forces which are patriotic and cherish democracy in carrying the struggle for independence and democracy through to the end. Our Party is fully confident that the proclamation of our current policy will rally the patriotic and democratic forces in a resolute fight against the enemy, thus promoting the development of the situation in our country in a direction more favorable to the victory of the revolution.

The Twelve Points of the Patriotic Front of Laos*

1. To consolidate and extend the United National Front and actively mobilize all the forces of the country to defeat North American imperialist aggression and overthrow the traitors who are its puppets.

2. To achieve equality in all areas, solidarity and mutual aid among the various nationalities for the purpose of fighting together against the imperialists, for national salvation, and the construction of a life of common well-being.

3. To respect and preserve the Buddhist religion and unite the various religions to contribute to the achievement of the unity of the entire people and the strengthening of the national forces in the anti-Yankee resistance for national salvation.

*Reprinted from *Tricontinental Bulletin,* April 1970.

4. To assure the complete realization of the people's democratic rights and liberties.

5. To achieve sexual equality; to develop the role and the capabilities of women in all aspects of the struggle.

6. To establish a democratic administration of national unity, guaranteeing national sovereignty and serving the interests of the people.

7. To create truly patriotic and popular armed forces and security forces capable of insuring the country's defense and also its internal order and security.

8. To build and develop a national and sovereign economy and finances; to improve the people's standard of living.

9. To develop a culture and an education with a national and progressive character; to raise the cultural and scientific level; to develop public health and improve the sanitary conditions of the population.

10. To guarantee the rights and interests and conscientiously watch over the people's living conditions.

11. To protect the interests of Laotian citizens abroad and guarantee the legitimate rights of foreigners living in Laos.

12. To apply a peaceful, independent, and neutral foreign policy; to establish ties of solidarity and friendship with the peoples and governments of the peace-loving and justice-loving countries of the world.

71 72 73 74 12 11 10 9 8 7 6 5 4 3 2 1